Quality Physical Education

This book represents the culmination of a two-decade effort to describe, define and measure 'quality physical education' (QPE). Presenting in-depth research and analysis from 24 countries across five continents, it offers a truly comparative analysis that shines important new light on policy and practice in contemporary physical education.

Opening with an introduction that explores the concept of 'quality' in relation to education and that traces the history of the QPE project, the book then presents country-specific chapters that drill down into the evidence. Each chapter outlines the geographical, political, economic, cultural and demographic background of that country, and analyses the development of physical education, sport education and school-based physical activity, as well as the contemporary situation regarding equity, teaching quality, professional training and curriculum development. Each chapter then offers an assessment of the eight factors that constitute the QPE index, including skill development, facilities, accessibility, cultural practices, governmental input, cognitive skill development and habituated behaviour.

With a global reach, this book is an invaluable resource for policymakers, curriculum coordinators, administrators, teachers and researchers looking to better understand the enablers and barriers to developing QPE and to develop evidence-based strategies and interventions for promoting and implementing QPE.

Walter Ho is Invited Research Fellow at Tokyo Gakugei University, Tokyo, Japan.

ISCPES International Studies in Sport and Physical Education Series

Editorial Board
Lead Editor
Rosa Lopez de D'Amico, President, ISCPES

Associate Editors
Walter Ho, Tokyo Gakugei University, Japan
Usha Nair, National Sports University, Central University Under the Ministry of Youth Affairs and Sports, India

Available in this series:
Quality Physical Education
Global Perspectives
Edited by Walter Ho

Quality Physical Education

Global Perspectives

Edited by Walter Ho

LONDON AND NEW YORK

First published 2025
by Routledge
4 Park Square, Milton Park, Abingdon, Oxon OX14 4RN

and by Routledge
605 Third Avenue, New York, NY 10158

Routledge is an imprint of the Taylor & Francis Group, an informa business

© 2025 selection and editorial matter, Walter Ho; individual chapters, the contributors

The right of Walter Ho to be identified as the author of the editorial material, and of the authors for their individual chapters, has been asserted in accordance with sections 77 and 78 of the Copyright, Designs and Patents Act 1988.

All rights reserved. No part of this book may be reprinted or reproduced or utilised in any form or by any electronic, mechanical, or other means, now known or hereafter invented, including photocopying and recording, or in any information storage or retrieval system, without permission in writing from the publishers.

Trademark notice: Product or corporate names may be trademarks or registered trademarks, and are used only for identification and explanation without intent to infringe.

British Library Cataloguing-in-Publication Data
A catalogue record for this book is available from the British Library.

ISBN: 978-1-032-84511-1 (hbk)
ISBN: 978-1-032-84514-2 (pbk)
ISBN: 978-1-003-51358-2 (ebk)

DOI: 10.4324/9781003513582

Typeset in Times New Roman
by Newgen Publishing UK

Contents

List of Contributors	ix
Series Editor Introduction	xiii
Foreword	xv
Acknowledgements	xvii

PART I
Background and Initiatives — 1

1 Quality Physical Education: Global Perspectives — 3
   WALTER HO, KLAUDIA RAFAEL, JENNIE YANG YANG XIE, AND LING QIN

PART II
Quality Physical Education and Country Reports — 13

2 Quality Physical Education in Australia — 15
   VALERIA VAREA

3 Physical Education in Brazil: The Turning Points and Dimensional Development in Quality of Teaching — 27
   ELIANA LUCIA FERREIRA AND MARIA BEATRIZ ROCHA FERREIRA

4 Quality Physical Education in the Province of Diguillín, Ñuble Region, Chile — 37
   ALIXON REYES RODRÍGUEZ

5	The Present and Future of Quality Physical Education in China TAO WANG, XIAOLIN ZHANG, QINGWEN GUAN, LULU LIU, AND XUETING ZHANG	49
6	Quality Physical Education in Colombia DIANA FELICIANO FUERTES, LUZ AMELIA HOYOS CUARTAS, AND CAROLINA GUERRERO REYES	59
7	Global Perspectives and Local Challenges of Quality Physical Education in the Dominican Republic MIGUEL ISRAEL BENNASAR-GARCÍA	70
8	Quality Physical Education Development in Greece EFTHALIA (ELIA) CHATZIGIANNI AND KRINANTHI GDONTELI	80
9	Quality Physical Education in India USHA SUJIT NAIR, KISHORE GOPINATHAN, AND SANDEEP TIWARI	91
10	Quality Physical Education and Development in Japan NAOKI SUZUKI, YUTAKA SATO, SEIJI HIROSAWA, AND YU FURUTA	101
11	Quality Physical Education in Jordan: Challenges and Evolutions EID MOHAMMED KANAAN AND MD. DILSAD AHMED	111
12	Understanding and Advancement of Quality Physical Education in Madagascar KLAUDIA RAFAEL, WALTER HO, JENNIE YANG YANG XIE, PATRICE RANAIVASON, HARISON P. ANDRIANARIVAO, LAURENT RABARIVELO, AND MIN LIU	123
13	Towards Quality Physical Education in Malaysia SELINA KHOO AND THARIQ KHAN BIN AZIZUDDIN KHAN	133
14	Analysis of Quality Physical Education in Mexico OSWALDO CEBALLOS GURROLA, ROSA ELENA MEDINA RODRÍGUEZ, OSWALDO CEBALLOS MEDINA, AND ERNESTO CEBALLOS GURROLA	142

15	Quality Physical Education Development in New Zealand FRANCISCO SERRANO ROMERO	153
16	Quality Physical Education in Nigeria FRANZ U. ATARE AND BELLO ODUNOLA	166
17	Quality Physical Education in the Philippines: Challenges and Opportunities MARVIN LUIS C. SABADO, ZYRA RUTH T. BREBANTE, MARIE ELOISA D. ULANDAY, HENRY C. DAUT, MILA A. GALLARDO, ATREJU MIKHAIL SAM A. GALLARDO, MICHELLE LAYAO, AND ABDULRASID T. LUCMAN	175
18	Quality Physical Education in Puerto Rico LUISA VELEZ	187
19	Nurturing Holistic Development through Quality Physical Education in Saudi Arabia: A Dialectical Approach Considering Gender and Cultural Diversity MD. DILSAD AHMED	197
20	Quality Physical Education in Slovakia and Its Challenges KLAUDIA RAFAEL AND BRANISLAV ANTALA	208
21	Quality Physical Education in South Africa APHIWE JADEZWENI AND RUDOLPH LEON VAN NIEKERK	218
22	The Development of Quality Physical Education in South Korea HYUN-JOO CHO AND SU-JIN KIM	229
23	Quality Physical Education in Spain ANTONIO CAMPOS-IZQUIERDO, MARÍA-DOLORES GONZÁLEZ-RIVERA, AND MARÍA GUTIÉRREZ-CONEJO	240
24	A Glance at Quality Physical Education in Venezuela ROSA LÓPEZ DE D'AMICO, ARGENIRA RAMOS, AND ALIXON REYES RODRÍGUEZ	250

25 Quality Physical Education in Zambia 261
KATONGO BWALYA AND MWANGALA KEBBY LISEKA

PART III
Conclusion and Forward **271**

26 Quality Physical Education and the Global Perspectives:
Conclusion and Future Outlook 273
WALTER HO, KLAUDIA RAFAEL, SELINA KHOO, USHA SUJIT NAIR,
ROSA LOPEZ DE D'AMICO, AND LING QIN

Index *279*

Contributors

Md. Dilsad Ahmed is Assistant Professor at Prince Mohammed Bin Fahd University, Al-Khobar, Saudi Arabia.

Harison P. Andrianarivao is Inspecteur de la Jeunesse et des Sports, Antananarivo, Madagascar.

Branislav Antala is Professor at Comenius University in Bratislava, Bratislava, Slovakia.

Franz U. Atare is Associate Professor at University of Uyo, Akwa Ibom State, Nigeria.

Miguel Israel Bennasar-García is Instituto Superior de Formación Docente Salomé Ureña, República Dominicana.

Zyra Ruth T. Brebante is Assistant Professor at University of the Philippines-Diliman, Quezon City, Philippines.

Katongo Bwalya is Lecturer at University of Zambia, Lusaka, Zambia.

Antonio Campos-Izquierdo is Professor and Researcher at Technical University of Madrid, Madrid, Spain.

Efthalia (Elia) Chatzigianni is Professor at University of the Peloponnese, Tripoli, Greece.

Hyun-joo Cho is Senior Researcher at Korea Institute of Sport Science, Seoul, South Korea.

Luz Amelia Hoyos Cuartas is Research Professor at Universidad Pedagógica Nacional de Colombia, Bogotá, Colombia.

Rosa Lopez de D'Amico is Emeritus Professor at Universidad Pedagógica Experimental Libertador, Maracay, Venezuela.

Henry C. Daut is Retired Professor at Mindanao State University, Marawi City, Philippines.

Eliana Lucia Ferreira is Professor at Federal University of Juiz de Fora, Juiz de Fora, Brazil.

Maria Beatriz Rocha Ferreira is Professor at Federal University of Juiz de Fora, Juiz de Fora, Brazil.

Diana Feliciano Fuertes is Professor at Universidad Pedagógica Nacional de Colombia, Bogotá, Colombia.

Yu Furuta is Post-doctoral Researcher at Seijo University, Tokyo, Japan.

Atreju Mikhail Sam A. Gallardo is Associate Professor at Mindanao State University, Marawi City, Philippines.

Mila A. Gallardo is Associate Professor at Mindanao State University, Marawi City, Philippines.

Krinanthi Gdonteli is Assistant Professor at University of the Peloponnese, Tripoli, Greece.

María-Dolores González-Rivera is Professor at University of Alcalá, Alcalá de Henares, Spain.

Kishore Gopinathan is Principal and Regional Head at Lakshmibai National College of Physical Education and Sports Authority of India, Thiruvananthapuram, India.

Qingwen Guan is Ph.D. candidate at Fujian Normal University, Fuzhou, China.

Ernesto Ceballos Gurrola is a Teacher at Manuel Ávila Camacho Benemérita Normal School, Zacatecas, Mexico.

Oswaldo Ceballos Gurrola is Professor at Universidad Autónoma de Nuevo León, Nuevo León, Mexico.

María Gutiérrez-Conejo is Associate Professor at Autonomous University of Madrid, Madrid, Spain.

Seiji Hirosawa is Senior Lecturer at Toin University of Yokohama, Tokyo, Japan.

Aphiwe Jadezweni is a graduate student at University of Fort Hare, Eastern Cape, South Africa.

Eid Mohammed Kanaan is Dean of Student Affairs at University of Sharjah, Sharjah, United Arab Emirates.

Thariq Khan Bin Azizuddin Khan is Associate Professor at Sultan Idris Education University, Tanjung Malim, Malaysia.

Selina Khoo is Associate Professor at Universiti Malaya, Kuala Lumpur, Malaysia.

Su-jin Kim is Research Assistant at Sports Policy Science Institute, Seoul, South Korea.

Michelle Layao is Associate Professor at Mindanao State University, Marawi City, Philippines.

Mwangala Kebby Liseka is Teacher at Mwami Secondary School and Part-time Lecturer at Jubeva College of Education, Lusaka, Zambia.

Lulu Liu is a graduate student at Fujian Normal University, Fuzhou, China.

Min Liu is Post-doctoral Researcher at Peking University, Beijing, China.

Abdulrasid T. Lucman is Associate Professor at Mindanao State University, Marawi City, Philippines.

Oswaldo Ceballos Medina is Professor at Universidad Autónoma de Nuevo León, Nuevo León, Mexico.

Usha Sujit Nair is Professor and Vice Chancellor (Officiating) at National Sports University, India.

Bello Odunola is Retired Chief Lecturer at FCT College of Education, Zuba-Abuja, Nigeria.

Ling Qin is Lecturer at Chongqing Normal University, Chongqing, China.

Laurent Rabarivelo is Retired Inspector General at de la Jeunesse et des Sports, Antananarivo, Madagascar.

Klaudia Rafael is Invited Researcher at EDUFISADRED, Venezuela.

Argenira Ramos is member of EDUFISADRED, Universidad Pedagógica Experimental Libertador – Campus El Mácaro, El Mácaro, Venezuela.

Patrice Ranaivason is Président de la Commission Politique à la Coalition de la Société Civile pour le Progrès des Malgaches, Antananarivo, Madagascar.

Carolina Guerrero Reyes is Associate Professor at Universidad Pedagógica Nacional de Colombia, Bogotá, Colombia.

Alixon Reyes Rodríguez is Adjunct Research Professor at Adventist University of Chile, Ñuble, and Arturo Prat University in Chile, Iquique, Chile.

Rosa Elena Medina Rodríguez is Professor at Universidad Autónoma de Nuevo León, Nuevo León, Mexico.

Francisco Serrano Romero is Senior Lecturer at Manukau Institute of Technology, Auckland, New Zealand.

Marvin Luis C. Sabado is Chair of the CHK Varsity Sports Program at University of the Philippines-Diliman, Quezon City, Philippines.

Yutaka Sato is Professor at Toin University of Yokohama, Tokyo, Japan.

Naoki Suzuki is Associate Professor at Tokyo Gakugei University, Tokyo, Japan.

Sandeep Tiwari is Professor and Officiating Principal at Indira Gandhi Institute of Physical Education and Sports Sciences, University of Delhi, New Delhi, India.

Marie Eloisa D. Ulanday is College Secretary at University of the Philippines-Diliman, Quezon City, Philippines.

Rudolph Leon van Niekerk is Professor at University of Fort Hare, Eastern Cape, South Africa.

Valeria Varea is Senior Lecturer at Edith Cowan University, Perth, Australia.

Luisa Velez is Lecturer at Sacred Heart University, San Juan, Puerto Rico.

Tao Wang is Associate Professor at Fujian Normal University, Fuzhou, China.

Jennie Yang Yang Xie is Ph.D. candidate at Universiti Malaya, Kuala Lumpur, Malaysia.

Xiaolin Zhang is Professor at Sichuan Normal University, Chengdu, China.

Xueting Zhang is a graduate student at Sichuan Normal University, Chengdu, China.

Series Editor Introduction

The International Society for Comparative Physical Education and Sport (ISCPES) presents the Book Series entitled *ISCPES International Studies in Sport and Physical Education*. It continues the successful Series that started in 1999 and was interrupted in 2003; it was led by Ken Hardman. The ISCPES Book Series embraced volumes with a mono-national (or country), so-called 'Area approach' and specific themes in an international dimension (e.g., Women and Sport), so-called 'Problem approach.' *Sport and Physical Education in China* was published in 1999; the second volume, *Sport and Physical Education in Germany*, was published in 2002; the third volume, *Social Issues in Women and Sport – International and Comparative Perspectives*, was published in 2003.

ISCPES was founded in 1978; it is a research and educational organization. Its purpose is to support, encourage and assist those seeking to initiate and strengthen research and teaching programmes in comparative, cross-cultural and international physical education and sport worldwide. The academic and professional interest in international issues in physical education physical activity and sport (PEPAS) has produced a need for texts aligned with the expressed purposes of international, comparative and cross-cultural study, which progress international studies beyond description to analysis and interpretation. While PEPAS have a global presence, they are subject to culturally specific 'local' variations in interpretation, policies and practices.

The primary purpose of the titles in the Series is, respectively and collectively, to extend knowledge of issues, themes and topics in a systematic way. The over-riding aim is to facilitate more profound awareness and understanding of physical education sport and physical activity in various topical socio-cultural, geographical, political arena and thematic issue settings. Each volume will focus on a thematic issue in different national or regional political entity settings. Each text can be used separately to extend knowledge or can be taken together to form an integrated basis for informed comparisons of thematic issues, thereby contributing to critical awareness and analysis amongst confirmed and potential comparativists and young scholars at under- and post-graduate levels. In general, the volumes in the series will provide a platform for a better understanding of peculiar factors and features of issues in a variety of geographical and cultural entity settings. Concomitantly, they will provide authentic material for critical comparisons and test the generality of statements about common patterns of development and issues in sport and physical education in different cultures. Another essential distinctive feature of the Series is to set issues and/or themes in a truly international dimension or treat them from an international perspective, thus avoiding, for example, traditional mainstream literature and, thereby, expanding to the area where the local academics can be incorporated with their voices, extending readership potential and providing a sound and informed basis for critical comparative, trans-national and cross-cultural understanding.

There is academic and professional interest in international and cross-cultural issues in the domain of sport and physical education. The interest has both broadened and deepened as concepts surrounding the globalization vs. localization debate have been applied to thematic subjects and issues. Testimony to the increased interest is the extended number of international academic and professional associations, but also growth in membership numbers and formation of regional bodies that look at PEPAS. In all regions of the world, academic organizations and PE, PA and/or sport are included in the education system. Besides that, the relevance that Ministers and Senior Officials Responsible for Physical Education and Sport (MINEPS) and World Health Organization have included international guidelines or themes to focus on the national agendas that impact PEPAS. The relevance of the Sustainable Development Goals (SDGs) and their impact on the international and national agendas has also promoted PEPAS to a more visible area, as research has also indicated that they are relevant to achieving the 2030 Agenda.

Essentially, each volume will have an introduction, which will provide general ideas and point to theoretical and policy frameworks, thus setting the structural scene and issues for subsequent chapters; as appropriate, these will provide data on and analyse structures, trends and dynamics of the thematic topics and issues, so those common or similar criteria for international and cross-national/cultural comparative research can be adhered to. Generally, the content will be multi-/international, representing different socioeconomic and political structures and cultural contexts. It is the purpose of ISCPES to have global representation in all its publications.

Foreword

In an era where the importance of holistic development is increasingly recognized, the significance of quality physical education (QPE) transcends borders, offering a powerful means to promote health, social equity and personal development. *Quality Physical Education: Global Perspectives* presents a timely and essential discourse on how physical education serves as a cornerstone for fostering not just physical well-being, but also social, emotional and cognitive growth. A rich tapestry of insights from diverse countries highlights different cultures and educational systems.

As we navigate the complexities of a rapidly changing world, the insights within this book illuminate the diverse ways in which QPE is approached across different cultures and educational systems. Each chapter offers a unique lens through which we can understand the myriad of factors that influence physical education, from policy and curriculum development to the lived experiences of students and educators.

This collection is not merely an academic exploration; it is a call to action for educators, policymakers and stakeholders to recognize the transformative potential of physical education. By embracing innovative practices and promoting inclusive environments, we can empower all students to thrive, fostering lifelong habits of health and well-being.

As you delve into the pages ahead, may you be inspired by the stories and research presented here. Together, we can advocate for a future where QPE is accessible to all, cultivating generations that are not only physically fit but also equipped with the skills necessary to navigate the challenges of the 21st century.

This book explores the diversity of countries around the world, bringing a wide range of perspectives, resources and challenges to QPE, each contributing uniquely to the development and implementation of effective programs. Diversity can influence and enhance QPE globally through cultural perspectives on physical activity, educational policy and curriculum, access to resources and infrastructure, social and economic influences, professional education and standards for educators, health and development goals, inclusivity and accessibility, as well as international collaborations and appropriate practices.

As you engage with this book, I hope you find inspiration in the diverse practices and research perspectives shared within these chapters. Together, they affirm that quality physical education is not just a privilege but a right for all students, essential for fostering healthier, more equitable societies.

Darlene A. Kluka, DPhil, PhD
Research Associate, Department of Humanities Education
University of Pretoria, South Africa

Acknowledgements

With utmost gratitude and depth, thanks are offered to all the contributors who committed their time and hard efforts in collecting, writing, translating and revising their works into something concrete which is important for the development of physical education. Because of the commitment of you all, it starts a global collaborative moment to study about the advancement of quality physical education (QPE).

Deep appreciation is expressed to Rosa Lopez de D'Amico, Usha Sujit Nair, Selina Khoo and Klaudia Rafael for your support in communications, connecting and editing. It will be hardly possible to complete this publication without all your kind works behind. Sincere thanks are extended to Ivan Ling Qin and Jennie Yang Yang Xie. Despite your busy schedule, your generous assistance is deeply appreciated.

Special thanks are extended to the International Society for Comparative Physical Education and Sport (ISCPES) for supporting this initiative and to the Tokyo Gakugei University for accepting this project.

Part I

Background and Initiatives

Chapter 1

Quality Physical Education
Global Perspectives

Walter Ho, Klaudia Rafael, Jennie Yang Yang Xie, and Ling Qin

The desire to have meaningful learning through physical education has continued to be developed as a standalone subject in schools to enhance students' growth physically, mentally, and socially to lay the groundwork for active living for a lifetime. Appropriate and effective arrangement of curriculum, pedagogy, assessment, and policies for equitable access and opportunities of physical activity have been regarded as a key linking to successful mastery of quality development through physical education.

The movement for quality physical education (QPE) can be traced back to 1978 when the United Nations Educational, Scientific, and Cultural Organization (UNESCO) initiated the International Charter of Physical Education and Sport (UNESCO, 1978). The Charter marked significant advancements in physical and sport education as a fundamental right for all. The Charter focused on curriculum design, pedagogy, community support, facilities building, access and opportunities for sport experiences and physical activities, policies for equitable opportunities for all students, and support for professionals in the field of physical education. Such initiative of quality pursuit was revised in 2015 and extended the scope to cover physical activity and sports with an extra article (UNESCO, 2015a).

The Charter introduced discussion in sports and physical education, emphasizing the effective use of the subject as a lifelong supplement to active living. The learning experiences of students and the inter-relationship of curriculum, pedagogy, assessment, access and opportunity for physical activity, and professional knowledge of teachers were continued concern. Research conducted by Gabbard (2001) suggested a structured programme of at least 150 minutes of physical education per week; National Association for Sports and Physical Education (NASPE)'s determinant of QPE in NASPE (2004) involving meaningful content arrangement, delivery of appropriate instruction, and effective education of professionals in the field of physical education; and Penney et al.'s (2009) discussion on the fundamental dimensions of curriculum, pedagogy, and assessment in physical education continue to be examples of discourses.

While discussing fundamental issues in teaching physical education, Marsden and Weston (2007) and Dyson (2014) suggested considering curricular that encompass physical, cognitive, and social development, as well as advocating for inclusive teaching methods that respect diversity of learning. This perspective significantly enriched the discourse on QPE from sport education to a holistic and multifaceted approach for life education. This shift in emphasis towards an inclusive and holistic framework for QPE prioritized students' well-being, equity, and lifelong engagement in physical activity as central concerns. Consequently, several investigations provided a pivotal implication for QPE development when guiding policymakers, educators, and researchers for adopting practices that ensure every student experience the full spectrum of benefits in association with QPE. The milestone of such discourse in QPE can be seen in the UNESCO's development of the Quality Physical Education: Guidelines for Policy Makers in 2015 (UNESCO, 2015b). This guideline emphasized QPE as a foundational element for lifelong engagement in physical activity and sport by advocating an effective management of teaching and learning with proper planning for inclusion, curriculum design flexibility, and partnerships with community resources. The UNESCO Guidelines for Policy Markers in QPE adopted the 2008 Health Position Paper of the Association for Physical Education (afPE) and considered QPE as a planned, progressive, inclusive learning experience that forms part of the curriculum in preschool, primary, and secondary education.

In response to such QPE development, subsequent planning in curriculum, pedagogy, participation time in sport and physical education, and inclusion appeared in many of the curriculum documents for government officers, school administers, and frontline teachers. For example, the message from Michigan Department of Education (2024) indicated the need of all students, pre-kindergarten to grade 12, to participate in QPE classes every school day, and a QPE programme included curriculum aligned instruction and assessment, safe environment, and access and opportunities for all to learn. The Physical and Health Education Canada (PHE Canada) (2024) regarded QPE as a well-planned school programme which was compulsory and provided regularly for all students (Kindergarten to Grade 12) throughout the school year. QPE programmes were to include regular curricular instruction, well-planned lessons, holistic assessment, lesson of fun, enjoyment, success and fair play, as well as taught by qualified teacher. The Victoria Government, Australia (2024) indicated the need for all students to participate in QPE for skills, knowledge, and confidence for active and healthy life development. The criteria of meeting minimum time for class in physical education, delivery of the Victorian Curriculum, teaching by competent teachers, and study in a safe and inclusive environment became the norm in QPE programme in the state of Victoria.

To support quality development in physical education, it is hardly possible with a simple advisory document. A comprehensive plan with focus on different issues is essential. In China, for example, a national survey was conducted to assess physical activities levels among students from primary to secondary school (Liu et al., 2023). This extensive survey included a representative sample of 133,006 school students (aged 9–17 years). Results indicated significantly low physical activity levels among Chinese youth, with only 14% meeting World Health Organization's

(WHO, 2022) guidelines. It also identified an age-related decline in physical activity compliance, decreasing from 58.5% among primary to 35.5% in upper secondary school students. The Chinese government recognized the challenge in 2000, and adopted 'quality education' (suzhi jiaoyu) when the country began to reform the education. Reforms indicated the goals of generic and life skills as the target of development in physical education (National Center for Education Development, 2000). Wang and her colleagues (2011) described the former physical education curriculum in China as a sports-based programme. Recent changes focused on the improvement of overall wellness as a goal in overall education. The Central Government of China recognized the benefits and included physical education as a compulsory subject in the national curriculum (Ministry of Education, 2002). Physical education was then made compulsory for all students in primary and secondary schools and extended the requirement to students in the second year of university (Ministry of Education, 2002, 2020, 2022). To ensure the goal of active living was adhered to in health and physical development, university students must complete 144 hours of physical education every semester in their first and second years, which resulted in at least two physical education classes weekly and each lasting no less than 45 minutes (Ministry of Education, 2014a).

In the city of Hong Kong SAR, the government promoted the development of quality school education in 1997 (Education Commission, 1997). The concept was adopted in the curriculum reform of 'Learning to Learn' in 2000 by the Curriculum Development Council to indicate the developmental need of life abilities that every student should have to provide necessities in the 21st century. These life abilities were referred to as the development of generic skills in documents that highlighted reforms and encompassed the features of learning in collaboration, communication, creativity, critical thinking, information technology, numeracy, problem-solving, self-management, and information collection. The focus of these skills was expected to be the main task of development throughout the different learning stages from junior primary to senior high school (Curriculum Development Council, 2001). Physical education was officially announced as one of the key learning areas in this curriculum reform to support the goal of 'Learning to Learn' and shared the responsibilities to achieve the expected goals of lifelong learner in sport, exercise and physical activities (Curriculum Development Council, 2017). Such a proposal for physical education to support lifelong learning in exercise, sport, and physical activities became the norm of practice since the introduction of the curriculum arrangement for students (Education Bureau, 2024).

While the Singapore government advocated for the 'Total Curriculum for the 21st Century Framework of New Character and Citizenship Curriculum', goals to nurture the citizens with good characters, as self-directed learner, as confident person, and concerned citizens were anticipated (Ministry of Education, 2014b, 2021). The government invested substantial funding to provide quality infrastructure and facilities in schools, such as indoor sports halls and synthetic turf fields. Infrastructure development then expanded to cover facilities to include of dance studios, outdoor running tracks, etc. The establishment of the Physical Education and Sports Teacher Academy provided teachers with in-service training and professional development to support the Programme of Active Learning (Tan et al., 2017). The primary goal has been to develop responsible citizen for their health growth while they are still at the young age.

The evolving nature of QPE, from the UNESCO's Charter to a detailed elaboration and purpose-driven curriculum development in countries reflected a growing interest and consensus on the importance of comprehensive, inclusive, and adapted physical education programmes in school. Recent physical education programme development in Australia, Canada, China, Hong Kong SAR, and Singapore are just some of the examples to reflect our understanding in implementing QPE in schools. Purpose-driven focus in the teaching and learning of diversified skills and cognitive understanding for a physically active lifestyle development was incorporated. These programmes shared similar circumstances of mandatory minimum time allocation for physical education, delivery of programme aligned to national standards, employment of specialized/professional teachers, adoption of community-based programmes/extra-curricular activities for active lifestyle development, and the creation of safe, inclusive environments for learning.

Although there were substantial developments in QPE research, there continue to be concerns. Hardman (2008) indicated that a 'mixed message' was found through legislative efforts to protect physical education teaching. Findings reflected a weakness in consolidating quality work with concrete plans or were slow in progress to achieve the expected goals. Such a threat was also observed in the 2013 UNESCO-NWCPEA (North-Western Counties Physical Education Association) Worldwide Survey of School Physical Education (UNESCO, 2014). Many nations had the compulsory physical education policy in schools but lacked consistent plans to allocate learning time for the subject. For example, the time allocated for physical education varies across nations, with an average record of 86 minutes per week in primary schools in Africa, 109 minutes in Europe, and 111 minutes in Oceania. Countries in Africa, Asia, and Latin America had similar time allocations of 85–96 minutes for students in high school, but more time was allocated for high school students in Europe, North America, and Oceania with about 105, 125, and 100 minutes respectively. A drop in overall curriculum time was reported: from 116 to 97 minutes in primary school and 143 to 99 minutes in high school physical education from 2000 to 2013 (UNESCO, 2014).

Similar concerns were also observed by Barroso and colleagues (2005), DeCorby et al. (2005), and Morgan and Hansen (2008). Each discussed issues of oversized classes, inadequate funding, generalist teachers' lack of specialized education background in training physical education, and the need for systemic improvements as the sources in preventing the quality development of physical education. Such observation was also noted by McNeil and colleagues (2009) in their study of QPE in Singapore. The efficiency and effectiveness for quality development of physical education were limited because of the staffing issues, inadequate duration for physical education lessons, and class size. In the Taiwan region, cultural bias, facilities, equipment, and resources were challenges to the development of physical education (Holzweg et al., 2013). Khan et al. (2012) studied female physical education teachers in the Khyber Pakhtunkhwa Province of Pakistan. Female teachers mainly assisted in organizing sporting events and taught physical education lessons at higher secondary levels. Although teaching responsibilities were assigned, many had no sporting background or were not from sports-related fields. They entered the teaching field by chance rather than by choice or to have a job quickly. Williams and Pill (2019) studied professional understanding of QPE in Australia. Their finding indicated difficulty of teachers' abilities in QPE, and teachers' understanding were largely individual or collective experiences and personal beliefs in physical education. Williams and Pill (2019)'s study resulted in the question of what was the pedagogical approach that the teachers used while teaching QPE. Uhlenbrock and Meier's (2021) discussion even went further by criticizing the UNESCO QPE project in South Africa a failure to reinstate physical education as standalone subject because of the difficulty to solve the substantial coordination and resource allocation between ministers, universities, and school sector and seemingly to reinforce sport as extra-curricular school sport rather than physical education.

The discussion of all issues has led to the following questions to be answered:

1 What is QPE?
2 Is there support for the movement outside of physical education?
3 What is the status of QPE in schools? And
4 What is being achieved?

In answering these questions and when the representatives of the four international associations of the International Society for Comparative Physical Education and Sport (ISCPES), International Association of Physical Education and Sport for Girls and Women (IAPESGW), International Federation of Adapted Physical Activity (IFAPA), and Federation Internationale d' Education Physique (FIEP) met in Brisbane in 2009 during the meeting of International Committee of Sport Pedagogy (working group of the International Council of Sport Science and Physical Education), it was decided to conduct a research project on QPE in schools. The study was executed by the international research team from ISCPES, and together with the research partners from the three international sport associations, the investigation on QPE was launched in 2010.

QPE was identified by the research team as the desire to have the best and most practical practice for physical education in schools. The aim of QPE was to achieve quality student growth physically, mentally, emotionally, and socially as well as the teaching and learning of the subject. The project conducted by the ISCPES international research team consisted of several phases and Global Voices in QPE from 2010 to 2012 was the first project in QPE. Four hundred and thirty-six professionals from 44 countries in physical education and sport were invited to answer a questionnaire with following questions on QPE (Holzweg et al., 2013; D'Amico et al., 2014).

1 What makes high QPE/school sport?
2 What are the challenges for physical education/school sport?
3 How do you manage those challenges?

After receiving substantial amounts of statements, the research team adopted the two-stage content-validity process containing the developmental and judgement process to analyse the statements in 2013. Based on the works in item identification, 65 items were transformed into a questionnaire known as the Professional Perceptions Toward Quality Physical Education (PPTQPE) in 2014–2015. One thousand six hundred and sixty-nine professionals of physical education answered the questionnaire. Results were published by Ho and colleagues (2016, 2017, 2018, 2019). The 2014 survey helped identify 48 items in 8 dimensions as a good fit for study (Ho et al., 2021, 2023). These items were distributed in the eight dimensions with references to Skill Development and Body Awareness, Facilities and Norms in Physical Education, Quality Teaching of Physical Education, Plans for Feasibility and Accessibility of Physical Education, Social Norms and Cultural Practice, Governmental Input for Physical Education, Cognitive Skill Development, and Habituated Behaviour in Physical Activities.

The editorial team of this book invited researchers from 24 countries to prepare executive summaries of the latest developments in physical education in their countries. Different regions of the world were represented: Africa – Nigeria, Madagascar, South Africa, and Zambia; Asia – China, India, Japan, Malaysia, Philippines, and South Korea; the Americas – Brazil, Chile, Colombia, Dominican Republic, Mexico, Puerto Rico, and Venezuela; Europe – Greece, Slovakia, and Spain; Middle East – Jordan and Saudi Arabia; and Oceania – Australia and New Zealand. The invited countries have diversified backgrounds in economic status, colonization experiences, complexity of demographic structure, and cultural and religious traditions. All contributors prepared country backgrounds and latest developments in physical education as well as description of the eight dimensions of development in QPE.

Each chapter of this book presents a unique background of the country, economic situation, demographic information, and general view of education development. The chapter also contains discussion of the latest development, legislation structure, and reform information in physical education. The writing of the eight dimensions offers country specific information on various issues in sports, health, and physical learning, works on facilities and venues, teaching quality, professional training, issues in gender, interrelationship with culture and economic development, governmental support, cognitive development in students, and lastly the behavioural habits development in physical activities. The writing offers scholars, administrators, and policy workers with intrinsic understanding of the relationship between culture, historical background, and physical education development and the situation of the eight dimensions provide particular attention to the foundation works in QPE. This is a challenging work as it is the first piece of writing with experiences from diverse countries from around the world on QPE and the collaborative moment to think of the QPE as topic for improvement.

References

Association for Physical Education (afPE). (2008). *Health position paper*. Worcester: Association for Physical Education.

Barroso, C.S., McCullum-Gomez, C., Hoelscher, D.M., Kelder, S.H., & Murray, N.G. (2005). Self-reported barriers to quality physical education by physical education specialists in Texas. *The Journal of School Health*, *75*(8), 313–319. https://pubmed.ncbi.nlm.nih.gov/16179081/

Curriculum Development Council. (2001). *Learning to learn – the way forward in curriculum development*. Hong Kong SAR: Curriculum Development Council. www.edb.gov.hk/attachment/en/curriculum-development/cs-curriculum-doc-report/wf-in-cur/CDC_LtL_Report_2001(web)_e.pdf

Curriculum Development Council. (2017). *Physical education key learning area curriculum guide (Primary 1 – Secondary 6)*. Hong Kong SAR: The Education Bureau. www.edb.gov.hk/attachment/en/curriculum-development/kla/pe/curriculum-doc/PEKLACG_e.pdf

D'Amico, R., Ho, W.K.Y., Branislav, A., Dinold, M., Benn, T., & Holzweg, M. (2014). Voces acerca de la educación física en América Latina. *Des-encuentros*, *II*, 6–14.

DeCorby, K., Halas, J., Dixon, S., Wintrup, L., & Janzen, H. (2005). Classroom teachers and the challenges of delivering quality physical education. *The Journal of Educational Research*, *98*(4), 208–221. www.tandfonline.com/doi/abs/10.3200/JOER.98.4.208-221

Dyson, B. (2014). Quality physical education: a commentary on effective physical education teaching. *Research Quarterly for Exercise and Sport*, *85*(2), 144–152. www.tandfonline.com/doi/abs/10.1080/02701367.2014.904155

Education Bureau. (2024). *Physical education*. Hong Kong Special Administration Region: Education Bureau. Retrieved on 27 September 2024. www.edb.gov.hk/en/curriculum-development/kla/physical-education/index.html

Education Commission. (1997). *Education Commission Report No.7: education administration – education standard – quality assurance – school management*. Education Commission Hong Kong SAR: Printing Department of the Hong Kong Special Administration Region Government. www.eduhk.hk/cird/publications/edpolicy/27.pdf

Gabbard, C. (2001). The need for quality physical education. *The Journal of School Nursing*, *17*(2), 73–75. https://doi.org/10.1177/105984050101700203

Hardman, K. (2008). Physical education in schools: a global perspective. *Kinesiology*, *40*(1), 5–28. www.academia.edu/19622196/Physical_education_in_schools_A_global_perspective

Ho, W., Ahmed, D., Carvalho, P.G., Antala, B., Imre, M., Valeiro, M.G., Kougioumtzis, K., Cazzoli, S., Van Niekerk, R.L., Morris, T., Huang, F., & Wong, B. (2019). Development of an instrument to assess perception of quality physical education (QPE) among the European professionals. *South African Journal for Research in Sport, Physical Education and Recreation*, *41*(1), 31–49.

Ho, W., Ahmed, D., de D'Amico, R.L., Antala, B., Dinold, M., Wong, B., & Huang, F. (2016). Quality physical education and global concern – ways ahead and future development. *Actividad Fisca y Ciencias*, *8*(1), 60–70.

Ho, W., Ahmed, D., de D'Amico, R.L., Ramos, A., Ferreira, E.L., Ferreira, M.B.A., Amaral, S.C.F., Gurrola, O.C., Diaz, G.B., Ramos, A., Hoyos, L.A., Jasmin, A., Duque, A.R., Van Nielerk, R.L., Huang, F., & Wong, B. (2018). Measuring the perception of quality physical education in Latin American professionals. *Revista Brasileira de Ciencias do Esporte*, *40*(4), 361–369.

Ho, W., Ahmed, D., Keh, N.C., Khoo, S., Tan, C.H., Dehkordi, M.R., Gallardo, M., Lee, K.C., Yamaguchi, Y., Wang, J., Liu, M., & Huang, F. (2017). Professionals' perception of quality physical education learning in selected Asian cities. *Cogent Education*, *4*(1), 1–17. https://doi.org/10.1080/2331186X.2017.1408945

Ho, W., Ahmed, D., Rafael, K., de D'Amico, R.L., Antala, B., Liu, M., Dong, X.X., & Xie, Y.Y. (2023). Quality physical education (QPE) measuring tool development. *International Sports Studies*, *45*(2), 6–27. https://doi.org/10.30819/iss.45-2.02

Ho, W., Ahmed, Md. D., & Kukurova, K. (2021). Development and validation of an instrument to assess quality physical education. *Cogent Education*, *8*(1), 1–25. https://doi.org/10.1080/2331186X.2020.1864082

Holzweg, M., Ho, W.K.Y., Antala, B., Benn, T., Dinold, M., de D'Amico, R., Saunders, J., & Bumm, K. (2013). Sharing global voice: perception of physical education and school sport worldwide. *International Journal of Physical Education*, *L*(3), 29–39.

Khan, S., Qureshi, Y.I., Ui-Islam, Z., Khan, W., & Abbass, S.A. (2012). Attitude of female lecturers in physical education towards profession. *International Journal of Learning & Development*, *2*(4), 17–23. https://doi.org/10.5296/ijld.v2i4.2050

Liu, Y., Ke, Y.Z., Liang, Y.H., Zhu, Z., Cao, Z.B., Zhuang, J., Cai, Y.J., Wang, L.J., Chen, P.J., & Tang, Y. (2023). Results from the China 2022 report card on physical activity for children and adolescents. *Journal of Exercise Science and Fitness*, *21*(1), 1–5. www.sciencedirect.com/science/article/pii/S1728869X22000570

Marsden, E., & Weston, C. (2007). Locating quality physical education in early years pedagogy. *Sport, Education and Society*, *12*(4), 383–398. www.tandfonline.com/doi/abs/10.1080/13573320701600621

McNeill, M., Lim, B.S., Wang, C.K., Tan, W.C., & MacPhail, A. (2009). Moving towards quality physical education: physical education provision in Singapore. *European Physical Education Review*, *15*(2), 201–223. https://doi.org/10.1177/1356336 X09345224

Michigan Department of Education. (2024). *Physical education*. Michigan, USA: Department of Education. Retrieved on 26 September 2024 www.michigan.gov/mde/services/health-safety/curriculum/physed

Ministry of Education. (2002). *National general higher education physical education course teaching guidelines [全国普通高等学校体育课程教学指导纲要]*. China: Ministry of Education. Retrieved on 26 September 2024 www.moe.gov.cn/s78/A17/twys_left/moe_938/moe_792/s3273/201001/t20100128_80824.html

Ministry of Education. (2014a). *Basic standards for physical education work in higher education institutions [高等学校体育工作基本标准]*. China: Ministry of Education. Retrieved on 26 September 2024 www.moe.gov.cn/srcsite/A17/moe_938/s3273/201406/t20140612_171180.html

Ministry of Education. (2014b). *Character and citizenship education syllabus – primary*. Singapore: Ministry of Education. www.moe.gov.sg/-/media/files/primary/characterand-citizenshipeducationprimarysyllabusenglish.pdf

Ministry of Education. (2020). *Senior secondary school physical education and health curriculum standards [普通高中体育与健康课程标准]*. Beijing, China: People's Education Press.

Ministry of Education. (2021). *Character and citizenship education (CCE). Syllabus – secondary*. Singapore: Ministry of Education. www.moe.gov.sg/-/media/files/secondary/syllabuses/cce/2021-character-and-citizenship-education-syllabus-secondary.pdf

Ministry of Education. (2022). *Physical education and health programme standards for compulsory education [义务教育体育与健康课程标准]*. Beijing, China: Beijing Normal University Press.

Morgan, P., & Hansen, V. (2008). Physical education in primary schools: classroom teachers' perceptions of benefits and outcomes. *Research Quarterly for Exercise and Sport, 79*(4), 506–516. www.tandfonline.com/doi/abs/10.1080/02701367.2008.10599517

National Association for Sport and Physical Education (NASPE). (2004). *Moving into the future: National standards for PE* (2nd ed.). https://wheresmype.org/downloads/NASPE%20Standards%202004.pdf

National Center for Education Development. (2000). *Green paper on education in China*. Beijing, China: Educational Science Publishing House.

Penney, D., Brooker, R., Hay, P., & Gillespie, L. (2009). Curriculum, pedagogy and assessment: three message systems of schooling and dimensions of quality physical education. *Sport, Education and Society, 14*(4), 421–442. www.tandfonline.com/doi/abs/10.1080/13573320903217125

Physical and Health Education Canada (PHE Canada). (2024). *Quality physical education*. Canada: PHE Canada. Retrieved on 26 September 2024 https://phecanada.ca/professional-learning/qpe

Tan, J.P.L., Koh, E., Chan, M., Costes-Onishi, P., & Hung, D. (2017). *Advancing 21st century competencies in Singapore. Center for Global Education*. Singapore: National Institute of Education, Nanyang Technological University. https://asiasociety.org/sites/default/files/2017-10/advancing-21st-century-competencies-in-singapore.pdf

Uhlenbrock, C., & Meier, H.E. (2021). The difficulty of policy transfer in physical education: the failure of UNESCO's Quality Physical Education in South Africa. *Physical Education and Sport Pedagogy, 28*(2), 139–152. https://doi.org/10.1080/17408989.2021.1958176

United Nations Educational, Scientific and Cultural Organization (UNESCO). (1978). *International Charter of Physical Education and Sport*. Paris, France: UNESCO. https://unesdoc.unesco.org/ark:/48223/pf0000216489/PDF/216489eng.pdf.multi

United Nations Educational, Scientific and Cultural Organization (UNESCO). (2014). *UNESCO-NWCPEA: Worldwide survey of school physical education – final report 2013*. Paris. France: UNESCO. https://unesdoc.unesco.org/ark:/48223/pf0000 229335/PDF/229335eng.pdf.multi

United Nations Educational, Scientific and Cultural Organization (UNESCO). (2015a). *International Charter of Physical Education, Physical Activity and Sport*. Paris, France: UNESCO. https://unesdoc.unesco.org/ark:/48223/pf0000235409/PDF/235409eng.pdf.multi

United Nations Educational, Scientific and Cultural Organization (UNESCO). (2015b). *Quality physical education (QPE): guidelines for policy makers*. Paris, France: UNESCO. https://unesdoc.unesco.org/ark:/48223/pf0000231101

Victoria Government. (2024). *Quality physical education*. Australia: Victoria Government. Retrieved on 26 September 2024. www.schools.vic.gov.au/quality-physical-education

Wang, X.Z., Housner, L., Ji, L., Torsney, C., & Mao, F. (2011). Reform of physical education in China. *International Sport Studies*, *33*(1), 11–27.

Williams, J., & Pill, S. (2019). What does the term 'quality physical education' mean for health and physical education teachers in Australian Capital Territory schools? *European Physical Education Review*, *25*(4), 1193–1201. https://journals.sagepub.com/doi/abs/10.1177/1356336X18810714

World Health Organization (WHO). (2022). *Physical activity*. Retrieved on 26 September 2024. www.who.int/news-room/fact-sheets/detail/physical-activity#:~:text=Levels%20of%20physical%20inactivity%20globally&text=That%20is%2C%20they%20do%20not,points%20between%202010%20and%202022

Part II

Quality Physical Education and Country Reports

Chapter 2

Quality Physical Education in Australia

Valeria Varea

Introduction

Quality physical education (QPE) is a worldwide debate. While some definitions of QPE exist, there is a lack of consensus about what the term means (Marsden & Weston, 2007). QPE has been defined, for example, as 'the planned, progressive, inclusive learning experience that forms part of the curriculum in early years, primary and secondary education' (United Nations Educational, Scientific and Cultural Organization, 2014, p. 9). According to this definition, QPE is linked to both, experiences and curriculums. In so doing, QPE is context- and country-specific, as different countries (and sometimes also states) have different curriculums.

In Australia, QPE has also been informed through theoretical frameworks (e.g. Light et al., 2014; Pill, 2011, 2016). According to the Australian National Health and Physical Education Curriculum (AC: HPE), at the core of the subject is the acquisition of movement skills and concepts to enable students to participate in a range of physical activities confidently, competently and creatively (Australian Curriculum, Assessment and Reporting Authority [ACARA], 2024). The AC: HPE also states that in an increasingly complex, sedentary and rapidly changing world, it is critical for every young Australian to be able to not only cope with life's challenges but also flourish as a healthy, safe, and active citizen in the 21st century.

The Australian Background

Australia comprises the mainland of the Australian continent and the island of Tasmania. Australia is the largest country by area in Oceania and the world's sixth-largest country, and it is a federal parliamentary constitutional monarchy comprising six states and ten territories. Its population of nearly 27 million (Australian Bureau of Statistics [ABS], 2023a) is highly urbanised and heavily concentrated on the eastern seaboard (ABS, 2012). Canberra is the national capital, while its most populous cities are Sydney, Melbourne, Brisbane, Perth and Adelaide (ABS, 2023b).

European settlement in Australia began in 1788 when the first 11 convict ships, known as the 'First Fleet', arrived from Great Britain on 26 January to the colony of New South Wales (NSW). Early free settlers came predominantly from Great Britain and Ireland. In 1901, the six different self-governing British colonies were united into a federation of states called the Commonwealth of Australia. Until 1950, migration levels rose and fell, and waves of non-British migration arrived after the Second World War. Since this early period, individuals from more than 200 countries have migrated to Australia and, as a result, Australian society is currently one of the most diverse in the world (Commonwealth of Australia, 2014).

Since the founding of the first colony of NSW in 1788, the British government had definite ideas of how education was to be developed in the colony. During the first decades of the 20th century, radical structural and ideological shifts in Australia influenced the relationship between church and state, family relations and relationships between the state and families (Wright, 2011). To understand Australian schooling, it is necessary to take into account British and wider European influences (Miller & Davey, 1990). The first colonists, colonial governors and educators were from Britain or educated in Britain, and, until the 1940s, the Australian states used mainly British syllabi. The colonists also brought with them a sports ethos that was already well established in England and marked by social class (Wright, 2011).

School Health and Physical Education

There is no single origin in how HPE developed in Australian schools (Scharagrodsky & Varea, 2016). Drills and cadet movements were scarcely mentioned in key education texts before the 1900s (Wright, 2011). As early as in 1858, there were some semblances of PE in the public schools in the suggestions to teachers concerning the orderly conduct of pupils entering and leaving school, and the importance of the playground (Scharagrodsky & Varea, 2016). During the 1900–1950 period in Australia, the development of the HPE subject in state schools was dependent upon teachers' ability and interest in the subject. A 1921 revision of the syllabus in NSW included 'the addition of Eurythmic Steps and Movement, Folk Dancing, and Dancing generally with special attention to deportment' (Rodwell, 1999). Additionally, organised games such as cricket, football, tennis and hockey were included (Kennedy, 1921).

Currently, the hours allocated in Australian schools for HPE may vary according to the state and year level. In Western Australia, for example, there are 2 hours per week allocated for HPE from pre-primary to Year 10. According to the current AC: HPE, students develop the skills, knowledge and understanding to strengthen their sense of self, and build and manage satisfying, respectful relationships in HPE. They learn to build on personal and community strengths and assets to enhance safety and wellbeing. They critique and challenge assumptions and stereotypes, and they learn to navigate a range of health-related sources, services and organisations. As a foundation for lifelong physical activity participation and enhanced performance, students acquire an understanding of how the body moves and develop positive attitudes towards physical activity participation. They develop an appreciation of the significance of physical activity, outdoor recreation and sport in Australian society and globally. Movement is a powerful medium for learning, through which students can practise and refine personal, behavioural, social and cognitive skills (ACARA, 2024).

The AC: HPE is organised into two interrelated strands: 'Movement and Physical Activity' and 'Personal, Social and Community Health'. Each of these strands includes different sub-strands with a wide variety of content according to the different school levels. Examples of this content are included in the following section to illustrate how the AC: HPE addresses the 8-dimensional development in QPE.

The 8-Dimensional Development in Quality Physical Education

Dimension 1: Skill Development and Bodily Awareness (SDBA)

Value learning in, about and through movement is a central proposition in the AC: HPE with movement being both a focus of learning and a medium for learning across the HPE curriculum and other curriculum areas (Macdondald, 2013). The centrality of learning in the movement to lay a foundation for lifelong participation is thus key for Australian HPE. The sub-strand 'Understanding movement' includes content related to fitness and physical activity, such as exploring how regular physical activity keeps individuals healthy and well (Foundation level). Moreover, discussions about the body's reactions to participating in physical activities are included as content for Years 1 and 2, and the benefits of physical activity to health and wellbeing in Years 3 and 4. The curriculum also emphasises the participation in physical activities designed to enhance fitness, and to discuss the impact regular participation can have on health and wellbeing. However, research has shown that the legitimisation of HPE as school subject as a place for health promotion is problematic (Pringle & Pringle, 2012) and it has perpetuated a healthism discourse (Lee & Macdonald, 2010). The use of fitness tests has also been widely criticised (Gard & Wright, 2001; Garrett & Wrench, 2008) and Australian HPE teachers have been shown to negotiate the use (or non-use) of fitness testing in secondary HPE (Alfrey & Gard, 2014). Nevertheless, older students in Australia are also expected to design, implement and evaluate personalised plans for improving or maintaining their own and others' physical activity and fitness levels according to the HPE curriculum.

The sub-strand 'Understanding movement' includes content related to elements of movement, such as identifying and describing how their body moves in relation to effort, space, time, objects and people, and incorporating elements of effort, space, time, objects and people in performing simple movement sequences. The manipulation and modification of elements of effort, space, time, objects and people to perform movement sequences are listed as content for Years 5 and 6, and to demonstrate and explain how the elements of effort, space, time, objects and people can enhance movement sequences for Years 7 and 8. Older students are also expected to analyse the impact of effort, space, time, objects and people when composing and performing movement sequences.

Dimension 2: Facilities and Norms in Physical Education (FNPE)

There is disagreement throughout the literature about the greatest inhibitors to implementing QPE programmes. A number of major barriers inhibit teachers' efforts and capacity to implement regular and developmentally appropriate PE lessons. The allocation of time and other resources to PE has remained a matter of worldwide professional concern (Hardman, 2000, 2001). Some of these inhibitors in Australia are related to institutional factors and are often beyond teachers' control (Morgan & Hansen, 2008).

The AC: HPE also addresses safety issues that students may encounter in their daily lives. The content supports students to develop knowledge, understanding and skills to assess risk, make safe decisions and behave in ways that protect their own safety and that of others. It is expected that all students at appropriate intervals across the continuum of learning from Foundation to Year 10 will learn about the following:

- safety at school
- safe practices at home, in road or transport environments, in the outdoors and when near water
- safe and unsafe situations at home, school and parties and in the community
- strategies for dealing with unsafe or uncomfortable situations
- safe practices when using information and communication technologies (ICT) and online services, including dealing with cyberbullying
- managing personal safety
- first aid and emergency care, including safe blood practices
- safety when participating in physical activity, including sports safety, sun safety, use of protective equipment and modifying rules
- relationship and dating safety (ACARA, 2024).

The AC: HPE also includes content related to ethical behaviour in movement settings under the sub-strand 'Learning through movement'. It is expected for students to follow rules when participating in physical activity in Foundation level, and to identify rules and fair play in Years 1 and 2. Furthermore, students should apply basic rules and scoring systems, demonstrate fair play when participating in physical activities in Years 3 and 4, and demonstrate ethical behaviour and fair play that aligns with rules when participating in a range of physical activities in Years 5 and 6. Students in Years 7 and 8 are expected to modify rules and scoring systems to allow for fair play, safety and inclusive participation, and to reflect on how fair play and ethical behaviour can influence the outcomes of movement activities in

Years 9 and 10. In particular, literature has demonstrated how notions of inclusion, responsibility and ownership, personal and social development and social justice are part of the pedagogical model of sports education which can be implemented in PE classes (Harvey et al., 2014).

Dimension 3: Quality Teaching of Physical Education (QTPE)

Interests in and conceptualisations of quality vary across educational arenas, and understandings of quality are intended to be framed in relation to dominant policy. However, curriculum, pedagogy and assessment are three fundamental dimensions of QPE (Penney et al., 2009), and quality teaching in PE is very closely related to this. In some respects, PE appears notable for pedagogical innovation, with internationally recognised developments focusing on pedagogy and driven by concerns regarding 'quality'. Models such as Teaching Games for Understanding (Bunker & Thorpe, 1982), Sport Education (Siedentop, 1994) and Teaching for Personal and Social Responsibility (Hellison, 1995) are some relevant examples.

The AC: HPE includes content for students to refine their movement skills. Examples of this are to practice fundamental movement skills and movement sequences using different body parts for Foundation level, and to perform fundamental movement skills in a variety of movement sequences and situations for Years 1 and 2. Similarly, in Years 3 and 4, students are expected to perform fundamental movement skills in a variety of movement sequences and situations, and to refine these ones in Years 5 and 6. In years 7 and 8, students should use feedback to improve body control and coordination when performing specialised movement skills in a variety of situations, and to provide and apply feedback of these in Years 9 and 10.

Some more content included in the AC: HPE that relates to quality teaching in PE is the expectation for students to understand emotions. In so doing, students in Foundation level should identify and describe emotional responses people may experience in different situations, and practise emotional responses that account for their own and others' feelings in Years 1 and 2. Similarly, students should investigate how emotional responses vary in depth and strength in Years 3 and 4, and examine the influence of emotional responses on behaviour and relationships in Years 5 and 6. Similarly, it is expected for students to analyse factors that influence emotions, and develop strategies to demonstrate empathy and sensitivity in Years 7 and 8, to evaluate situations and propose appropriate emotional responses, and then reflect on possible outcomes of different responses in Years 9 and 10.

Over the years, Rink (2013) has drawn our attention to the notion of quality instruction for quality PE classes. However, the quality teaching of PE is more than that. Following Dyson (2014), it is imperative to educate the whole child. Wright et al. (2018) have also explored the conditions of possibility for a socially critical approach to health education in HPE.

Dimension 4: Plans for Feasibility and Accessibility of Physical Education (PFAPE)

The Australian Council for Health, Physical Education and Recreation (ACHPER) supports the Active and Healthy Schools Committee (AHSC). The overall role of the AHSC is to assist in advancing ACHPER's engagement with health education communities relevant to the Health and Physical Education, Recreation and Sports fields and professional contexts, and to thereby support work aligned with ACHPER's identified strategic priorities. More specifically, the Charter established for the AHSC reflects and advises on strategies to extend ACHPER connectedness with those who work in the health education sector. ACHPER plays an active role in fostering connections between health education and promotion and those who work in HPE and related fields.

Furthermore, the Australian Sports Commission is the Australian Government agency responsible for supporting and investing in sports at all levels, and it has a programme called 'Sporting Schools'. Sporting Schools is an Australian Government initiative designed to help schools increase children's participation in sports and connect them with community sports opportunities. Sporting Schools programmes are provided free to children and their families to help students build the confidence and capability to be active for life. To help achieve this, the Australian Sports Commission has partnered with more than 35 national sporting organisations. There is a programme for primary schools, and a targeted programme for Year 7 and Year 8 students (Australian Sports Commission, 2024).

While there is a plethora of research about feasibility and accessibility to physical activity in Australian schools (e.g. Eather et al., 2013; Elliot et al., 2023), there is more limited research that focusses specifically on PE classes. Jenkinson and Benson (2010), for example, studied the barriers to providing PE in Victorian state secondary schools, and Martin and Kudláček (2010) investigated the attitudes of Australian pre-service teachers towards inclusion of students with physical disabilities in PE programmes. However, feasibility and accessibility of PE in Australia is still an ongoing issue.

Dimension 5: Social Norms and Cultural Practice (SNCP)

In Australia, approximately 26% of school students are from culturally and linguistically diverse backgrounds (Wrench & Garrett, 2021). In adopting socio-cultural understandings of learning, culturally responsive pedagogies are underpinned by the notion that all curriculum is culturally based (Gay, 2002).

The AC: HPE includes content related to cultural significance of physical activity, and valuing diversity. For example, students are expected to participate in physical activities from their own and other cultures in Years 3 and 4, and to examine how involvement creates community connections and intercultural understanding in Years 5 and 6. In Years 7 and 8, students should participate in and investigate cultural and historical significance of a range of physical activities, and examine the role physical activity, outdoor recreation and sport play in the lives of Australians, and investigate how this has changed over time in Years 9 and 10.

According to the AC: HPE, students are expected to recognise similarities and differences in individuals and groups, and explore how these are celebrated and respected in Years 1 and 2. Students should also research their own heritage and cultural identities, explore strategies to respect and value diversity in Years 3 and 4, and identify how valuing diversity positively influences the wellbeing of the community in Years 5 and 6. In Years 7 and 8, students investigate the benefits to individuals and communities of valuing diversity and promoting inclusivity, and they critique behaviours and contextual factors that influence health and wellbeing of diverse communities in Years 9 and 10.

Recently, there has been an emphasis not only in recognising Indigenous knowledge in Australian society in general but also in PE. For example, Whatman et al. (2017) have used Indigenous knowledge as a way to disrupt norms in physical education teacher education. Similarly, Hart et al. (2012) explored pre-service teachers' pedagogical relationships and experiences of embedding Indigenous Australian knowledge in teaching practicum.

Dimension 6: Governmental Input for Physical Education (GIPE)

The Australian Professional Standards for Teachers is a public statement of what constitutes teacher quality in Australia (HPE included). The Standards define the work of teachers and make explicit the elements of high-quality, effective teaching in 21st-century schools, which result in improved educational outcomes for students. The Standards do this by providing a framework that makes clear the knowledge, practice and professional engagement required across teachers' careers. They present a common understanding and language for discourse between teachers, teacher educators, teacher organisations, professional associations and the public (ACHPER, 2024).

The professional standards are organised in three areas: (1) Professional knowledge, (2) Professional practice and (3) Professional engagement. Professional knowledge includes issues related to knowing students and how they learn (e.g., physical, social and intellectual development and characteristics of students, and strategies for teaching Aboriginal and Torres Strait Islander students), and knowing the content and how to teach it (e.g., content and teaching strategies of the teaching area; curriculum, assessment and reporting, etc.). Professional practice includes the planning and implementation of effective teaching and learning, the creation and maintenance of supportive and safe learning environments, and the assessment, feedback and reporting of student learning. Finally, professional engagement includes engaging in professional learning and engaging professionally with colleagues, parents/carers and the community.

Dimension 7: Cognitive Skill Development (CSD)

The AC: HPE includes content related to critical and creative thinking in movement. In Foundation level, students are expected to test possible solutions to movement challenges through trial and error. In Years 1 and 2, they should propose a range of alternatives, test their effectiveness when solving movement challenges, and apply innovative and creative thinking in solving movement challenges in Years 3 and 4. In Years 5 and 6, they are expected to apply critical and creative thinking processes in order to generate and assess solutions to movement challenges, and to evaluate and justify reasons for decisions and choices of action when solving movement challenges in Years 7 and 8. Finally, they should transfer understanding from previous movement experiences to create solutions to movement challenges in Years 9 and 10.

The AC: HPE also includes content related to interaction with others. For example, students are expected to practise personal and social skills to interact positively with others in Foundation level, and to describe ways to include others to make them feel they belong in Years 1 and 2. Students should be able to describe how respect, empathy and valuing diversity can positively influence relationships in Years 3 and 4, and to practise skills to establish and manage relationships in Years 5 and 6. Students are also expected to investigate the benefits of relationships and examine their impact on their own and others' health and wellbeing in Years 7 and 8, and to investigate how empathy and ethical decision making contribute to respectful relationships in Years 9 and 10.

Wright et al.'s (2004) book is a relevant example of the application of critical inquiry and problem-solving in PE. The authors emphasise the rapid changes in values across generations and social groups, the exposure to diverse values and the implications for PE. Furthermore, Welch et al. (2020) particularly analyse how the key ideas and propositions from the Australian curriculum for HPE and the critical and creative thinking capability raise relevant questions regarding the social emergence of educative creative purpose and potential in HPE.

Dimension 8: Habituated Behaviour in Physical Activities (HBPA)

The AC: HPE includes content related to developing movement concepts and strategies, which may lead to developing habituated behaviour in physical activities. Students are expected to participate in games with and without equipment in Foundation level, and to create games in Years 1 and 2. In Years 3 and 4, students should practise and apply movement concepts and strategies with and without equipment, and to propose these in Years 5 and 6. By years 7 and 8, students are expected to practise, apply and transfer movement concepts and strategies, and to develop and evaluate these ones for successful outcomes by Years 9 and 10.

The AC: HPE also includes content related to making healthy and safe choices. In Years 1 and 2, students should recognise situations and opportunities to promote health, safety and wellbeing, and to identify and practise strategies to promote health, safety and wellbeing in Years 3 and 4. In Years 5 and 6, students are expected to plan and practise strategies to promote health, safety and wellbeing, and to investigate and select these strategies in Years 7 and 8. By Years 9 and 10, students should propose, practise and evaluate responses in situations where external influences may impact on their ability to make healthy and safe choices.

There is abundant literature in relation to forming habits to increase physical activity behaviour (e.g. Carballo-Fazanes et al., 2020; Schroé et al., 2020). Specifically in Australia, several intervention programmes have been conducted in schools to try to increase physical activity time among children. Some examples of these are the Health-Related Quality of Life programme (Casey et al., 2014), two high-intensity interval training protocols (Costigan et al., 2016) and the Lunchtime Enjoyment Activity and Play intervention (Hyndman et al., 2014).

Conclusion

The promotion of QPE is important because it has been claimed to play a role in bolstering the credibility of PE as a subject area. Further, the provision of QPE can help achieve the reality of a subject claiming to be a platform for physical activity participation and social inclusion beyond the school limits (Drummond & Pill, 2011).

The future of Australian (and worldwide) PE has been questioned in the literature, particularly in relation to the development of digital technology, the commercialisation of education, the spread of surveillance culture and medicalisation (Gard, 2014).

Throughout this chapter, QPE in Australia has been linked to the content of the AC: HPE, showcasing how QPE is context-specific. While the debates of what QPE means continue, research like the chapters of this book show attempts to unpack what QPE implies in different countries.

References

Alfrey, L., & Gard, M. (2014). A crack where the light gets in: a study of Health and Physical Education teachers' perspectives on fitness testing as a context for learning about health. *Asia-Pacific Journal of Health, Sport and Physical Education*, 5(1), 3–18.

Australian Bureau of Statistics [ABS]. (2012). *Geographic distribution of the population.* www.abs.gov.au/ausstats/abs@.nsf/Lookup/by%20Subject/1301.0~2012~Main%20Features~Geographic%20distribution%20of%20the%20population~49

Australian Bureau of Statistics [ABS]. (2023a). *National, state and territory population.* www.abs.gov.au/statistics/people/population/national-state-and-territory-population/sep-2023

Australian Bureau of Statistics [ABS]. (2023b). *Regional population.* www.abs.gov.au/statistics/people/population/regional-population/latest-release

Australian Council for Health, Physical Education and Recreation [ACHPER]. (2024). achper Australia. www.achper.org.au

Australian Curriculum, Assessment and Reporting Authority [ACARA]. (2024). *Australian curriculum for health and physical education.* www.australiancurriculum.edu.au/f-10-curriculum/health-and-physical-education/

Australian Sports Commission. (2024). *Sporting schools. Bringing schools and sports together to help Aussie children get active.* www.sportaus.gov.au/schools

Bunker, D., & Thorpe, R. (1982). A model for the teaching of games in the secondary school. *Bulletin of Physical Education, 18*(1), 5–8.

Carballo-Fazanes, A., Rico-Díaz, J., Barcala-Furelos, R., Rey, E., Rodríguez-Fernández, J.E., Varela-Casal, C., & Abelairas-Gómez, C. (2020). Physical activity habits and determinants, sedentary behaviour and lifestyle in university students. *International Journal of Environmental Research and Public Health, 17*(9), 3272.

Casey, M.M., Harvey, J.T., Telford, A., Eime, R.M., Mooney, A., & Payne, W.R. (2014). Effectiveness of a school-community linked program on physical activity levels and health-related quality of life for adolescent girls. *BMC Public Health, 14*, 649.

Commonwealth of Australia. (2014). *Australian citizenship. Our common bond.* Belconnen: National Communications Branch of the Department of Immigration and Border Protection. https://immi.homeaffairs.gov.au/citizenship/test-and-interview/our-common-bond

Costigan, S.A., Eather, N., Plotnikoff, R.C., Hillman, C.H., & Lubans, D. (2016). High-intensity interval training for cognitive and mental health in adolescents. *Medicine & Science in Sports & Exercise, 48*(10), 1985–1993.

Drummond, M.J., & Pill, S.A. (2011). The role of physical education in promoting sport participation in school and beyond. In S. Georgakis & K. Russell (Eds.), *Youth Sport in Australia: history and culture* (pp. 165–178). Sydney University Press.

Dyson, B. (2014). Quality physical education: a commentary on effective physical education teaching. *Research Quarterly for Exercise and Sport, 85*(2), 144–152.

Eather, N., Morgan, P.J., & Lubans, D.R. (2013). Feasibility and preliminary efficacy of the Fit4Fun intervention for improving physical fitness in a sample of primary school children: a pilot study. *Physical Education and Sport Pedagogy, 18*(4), 389–411.

Elliott, K., Norman, J., Wardle, K., Budgen, P., Callahan, H., Camilleri, M., Romeo, A., Trinh, K., Okely, A., & Kariippanon, K.E. (2023). Feasibility, acceptability and potential efficacy of a virtual physical activity program in primary and secondary schools in New South Wales, Australia: a quasi-experimental study. *Health Promotion Journal of Australia, 34*(1), 70–84.

Gard, M. (2014). eHPE: a history of the future. *Sport, Education and Society, 19*(6), 827–845.

Gard, M., & Wright, J. (2001). Managing uncertainty: obesity discourses and physical education in a risk society. *Studies in Philosophy and Education, 20*(6), 535–549.

Garrett, R., & Wrench, A. (2008). Fitness testing: the pleasure and pain of it. *ACHPER Healthy Lifestyles Journal, 55*(4), 17–22.

Gay, G. (2002). Preparing for culturally responsive teaching. *Journal of Teacher Education, 53*(2), 106–116.

Hardman, K. (2000). The world-wide survey of physical education in schools: findings, issues and strategies for a sustainable future. The fellows lecture (part 1). *The British Journal of Teaching Physical Education, 31*(4), 29–31.

Hardman, K. (2001). The world-wide survey of physical education in schools: findings, issues and strategies for a sustainable future. The fellows lecture (part 2). *The British Journal of Teaching Physical Education, 32*(1), 29–31.

Hart, V., Whatman, S., McLaughlin, J., & Sharma-Brymer, V. (2012). Pre-service teachers' pedagogical relationships and experiences of embedding Indigenous Australian knowledge in teaching practicum. *Compare: A Journal of Comparative and International Education, 42*(5), 703–723.

Harvey, S., Kirk, D., & O'Donovan, T.M. (2014). Sport Education as a pedagogical application for ethical development in physical education and youth sport. *Sport, Education and Society, 19*(1), 41–62.

Hellison, D. (1995). *Teaching responsibility through physical activity*. Human Kinetics.

Hyndman, B.P., Benson, A.C., Ullah, S., & Telford, A. (2014). Evaluating the effects of the Lunchtime Enjoyment Activity and Play (LEAP) school playground intervention on children's quality of life, enjoyment and participation in physical activity. *BMC Public Health, 14*, 164.

Jenkinson, K.A., & Benson, A.C. (2010). Barriers to providing physical education and physical activity in Victorian state secondary schools. *Australian Journal of Teacher Education, 35*(8), 1–17.

Kennedy, W.M. (1921). Physical Education. *Journal of the Institute of Inspectors of Schools, 3*(1), 22.

Lee, J., & Macdonald, D. (2010). 'Are they just checking our obesity or what?' The healthism discourse and rural young women. *Sport, Education and Society, 15*(2), 203–219.

Light, R., Curry, C., & Mooney, A. (2014). Game Sense as a model for delivering quality teaching in physical education. *Asia-Pacific Journal of Health, Sport and Physical Education, 5*(1), 67–81.

Macdondald, D. (2013). The new Australian Health and Physical Education Curriculum: a case of/for gradualism in curriculum reform? *Asia-Pacific Journal of Health, Sport and Physical Education, 4*(2), 95–108.

Marsden, E., & Weston, C. (2007). Locating quality physical education in early years pedagogy. *Sport, Education and Society, 12*(4), 383–398.

Martin, K., & Kudláček, M. (2010). Attitudes of pre-service teachers in an Australian university towards inclusion of students with physical disabilities in general physical education programs. *European Journal of Adapted Physical Activity, 3*(1), 30–48.

Miller, P., & Davey, I. (1990). Family formation, schooling and the patriarchal state. In M. Theobald & R. Selleck (Eds.), *Family, school and state in Australian history* (pp. 83–99). Allen & Unwin.

Morgan, P.J., & Hansen, V. (2008). Classroom teachers' perceptions of the impact of barriers to teaching Physical Education on the Quality of Physical Education Programs. *Research Quarterly for Exercise and Sport, 79*(4), 506–516.

Penney, D., Brooker, R., Hay, P., & Gillespie, L. (2009). Curriculum, pedagogy and assessment: three message systems of schooling and dimensions of quality physical education. *Sport, Education and Society, 14*(4), 421–442.

Pill, S. (2011). Seizing the moment: Can Game Sense further inform sport teaching in Australian physical education? *PHENex Journal/Revue phenEPS, 3*(1), 1–15.

Pill, S. (2016). Exploring the challenges in Australian physical education curricula past and present. *Journal of Physical Education & Health: Social Perspective, 5*(7), 5–18.

Pringle, R., & Pringle, D. (2012). Competing obesity discourses and critical challenges for health and physical educators. *Sport, Education & Society, 17*(2), 143–161.

Rink, J.E. (2013). Measuring teacher effectiveness in physical education. *Research Quarterly for Exercise and Sport, 84*, 407–418.

Rodwell, G. (1999). The Eugenic and political dynamics in the early history of physical education in Australia, 1900–50. *Critical Studies in Education*, *40*(1), 93–113.

Scharagrodsky, P.A., & Varea, V. (2016). Tracking the origins of physical education in Argentina and Australia. *The International Journal of the History of Sport*, *33*(8), 777–796.

Schroé, H., Van Dyck, D., De Paepe, A., Poppe, L., Loh, W.W., Verloigne, M., ... & Crombez, G. (2020). Which behaviour change techniques are effective to promote physical activity and reduce sedentary behaviour in adults: a factorial randomized trial of an e-and m-health intervention. *International Journal of Behavioral Nutrition and Physical Activity*, *17*, 1–16.

Siedentop, D. (1994). *Sport education: quality PE through positive sport experiences*. Human Kinetics.

United Nations Educational, Scientific and Cultural Organization. (2014). *Quality physical education*. http://unesdoc.unesco.org/images/0023/002311/231101E.pdf

Welch, R., Alfrey, L., & Harris, A. (2020). Creativity in Australian health and physical education curriculum and pedagogy. *Sport, Education and Society*, *26*(5), 471–485.

Whatman, S., Quennerstedt, M., & McLaughlin, J. (2017). Indigenous knowledges as a way to disrupt norms in physical education teacher education. *Asia-Pacific Journal of Health, Sport and Physical Education*, *8*(2), 115–131.

Wrench, A., & Garrett, R. (2021). Culturally responsive pedagogy in health and physical education. In J. Stirrup & O. Hooper (Eds.), *Critical pedagogies in physical education, physical activity and health* (pp. 196–209). Routledge.

Wright, J. (2011). Educación Corporal en Australia: 1870–1910. In P. Scharagrodsky (Ed.), *La Invención del "Homo Gymnasticus". Fragmentos Históricos sobre la Educación de los Cuerpos en Movimiento en Occidente* (pp. 321–345). Prometeo.

Wright, J., Macdonald, D., & Burrows, L. (2004). *Critical inquiry and problem-solving in physical education*. Routledge.

Wright, J., O'Flynn, G., & Welch, R. (2018). In search of the socially critical in health education: exploring the views of health and physical education preservice teachers in Australia. *Health Education*, *118*(2), 117–130.

Chapter 3

Physical Education in Brazil
The Turning Points and Dimensional Development in Quality of Teaching

Eliana Lucia Ferreira and Maria Beatriz Rocha Ferreira

Introduction

Country Background

The current Constitution, promulgated in 1988, conceives of Brazil as a presidential federative republic, formed by the union of 26 states, the Federal District, and 5,570 municipalities. Officially called the Federative Republic of Brazil, it is the largest country in Latin America and the fifth largest in the world in terms of land area, with 8,500 square kilometers. The Brazilian population is projected at 212 million inhabitants (IBGE, 2024), with a high degree of ethnic and racial crossbreeding, mutual assimilation of cultures, syncretism, and racial miscegenation (Brasil, 1988).

Historically, a significant milestone was the arrival of the Portuguese in 1500. The idea of expanding new territory in search of riches was an objective of the colonizers. The original people, called Indians, a generic terminology, needed to be dominated – whether by force of the sword, catechization, miscegenation, or destruction of culture. They were considered primitive, soulless, cannibalistic people by the European invaders. Different actions and policies have been developed over the centuries. The legal recognition of indigenous people was only enacted by the 1988 Constitution, which recognizes the cultural diversity and rights of these people.

Summarizing history, African slavery from the 16th to the 19th century (1888), French, Dutch, and English invaders under the rule of the Portuguese crown, the reign of the Portuguese crown that moved to the country in 1808, independence from Portugal on September 7, 1822, and the proclamation of the Republic on November 15, 1889, and obviously the post-Republic phase were important milestones in the formation of the Brazilian state.

In the 19th century, the country developed an assimilationist policy, aimed especially at wage-earning jobs, with a focus on agriculture. This process contributed to urbanization and industrialization. Italians, Japanese, Portuguese, Germans and, at the beginning of the 20th century, Syrian Lebanese responded to a call, and also the influx of Portuguese increased. At the end of the 20th century, Bolivians, Haitians, and Venezuelans arrived. All these ethnical groups had an important influence on

DOI: 10.4324/9781003513582-5

the culture and in the richness of traditional body practices, sports, and the processes of sportification.

Women played a fundamental role not only in building the country but also in the shadow of a macho society. This protagonism has become more visible in recent centuries and is interconnected with different factors that have contributed to women opening up new perspectives and empowerment in social life and obviously in physical education and sports, such as the acceleration of social changes in the country at the end of the 19th century and during the 20th century, the processes of urbanization and industrialization, the division of labor, the need for women to participate in work [outside the home], the right to vote in 1932 (Decreto, 2024).

The development of the educational process occurred interconnected with social changes in different areas of the country. The process of politicization, democratization, and secularization that occurred in the country throughout history influenced the educational area, in legislative and executive terms. The development of the educational system was processual, aiming to produce perspectives, knowledge, and innovations to grasp reality. Currently, physical education is anchored in inclusive and responsive principles, promoting a democratic, participatory, collaborative, adaptive, and socio-emotional approach.

Physical Education Development: The Turning Points

The roots of physical education in the country originated in the 18th century, during the transition from colonial Brazil to the Republic. At the time, important issues were being dealt with, such as the search for national identity and the country's geo-political formation, which influenced the field of physical education.

The first physical education schools were created at the end of the 19th century and were associated with military preparation and sports practice rather than formal academic training in the area. It was only in the 20th century that the first schools specializing in physical education appeared, such as the School of Physical Education at the State University of Sao Paulo in 1934, and the National School of Physical Education and Sports (ENEFD) in 1942, in Rio de Janeiro.

Until the 1940s, gymnastics and the so-called gymnastic methods developed by the European schools (Swedish, German, and French) were the main instruction and bodily training imparted to students in primary and secondary schools (Bracht, 1989).

School physical education was strongly influenced by the Austrian Natural Method developed by Karl Gaulhofer and Margarete Streicher, and by the Generalized Sports Method, developed by teachers at the Institut National des Sports (France) in the 1940s. Between 1952 and 1980, the Generalized Sports Method was the most widespread in Brazil. It advocated the integral formation of children and young people through the practice of sports games, based on the argument that teaching sports provides students with a set of attitudes such as teamwork, solidarity, discipline, respect for rules, as well as hygienic habits, and physical development (Bankoff et al. 2014).

In legislative terms, in a period prior to 1971, legal documents indicated that physical education was compulsory in all school years, according to Bracht (1989), until this time many schools barely had adequate physical spaces. With the enactment of the Law of Guidelines and Bases of National Education LDB no. 5.692/71 (Brasil, 1996) and Decree Law no. 69.540/71, it was then established that for physical education to work, it was mandatory to establish viable physical spaces for the practice of the activity. It was from 1971 onward that all schools looked for ways to offer the minimum necessary physical education to obtain authorization to operate. To meet this requirement, existing schools had to build their own spaces or sign agreements with clubs or other places where they could hold these classes, so 1971 became the milestone for the effective development of physical education in Brazil.

Decree-Law no. 69.540/71 regulated the teaching of physical education at all levels of the Brazilian education system, emphasizing that the development of physical fitness should be the fundamental reference for the planning, control, and evaluation of physical education; from the fifth grade onwards, sports initiation should be emphasized; and that in higher education, sports teaching should be improved. From this decree, with the encouragement given by the military government, the hegemony of sports teaching in school physical education was officially firmed.

The development of sport in the country also had repercussions on physical education classes. From 1970 onwards, the technical sports concept became dominant in physical education classes. According to Resende (2017), this scenario still exists, even though this concept has been strongly criticized since the end of the same decade.

From 1971 onwards, the emphasis of physical education classes was on the initiation of different sports, from the recreational perspective of the game (10–14 years old). Teaching focused on learning the technical and specific fundamentals of each sport (specific motor skills), while emphasizing the recreational learning of games, basic rules, and general notions of attack and defense (in the case of individual or collective confrontation games).

In high school (first to third year), students were expected to already have the experience and conditions to perfect the specific skills of each sport with a view to their technical-tactical application. The expectation was that the most skilled students would be directed toward forming training teams, with a view to taking part in the municipal, state, and national sports competitions, which the latest one was widespread after the 1970s (Daolio, 1996).

Dance was also a theme that was widely explored in physical education classes as part of the Technical Sports Concept. It was common for teachers (and not exclusively) with experience and skills as dancers to teach dance in physical education classes, especially to students. It is important to note that, until this period, classes were subdivided by gender, as it was thought that there were typically male or female practices.

Decree-Law no. 3.199 of 1965 influenced the curriculum of physical education classes and reinforced the idea that the physical differences between men and women made them much less competent to play sports than men and, secondly, that playing sports masculinized them, making them 'abnormal' women and/or lesbians, especially young unmarried women. These ideas have become intertwined with the development of Brazilian sport, whose gender inequalities are rooted in the structure and organization of Brazilian sport and disseminated in research such as Guedes (2020), Rubio et al. (2016) and Mourão (2000).

The barriers that sportswomen have had to face have been numerous, and these have been reflected in physical education at school. Here are a few episodes. In 1941, Decree-law no. 3.199 prohibited women from practicing sports that were 'incompatible with the conditions of their nature'. In 1965, the National Sports Council (CND) regulated this decree, establishing that women could practice sports established by international bodies and prohibiting wrestling of any kind, as well as soccer, indoor soccer, beach soccer, water polo, polo, rugby, weightlifting, and baseball. It wasn't until 1979 that the 3199 decree was repealed, allowing women to play any sport (Rubio et al., 2016). At this time, women's soccer and wrestling were not practiced at school.

Therefore, the two moments can be detected in the historical context of Brazilian school physical education. The first is characterized by the hegemony of two conceptions that fundamentally marked the discourse and pedagogical practice of physical education in the educational context: (a) the Biological-Functional conception of physical fitness (hygienist and militarist) and, later, (b) the pedagogization and sportivization of physical education, whose conception was called Technical-Sporting, which privileged selective competitiveness, motor standards and skills, productive rationalization and the search for efficiency, among other aspects, focused on profitability, productivity (Bracht, 1989).

But from the 1980s onwards, critics of these contexts pointed out that the aim of school could not be related to an education focused on strengthening and anatomical-physiological performance (these should be the missions of gyms and sports clubs). There was a struggle to defend the idea that the aim of the school should be more political (Betti & Zuliani, 2002). In this sense, we can mention the emergence of pedagogical proposals for the teaching of physical education from the perspective of psychomotricity, constructivist, developmental, formative-recreational, critical-emancipatory, critical-supervisory, and conceptions open to the experience of movement.

The 1988 constitution was an opening for government and democratic policies. This Constitution establishes the recognition of minorities with constitutional rights, such as people with disabilities, indigenous people, riverside dwellers, and *quilombolas* (afro-descendants who inhabit lands from the escape of slaves to free and generally isolated lands). Physical education and sport began to take on new perspectives.

The 9.394 Law of Guidelines and Bases in 1996 established new categories of Brazilian education: basic and university education (Table 3.1). The new categories required a review of educational guides. Evidently, the historical bases presented here served as the basis for changes and new perspectives.

Physical Education in Brazil 31

Table 3.1 LDB educational system in Brazil

Basic Education	Early Childhood Education	0–5 years old
	Elementary Education	I – First to fifth grade (6–10 years old)
	High School	II – Sixth to ninth grade (11–14 years old)
		First, second and third (15–17 years old)
University Education	Undergraduate programs	4–5 years (depending on the area)
	Graduate programs	Specializations
		Master, Ph.D.

In March 2004, the national curricular guidelines for physical education courses were introduced, which resulted in the curricular division, with two courses emerging at that time: bachelor's degree for coaches and training and educational (*licenciatura*) degree for schoolteacher.

After many discussions, the National Common Curricular Base – BNCC (2024) was created and began to come into force in Brazilian schools in 2018. Implementation was done gradually and progressively, with education networks and states adapting their curricula and pedagogical practices over the subsequent years. Thus, since 2018, schools have been working to incorporate the contents and guidelines established by the BNCC into their political pedagogical projects, aiming to offer an education more aligned with the contemporary demands and needs of Brazilian students. The final date for implementing the National Common Curricular Base in all schools in Brazil was December 2020. The legislation covers all the dimensions listed below, with greater emphasis on some segments.

The 8-Dimensional Development in Quality Physical Education

Dimension 1: Skill Development and Bodily Awareness (SDBA)

The literature indicates that physical education is the most effective way of providing children with the skills, attitudes, values, knowledge, and understanding to participate in physical and sporting activities throughout their lives, across all age groups. With regard to the development of body awareness, studies since the 1980s suggest that greater emphasis should be placed on activities that develop awareness of one's own body and increase relative autonomy. The suggestion is to use psychopedagogical or similar methods to develop body awareness (D'Avila, 1988; Melo, 1994; Cavalari, 2005). Basically, there is the development of agile methods that encourage bodily experimentation and the search for connections and autonomy (Gonzaga, 2024).

Dimension 2: Facilities and Norms in Physical Education (FNPE)

The BNCC recommends that the State guarantee free, compulsory basic education for 4–17 years old, organized as follows: early childhood education (3–5 years old), elementary education (first to fifth year from 6 to 10 years old), sixth or ninth year (11–14 years old), and high school (15–17 years old). Physical education is a mandatory curricular component of school years. Guiding content for the pedagogical practice of physical education teachers is to experience, enjoy, appreciate, and create different games, dances, gymnastics, sports, fights, and adventurous body practices, valuing collective work and protagonism.

It is recommended by legislation that schools have appropriate and safe equipment for physical education classes. However, there are differences between public and private schools, with the latter being better equipped with sports equipment.

The teacher must have a university degree to teach physical education at school, especially after the sixth grade, and supervised by the Minister of Education. Early years can be taught by the class teacher. The after-school program for public schools, called *Programa Segundo Tempo*, organized by the Ministry of Sports (2024), aims to democratize access to the practice and culture of sport, to promote the integral development of children, adolescents, and young people, as a factor in the formation of citizenship and improving quality of life, especially in areas of social vulnerability. The expectation for this new cycle is that 95 centers will be established in total, which will initially be able to serve around 10,000 students and generate employment for around 180 physical education and sports teachers and assistants.

Dimension 3: Quality Teaching of Physical Education (QTPE)

Quality Teaching is a core in all schools. The control is done by the director of school, supervised by the local secretary of education to fulfill the requirement of the BNCC. This includes human rights issues for all children, opportunities for broad involvement in physical activities according to age, respect for the academic learning period at school, the continued education in the area, such as participation in graduate programs (specialization, master, and doctorate). The research is the consequences of the involvement in graduate programs and universities. All the documents and programs emphasize that physical education is an opportunity to fulfill the human potential, health, and well-being of all citizens.

The current actions that have been developed in the school programs are based on the work of:

1 Collaboration: teamwork and the involvement of different stakeholders in decisions, valuing the diversity of perspectives.

2 Decentralization: empowering everyone to make decisions, promoting agility and commitment.
3 Innovation: stimulating creativity and experimentation, encouraging the implementation of new ideas and solutions.

It is important to remark that the desired model for achieving quality in physical education still needs to advance in the country due to the large population and socioeconomic differences.

Dimension 4: Plans for Feasibility and Accessibility of Physical Education (PFAPE)

The national collaboration plans and learning opportunities for teachers are offered by some public universities in specific areas, for instance in Special Education and Inclusion organized by the NGIME – Federal University of Juiz de Fora (2024). The National Physical Education Council CONFEF (2024) through state representatives (CREFs) offers courses for members. Note that membership in this council is mandatory only for bachelors (coaches, trainers) and optional school teachers. The public universities also organize congresses and symposiums with reasonable fees, which open the possibilities to discuss teaching experiences and develop an international network.

One of the most relevant objectives of physical education is that all children and adolescents have access to an excellent education that will allow them to succeed in life. The current changes in Brazilian education respond to multifactorial factors, among which the political, social, economic, cultural, and educational systems stand out.

Dimension 5: Social Norms and Cultural Practice (SNCP)

Inclusion is an important issue to be worked on in all schools, the classes are mixed with children from multicultural backgrounds, intellectual levels, and gender. (Ferreira, 2010). The Brazilian culture is based on many religious backgrounds which fact does not impair the access of the school system. However, economics is an issue in contributing to the development of unequal learning opportunities in our country, in the sense that most better schools are private. There is a growing movement to discuss different aspects of gender and how to deal with it in schools. (Rubio, 2016; Altmann, 2019; Mourão, 2000).

The current policy of inclusion is based on: the development of a democratic, participatory, collaborative, adaptive, and socio-emotional approach; providing personalized teaching and a more effective and inclusive school environment; involvement of all the actors in the teaching-learning process in sharing responsibilities, as everyone (government, schools, students and parents) must play the same role in improving the quality of teaching and learning in classrooms in an environment that is organized appropriately for the processes it is intended to develop.

In summary, the inclusion policy seeks to establish a culture of support for students, responding emotionally and socially to them, and showing appreciation for their needs and socio-emotional skills.

Dimension 6: Governmental Input for Physical Education (GIPE)

The government supports research in the area through graduate programs (specialization, master's, and doctorate). It offers scholarships and research funding from two main organizations: CNPq – National Research and Technology Council and CAPES – Coordination for the Improvement of Higher Education (Brasil, 2024). Brazilian states have also their own resources for the same purpose. The universities have several agreements abroad, which opens possibilities for professors and students to increase international networks.

The structure of government programs refers to the organizational and systemic aspects of the research area. The research context involves the establishment of collaborative structures, such as research partnerships, which bring together stakeholders from different areas of interest.

Dimension 7: Cognitive Skill Development (CSD)

Cognitive skill development is developed in all areas. According to the BNCC, the thematic unities of basic education are circus activities, plays and games, dance, sports, gymnastics, fights, and body practices. These units give opportunities to open ways to develop socially acceptable thinking and moral conduct, critical thinking skills, ability to solve problems, innovation and relative autonomy (there is no plain autonomy).

The educational process for cognitive development is constantly being updated. And it takes into account organizations, perspectives for producing knowledge of reality, pedagogical approaches, learning environments, relationships based on dialog, exchange and collective construction, pedagogical work, mediating teachers, working together and with work as an educational principle.

With these perspectives, the aim is to create conditions conducive to continually evaluating and analyzing situations and processes, listening to the expectations, opinions, and needs of people involved in the educational process, and responding and modifying actions in an agile manner, participatively building better projects and programs that meet everyone's needs and all contexts.

Dimension 8: Habituated Behavior in Physical Activities (HBPA)

We observe active and proactive behavior in children and young people in physical activities in the country. Although many cities already have parks, outdoor fitness equipment, bike paths, and sports courts, much still needs to be built considering the size of the country, population, and economy class. All cities need to be more welcoming, have more police security, and provide better conditions for an active and healthy life for everyone. We mention here the Agita Sao Paulo Program, a multi-level plan that promotes messages about the health benefits of physical activity. It was launched by CELAFISCS (2024) in 1966, based on scientific knowledge, movements of daily life, network (partnership), motivation of people involved, and messages (mascots, folders, YouTube), with low costs.

The aim of physical activity programs is to provide efficient responses to the demands generated by today's society, taking responsibility for new generations and overcoming challenges.

Conclusion

This chapter gives an idea of the size of Brazil, in a brief history of the formation of the Brazilian state, the laws that have been developed in the country in the area of physical education, and the influence of sport. The 8-dimensional development in Quality Physical Education gives an overview of the country's effort to improve the quality of physical education programs.

Physical education is the most effective way of providing children with skills, actions, values, and knowledge throughout their lives. Furthermore, physical education should continue to be accessible to all children regardless of their motor skills, race, religion, gender, age, culture, and religious, social, or economic background.

Government policies have advanced in several aspects of physical education, regarding teaching professionalization and specialization, national guidance programs and supervision. Inclusion, innovation, and opportunities are current themes that permeate the educational processes. Cities that have spaces for leisure, hospitality, and public safety for an active and healthy life deserve greater attention, especially in some areas of the country.

References

Altmann, H. (2019). Gênero na educação física escolar: a educação esportiva a partir da produção científica. En: Quintão, F., Lara, L.,Wachs, F. (eds.). *Democracia e emancipação: desafios para a educação física e ciências do esporte na América Latina.* p. 94–112. Jundiaí: Paco Editorial.

Bankoff, A. D. P., Ferreira, E. L., Rocha Ferreira, M. B. (2014). Physical Education in Brazil. En: Ferreira, E. L. (ed.). *Focuses on Physical Education.* p. 7–83. Juiz de Fora: NGIME/UFJF.

Betti, M., Zuliani, L. R. (2002). Educação física escolar: uma proposta de diretrizes pedagógicas. *Revista Mackenzie de Educação Física e Esporte*, 1(1), 73–81.

Bracht, V. (1989). Educação Física: a busca da autonomia pedagógica. *Revista da Educação Física/UEM*, 1(1), 12–18.

Brasil. (1988). *Constituição Federal.* Brasília, DF: Senado Federal. www.planalto.gov.br/ccivil_03/constituicao/ConstituicaoCompilado.htm

Brasil. (1996). *Lei de Diretrizes e Bases da Educação Nacional.* Brasília, DF: MEC. http://portal.mec.gov.br/seed/arquivos/pdf/tvescola/leis/lein9394.pdf

Brasil. Ministério da Educação e Cultura. (2024). *Base NacionalComum Curricular.* Brasília, DF: MEC. http://portal.mec.gov.br/conselho-nacional-de-educacao/base-nacional-comum-curricular-bncc

Cavalari, T.A. (2005). *Consciência corporal na escola.* [Tesis de Maestría, FEF, UNICAMP]. https://repositorio.unicamp.br/acervo/detalhe/338912

CELAFISCS. (2024). Centro de Estudos do Laboratório de Aptidão Física de São Caetano do Sul. https://celafiscs.org.br

Daolio, J. (1996). Educação física escolar: em busca da pluralidade. *Revista Paulista de Educação Física,* 2(1), 40–42.

D'Avila, C. (1998). *Consciência corporal e adolescência.* [Tesis de maestria, FEF, UNICAMP]. https://repositorio.unicamp.br/acervo/detalhe/337594

Decreto. (1932 [2024]). Decreto Nº 21.076, de 24 de Fevereiro de 1932. www2.camara.leg.br/legin/fed/decret/1930-1939/decreto-21076-24-fevereiro-1932-507583-publicacaooriginal-1-pe.html

Ferreira, E. L. (2010). *Esportes e atividades físicas inclusivas.* Niterói: Intertexto. v. 2.

Gonzaga, K. (2024). *Gestão escolar, responsividade e sociedade 5.0.* En: Ferreira, E. l. (org.). *Estratégias de instrumentos de ensino e aprendizagem para a Educação Inclusiva.* 1st ed. p. 31 – 40. Juiz de Fora: Ngime/UFJF.

Guedes, C. M. (2020). *Mulheres a cesta: história do basquetebol feminino no Brasil: 1892–1971.* [S. l.]: MissLily. https://mulheresacesta.com.br/documentario/

Instituto Brasileiro de Geografia e Estatística (IGBE). (2024). *Projeções da População.* IGBN. www.ibge.gov.br/

Melo, J. P. (1994). *Desenvolvimento da consciência corporal:uma experiencia da educação física na idade pré escolar.* [Tesis de maestria en, FEF, UNICAMP]. https://repositorio.unicamp.br/acervo/detalhe/135119

Mourão, L. (2000). Representação social da mulher brasileira nas atividades físico-desportivas: da segregação à democratização. *Movimento,* 7(13), 5–18.

Resende, Helder Guerra de. (2017). Saberes da educação física na educação escolar. En: Antunes, Marcelo Moreira, Miranda, Márcia. (org.). *A educação física escolar em colégios de aplicação: múltiplos olhares.* 1st ed. p. 15–30. Curitiba: CRV.

Rubio, K., Altmann, H., Mourão, L. A., Goellner, S. V. (2016). Women and sport in Brazil. En:D'Amico, R. L. de, Benn, T., Pfister, G. (ed.). *Women and Sport in Latin America.* p. 69–78. NewYork: Routledge.

Chapter 4

Quality Physical Education in the Province of Diguillín, Ñuble Region, Chile

Alixon Reyes Rodríguez

Introduction

The Republic of Chile is located in the southernmost part of South America. It shares borders with Argentina, Peru, and Bolivia, to the south with Antarctica, and to the west, it borders the Pacific Ocean. It is considered a tricontinental country, given the location of Easter Island, Sala Island, and the Juan Fernández Archipelago (Ministry of Education [MINEDUC], 2019).

Chile has been an independent country since February 12, 1818 (Britannica, 2024). According to the Political Constitution of the Republic of Chile (Chile, 1980), in Articles 3 and 4, Chile is constituted as a unitary state and as a democratic republic.

Chile is recognized for having one of the most stable economies in Latin America, estimating a 2% increase in its Gross Domestic Product by 2024, maintaining the trend of the last 10 years (World Bank, 2024).

Education is enshrined as a citizen's right in Chile, being compulsory up to secondary education (Law 20.370 establishing the General Education Law, 2009). The Chilean educational system is structured in five stages that cover different levels, namely: kindergarten education, school education (basic and secondary education), technical-professional education, higher education, and youth and adult education (MINEDUC, 2024a).

About the Disciplinary Field

The disciplinary area in Chile is currently covered by a subject called 'Physical Education and Health', which is taught throughout basic education and part of secondary education. In third and fourth year of secondary education, 'Physical Education and Health' is an optional subject, which is a measure adopted since 2020 under Agreement No. 057/2019 (Consejo Nacional de Educación de Chile [CNED], 2019), representing a contradiction in the framework of public policy on education and health in Chile, given the high rates of sedentary lifestyles and obesity in that age group (Aguilar-Farías et al., 2019, 2024; Reyes Rodríguez & Martínez, 2024).

According to the hourly dispensation of the curricula for basic education and secondary education in Chile (MINEDUC, 2023), the subject of 'Physical Education and Health' has an allocation of 4 hours per week for courses ranging from first to fourth year of basic education with Jornada Escolar Completa (JEC), and 3 hours per week for institutions without JEC. Between fifth and eighth grade, the allowance is 2 hours per week, with or without JEC. In the case of secondary education, the subject is assigned 2 hours per week for first and second grades, with or without JEC, while for third and fourth grades, the assignment is 2 hours per week, as long as this is one of the subjects selected from among the electives.

At the time of this writing, MINEDUC is conducting a public consultation process for a curricular updating proposal that covers all basic education and goes up to the second year of secondary education (MINEDUC, 2024b). This proposal also incorporates updates in the 'Physical Education and Health' syllabus. Although it is true that the proposal has no scope in relation to the increase or not of the number of hours assigned in the curricular architecture, it is also true that the debate was initiated in the Senate regarding a bill introduced in 2022 that seeks the increase of weekly hours for the subject, which can be seen in Bulletin No. 15502-04, introduced in November 2022 and declared 'Without urgency' (Senate, 2022).

From the epistemic point of view, Chile has historically experienced the course of different trends (rationalist-technical, through sports and hygienist), as has occurred in the rest of Latin America (Mujica et al., 2022; Castillo-Retamal et al., 2020). Currently, Chile has adopted the human motor sciences as an explanatory paradigm for Physical Education (PE). The Centro de Perfeccionamiento, Experimentación e Investigaciones Pedagógicas (CPEIP) has presented the 'Pedagogical and Disciplinary Standards for Physical Education and Health Pedagogy Careers' (CPEIP, 2021), a document that presents the standards for initial teacher training associated with the disciplinary field and in which, in addition, the explicit definition of the expected manifestations for each of the eight standards is presented. Seven of the eight standards make explicit the epistemic orientation of PE in Chile and account for the human motor sciences as a paradigm that orients the foundations of the field for professional performance. This document of disciplinary standards is relevant in that it presents 'those orientations that make explicit and define the set of skills, knowledge, and dispositions that an education professional should have once he or she has completed his or her initial training' (Decree 309, cited in CPEIP, 2021; p. 10).

On the Quality of Physical Education in Chile

According to Rodríguez-Rodríguez (2016) and Durán (2018), the evaluation of quality in education becomes complex given the polysemy of the term 'quality', having to do with the different notions that can be had around the elements that configure 'quality' in education.

In Chile, the 'Sistema Nacional de Evaluación de Resultados de Aprendizaje' was created in 1968 (Bravo, 2016; MINEDUC, 2024c), and the 'Prueba Nacional de Desempeño Escolar' was applied until 1971. By 1982, already in times of military dictatorship, the 'Programa de Evaluación de Desempeño' (PER) was created, being applied until 1984 (Bravo, 2016). Then, the 'Sistema de Evaluación de la Calidad de la Educación' (SECE) was created, in charge of the CPEIP, being applied between 1985 and 1986. Subsequently, it was followed by the 'Sistema de Medición de la Calidad de la Educación' (SIMCE), in charge of the Universidad Católica de Chile between 1988 and 2012, and then in charge of the 'Agencia de Calidad de la Educación Escolar' from 2012 to the present (Bravo, 2016).

The SIMCE includes tests for the curricular area of 'Physical Education and Health'. However, in consideration of Rodríguez-Rodríguez (2016), these tests are not coherent with the formative paradigms of PE in Chile, inasmuch as they ignore the complexity and integrality underlying the notion of human motricity. Insofar as this is so, he points out: '(…) it distances itself from the previously defined concept, and it even seems that part of the PE teaching staff agrees with the test or takes a passive attitude towards the problematic incoherence between the conceptualization of PE and its evaluation, and between the plans and programs of the subject and its evaluation' (p. 175).

The delivery of PE presents disparities in Latin America and the world (López-D'Amico, 2019). When in one country, the educational process advances well, it may happen that, in another, there are limitations, whether political, economic, cultural, or religious. Based on the studies by Hardman (2008) and Hardman and Marshall (2000, 2009), UNESCO, together with other organizations, worked on the proposal of a perspective that would reduce the gaps in PE at a global level. Thus, the quality physical education (hereafter, QPE) approach emerged, which has generated an entire intervention model (McLennan & Thompson, 2015).

Objective

Having already a context in relation to UNESCO's QPE model, this work has the purpose of analyzing the global index of QPE in the province of Diguillín, Ñuble region, Chile.

Methodology

Type of Approach and Design

The study corresponds to a quantitative approach and to a type of exploratory research with a cross-sectional design.

Technique and Instrument

The technique used for data collection was the survey, and the instrument was the questionnaire called 'Global Index of Quality Physical Education' (Ho et al., 2021), with the corresponding linguistic-semantic adaptation for its application in Latin America.

Table 4.1 Dimensions

Dimensions	Acronym
Quality Teaching of Physical Education	QTPE
Facilities and Norms in Physical Education	FNPE
Skill Development and Bodily Awareness	SDBA
Cognitive Skill Development	CSD
Habituated Behavior in Physical Activities	HBPA
Social Norms and Cultural Practice	SNCP
Governmental Input for Physical Education	GIPE
Plans for Feasibility and Accessibility of Physical Education	PFAPE

Source: Own elaboration (2024).

The instrument (Ho et al., 2021) contemplates 8 dimensions, with 50 items to be answered based on a gradation from lowest to highest (1–6), according to levels of agreement with the statements of the items, with the number 1 representing 'In total disagreement', and the number 6 'Totally agree'. The study dimensions are: quality of PE teaching; PE facilities and standards; skill development and body awareness; cognitive skill development; habitual behavior in physical activities; social norms and cultural practices; governmental contributions to PE; feasibility and accessibility plans for PE (see Table 4.1). Cronbach's alpha α was 0.952, presenting an excellent reliability of the instrument.

Population and Sample

This instrument was applied to 69 teachers in the communes of Chillán and San Carlos (considering that in Chile, there are 346 communes, 56 provinces, and 16 regions [Reyes Astudillo et al., 2022] and that Chillán is the capital of the Ñuble region), in the province of Diguillín of the Ñuble region, Chile, based on a non-probabilistic, accidental sampling.

Ethical Procedure

The instrument was applied considering the informed consent reported through a Google form. The study was approved by the Ethical-Scientific Committee of the Adventist University of Chile.

Results

There were the invitation of 69 teachers from the community of Chillán ($n = 53$) and San Carlos ($n = 16$) to participate in the questionnaire survey. Of this group, 20 (29%) were women and 49 (71%) were men. Sixty-five teachers said that they work in institutions in which mixed PE classes are taught, i.e., boys and girls together, while 4 teachers said they work in institutions in which the classes are taught in a

Table 4.2 Mean, standard deviation and variance of the dimensions

Dimensions	Half	Deviation Standard
QTPE	6,5	2,1
FNPE	5,3	2,3
SDBA	6,6	2
CSD	6	2,3
HBPA	6,1	2,8
SNCP	6,4	2
GIPE	5,4	2,4
PFAPE	5,5	2,4

Source: Own elaboration (2024).

differentiated manner. Furthermore, it should be noted that 42 teachers (60.87%) work in the public sector, 15 (21.74%) in the private sector, and 12 (17.39%) in institutions with mixed funding (Table 4.2).

As shown in Table 4.1, the dimension with the best performance is SDBA, followed by QTPE and SNCP, while the dimensions with the lowest average score are FNPE and GIPE. The standard deviation shows that the HBPA dimension stands out in relation to the other dimensions, and this is due to the fact that, just in this dimension, two of its items scored as the lowest and highest rated of the entire instrument, namely, items 31 ('Physical education is a compulsory subject for high school students in our city') and 45 ('Physical education is a compulsory subject for all elementary school students in our city'), respectively. Item 31 was the lowest rated in that it reveals what is a reality in Chile, because, although it is true that PE is taken in secondary education, it is compulsory only up to the second year of that level (CNED, 2019).

If each dimension is considered one by one, it should be noted that the comparisons of this work with international studies, such as those conducted in Ecuador and the Dominican Republic, should be properly contextualized as, in the latter two countries, these are national studies, while in the present study, only two communes of a province in Chile have been considered. With this in mind, it should be noted that, in relation to the QTPE dimension in the present study, the score is similar to the results of the evaluation made in Ecuador using the same instrument (Del Val Martín et al., 2023), and lower than the same evaluation made in the Dominican Republic (Reyes Rodríguez et al., in press). For the case under study, the dimension refers to the quality of PE teaching and implies that the subject should develop elements that encourage and allow students to value structured physical activity and the acquisition of active and healthy habits and lifestyles, adopting them in their daily lives.

In Chile, there are public policies such as the 'Choose to Live Healthy' program (Ministry of Social Development and Family, 2024), in addition to curricular implications, among which the differentiated program for third and fourth grades called 'Promotion of Active and Healthy Lifestyles' (MINEDUC, 2021) stands out.

According to the results of the study, the informant teachers have a clear perception of what can be achieved through the teaching of PE. However, there is a relevant gap between what is perceived and what has been achieved so far, given the data associated with physical inactivity, sedentary lifestyles, and obesity in Chilean children and adolescents.

However, it is understood that the quality of PE cannot be considered exclusively around the promotion of healthy life habits, but that other elements are incorporated, such as curriculum and didactics, without undermining others that are surely relevant. And, as previously highlighted, right now in Chile, a proposal for updating the curriculum for basic education up to the second year of secondary education is being discussed, hoping, of course, that what emerges as a ministerial decision will truly reflect the concerns of PE professionals and society in general, and that the aforementioned consultation process will not be just a checklist generated by the ministerial entity for illusory participation.

Finally, it should be noted that one of the items in this dimension refers to teacher training as a relevant factor for achieving QPE, according to UNESCO. In Chile, there is Law 20.903, 'which creates the National System of Professional Teacher Development', which generates a mechanism of continuous action of accompaniment, permanent training, and teacher evaluation that allows for the qualification of teaching.

The FNPE dimension reached an average of 5.3, which is surpassed in Ecuador (Del Val Martín et al., 2023) but is higher than the results in the Dominican Republic (Reyes Rodríguez et al., in press). This dimension refers to the existence of adequate facilities for the teaching and learning of PE, considering the existence of sufficient and quality equipment.

Montalvo et al. (2010), González-Calvo et al. (2018), and Bores-García et al. (2020) point out the importance of the existence of physical spaces for the teaching and learning of PE and the relevance of having safe spaces, consistent and appropriate to the requirements of the area and the ages of the students. On many occasions and in many institutions, the PE area ends up being sacrificed when budget allocations are limited, which is common. Institutions where there is no physical space for PE are improvised in inadequate places. It is not just about the existence of the space but about safety, suitability, and versatility to the learning needs of students.

This is a relevant issue, considering that infrastructure and equipment impact student motivation, the provision of education, and at the same time, restrict and reduce opportunities for action and freedom, and their impact on learning and the quality of learning (Development Bank of Latin America and the Caribbean, 2016). The study by Aguilar-Farías et al. (2024) shows that in Chile public sector facilities are available in the different municipalities (the private sector has its own), but there is no information on their use, accessibility, quality of the facilities, and suitability for educational purposes.

In another order, the SDBA dimension is shown to achieve the best performance in the province (6.6), slightly higher than the results in Ecuador (Del Val Martín et al., 2023) but lower than those obtained in the Dominican Republic (Reyes Rodríguez et al., in press). This dimension aims at the development of motor skills and body awareness. According to Reyes Rodríguez (2022) and the National Administration of Public Education (ANEP, 2023), body awareness emerges as the basis and hinge of all human development, and Meikahani et al. (2024) state that to address the development of body awareness, comprehensive education must be focused on. Hence, this relevant assessment has been very positive.

This indicates that one of the concerns of school PE is met in the province, although there is a degree of improvement to be achieved. Ideally, the proposed curricular update that will soon be approved in Chile should help reduce this gap, not only in terms of the dimension per se but also in relation to school segregation and inequality in Chile (Acuña and Falabella, 2022; González, 2018).

Regarding the CSD dimension, there is an average of 6, slightly below the study by Del Val Martin et al. (2023) in Ecuador and the study by Reyes Rodríguez et al. (in press) in the Dominican Republic. This dimension, which refers to the development of cognitive skills, obtained the fourth lowest rating, showing the need to deepen and qualify the attention of the dimension in regard to critical thinking, independent thinking, the development of problem-solving skills, problems, innovative thinking, moral thinking, etc. That is to say, it is very good to move toward the development of motor skills and body awareness, but the pedagogical act should not neglect cognitive skills. Reyes Rodríguez (2021, 2022) and Reyes Rodríguez et al. (2016) allude to the need to think about an EF that addresses human integrality, aiming at the formation of such cognitive skills without dissociating pedagogical action.

The HBPA dimension shows the fourth-best rating, equaled by the rating in Ecuador (Del Val Martin et al., 2023) and lower than that obtained in the Dominican Republic (Reyes Rodríguez et al., in press). This dimension refers to habitual behavior in physical activities. These results generate concern regarding mandatory PE in the last years of secondary education, given the background already mentioned regarding Agreement No. 057/2019 (National Council of Education of Chile [CNED], 2019), and which, according to Reyes Rodríguez and Martínez (2024), dissociates Chilean public policy insofar as it is not related to the focus on the focal problem of physical inactivity, overweight and obesity.

The SNCP dimension obtained the third-highest score in this study, with a mean of 6.4. This is higher than the study conducted in Ecuador (Del Val Martin et al., 2023) but lower than that obtained in the Dominican Republic (Reyes Rodríguez et al., in press). This dimension refers to the social commitment of students in the PE class, i.e., whether they develop coexistence, social norms, and appreciation of physical activity as a group, among others. As a derivation of this dimension, it can be interpreted as expressed by Reyes Rodríguez (2022) when he details the need to form the constitution of the political subject from the PE class. This concept is related to the need to be recognized as a relevant social actor, capable of integrating into the social dynamics of their community and intervening in it in relation to others, focusing on strategies that favor the active participation of students, the generation of community projects, the adoption of the service-learning methodology (Gómez, 2023).

In relation to the GIPE dimension (government contributions to PE), this dimension obtained the lowest average score in the study. The GIPE average is slightly higher than the result obtained in Ecuador (Del Val Martin et al., 2023) but lower than the result obtained in the Dominican Republic (Reyes Rodríguez et al., in press). When reviewing the results of this dimension in the three studies, the score is the second lowest in all of them. This is not an isolated case.

This dimension presents a view of the governmental contribution to providing QPE. Apparently, it is one of the lowest-rated dimensions and reveals the teachers' opinion regarding the participation of government bodies and agencies in helping to improve the quality of QPE. The governmental contribution involves several elements: support and search for internal and external funding; investment in the expansion, improvement, and adequacy of infrastructure; generation of policies that make QPE a right of children and adolescents, as well as inclusive gender policies to reduce the relative gaps in PE; promotion and support for research to improve the quality of PE; development of activities that complement PE classes and contribute to improving adherence to healthy lifestyles, etc. Now, it is true that there are contributions, and the teachers who reported them point out that their score is the second lowest of all dimensions, which suggests that the level of contribution is not even close to what is expected. Without a forward-looking vision of the State and its authorities, it will be impossible to achieve the fulfillment and satisfaction of everyone's right to quality education. In Chile, there are legal provisions, plans, and projects that emerge from the State, but it is not enough to talk and institutionalize if this does not translate into the realization of social and community needs.

Finally, the PFAPE dimension also obtained a low score in comparison with other dimensions under study. Comparing results with Ecuador (Del Val Martín et al., 2023), it is observed that the latter are lower than those obtained in this study, and the latter are lower, in turn than those obtained in the Dominican Republic (Reyes Rodríguez et al., in press). In Ecuador, this is the worst-rated dimension, while both in this study and in the Dominican case, it is the third worst-rated. These do not seem to be isolated cases. This dimension refers to EF viability and accessibility plans and refers to institutional and governmental plans for the development of social and community projects that expand the coverage of the right by making it accessible. This implies multifaceted and decisive political action. It must also involve all relevant actors in society.

Conclusion

It is true that in Chile, the results of QTPE are outstanding, this is certainly being questioned; this may be considered out of context, as there are paradigms that collide with the various national and international evaluation proposals, in addition to what the current proposal for curriculum update is doing from an epistemic level.

It will always be a challenge, not only for Chile, to improve the quality of EF, regulations, curriculum, facilities, inclusion, accessibility, investment, the increase in the time allocation of the subject and its place in Chilean curricular architecture, plus coverage of it and improvement plans. While it is true that the most descending dimensions of measurement in Chile were FNPE and GIPE, it is also true that there is a need for improvement in the overall rating of the exploratory factor analysis measurement. To give just one example: the fact that no dimension has reached 7 points says concretely that there are gaps and that there is a significant margin for improvement to be resolved. Thus, it is a matter of rights, the constitution of an emancipated citizen, and not less than that, public health.

Future Course of Action

The researcher is developing the study at the national level in Chile so that the data will have greater national coverage, allowing a better understanding of the educational phenomenon under study.

Conflict of Interest

The author declares that he has no conflict of interest.

References

Acuña Ruz, F.; & Falabella, A. (2022, 2 de mayo). *Y después del SIMCE, ¿qué camino seguir?* [Consulta: August 25, 2024]. www.ciperchile.cl/2022/05/02/y-despues-del-simce-que-camino-seguir/

Administración Nacional de Educación Pública. (2023). *Programa de Educación Básica integrada. Conciencia y conocimiento corporal. Tramo 4. Grados 5° y 6°.* Del autor.

Aguilar-Farías, N.; Miranda-Márquez S.; Sadarangani, K.; Martino-Fuentealba, P.; Cristi-Montero, C.; Cárcamo-Oyarzún, J.; Delgado-Floody, P.; Chandía-Poblete, D.; Mella-García, C.; Rodríguez-Rodríguez, F.; Von Oetinger, A.; Balboa-Castillo, T. ; Peña, S.; Cuadrado, C.; Bedregal, P.; Celis-Morales, C.; García-Hermoso, A.; & Cortínez-O'Ryan, A. (2019). *Reporte de Notas de Actividad Física Infantil de Chile – Díptico 2018.* https://urlc.net/JcCH

Aguilar-Farías, N.; Miranda-Márquez, S.; Toledo-Vargas, M.; Sadarangani, K. P.; Ibarra-Mora, J.; Martino-Fuentealba, P.; Carcamo-Oyarzun, J.; Cristi-Montero, C.; Rodríguez-Rodríguez, F.; Guarda-Saavedra, P.; Balboa-Castillo, T.; Von Oetinger, A.; & Cortinez-O'Ryan, A. (2024). Results from Chile's 2022 report card on physical activity for children and adolescents. *Journal of Exercise Science & Fitness*, 22, 390–396. https://doi.org/10.1016/j.jesf.2024.07.004

Banco de Desarrollo de América Latina y el Caribe. (2016, 4 de octubre). *La importancia de tener una buena infraestructura escolar.* [Consulta: August 25, 2024]. https://lc.cx/ju9DOw

Banco Mundial. (2024). *Chile. Panorama general.* [Consulta: August 15, 2024]. www.bancomundial.org/es/country/chile/overview

www.bcn.cl/siit/estadisticasterritoriales//resultados-consulta?id=340990

Bores-García, D.; Rojas A. L. M.; & Polo-Recuero, B. (2020). La influencia del espacio físico en el proceso de enseñanza-aprendizaje de la Educación Física. *Revista de Estilos de Aprendizaje, 13*(25), 200. https://doi.org/10.55777/rea.v13i25.1490

Bravo, J. (2016). *SIMCE: Pasado, presente y futuro*. ESTUDIOS PÚBLICOS. https://urlc.net/Jc2N

Britannica. (2024). *History of Chile*. Encyclopaedia Britannica. www.britannica.com/topic/history-of-Chile

Castillo-Retamal, F.; Almonacid-Fierro, A.; Castillo-Retamal, M.; & de Oliveira, A. A. B. (2020). Formación de profesores de Educación Física en Chile: una mirada histórica. *Retos, 38*, 317–324. https://doi.org/10.47197/retos.v38i38.73304

Centro de Perfeccionamiento, Experimentación e Investigaciones Pedagógicas. (2021). *Estándares Pedagógicos y Disciplinarios para-Carreras de Pedagogía en Educación Física y Salud*. Del autor.

Chile. (August 11, 1980). *Constitución Política de la República*. www.bcn.cl/procesoconstituyente/comparadordeconstituciones/constitucion/chl

Chile. (August 17, 2009). *Ley 20.370 que establece la Ley General de Educación*. www.bcn.cl/leychile/navegar?idNorma=1006043

Chile. (March 23, 2024). *Ley 20.903, que crea el Sistema Nacional de Desarrollo Profesional Docente y modifica otras normas*. www.bcn.cl/leychile/navegar?idNorma=1202123

Chile, Senado. (2022). *Boletín 15502-04*. [Consulta: August 15, 2024]. https://urlc.net/LnE0

Consejo Nacional de Educación de Chile. (2019). *Acuerdo N° 057/2019*. [Consulta: March 15, 2019]. www.cned.cl/sites/default/files/acuerdo_057_2019_res_159_2019_plan.pdf

Del Val Martín, P.; Kukurová, K.; Ho, W.; Blázquez Sánchez, D.; & Sebastiani Obrador, E. M. (2023). The perceptual understanding of quality Physical Education (QPE) from professional in Ecuador. *Retos, 48*, 16–23. https://doi.org/10.47197/retos.v48.96531

Durán Sanhueza, F. (2018). La Evaluación de la calidad educativa en Chile: instrumentos de control y rendición de cuentas. *Revista Educación, Política y Sociedad, 3*(1), 85–99. https://doi.org/10.15366/reps2018.3.1.005

Gómez Rijo, A. (2023). El Aprendizaje-Servicio en Educación Física: ¿simplemente un modelo pedagógico? *Revista Española de Educación Física y Deportes, 437*(3), 17–25. https://doi.org/10.55166/reefd.v437i3.1104

González, R. (2018). *Segregación educativa en el sistema chileno desde una perspectiva comparada*. Centro de Estudios del Ministerio de Educación.

González-Calvo, G.; Martínez-Álvarez, L.; & Hortigüela-Alcalá, D. (2018). La influencia de los espacios para el desarrollo del proceso de enseñanza/aprendizaje en educación física: una perspectiva autoetnográfica. *Retos, 34*, 317–322. https://doi.org/10.47197/retos.v0i34.63672

Hardman, K. (2008). Physical education in schools: a global perspective. *Kinesiology: International Journal of Fundamental and Applied Kinesiology, 40*(1), 5–28. https://bit.ly/36awjms

Hardman, K.; & Marshall, J. (2000). *World-wide Survey of the State and Status of School Physical Education: The Final Report to the International Olympic Committee*. University of Manchester. https://doi.org/10.1177/1356336x000063001

Hardman, K.; & Marshall, J. (2009). *Second World-wide Survey of School Physical Education. Final Report*. ICSSPE.

Ho, W.; Ahmed, D.; & Kukurova, K. (2021). Development and validation of an instrument to assess quality physical education. *Cogent Education,* 8(1), 1864082. https://doi.org/10.1080/2331186X.2020.1864082

López D'Amico, R. (2019). Educación Física de calidad: ¿De dónde surge este planteamiento? *RECIE. Revista Caribeña de Investigación Educativa,* 3(2), 33–45. https://doi.org/10.32541/recie.2019.v3i2.pp33-45

McLennan, N.; & Thompson, J. (2015). *Educación Física de Calidad. Guía para los responsables políticos.* UNESCO.

Meikahani, R.; Setyo, E.; & Dwi, D. (2024). Identifying the quality of lower-grade primary school rhythmic activity learning. *Retos,* 56, 40–46. https://doi.org/10.47197/retos.v56.101493

Ministerio de Desarrollo Social y Familia. (2024). *Elige Vivir Sano.* [Consulta: August 14, 2024]. https://eligevivirsano.gob.cl/

Ministerio de Educación. (2019). *Ciencias Sociales. Primer ciclo.* Del autor.

Ministerio de Educación. (2021). *Programa de Estudio Promoción de Estilos de Vida Activos y Saludables – 3° o 4° medio.* Del autor. www.curriculumnacional.cl/614/articles-140159_programa.pdf

Ministerio de Educación. (2023). *Planes de estudio vigentes.* Del autor. [Consulta: August 16, 2024]. https://urlc.net/JaaH

Ministerio de Educación. (2024a). *Etapas educativas.* [Consulta: August 15, 2024]. www.mineduc.cl/

Ministerio de Educación. (2024b). *Actualización Curricular.* [Consulta: August 18, 2024]. https://urlc.net/LmAk

Ministerio de Educación. (2024c). *SIMCE.* [Consulta: August 12, 2024]. www.ayudamineduc.cl/ficha/simce

Montalvo Panadero, J.; Felipe Hernández, J. L.; Gallardo Guerrero, L.; Burillo Naranjo, P.; & García Tascón, M. (2010). Las instalaciones deportivas escolares a examen: Una evaluación de los institutos de Educación Secundaria de Ciudad Real. *Retos,* 17, 54–58. www.redalyc.org/pdf/3457/345732283011.pdf

Mujica Johnson, F.; Santander Reveco, I.; Uribe Uribe, N.; Gajardo Cáceres, P.; Carreño Godoy, N.; & Russell Guzmán, J. (2022). Aprendizaje en Educación Física y Salud en Chile: estudio cualitativo del currículum de 7° básico a 2° medio. *Retos,* 46, 843–851. https://doi.org/10.47197/retos.v46.94801

Reyes Astudillo, C.; Salinas Berrios, M.; & Utreras Díaz, J. C. (2022). *Perfiles Comunales 2022. Caracterización de las Comunas de Chile.* Biblioteca del Congreso Nacional de Chile.

Reyes Rodríguez, A. D. (2021). Educación Física crítica: experiencias, aplicaciones y posibilidades. El caso venezolano. *Ágora para la Educación Física y el Deporte,* 23, 29–51. https://doi.org/10.24197/aefd.0.2021.29-51

Reyes Rodríguez, A. D. (2022). Constitución del sujeto, Educación Física y sociomotricidad: campos tensionados. *Retos,* 45, 767–778. https://doi.org/10.47197/retos.v45i0.93008

Reyes Rodríguez, A. D.; & Martínez Rojas, E. (2024). Contradictions in Chilean public education policy: physical education and health case. *Frontiers Sports in Active Living,* 6, 1410849. https://doi.org/10.3389/fspor.2024.1410849

Reyes Rodríguez, A. D.; Retamal, F.; López-D'Amico, R.; & Ho, W. (in press). Índice Global de la Educación Física de Calidad'. El caso de República Dominicana. En prensa.

Reyes Rodríguez, A. D.; Reyes, C.; & Reyes, A. (2016). Pensar la Educación Física. *Diálogos Pedagógicos, 14*(27), 107–129. https://revistas.bibdigital.uccor.edu.ar/index.php/dialogos/article/view/287/pdf

Rodríguez Rodríguez, F. (2016). Medición de la calidad de la Educación Física en Chile, un desafío pendiente. *Espacios en Blanco,* 26, 173–185. www.redalyc.org/articulo.oa?id=384547076009

Chapter 5

The Present and Future of Quality Physical Education in China

Tao Wang, Xiaolin Zhang, Qingwen Guan, Lulu Liu, and Xueting Zhang

Introduction

Background of the Development of School Physical Education in China

China, located in eastern Asia, covers approximately 9.6 million km^2, with a gross domestic product (GDP) of 17.69 trillion US dollars in 2023, making it the world's second-largest economy (National Bureau of Statistics of China, 2024). With a population of around 1.4 billion, China is the second most populous country in the world, and its rapid political and economic development have created a supportive environment in advancing the development of education in schools.

Various policies have promoted the standardised development of school physical education by emphasising the enhancement of physical literacy among children and adolescents. Key policies such as the *Medium- and Long-Term Youth Development Plan* (Central Government of the People's Republic of China, 2017) and *Opinions on Comprehensively Strengthening and Improving School Physical Education in the New Era* (General Office of the Central Committee of the Chinese Communist Party & General Office of the State Council of the People's Republic of China, 2020) have been essential in integrating physical education with students' physical and mental well-being. Following the global focus on health, China adopted the 'Health First' philosophy at the Fourth National Education Conference in 2011, establishing standards for compulsory physical education and health curricula. These standards divide compulsory education into four levels: sports participation, sports skills, physical and mental health and social adaptability (Ministry of Education of the People's Republic of China, 2022a). Such measures have strengthened the role of physical education in holistic education and led to improvements in young people's physical health. However, several challenges remain, including China's vast size, limited per capita resources, complex social demands and conflicting interests. The marginalisation of physical education teachers, the secondary status of physical education curricula and inequalities in resource allocation continue to impede the nationwide development of high-quality physical education.

DOI: 10.4324/9781003513582-7

Development of Physical Education in China

The development of quality physical education (QPE) programmes has gained significant attention due to its role in promoting effective learning for children and adolescents. Research on QPE in China can offer valuable insights into the contextual factors shaping its development, the unique challenges faced, and strategies for successful implementation. Ho et al. (2023) conducted a survey to explore strategic approaches to QPE in China, including methods to promote equal access to QPE across various regions. The study surveyed 437 PE teachers and curriculum developers from primary and secondary schools across six regions: North, Northeast, East, South Central, Southwest and Northwest China. At the same time, a number of Chinese literatures and studies have provided theoretical support for the eight dimensions of QPE in this study (Ma et al., 2021; Liu & Liu, 2019; Wang et al., 2020). The dimensions are Skill Development and Bodily Awareness (SDBA), Facilities and Norms in PE (FNPE), Quality Teaching of PE (QTPE), Plans for Feasibility and Accessibility of Physical Education (PFAPE), Social Norms and Cultural Practice (SNCP), Governmental Input for PE (GIPE), Cognitive Skill Development (CSD), and Habituated Behaviour in Physical Activities (HBPA) (Table 5.1).

The results revealed an overall mean score of 7.39 for QPE development. The highest mean scores were 7.73 for SDBA and 7.67 for HBPA. In contrast, the lowest scores were 7.16 for CSD and 7.14 for PFAPE. These findings indicate that school physical education in China primarily emphasises improving motor skills, enhancing physical education knowledge and fostering exercise habits. However, the lower score for PFAPE underscores the need for more inclusive and accessible fitness opportunities to ensure all students can fully participate in physical

Table 5.1 Average mean and standard deviation of the dimensions

Dimensions	Mean	Deviation Standard
SDBA	7.73	1.60
HBPA	7.67	1.67
QTPE	7.38	1.76
SNCP	7.30	1.85
FNPE	7.25	1.79
GIPE	7.24	1.87
CSD	7.16	1.83
PFAPE	7.14	2.07
Total score	7.39	1.68

Notes: SDBA = Skill Development and Bodily Awareness; HBPA = Habituated Behaviour in Physical Activities; QTPE = Quality Teaching of PE; SNCP = Social Norms and Cultural Practice; FNPE = Facilities and Norms in PE; GIPE = Governmental Input for PE; CSD = Cognitive Skill Development; PFAPE = Plans for Feasibility and Accessibility of Physical Education.

education. Addressing these barriers is crucial for achieving a more balanced and comprehensive QPE approach. Additionally, the findings highlight the need for improvement in enhancing cognitive skills development and the importance of improving fitness programmes that are accessible to students to support the overall development of QPE in China. The following expects to discuss the development in related dimensions and the importance of holistic planning of dimensions as prerequisite for success.

Focus on Skill Development and Bodily Awareness

The latest physical health data released by the Chinese Health Commission show that the nationwide myopia rate of children and adolescents was 53.6% in 2022—36% among primary school students and 71.6% among junior high school students; in 2023, the rate was 52.7%—35.6% among primary school students, 71.1% among junior high school students and 80.5% among senior high school students (Ministry of Education of the People's Republic of China, 2024). In recent years, myopia rates among adolescents have remained high, severely impacting their health, academics and lives and making them prone to psychological anxiety, depression and other negative emotions. Therefore, the problem of physical fitness and health among children and adolescents needs to be resolved urgently (Yin & Zeng, 2021). Consequently, the focus of physical education in Chinese schools tends to be on 'developing students' physical abilities' and 'cultivating students' motor skills' in an attempt to improve their physical and mental health through physical exercise (Cheng & Wang, 2023).

Improvement of Facilities and Norms in Physical Education

Many schools in China still face problems such as difficulty in replacing dated sports facilities with new ones, outdated equipment, geographical constraints on the construction of stadiums and homogenisation of sports facilities (Wang, 2019). Most of these schools are located in the western and northwestern parts of the country. However, China has an overall favourable rate of compliance with standards of sports equipment and facilities. According to data released by the Ministry of Education in 2022, 93.52%, 95.68%, and 94.46% of the primary, middle and high schools in China, respectively, had sports halls that meet the standards, and 97.07%, 98.08% and 96.50%, respectively, was equipped with sports equipment that meets the standards. This indicates that most primary and secondary schools in China can provide students with a safe and appropriate environment, equipment and facilities for physical education and meet the needs of young students to participate in physical activities. Therefore, it is necessary to implement the standard requirements for the provision of physical education facilities and equipment, build venues and special classrooms to meet the demand and establish a mechanism for replenishing, repairing and updating equipment to achieve full coverage of the school stadium facilities and equipment that meet the standards.

Governmental Input for Quality Physical Education

With China's socioeconomic development and the rise of global sports, the government has placed increasing emphasis on physical education. Governments at all levels have introduced a series of policies and initiatives to promote the development of physical education, investing funds and increasing support in the construction of school sports facilities and physical education training. Accordingly, China has issued several policies to promote young people's healthy development through high-quality physical education as an institutional guarantee and attached great importance to financial investment in school physical education. The most direct investment from the State General Administration of Sports is in the construction of sports venue infrastructure. According to the statistics on sports venues in China released by the 2023 Department of Sports Economics, the country has 4,592,700 sports venues with a total area of 4,071 million m^2 and a per capita area of 2,890 m^2 (Central People's Government of the People's Republic of China, 2024). The Chinese make full use of social resources to meet the needs of students for physical exercise and actively advocate the establishment of a mechanism of openness, mutual promotion and co-promotion between school gymnasiums and public gymnasiums. This indicates opening up the school stadiums to the community and free or low-fee public stadiums to students to enhance the openness and efficiency of stadiums. Regardless of the policy support or financial investment, China has demonstrated the importance and development of physical education in schools.

Importance of Developing Quality Physical Education Teaching and Learning

China's new curriculum standard emphasises that teaching and learning are processes of interaction between teachers and students, which coincides with the importance of teaching and learning in high-quality physical education. In the design and practice of physical education teaching strategies in China, there has been a gradual breakthrough in the traditional teaching model, with a greater emphasis on project-based learning, that is, teachers designing relevant scientific approaches and contexts, helping students experience, discover and explore so that they can judge, summarise, analyse and collect information and develop their thinking ability. Simultaneously, China's emphasis on physical education is also reflected in the curriculum textbooks, whereby teaching materials pay attention to students' sports skills, sports behaviour and sports moral core quality training and to the combination of teaching content and modern information technology. This is done by using diversified information technology means to improve the vitality and effectiveness of physical education classroom teaching (Ren, Yuan, & Chu, 2024). In curriculum design, the integration of structured and situational curriculum ideas ensures intercommunication between teachers' teaching content and students' learning activities, which further strengthens the role of physical education in students' skill promotion and healthy development.

Importance of Improving Cognitive Skill Development

Participation in sports can help students develop critical and innovative thinking, which is an important goal of compulsory physical education in China. The policy promulgated by China in the *Guiding Opinions on Promoting the Reform of the Educational Methods of Ordinary Senior High Schools in the New Era* expects ordinary senior high school education to lay a favourable foundation for students to adapt to society, obtain higher education and develop their future careers. The policy strives to cultivate students into socialist builders and successors with all-round development in morality, intelligence, physical fitness, aesthetics and aptitude (Central People's Government of the People's Republic of China, 2019a). After years of educational reform in China, most primary and high schools already have a physical education teaching environment that fosters critical thinking; however, there has been no fundamental change in the way students learn and train. The compulsory physical education reform in China should focus on the training of 'specific ability' or 'specific thinking'. Meanwhile, education and teaching reform has entered the stage of internal development, focusing on more implicit education and teaching activities.

Demonstration of Habitual Behaviour in Physical Activities

With the rapid development of China's economy, the dietary structures and patterns of adolescents and young people have changed, indicating excessive intake of high-fat, high-sugar and high-salt foods; changes in lifestyle and transportation; increased time for sedentary activities; reduced physical activity; an imbalance between energy intake and consumption; and overweight and obesity issues (Zhang & Ma, 2017). According to the *Report on the Status of Nutrition and Chronic Diseases in China (2020)* released by the National Health Commission, the prevalence of overweight and obesity issues among children and adolescents aged 6–17 in China is approximately 20% (Central People's Government of the People's Republic of China, 2020). For children and adolescents, long-term overweight and obesity issues hasten the growth and development period with rapid bone age growth, resulting in the compression of the height development period. Other obesity-related diseases also affect the physical and mental health of children and adolescents. Therefore, China has begun motivating young students to participate in sports activities using a policy-oriented approach. The *Outline of Healthy China 2030 Plan* proposes: 'By 2030, young students will participate in moderate-intensity sports activities more than three times a week and mastery in1–2 sports skills' (Central People's Government of the People's Republic of China, 2019b). This is how

China intends to increase the intensity of young students' sports participation, helping them maintain a healthy lifestyle, develop the habit of regular exercise, and understand the relationship between physical activity and personal and social development and practice the same.

Plans for Feasibility and Accessibility of Physical Education

Currently, the *Physical Education and Health Curriculum Standards for Compulsory Education (2022 Edition)* requires the use of information-based teaching tools and methods to conduct real-time and accurate evaluations in the implementation of physical education curriculum (Ministry of Education of the People's Republic of China, 2022b). With the advancement and popularisation of the Internet of Things, information and communication technology, and wearable devices, it is possible to obtain real-time and convenient youth sports data in the physical education classroom, which is mainly embodied in the intelligent analysis of real-time youth sports data and feedback on the learning of sports skills during the linking process of the three scenarios of 'teaching, practising and competing' in the physical education classroom. China has also started focusing on the technology-enabled development of QPE in schools with innovative teaching methods and modes in the classroom. This seems to be the primary means of improving teaching efficiency and increasing the sense of participation and satisfaction among the youth and students in sports as the main teaching objectives, which is the current direction of the development of China's QPE.

Analysis of Differences in the Development of Quality Physical Education in China

During the Seventh Five-Year Plan period, China was divided into three major economic zones—Eastern, Central and Western—based on differences in natural conditions, economic resources or advantages, levels of economic development and transport conditions.

The results in Table 5.2 show that the eight dimensions of the development of QPE in China exhibited significant differences at the economic level ($p < 0.05$). This indicates that QPE was significantly influenced by the regional economic level. Consequently, the quality of physical education in the more economically developed regions, such as the eastern region, was found to be significantly higher than that in the central and western regions. Multiple comparative analyses indicated the presence of a distinctive feature in 'cognitive skill development'. This is evidenced by the close proximity of the mean values observed in the eastern region to those observed in the central region and a large discrepancy observed between the eastern and western regions. The remaining dimensions exhibited a distinct divergence between the mean values observed in the eastern and western regions (1 > 2, 2, 3), with the disparity between the eastern and western regions being more pronounced than that observed between the eastern and central regions

Table 5.2 Analysis of regional variability in the eight dimensions of quality physical education development (M ± SD)

	1 (n = 9)	2 (n = 7)	3 (n = 4)	F	p	Least Significant Difference	Variance Chi-square
SDBA	7.85 ± 0.45	7.23 ± 0.49	7.07 ± 0.52	5.688*	0.012	1 > 2, 3	0.854
FNPE	7.91 ± 0.45	7.39 ± 0.51	7.22 ± 0.50	4.166*	0.032	1 > 2, 3	0.905
QTPE	7.67 ± 0.50	7.11 ± 0.55	6.99 ± 0.49	3.862*	0.039	1 > 2, 3	0.778
PFAPE	7.26 ± 0.66	6.56 ± 0.62	6.42 ± 0.75	3.584*	0.048	1 > 2, 3	0.932
SNCP	7.70 ± 0.45	7.17 ± 0.54	6.95 ± 0.59	4.332*	0.028	1 > 2, 3	0.800
GIQPE	7.44 ± 0.54	6.84 ± 0.58	6.64 ± 0.75	3.772*	0.042	1 > 2, 3	0.837
CSD	7.43 ± 0.47	6.97 ± 0.41	6.69 ± 0.53	4.567*	0.024	1 > 3	0.933
HBPA	7.70 ± 0.45	7.18 ± 0.48	6.86 ± 0.58	5.377*	0.014	1 > 2, 3	0.900

Note: *$p < 0.05$; 1 = the eastern region, 2 = the central regions, 3 = the western regions.

(1 > 2, 4). In contrast, the level of development of QPE was relatively balanced within the eastern economic region, likely because areas with more developed economies have better educational environments and more advanced resources for physical education. They also trade and exchange cultures with other places more frequently. In addition, there is a strong culture of physical exercise involvement in the social environment related to physical culture, which places a high value on physical activity and a significant willingness to invest in physical education. Furthermore, the mean value of 'cognitive skill development' showed no obvious difference between the eastern and western regions and eastern and central regions.

Conclusion and Recommendations

The development of QPE in China has attracted considerable attention from various stakeholders, including the government, society and schools. The eastern region of China, which is home to the country's most economically developed provinces and cities, has demonstrated a higher level of development in eight key dimensions of QPE than the national average. This suggests that the advancement of China's QPE is influenced by a number of factors, including the economic level, prevailing concepts of education, and investment in sports venues and facilities. It is imperative to address the limitations of uneven development and the insignificant improvements in the quality of physical education in China. The future development of physical education in schools will undoubtedly be characterised by an increasing focus on inclusive and high-quality physical education. To realise the quality development of physical education in China, a collaboration among policies, concepts and mechanisms is necessary.

1 At the policy level, it is necessary to conduct comprehensive research on QPE and compile data and scientific evidence regarding the development of QPE in China. This will ensure the scientific and effectiveness of policy design. Concurrently, the Chinese government should reinforce the interconnection of policies with the international QPE advocacy sector, coupled with the youth policy advocacy document launched by UNESCO, to enhance synergy between policies.
2 At the conceptual level, it is important to promote QPE implementation in China. The reform and development of school physical education should be guided by the principles of fairness and inclusiveness to ensure equity in physical education. To achieve this goal, it is essential to provide targeted assistance to areas that may lag behind and leverage the available resources.
3 At the mechanism level, the guarantee mechanism of physical education in Chinese schools can be based on the linkage of family, school and society, following the supportive behaviours of the stakeholders in the development of QPE to stimulate the vitality of powerful social forces and encourage the growth of more social forces. Furthermore, it can encourage the involvement of additional social sports organisations in school sports activities and facilitate multiparty collaboration and comprehensive participation.

References

Central Government of the People's Republic of China. (2017). *The Central Committee of the Communist Party of China and the State Council Issued the Medium- and Long-term Youth Development Plan (2016–2025) [中共中央 国务院印发《中长期青年发展规划（2016－2025年）]*. www.gov.cn/zhengce/202203/content_3635263.htm#1

Central Government of the People's Republic of China. (2019a). *Guiding Opinions on Promoting the Reform of Parenting Methods in General Senior Secondary Schools in the New Era [关于新时代推进普通高中育人方式改革的指导意见]*. www.gov.cn/zhengce/content/2019-06/19/content_5401568.htm

Central People's Government of the People's Republic of China. (2019b). *Action for a Healthy China (2019–2030) [健康中国行动 (2019–2030)]*. www.gov.cn/xinwen/2019-07/15/content_5409694.htm

Central People's Government of the People's Republic of China. (2020). *The State Council Information Office Held a Briefing on the Report on Nutrition and Chronic Disease Status of Chinese Residents (2020) [国务院新闻办就《中国居民营养与慢性病状况报告（2020年）》有关情况举行发布会]*. www.gov.cn/xinwen/2020-12/24/content_5572983.htm

Central People's Government of the People's Republic of China. (2024). *Statistics on Sports Venues Across the 2023 [2023年全国体育场地统计调查数据]*. www.gov.cn/lianbo/bumen/202403/content_6941155.htm

Cheng, X., Wang, L. (2023). Characteristics, challenges and strategies for the Development of School Sports in Primary and Secondary Schools under the Perspective of Sports and Health Integration [体卫融合视域下中小学学校体育的发展特征、挑战及策略]. *Journal of Guangzhou Sports Institute*, 43(3), 102–108.

General Office of the Central Committee of the Chinese Communist Party, General Office of the State Council of the People's Republic of China. (2020). *Opinions on Comprehensively Strengthening and Improving School and University Physical Education Work in the New Era [关于全面加强和改进新时代学校体育工作的意见]* www.gov.cn/gongbao/content/2020/content_5554511.htm

Ho, W., Hu, J., Rafael, K., Xie, Y.Y., Ahmed, D., Liu, M., Wang, T., Wang, Y. (2023). The perception of quality physical education in China. *International Sports Studies*, 45(2), 69–87.

Liu, B., Liu, S.J. (2019). Evaluation research on the teaching quality of physical education classes in primary and secondary schools [中小学体育课教学质量的评价研究]. *Teaching and Management*, 30, 122–124.

Ma, R., Hu, J., He, J. (2021). From movement screening to educational integration: the developmental flux of international children's basic motor skill assessment [从动作筛查到教育融合：国际儿童基本动作技能评价的发展流变]. *Journal of Guangzhou Sports Institute*, 41(5), 82–86.

Ministry of Education of the People's Republic of China. (2022a). *Circular of the Ministry of Education on the Issuance of the Compulsory Education Curriculum Programme and Curriculum Standards (2022 version) [教育部关于印发义务教育课程方案和课程标准（2022年版）的通知]*. www.moe.gov.cn/srcsite/A26/s8001/202204/t20220420_619921.html

Ministry of Education of the People's Republic of China. (2022b). *General Office of the Central Committee of the Communist Party of China General Office of the State Council Issues Opinions on Comprehensively Strengthening and Improving School Sports Work in the New Era [关于全面加强和改进新时代学校体育工作的意见]*. www.moe.gov.cn/jyb_xxgk/gk_gbgg/moe_0/moe_7/moe_445/tnull_6327.html

Ministry of Education of the People's Republic of China. (2024). *How Has the 'Big Problem' of 'Small Glasses' Been Solved with a Drop of 1.7 Percentage Points? [降了1.7个百分点"小眼镜"的"大问题"解决得如何了？]*. www.moe.gov.cn/jyb_xwfb/s5147/202406/t20240603_1133754.html

National Bureau of Statistics of China. (2024). *The 2023 Statistical Communiqué on the National Economic and Social Development of the People's Republic of China [中华人民共和国2023年国民经济和社会发展统计公报]*. www.stats.gov.cn/sj/zxfb/202402/t20240228_1947915.html

Ren, Y., Li, D.S., Chu, J. (2024). Characteristics, structural features and teaching suggestions of physical education and health textbooks for general senior high schools published by people education press [人教版普通高中体育与健康教材编写特色、结构特征与教学建议]. *Theory and Practice in Education*, 44(20), 36–41.

Wang, C.Z., Wang, S., Xing, J.M. (2020). Research on the governance structure of school sports field facilities under the background of multiple governance [多元治理背景下学校体育场地设施治理结构研究]. *Sports Culture Guide*, 12, 38–43.

Wang, J.W. (2019). Dilemma and way out of school sports development in China under the background of healthy China [健康中国背景下我国学校体育发展的困境与出路]. *Journal of Guangzhou Sports Institute*, 39(4), 1–4.

Yin, X.J., Zeng, Z.P. (2021). Joint attention to physical and mental health to promote comprehensive development of Chinese adolescents [共同关注体质与心理健康促进中国青少年全面发展]. *China School Health*, 42(1), 5–9.

Zhang, N., Ma, G.S. (2017). An interpretation of the China childhood obesity report [《中国儿童肥胖报告》解读]. *Journal of Nutrition*, 39(6), 530–534.

Chapter 6

Quality Physical Education in Colombia

Diana Feliciano Fuertes, Luz Amelia Hoyos Cuartas, and Carolina Guerrero Reyes

Introduction

Country Background

Currently, Colombia is recognized as the fifth growing economy in Latin America, after Brazil, Mexico, Chile, and Argentina. The country's economic development is mainly supported by the export of oil and agricultural products such as coffee, emeralds, and flowers. In relation to political organization, the country has a democratic system and is considered well-grounded compared to other countries in the region. For the first time in history, a left-wing government, calling itself *moderate left*, is now the head of the government. Regarding population, Colombia has approximately 52 million inhabitants, of which a high percentage is located in the Andean region of the country, where two of the main and developed cities are located and where the largest number of populations is concentrated. For access to public services, the population is distributed in socio-economic strata scaled from 1 to 6, with the most vulnerable population being those belonging to strata 1 (poor) and 2 (vulnerable); they receive subsidies from the government, and correspond to 33.6% and 21.1%, respectively, according to the report presented by the National Department of Statistics DANE (DANE, 2022, p. 3).

The geographical location of the country is considered strategic and privileged due to two particular situations: first, Colombia is considered to be the connecting bridge between the north and south countries of the American continent, and, second, it has an extensive continental platform, which is divided into two oceans, the Atlantic (Caribbean Sea) and the Pacific, making it the gateway to South America and setting communications with the rest of America, Europe, and the countries of the Pacific basin (DANE, 2023). Furthermore, its location in the Equatorial Torrid Zone determines the existence of a great variety of climates and ecosystems, almost the opposite of the other tropical zones of the planet (Molano-Barrero, 1995).

The equatorial location of the country has an equatorial climate that remains constant throughout the year, but its relief conditions and geographical formations cause the climate to vary depending on the altitude, finding tropical humid dry temperatures, and mountain climates, which makes Colombia hosting between 10% and 14% of the world's biodiversity (Viceministerio de Turismo, 2021, p. 21).

Likewise, the geographical location of Colombia also defines the multiculturalism and multiethnicity of the territory, where there are indigenous communities, black communities, Afro-Colombian, *Palenqueras, Raizales,* and *Gypsy Rom* communities whose practices and traditions constitute the basis of the culture of the country (Ministerio de Cultura, 2013).

The Colombian territory is divided into six regions that are defined by the conditions of relief, altitude, average rainfall, and soil conditions (DANE, 2023), which favors agricultural production and promotes tourism. In the last two decades, after the peace treaty was signed between the government and the Revolutionary Armed Forces of Colombia (FARC) guerrillas, the country has experienced a significant increase in tourists coming from all over the world, a fact that has had an impact on the economic development of the country.

The Colombian educational system is governed by public policies formulated by the Ministry of Education, an entity whose purpose is; "*State education policies and monitor education quality indicators*" (Decreto 2230, 2003, p. 1). In this sense, one of the Ministry of National Education (MEN)'s responsibilities is to monitor the development of public and private systems that provide educational services at five levels: (a) nursery; (b) elementary; (c) secondary; (d) university education; and (e) education for employment and human development. The country currently has a high level of literacy, 91.8% in women and 91.2% in men, according to the DANE report. The percentage of people who do not know how to read or write is found in areas that are difficult to access due to their geographical or cultural conditions (DANE, 2022).

School Physical Education/or Sports Education/or Learning of Physical Activities

Physical education in Colombia, as an academic discipline and as part of the school curriculum, was made official in 1928 under the decree 710 of 1928 (Decreto, 1928). However, within the different educational models implemented in the country during the time of the Spanish Colony, and during the course throughout the 17th and 19th centuries, it is possible to identify some physical and sports practices, which had as their purpose the integral formation of the subject, the acquisition of healthy lifestyle habits, and specifically during the colony, including preparation for war (Hoyos, 2020).

Throughout the 20th and into the 21st centuries, physical education in Colombia has been influenced by the different dominant epistemological paradigms coming from abroad. Thus, in the first decades of the 20th century, and according to González-Boto, Madrera-Mayor, and Salguero del Valle (2004), there were the great European gymnastic movements that governed the body practices carried out in Colombian schools, among them were the German gymnastics of Guts Muths (1759–1859) and Ludwin Jahn (1778–1852), and the Swedish gymnastics of Henrik Ling (1776–1839). It was precisely in the 1920s when physical education was formalized as a school subject in the country. This fact generated the formalization of the first university program to train physical education teachers in 1936.

By the middle of the 20th century, the current approaches of physical education developed in the United States from a medical perspective arrived in the country to decisively influence the first school curricula, in which psychomotor theories and, later, the fitness theories, could be identified. In 1970, the proposal of the Spanish, José María Cajigal (1928–1983), cited in Chávez-Ligña (2023) gave a new twist to Colombian physical education, transforming the curricula from a humanistic vision of body practices, giving an educational nature to sport and school physical education. Already in the 1990s, the training curricula for graduates in physical education in Colombia showed a tendency toward the science of motor action, supported by the works of Pierre Parlebas which, internationally, are known as the motor praxeology. Also, Cajigal's sociological theories and his analysis of games and sports were fundamental for the development of new training programs at the university level, in the professional qualification of graduates in Sports and professionals in Sports Sciences (Martines, De Caravalho-Figi, & DeSouza, 2020).

In the first decade of the 2000s, physical education in Colombia continued to be greatly influenced by Parlebas; nonetheless, the notion of human motor skills emerged, led by Manuel Sergio and Eugenia Trigo. This paradigmatic current, supported by the premise of considering human motor skills as a science that studies the subject's ability to intentionally reveal themselves in the world, places physical education as its predecessor, which has had a relative influence on some programs of undergraduate and postgraduate studies in the area.

Dimensions in Quality Physical Education

Skill Development and Body Awareness

The development of motor skills and body awareness are considered fundamental components in physical education programs in Colombian schools (Ministerio de Educación Nacional, 2022). It is also fundamental for school children by linking their body experience with the opportunity to transfer these learnings to other movement potentials in a more complex way, where aspects such as technique, harmony, efficiency, and effectiveness are combined during the performance of movements and motor schemes, as for instance, those carried out in sports, recreational practices, and body expression, among others.

However, these practices on skill development and body awareness are not made visible homogeneously in the physical education curricular plan. In the country, not all schools have physical education teachers. It may depend on the type of educational institution, whether it is public or private.

For the specific case of public schools, some factors are identified that may affect the teacher's assignment, for example, the levels of schooling served by the institution, the physical infrastructure, the geographical location, whether it is rural or urban, and so on.

However, private schools have different conditions compared to the public sector. In private schools, the hiring process of a physical education professional depends on the financial solvency of the institution. With this, two situations may arise: first, if the institution has sufficient financial capacity and has specialized personnel in the area; or, the second, when the development of the academic space is assigned to another teacher who does not have the expertise and knowledge.

Physical Scenarios for the Practice of Physical Education

The infrastructure for the area of physical education varies significantly, depending on the public or private nature of the school. At a general level, educational institutions have a sports space, which is used for students' recreation time, and also as a classroom for physical education class. In public schools, there is at least one sports field; however, there are great variations in their dimensions, quality, and maintenance (Hoyos, 2012). Unfortunately, government entities do not understand the importance of having the appropriate settings and the provision of necessary implements for the development of the physical education class.

However, some physical education teachers, especially in rural areas, make use of geographical and natural resources by proposing a disruptive physical education in relation to the traditional contents of the class, also managing to develop a sense of relevance and identity in the students who live in those regions (Estevez & Hoyos, 2021).

Finally, at the municipal level, the following is promoted: "*Physical Education Development Centers*" (Vicepresidencia de la Nación, 2023). This strategy is an opportunity to bring educational communities closer to making use of facilities such as coliseums, multiple fields, and sports fields, which are little used. The strategy is directly linked to municipal development plans through structures such as sports committees and more directly with the municipal education secretary.

Quality of Physical Education Teaching

The quality of physical education teaching can be approached from the following angles:

1 *Teacher's performance:* This is associated with the teacher's expertise in his or her disciplinary field, that is, the mastery of the contents according to the conditions and needs of the student population and/or the school where you work. Therefore, in some schools in the country, there are teachers who have extensive experience, and in this way, they facilitate offering content for physical education, contextualized to the realities of the school.
2 *Graduate education of teachers*: teachers who opt for a degree such as specialization, master's, or doctorate, contribute significantly from the research

teachers carried out in school contexts to the resolution of problems related to physical education, or student´s coexistence.

3 *Contract modality is presented as a determining factor.* Thus, as there are full-time teachers hired by the State, with an indefinite contract with a salary that covers 12-month fully paid, there are other teachers who are hired only for 11 months, which is the time when the students are enrolled, leaving their contract for the following year in the power of the institution with no certainty. These working conditions directly influence the quality of physical education teaching, as they affect the teacher in his or her personal and professional development.

4 *Government commitments regarding the quality of physical education.* In some schools in Colombia, physical education has low recognition in the general education curriculum. Ignorance and invisibility of the significant contributions of physical education for the development of students in all its dimensions generate tensions for teachers in the area.

The aforementioned discussion shows that most schools have only 2 hours of physical education a week. It is necessary, of course, to recognize that there are experiences in schools in Bogotá, which, because of the leadership of the teachers and particular institutional conditions, have achieved a greater number of hours per week, and even develop the Institutional Educational Project (PEI) of the school with emphasis on physical education. This is how, for instance, the Agustín Fernández public school and Los Nogales private school stand out (Guío-Gutiérrez, Díaz-Marín, & Mejía-Ortiz, 2010).

5 *Networking, associations, and organizations.* These promote the development of physical education in schools. These academic organizations have set networks of researchers that generate knowledge and alternative proposals to solve school problems. Also, it has allowed the dissemination, recognition, and consolidation of groups of physical education professionals focus on both theory and practice on the body, play, movement, and sport, generating a dialogue with other disciplines that enrich the practices, senses, and meanings of physical education.

It can be concluded that the quality in the teaching of physical education in Colombia depends on the experience, expertise, and continuous improvement of the physical education teacher, and the place it occupies within the general structure of formal education—in terms of the allocation of time to physically educate students and ending with the self-management capacity that teachers have when energizing academic organizations interested in contributing to the development of the discipline.

Physical Education Inclusion and Accessibility Programs

During the 18th and 19th centuries in Colombia, people with disabilities were relegated from the school system. Merely a small percentage of the population with disabilities received care in hospices, shelters, or orphanages, organized mainly by religious communities, which considered *disability care* as an act of charity. In the middle of the 20th century, children and young people with disabilities began to be looked after by specialized institutions according to the type of disability, as for instance, the National Institute for the Deaf (INSOR), the National Institute for the Blind (INCI), and the Foundation in charge of care for children with Down syndrome (CSD), whose main purpose was to guarantee their access to a comprehensive education process.

The Political Constitution of 1991 defines that all people have the same rights, regardless of race, sex, or disability. This regulatory framework generates a favorable social and political environment, with the perspective of guaranteeing the rights of people with disabilities, and the inclusion to society in different areas of life in educational, social, and work contexts. Consequently, the General Education Law (1994) states that all children with disabilities must be placed in regular schools, either public or private.

From 1995 and till date, the Colombian educational system has made an important progress by establishing different modalities of inclusion for students with disabilities in schools. It has found a wide spectrum of schools with different levels of care and specialized attention, according to the different functional levels of the students and the human and material resources available in each school. Despite numerous governmental efforts to efficiently meet the needs to the inclusion processes that the population requires, it seems to be insufficient (MINSALUD, 2019).

It is important to highlight that adaptation processes have been initiated in school facilities to enable ace ss for people with disabilities; especially those who have mobility limitations. Similarly, professionals have been linked to comprehensive care teams that include experts in Special Education, Thypholology, or Colombian sign language.

Regarding the attention of students with disabilities from physical education, it is identified that the type of curricular adaptations, and the contents offered to guarantee the full participation of these students in the physical education class, depends in a high percentage on the positive attitude that teachers have toward working with people with disabilities. The study carried out with physical education teachers in Colombia by Columna y otros (2016) found that the attitude that favors the inclusion of students with disabilities depends on the knowledge acquired in their professional pre-service training process, related to the types of disabilities, the characteristics of the people, the methods of adaptation to sports, and, in general, it is related to the amount of experiences gained from schoolchildren with disabilities in physical and sports practices.

Regarding the training of physical education teachers in the care of people with disabilities, it is possible to determine that, currently, more than 70 undergraduate training programs in physical education and sports-related careers at the national level have at least one course related to disability, adapted physical activity, and Paralympic sports. Relevant information on teacher training in inclusive education in Colombia can be found from Calvo's (2024) writing.

Finally, public sports policy in Colombia has taken a fundamental step in making people with disabilities visible, through Paralympic sports, making Colombia the second power at the South American level at present. A fact that contributes not only to the increase in the participation of schoolchildren with disabilities in adapted physical education activities, but also to the fact that these Paralympic athletes become role models and public figures, who speak of the empowerment of people with disabilities and the fundamental role they can play within their families and society in general (Hoyos & Guerrero, 2023).

Social Norms and Cultural Practices of Physical Education

Public policies for physical education in the school environment can be identified in the approaches proposed in the official documents of the area called Curricular Guidelines, which, to date, the Ministry of Education has published three versions: 2000; 2010; and 2022.

In these Curricular Guidelines of the area, the following are found as fundamental axes: (1) the flexibility to determine the contents of the curriculum, (2) the recognition of the idiosyncrasy of the population in the regions of the country as when finding diversity of customs, traditions, and possibilities of particular bodily practices, the teacher of physical education is presented as an agent who proposes and actively participates in the proposal for the construction of the contextualized curriculum.

The interpretations and understandings of the new body practices that have been emerging in the country and that depend on the epistemological constructions of the body are increasingly relevant. The body moves from identifying the body solely from a biological perspective to being understood as a phenomenon that, through hermeneutics, exalts subjectivities and new bodily practices. This is how the curricular guidelines of the Ministry of Education (MEN, 2022) invite the practices carried out in the school environment to be permeated by new perspectives from the social sciences such as anthropology, philosophy, and sociology.

For the Colombian education, and particularly for the area of physical education, it has been a challenge to make the contents of the programs more flexible, as traditionally the curriculum of the area focuses on teaching sports practices. Currently, and as a result of the emergence of new body practices, other contents of physical education are visibly addressed: the aesthetic, the culture of body care, the development of physical condition, and the maintenance of health, vertigo body practices, and body practices in nature, which are developed in both the urban and rural context.

Current school physical education contributes to the dialogue processes between the learning subject and the environment in which he or she is located. In particular, the area, from its didactics, promotes individual and collective participation during the implementation of the activities proposed in the class.

Regarding the learning processes related to the norm as a component that allows coexistence at school, physical education contributes significantly to the understanding of the meaning of the norm as a means for the acquisition of own behaviors for a citizen who interacts with others and these teaching practices located in different contexts during their school life.

Based on the above, Colombian physical education teachers have found various alternatives to contribute to the construction of environments for coexistence where communication and interpersonal and intrapersonal relationships are crossed by the conception of the norm as a dynamic element. Nowadays, it is common to find school teachers who carry out graduate studies, developing research with pedagogical and/or didactic proposals that improve school environments related to coexistence, and the training of students in their ethical and social dimensions.

Social norms and cultural practices contribute to the quality of physical education from two angles: those related to new body practices that emerge from experimentation with the body from other approaches and with other purposes and the learning environments of physical education, where coexistence is mediated by the capacity of the subjects who find themselves sharing spaces, times, and challenges of motor learning individually and collectively. Physical education reflects the proposal for the formation of "human beings" that the Colombian society requires.

Government Contribution to Physical Education

In Colombia, the education system is regulated by the MEN. It is from there that public policies guide the school educational system and the development of the PEI. In particular, the area of physical education contributes to the quality of education in the Colombian population, as it is considered a fundamental area in the school curriculum, which aims at the comprehensive development of the Colombian population.

The Secretaries of Education at the departmental level are the entities in charge of designing, planning, executing, and evaluating the implementation of the policy established for the improvement of education and achieving the desired level of quality. Regarding physical education, the government, through the allocation of economic resources, guarantees access to education for the Colombian population and therefore the development of the area of school physical education.

MEN and the Secretaries of Education carry out teacher competitions to increase the number of professional personnel in the area, in the various regions of the country, thus covering schools located in the marginal areas of cities and rural schools. The MEN allocate resources for the improvement or construction of sports venues, which allow physical education to be carried out. It is of course understood that the budget allocation is not enough, but the government's effort is recognized.

The Secretaries of Education and the Sports and Recreation Institutes of the main cities of Colombia implement extracurricular programs that encourage the practice of sports for training purposes, and participation in artistic activities. This project includes the allocation of resources for hiring teachers, and transporting students to the city's sports venues, and is offered free of charge to schoolchildren. Currently, approximately 20% of public school students participate in these programs.

As a general policy, the government grants scholarships for postgraduate training of public school teachers, thus providing teacher qualifications. In relation to teachers in the area of physical education, there is already a high percentage of teachers with a master's degree; however, the percentage of area teachers with a doctorate is very low.

Conclusion

The enormous influence of European gymnastic movements throughout the 20th century, combined with the different paradigms of physical education at an international level, is reflected in multiple curricular orientations that coexist in the school programs. In this perspective, the Ministry of National Education recognizes this curricular diversity by working to guarantee the quality of school physical education, facing great challenges, which are related to budgetary limitations, the high percentage of school institutions located in the rural areas, the small number of schools that have elementary physical education teachers, among other challenges.

Physical education teachers linked to public and private schools constantly push for an increase in the number of weekly hours for physical education class that schoolchildren receive, decisively combating the trend toward physical inactivity, which is present in a high percentage of schoolchildren and face important challenges such as the inclusion of children with disabilities and other vulnerable conditions, caused by their socio-economic condition and even by the forced displacements suffered by some sectors of the population in the country.

References

Calvo, G. (2024). Training teachers for inclusive education in Colombia: From policy to practice. In S. Romero-Contreras, I. Garcia-Cedillo, & L. M. Moreno-Medrano (Eds). *Intercultural and Inclusive Education in Latin America* (pp. 81–95). Emerald Publishing Limited. www.emerald.com/insight/content/doi/10.1108/s1479-363620240000024006/full/html

Chávez-Ligña, D. (2023). La gimnasia educativa y su influencia en el desarrollo de las capacidades físicas básicas: revisión sistemática. *GADE: Revista Científica, 3*(2), 89–107. https://revista.redgade.com/index.php/Gade/article/view/215

Columna, L. H., Prado-Perez, J., Chavarro-Bermeo, D., Mora, A., Ozols-Rosales, M., Álvarez-Del Cid, L., & Rivero, I. (2016). Latin American physical educators' intention to teach individuals with disabilities. *Adapted Physical Activity Quarterly, 3*(33), 213–232. https://doi.org/10.1123/APAQ.2014-0167

DANE. (2022). *Análisis de las Clases Sociales de Colombia.* Bogotá: Gobierno de Colombia. www.dane.gov.co/files/investigaciones/condiciones_vida/pobreza/2021/analisis_clases_sociales_23_ciudades.pdf

DANE. (2023). *Atlas Estadístico Tomo I Domografía*. https://geoportal.dane.gov.co/servic ios/atlas-estadistico/src/Tomo_I_Demografico/%E2%80%A2regiones-geogr%C3%A1fi cas.html

Decreto, 710 (República de Colombia Mayo 5, 1928). www.suin-juriscol.gov.co/viewD ocument.asp?ruta=Decretos/1151342

Decreto 2230, *Funciones del Sistema Educativo en Colombia (Agosto 08*, 2003). www. mineducacion.gov.co/1759/articles-86029_archivo_pdf.pdf

Estevez, F., & Hoyos, L. (2021). Caracterización de las actividades de tiempo libre de los adolescentes del municipio del Valle de San José-Santander y las expectativas frente a los programas de actividad física. *Revista de Actividad Física y Deportes, 7*(1), 1–14. https://doi.org/10.31910/rdafd.v7.n1.2021.1793

González-Boto, R., Madrera-Mayor, E., & Salguero del Valle, A. (2004). Las escuelas gimnásticas y su relación con la actividad física y educación física actuales. *Revista Digital Efdeportes, 10*(73), 1. www.efdeportes.com/efd73/gimn.htm

Guío-Gutiérrez, F., Díaz-Marín, J. M., & Mejía-Ortiz, M. (2010). Experiencias significativas en la enseñanza de la Educación Física en colegios oficiales de Bogotá. *HALLAZGOS – Revista de investigaciones, 7*(14), 161–182. www.redalyc.org/pdf/4138/413835202009.pdf

Hoyos, L. (2012). *Caracterización de los programas de deporte escolar en Bogotá, análisis de los modelos didácticos empleados para su enseñanza*. Tesis Doctoral, Facultad de Ciencias de la Actividad Física y el Deporte, Universidad de León. https://buleria.unileon.es/handle/10612/9967

Hoyos, L. (2020). La Formación de Licenciados en Educación Física en Colombia. *Italian Journal of Sports Pedagogy x, 1*, 55–61. https://doi.org/10.5281/zenodo.4367219

Hoyos, L., & Guerrero, C. (2023). Desarrollo del deporte en Colombia a través de la perspectiva de cinco atletas de alto rendimiento. *STAPS. Perspectivas sociales del deporte en latinoamericana, 1*, 87–107. www.cairn-mundo.info/revue-staps-2023-HS-page-87.htm&wt.src=pdf

Ley 115, Ley General de Educación (Congreso de la República Febrero 08, 1994). www. mineducacion.gov.co/1621/articles-85906_archivo_pdf.pdf

Martines, M. C., De Caravalho-Figi, N., & DeSouza, J. (2020). The José María Cagigal research program for the field of Physical Education. *Movimento: Revista da Escola de Educação Física, 26*, 1–13. https://seer.ufrgs.br/Movimento/article/view/92691

MEN. (2000). *Lineamientos Curriculares:Educación Física, Recreación y Deporte*. www. mineducacion.gov.co/1780/articles-339975_recurso_10.pdf

MEN. (2010). *Orientaciones Pedagógicas para la Educación Física, Recreación y Deporte*. Ministerio de Educación. https://descubridor.idep.edu.co/Record/6338

MEN. (2022). *Orientaciones Curriculares para la Educación Física, Recreación y Deportes en educación básica y media*. Ministerio de Educación. www.mineducacion.gov.co/1780/articles-411706_recurso_3.pdf

Ministerio de Cultura. (2013). *Diversidad Cultural*. Bogotá: MinCultura. www.mincultura. gov.co/areas/poblaciones/publicaciones/Documents/Cartilla%20Diversidad%20Cultural.pdf

Ministerio de Educación Nacional. (2022). *Orientaciones Curriculares para la Educación Física, Recreación y Deportes en la Educación básica y media*. Bogotá: Gobierno de Colombia. www.mineducacion.gov.co/1780/articles-411706_recurso_3.pdf

MINSALUD. (2019). *Normograma de Discapacidad República de Colombia.* República de Colombia. www.minsalud.gov.co/sites/rid/Lists/BibliotecaDigital/RIDE/DE/PS/Normograma-discapacidad.pdf

Molano-Barrero, J. (1995). Arqueología del Paisaje. *Cuadernos de Geografía: Revista Colombiana de Geografía,* 5(2), 1–10. https://revistas.unal.edu.co/index.php/rcg/article/view/70762/64943

Viceministerio de Turismo. (2021). *Contemplar, Comprender, Conservar. Manual ilustrado para guías de naturaleza en Colombia.* Bogotá: Puntoaparte SAS. https://guianaturaleza.colombia.travel/manual

Vicepresidencia de la Nación. (2023). *Proyecto Reforma a la Ley 11 del Deporte.* Bogotá. https://indeportesantioquia.gov.co/archivos/observatorio/Proyecto%20Reforma%20Ley%20181-min.pdf

Chapter 7

Global Perspectives and Local Challenges of Quality Physical Education in the Dominican Republic

Miguel Israel Bennasar-García

Country Background and Education Development

The Dominican Republic achieved its independence in 1884 and is located in the Caribbean, occupying the eastern part of the island of Hispaniola, which it shares with Haiti, presenting a remarkable geographic diversity, including mountains, coastal plains, fertile valleys, and an extensive coastline. The climate is tropical, with well-defined rainy and dry seasons.

In the political sector, it is a democratic and representative republic, with a system of government divided into three branches: executive, legislative, and judicial. The president is the head of state and government and is elected every 4 years through popular elections (Wikipedia, 2024). The Dominican education system at the primary level has a duration of 6 years, where children between 6 and 12 years of age are served; the secondary level has a duration of 5 years and serves young people between 12 and 18 years of age (IDEICE, 2020).

For the development of education, the government has implemented policies to address these problems and improve educational standards throughout the country. Therefore, educational institutions have been built at the primary and secondary levels, as well as the endowment of universities, where the areas of technology and sports are included (Gobierno de la República Dominicana, 2023).

Regarding demographics, the Dominican population is diverse and is composed primarily of people of African, European, and Amerindian descent. The majority of the population is urban, with the capital, Santo Domingo, being the largest city in the country. The population growth rate is moderate, and the youth population is significant (National Statistical Office, 2021).

In the Dominican educational system, the integral development of students, including their intellectual, physical, emotional, and social well-being, is fundamental. In this context, physical education plays a relevant role. Throughout history, the way of conceiving and teaching this discipline has changed, reflecting advances in the knowledge of human development and social needs. What was once focused on military training has evolved into a more holistic approach that promotes the physical, emotional, and social development of students.

The Development of Quality Physical Education in the Dominican Republic

Physical education is a dynamic field that promotes healthy habits, teamwork, leadership, and the strengthening of self-esteem. Its regular implementation in educational institutions contributes to the well-being of students (Bernate et al., 2020). Ensuring equity implies offering inclusive programs that allow the participation of all students, regardless of gender, abilities, or socioeconomic context, through adaptations and the elimination of barriers.

Physical education curriculum design should be broad, offering varied activities that promote the development of motor skills, physical well-being, and values such as cooperation and respect. It should also be flexible to respond to the needs and interests of students. The following discussion expects to capture the latest physical education development in the Dominican Republic and shares the view while the country is on the way to quality improvement for sport and health success in students.

Dimension 1: Development of Skills and Body Awareness (DHCC)

Several studies in the Dominican Republic point to the exploration of skills and body awareness at the educational level, which is indicative of the awareness of both teachers and learners of the importance of this orientation in the formation of mechanisms for the consolidation of quality physical education (QPE) at the national level (Ramírez-Rodríguez et al., 2023; Santana, 2021). The developments of the curricula are oriented toward the improvement of motor skills in the context of QPE, which advocates the development of body awareness that is materialized in the continuous adherence to the knowledge of sports culture, the cultivation of the body, the importance of sports habits, as well as leisure as a recreational activity (INEFI, 2023; Prada Rozo, 2021; Zamora-Mota et al., 2022a).

Body awareness in students at all levels of Dominican education is a permanent task for teachers working in physical education, given that 58% of the curricular content responds to motor development and the acquisition of skills to manage a particular sport discipline (Ramírez-Rodríguez et al., 2023). "Being aware of what one feels not only helps one's motor development but also to develop in a society where our decisions have great repercussions both internally and externally" (Dyck Estigarribia, 2023, p. 10).

Another important element is provided for in the "National Intersectoral Physical Activity Plan 2023–2030" in the Dominican Republic, where it is estimated to involve the formal school sectors and the community in general, covering more than 80% of the population within the program of body and sports awareness in schoolchildren (Ministry of Public Health and Social Assistance [MISPAS], 2023).

Dimension 2: Facilities and Standards in Physical Education (INEF)

In the country, research has been developed that has addressed in a scientific manner what is related to facilities and standards in physical education, in the case of primary education, where proactive attitudes and values whose correlation with sports activity is one of the purposes of both Dominican institutions and INEFI authorities.

Joaquín Tineo (2020) points out the need to create awareness among state agencies about the key element that this area plays as a preventive tool in the field of health, which implies recognizing that regular physical activity can contribute significantly to preventing diseases and promoting a healthy lifestyle.

With respect to sports facilities in general, within the framework of a quality sports service in the country, certain restrictions are perceived that are manifested in the inadequate or optimal conditions, which can indeed mean an important hurdle in the purpose of developing a QPE, these deficiencies can be overcome in terms of the comprehensive training of young Dominicans (Morel, 2024).

The Constitution of the Dominican Republic (2015), in its Article 65, establishes the right to sport, in which the quality of education is measured not only in numerical or percentage terms but also in the various curricular modifications implemented both in teacher training institutions and in the different educational levels of the country.

The General Law of Sport, No. 356-35 (2005), in its Article 11, highlights the importance of the adequacy of sports facilities, which is in line with Article 40 that school sport is specialized physical activity that has the purpose of contributing to the integral formation of children and young people, and INEFI must coordinate such actions. Sport is an integral part of the Dominican educational system, and collaboration between educational and sports authorities to promote its practice and development is important.

One of the functions of the Ministry of Sports and Recreation (MIDEREC) is to assist both INEFI and the different educational institutions in the promotion and development of the physical attitude to strengthen the development of the motor functions of students.

The World Health Organization (WHO, 2020) identifies the importance of infrastructure in the different countries of the region and particularly in the Dominican Republic, arguing that governments and educational institutions should make efforts in the direction of having adequate sports facilities that allow the planning and execution of the country's legal norms (Morel, 2024).

The public policies of any nation should include physical activity as one of its main objectives, given that it improves the well-being and quality of life of people, especially adolescents. To achieve effective development of QPE, it is essential to have qualified teachers and adequate conditions (García Quezada, 2020).

Dimension 3: Quality Teaching in Physical Education (ECEF)

To achieve QPE in the Dominican Republic, adequate teacher training in this area is essential. The perception of quality is subjective and varies according to the expectations of each community (López-D'Amico, 2019). This requires an adequate educational environment in different institutions (UNESCO, 2015). The QPE assessment includes indicators such as sports infrastructures, teacher training programs, didactic resources, and the pedagogical skills of teachers. Although research shows that the current situation is not ideal, there are institutional and governmental efforts to improve it (Zamora-Mota et al., 2022b).

The Dominican educational system has developed a legal framework to consolidate the project of a QPE, aligned with the ethical values of the country (Bennasar-García et al., 2023). "With physical education and physical activity, more time should be devoted to both the subject and school sports practice in all programs" (Rodríguez Peña, 2020, p. 76).

In various educational institutions, physical education classes in the country are oriented to promote the knowledge and practice of different disciplines for individual initiatives (López-D'Amico, 2019). This configures a positive spectrum toward the achievement of the greater goal that is OBE (Santana, 2021). It is consequently "A multi-stakeholder approach to QPE policy development and implementation should extend to collaboration with other appropriate stakeholders..." (UNESCO, 2015, p. 22).

Dimension 4: Plans for the Feasibility and Accessibility of Physical Education (PFAPE)

Among the policies that have been implemented in the country as a link between state institutions and international organizations is the National Action Plan for Physical Activity (2023), which was built last year and which came to fill a gap of a normative nature within the philosophy of QPE, which is one of the imperatives in the country.

The General Sports Law No. 356-35 (2005) establishes that adaptations must be made in the contents and curriculum orientations in schools and universities, to make viable the actions tending to establish the different policies that will give legal character to the activities in the discipline of physical education.

Dimension 5: Social Norms and Cultural Practices (NSPC)

Social norms are a set of rules that guide the interactions and behaviors of people within a community, with the purpose of promoting harmonious coexistence (Law, 2024). Article 64 of the Constitution of the Dominican Republic (2015) sets out in general terms the right of every citizen to practice the sport of their choice and guarantees freedom of action and formative processes in particular disciplines.

In Dominican culture, for the purposes of practicing sports or performing any productive activity, as well as study opportunities, among others, there are no attitudes of rejection due to gender issues (Zamora-Mota et al., 2022b). As for religious manifestations, Catholicism dominates the preferences of citizens, where there is a kind of tolerance with respect to the existence in the country of beliefs or religions (Rodríguez Peña, 2020).

In the Dominican Republic, economic factors limit access to goods and services, including education. Costs such as transportation, food, teaching materials, and technology impose restrictions, even with public institutions. The government has partially addressed this by providing scholarships and financial support (MISPAS, 2023). Socially and culturally, Dominicans are generally noted for their peaceful society.

Dimension 6: Government Contributions to Physical Education (GIPE)

The activities and resources needed in the country for the adequate development of physical education in the country, in the National Report on the Evolution of Education Expenditure 2015–2021 in the Dominican Republic, some allocations can be observed that, by way of fact, benefit the conditions of this area of continuing education and, of course, the users. In this sense, "The Ministry of Education has presented an accumulated expenditure in the period 2015–2021 of 1,094,761.90 million pesos (21,517.77 million dollars), at current prices" (Sánchez Jáquez, 2023, p. 8), which indicates the effort to improve investment in this sector.

There is recognition of the importance of physical education as a fundamental part of the curriculum and study programs at all levels in the Dominican Republic, because the integral formation of students depends on it, promoting sports and cultural conditions in a progressive and sustainable manner (Sánchez Jáquez, 2023).

At the Latin American level, there are organizations with which it is possible to establish strategic collaborations, such as the Bolivarian Alliance for the Peoples of the Americas (ALBA), the Common Market of the South (MERCOSUR), the Community of Latin American and Caribbean States (CELAC), the Union of South American Nations (UNASUR), the Latin American Social Sciences Council (CLACSO), UNESCO's Regional Bureau of Education for Latin America and the Caribbean (OREALC), the Organization for Economic Cooperation and Development (OECD), the Latin American Social Sciences Council (CLACSO), the UNESCO Regional Bureau of Education for Latin America and the Caribbean (OREALC), and the Inter-American Planning Center of the Organization of American States (CINTERPLAN-OAS), with the objective of advancing the improvement of QPE. These alliances make it possible to strengthen joint work to deepen regional and global initiatives in education, involving both teachers and authorities in the construction of high-level educational networks (López-D'Amico, 2019).

Responding to state policies, institutions such as the Instituto Superior de Formación Docente Salomé Ureña (ISFODOSU) and the Universidad Autónoma de Santo Domingo (UASD) have developed specialization programs and research projects in the area of physical education, on a recurring basis, covering 12% of studies in this area (Sánchez Jáquez, 2023).

The budget allocated to the Ministry of Sports includes 29% directed toward several important aspects, including technical and sports training for teachers, construction and maintenance of sports facilities, promotion of school and university sports, as well as recreation, physical activity, and leisure time sports (Mathiasen, 2023). This is why there are agreements with institutions such as the World Bank, the International Monetary Fund, to name a few, to establish alliances and cooperation programs to provide financial assistance to physical education activities in the country (Fulcar, 2022).

Dimension 7: Development of Cognitive Skills (DCS)

When referring to the development of cognitive skills, it implies developing the set of innate potentialities of people, which are strengthened to the extent that knowledge is acquired, using learning processes and developing meaningful experiences (García Montero, 2023; Torres Santomé, 2006, p. 20).

In the Dominican case, it is about executing relationships that emerge from the processes to apprehend and access knowledge, more specifically developing elements that fortify memory, the improvement of ways of expressing ideas and language, forms of perception, and systematization of ideas to face conflicts or problems, among others (Gil et al., 2018; Jiménez et al., 2020). UNESCO (2020) addressed this juncture as a turning point in the Latin American educational development, where it suggests that the education of the 21st century should emphasize the cognitive skills of students as an assertive proceeding in this sector, which implies a change in the informative version of the formative processes.

Dimension 8: Habituated Behavior in Physical Activities (HBPA)

In physical education, students have spaces to engage in various sports activities, allowing them to make decisions for their personal well-being and development (García Quezada, 2020). In the Dominican Republic, students follow specific protocols for school activities, promoting the acquisition of social, cognitive, and affective skills relevant to their life development (Posso et al., 2023). Additionally, students can form sports clubs or teams, build social relationships, develop sports and health habits, and enhance their self-esteem and cognitive and motor skills (Rodríguez Peña, 2020).

Conclusion

QPE is perceived with a possibility of success, especially when the traditional conception of school physical education is strengthened, when there is a strong desire in providing spaces for success and achievement, and when there is the introduction of curricular projects to consolidate and ensure the comprehensive development and holistic training of students at different educational levels in the Dominican Republic.

The sociocultural and geopolitical context of the Dominican Republic has played a key role in the configuration of its educational system, particularly in the field of physical education. Historically, physical education in the country has shifted from a militaristic and disciplinary approach to a more holistic one that seeks the integral development of students, including physical, emotional, and social aspects. This change has been driven by educational policies that seek to align with international standards and improve the quality of education in the country.

Despite significant advances, such as improved sports infrastructure and teacher training, there are still notable challenges, such as unequal access to educational resources and the need for greater inclusion and equity in education. These challenges highlight the importance of a continued commitment on the part of the government, educational institutions, and the community at large to promote QPE that contributes to the integral well-being of students and the sustainable development of Dominican society.

References

Bennasar-García, M., Cruceta Gutiérrez, J., García Quezada, R., López Guillén, R., Arias Ureña, J., Pacheco-Ferreira, L., Díaz-Vásquez, M., Caba Quiroz, L., Brito Mejía, L., Jiménez Ramírez, C., Minaya Sosa, P., Frías Marte, D., Santos Viñas, E., Burgos De Asís, A., Acosta de la Cruz, J., Contreras Contreras, R., Lora Cruz, J., Ramírez de los Santos, D., Sierra Ventura, K., Pérez Santana, C., Tavera, F., Hernández Valerio, A., Núñez Abreu, D., Leyba Medrano, C., Valdez Peña, F., Vargas Céspedes, A., Torres Peralta, S., y Castillo Javier, F. (2023). *EDUCACIÓN FÍSICA DE CALIDAD EN EL SISTEMA EDUCATIVO DE LA REPÚBLICA DOMINICANA. Experiencia académica desde el recinto "Luís Napoleón Núñez Molina" (Primera Edición digitalizada)*. Unidad de Publicaciones UPEL; IPB, FEDUPEL, Fondo Editorial UPEL, Barquisimeto, Estado Lara, Venezuela. https://publicacionesipb.investigacion-upelipb.com/index.php/libros/catalog/view/33/31/31

Bernate, J., Fonseca, I., y Jiménez, M. (2020). Impacto de la actividad física y la práctica deportiva en el contexto social de la educación superior. *Retos: nuevas tendencias en educación física, deporte y recreación*, (37), 742–747. https://dialnet.unirioja.es/servlet/articulo?codigo=7243345

CF Law Firm. (2024). *¿Qué son las normas sociales?* https://fc-abogados.com/es/que-son-las-normas-sociales/

Constitución de la República Dominicana. (2015). *Votada y Proclamada por la Asamblea Nacional en fecha trece (13) de junio de 2015 Gaceta Oficial No. 10805 del 10 de julio de*

2015. https://presidencia.gob.do/sites/default/files/statics/transparencia/base-legal/Const itucion-de-la-Republica-Dominicana-2015-actualizada.pdf

Dyck Estigarribia, D. (2023). La consciencia corporal como método de autoconocimiento emocional a través de la expresión corporal propuesta didáctica diseñada para 3º de educación primaria. *[Trabajo de fin de Grado en Educación Primaria con mención de Educación Física]*. Facultad de Educación de Palencia. Universidad de Valladolid, España https://uvadoc.uva.es/bitstream/handle/10324/62551/TFG-L3601.pdf?sequence= 1&isAllowed=y

Fulcar, R. (2022). Ministros de Educación, Deportes e Interior reafirman respaldo del Gobierno al deporte escolar y comunitario / Entrevistado por Jesús -Chu- Vásquez. https:// presidencia.gob.do/noticias/ministros-de-educacion-deportes-e-interior-reafirman-respa ldo-del-gobierno-al-deporte

García Montero, L. D. (2023). Estrategias para fomentar el análisis crítico en estudiantes del área ciencias sociales de 6to grado. *MENTOR Revista De investigación Educativa Y Deportiva, 2*(Especial), 618–644. https://doi.org/10.56200/mried.v2iEspecial.6471

García Quezada, R. (2020). Los motivos de abandono de la práctica de actividad física del alumnado de primaria y secundaria en República Dominicana. *[Trabajo de Grado de Maestría en Educación Física Integral]*. Instituto Superior de Formación Docente Salomé Ureña, Recinto Eugenio María de Hostos, República Dominicana.

Gil, L., Páez, R., Rondón, G., y Trejo, J. (2018). Formación docente y pensamiento crítico en Paulo Freire. CLACSO, Buenos Aires.

Gobierno de la República Dominicana. (2023). *Plan Nacional Intersectorial de Actividad Física (PIAF) 2023–2030*. https://repositorio.msp.gob.do/bitstream/handle/123456789/ 2331/9789945644456.pdf?sequence=1&isAllowed=y

IDEICE. (julio 2020). SISTEMA EDUCATIVO DOMINICANO: PERFIL DE LA EDUCACIÓN INICIAL, PRIMARIA Y SECUNDARIA. Unidad de Seguimiento y Evaluación de la Política Educativa – USEPE. https://ideice.gob.do/lineas-de-investigacion

Instituto Nacional de Educación Física [INEFI]. (2023). *INEFI IMPULSÓ EL DESARROLLO DE LOS DOCENTES CON PROYECTOS DE CAPACITACIÓN E INCENTIVOS SALARIALES*. https://inefi.gob.do/2023/12/26/inefi-impulso-el-desarrollo-de-los-docen tes-con-proyectos-de-capacitacion-e-incentivos-salariales/

Jiménez, M., Angelini, M., y Tasso, Ch. (2020). Orientaciones metodológicas para el desarrollo del pensamiento crítico. Octaedro, Barcelona.

Joaquín Tineo, H. (2020). Análisis de la actividad física realizada por el alumnado de 6to. grado de la primaria en edades de (10-12 AÑOS) en la República Dominicana atendiendo al género. Año escolar 2019–20. *[Trabajo de Grado de Maestría en Educación Física Integral]*. Instituto Superior de Formación Docente Salomé Ureña, Recinto Eugenio María de Hostos, República Dominicana.

Ley General del Deporte No. 356-35. (2005). *EL CONGRESO NACIONAL*. En Nombre de la República. https://biblioteca.enj.org/bitstream/handle/123456789/79890/LE356-2005. pdf?sequence=1

López-D'Amico, R. (2019). Educación Física de calidad: ¿De dónde surge este planteamiento?. *RECIE. Revista Caribeña De Investigación Educativa, 3*(2), 33–45. https://doi.org/ 10.32541/recie.2019.v3i2

Mathiasen, P. (2023). Incrementan en 700 millones presupuesto Miderec 2024. *Listin Diario*. https://listindiario.com/el-deporte/olimpismo/20231219/incrementan-700-millo nes-presupuesto-miderec-2024_787680.html

Ministerio de Salud Pública y Asistencia Social (MISPAS). (2023). *Plan Nacional Intersectorial de Actividad Física 2023–2030*. 1era Edición. https://repositorio.msp.gob.do/bitstream/handle/123456789/2331/9789945644456.pdf?sequence=1&isAllowed=y

Morel, M. (2024). Procesos de capacitación y la calidad de la gestión estratégica del instituto nacional de educación física (INEFI) República Dominicana. *Revista Actividad Física y Ciencias*, *16*(1), https://revistas.upel.edu.ve/index.php/actividadfisicayciencias/article/view/2429/2572

Oficina Nacional de Estadística. (12 de julio 2021). República Dominicana: una población joven con tendencia al envejecimiento. www.one.gob.do/noticias/2021/republica-dominicana-una-poblacion-joven-con-tendencia-al-envejecimiento/

Organización Mundial de la Salud OMS. (2020). *Actividad física*. www.who.int/es/news-room/fact-sheets/detail/physical-activity

Posso, R. J., Cóndor, M. G., Rojas, M. D. C. H., Ronquillo, N. D. y Machado, P. E. (2023). La nivelación de conocimientos: Retos de la educación postpandemia. *Revista EDUCARE-UPEL-IPB-Segunda Nueva Etapa* 2.0, *27*(1), 94–110. https://doi.org/10.46498/reduipb.v27i1.1861

Prada Rozo, M. J. (2021). Las competencias ciudadanas en la clase de Educación Física: entre las miradas desde la docencia y el discurso planteado en el currículo dominicano. *Revista Educación*, *45*(1), 257–269. https://doi.org/10.15517/revedu.v45i1.41

Ramírez-Rodríguez, Y., Capellán-Caraballo, R., y Bennasar-García, M. (2023). Desafío social de las competencias educativas en educación física, niveles primario y secundario, República Dominicana. *Revista revoluciones*, *5*(12):20–39. https://doi.org/10.35622/j.rr.2023.012.002

Rodríguez Peña, A. (2020). Estudio de la relación del índice de actividad física y hábitos de la alimentación en función del género, para identificar los escolares activos o sedentarios del segundo ciclo, nivel secundario de la República Dominicana. *[Trabajo de Grado de Maestría en Educación Física Integral]*. Instituto Superior de Formación Docente Salomé Ureña, Recinto Eugenio María de Hostos, República Dominicana.

Sánchez Jáquez, R. (2023). *Informe Nacional de la Evolución del Gasto en Educación 2015–2021 en República Dominicana. Justicia fiscal y derecho humano a la educación: diagnóstico, participación e incidencia desde América Latina y Caribe*. https://redclade.org/wp-content/uploads/11-RD-gasto-en-educacion.pdf

Santana, I. (2021). *Diseño Curricular Centrado en el Aprendizaje y Diseño Curricular por Competencias*. Universidad Autónoma de Santo Domingo. https://cutt.ly/fwqRrilY

Torres Santomé, J. (2006). *Globalización e interdisciplinariedad*. Morata, Madrid.

UNESCO. (2015). *Educación Física de Calidad–Guía para los responsables políticos. UNESCO. Guía para los responsables políticos*. http://unescoittralee.com/wp-content/uploads/2017/11/QPE-for-policy-makers-Spanish.pdf

UNESCO. (2020) *¿Qué se espera que aprendan los estudiantes de América Latina y el Caribe? Análisis curricular del Estudio Regional Comparativo y Explicativo (ERCE2019)*. https://unesdoc.unesco.org/ark:/48223/pf0000373982

Wikipedia. (2024). *President of the Dominican Republic*. Wikipedia. https://en.wikipedia.org/wiki/President_of_the_Dominican_Republic#:~:text=The%20president%20is%20elected%20by,of%20president%20more%20than%20twice

Zamora-Mota, H., Santana-Álvarez, J., y Miranda-Ramos, M. (2022a). Hábitos de alimentación y práctica de actividad física del alumnado de nivel secundario. *Archivo Médico Camagüey, 26.* https://revistaamc.sld.cu/index.php/amc/article/view/8838

Zamora-Mota, H., Santana-Álvarez, J., Ventura-Cruz, V., Fernández-Villarino, M., Miranda-Ramos, M., y Joaquín-Tineo, H. (2022b). Influencia del modelo social, actividad físico-deportiva y salud en alumnos de secundaria. Archivo Médico Camagüey, *27.* https://revistaamc.sld.cu/index.php/amc/article/view/9263

Chapter 8

Quality Physical Education Development in Greece

Efthalia (Elia) Chatzigianni and Krinanthi Gdonteli

Introduction

Greece is a European country in the southeastern Mediterranean and lies in the Balkan peninsula. It is located at the point where three continents meet: Europe, Asia, and Africa, which is why Greece is considered a crossroads of people and cultures. According to Eurostat 2023 data, Greece has a geographical size of 131,694 km^2 and a population of 10,394,055.

Modern Greece has been an independent state for about two centuries. Following the Greek War of Independence (1821–1828), the first Hellenic Republic (1828–1832) was established, followed by the Kingdom of Greece (1832–1924). The second Hellenic Republic (1924–1935) was followed by the restored Kingdom of Greece (1935–1967) and a military dictatorship (1967–1974). In 1974, democracy in Greece was restored under the Third Hellenic Republic. Since then, Greece has been a parliamentary democracy. Administratively, the country is divided into 13 regions, which are secondary local organizations of the Greek state. Greece has been a member of the European Union (EU) since January 1, 1981, and a member of the Eurozone since January 1, 2001.

Greece went into a full-scale economic crisis in 2009 as a result of the 2007–2009 global economic recession and the subsequent default on public debt. For some, 2018 is considered the end of the debt crisis, while for others, September 2019, when the complete lifting of the imposed capital controls took place. Since then, the Greek economy has shown significantly improved yearly economic performance. According to the International Monetary Fund (2024), Greek economic activity has been robust post-pandemic, and in 2023, the projected real gross domestic product (GDP) growth was at 2.3%, while in 2024 at 2.1%. Tourism and shipping are very important "industries" for the Greek economy.

Physical Education (PE) and Sports have been an integral part of the Greek education system under the Third Hellenic Republic. According to the Greek Constitution, PE is a main component of the structure of the school and education in general and "constitutes a basic mission of the State aiming at the moral, spiritual, professional and PE of Greeks" (Constitution of Greece, Article 16, par. 2). Furthermore, Greece follows guidelines and policies implemented by the EU

DOI: 10.4324/9781003513582-10

according to which PE is more than physical skills and recreational activities; it is also related to learning concepts such as fair play, the "rules of the game", respect, tactical and bodily awareness, and the social awareness linked to personal interaction and team effort in many sports (European Commission, 2007, 2008).

According to the World Health Organization (2016), all 27 EU countries have PE as mandatory in their school curricula, even though with differences in the number of mandatory hours. EU data (2013) shows that, while in some countries, the amount of indicated taught time is decreased after the first 4–6 years of compulsory education, in Greece, Denmark, and Cyprus, the amount of teaching hours increases.

The Evolution of PE in Greece: Context for Sport and PE

Greece is the birthplace of the ancient Olympic Games. Consequently, the reality of sports development in recent years has mirrored the considerable influence of the Olympics on Greek sports mentality and ideology.

Yet, PE in schools has not always been a priority in the history of modern Greece. When the first Hellenic Republic was established, under the influence of the intellectuals of the time, the main focus of school life was on learning to become educated human beings (Pavlinis, 1927). PE was considered a secondary activity, often regarded with contempt, by the organizers of the educational system at the time until about 1880, when PE was first introduced in high schools as a core subject.

In 1929, Law 4371 clearly recognized the significance of PE to the physical and mental well-being of all students and rendered PE compulsory in all state schools, public and private, and recognized for all grades and genders. Still, in the years to follow, like in many other European countries, the main goal of PE was to prepare the youth for the army. Following the Second World War, Greece was in the midst of a civil war that had a huge negative impact not only on the financial situation of the country but also on the educational system. Schools had no equipment of any kind. PE took place in an environment of strict discipline and was mainly based on military walking, national dances, Swedish gymnastics, horizontal bars, and gymnastic performances at the end of the school year (Avgerinos, 2000).

The situation changed in 1974, with the end of the dictatorship when the third Hellenic Republic was established. Among many reforms, one was exemplary of the importance attributed to PE in modern Greece: the years of study at The National Academy of PE were increased from 3 to 4.

In 1985, Law 1566, Article 1 about the "Structure and operation of primary and secondary education", notes that the primary goals of education are to contribute to the harmonious and balanced development of students' intellectual and psychophysical qualities, regardless of their gender and descent in a way that they have the potential to develop all aspects of their personalities and live creatively. Article 5 notes that high school students should have the opportunity to develop their bodies smoothly so as to safeguard their functional development and cultivate their motor inclination and activities.

However, the main step forward in the field of PE in schools took place with the publication of the presidential degree (PD) 377/1995 on a "Detailed program of PE in Primary Schools" based on the work of the PE Committee of the Pedagogical Institute established in 1994. Article 1 of the PD notes that *the primary purpose of teaching PE in schools through various sports activities and programs is not only the physical but also the mental and spiritual development of the students and their balanced and harmonious integration in the society.* Since then, the development of PE in Greece has evolved in accordance with the European standards and criteria set by the Hellenic Institute of Educational Policy, which supports the Ministry of Education, Religious Affairs, Sports, and related bodies in areas concerning school education, including PE. According to the European Commission (2013), the curricular reform in Greece aimed not only to increase PE taught time but also to the enlargement and diversification of its content by combining traditional sports practiced at school with new activities. These reforms extended school autonomy in terms of organizing PE both in the framework of the school curriculum and in extracurricular activities. Nowadays, sports and PE represent significant components of Greek national life, from school to elite sports.

The Development of Quality Physical Education Eight Dimensions in Greece

Dimension 1: Skill Development and Bodily Awareness (SDBA)

The central purpose of the new Analytical Program of the Ministry of Education (2016 – revised in 2024, Official Government Gazette) is the formation of physically literate students through their encouragement for physical activity within and outside school and the use of PE to the evolution of the individual's knowledge, skills, and attitudes, as well as the development of autonomy and the pursuance of physical fitness, self-confidence, morals, and of self-regulation skills in various physical activity areas.

To achieve this, the program requires PE teachers at all levels, besides teaching the most popular sports, to enhance knowledge of sports, teamwork, personal development, and lifelong exercise. In addition, all new curricula incorporate physical literacy as a core orientation in the PE course.

For the elementary school, modules include psychomotor and music-motor education, group/individual and traditional games, gymnastic exercises, an introduction to physical activities that are linked to health and recreational sports, music-motor education via Greek traditional dances, gymnastics, track and field, and team sports including football, volleyball, basketball, and handball. Furthermore, the module aims at the familiarization with non-common sports for the disabled, as well as swimming training. For the last 2 years of elementary school, a direction has been given to deepen the knowledge of the most popular sports.

During the first three grades of High School (Gymnasium), emphasis is given to the following: the development of motor skills, the satisfactory execution of exercises, the acquisition of knowledge from sports science and its application for effective participation in future physical activities, the knowledge and development of a good level of physical condition for health, the development of self-expression and sociability, the understanding and respect of diversity, and finally the demonstration of sports and social behavior. The main purpose of PE in the last 3 years of High School (Lyceum) is defined as "lifelong exercise for health and quality of life".

Given that Greece has a coastline of 13,676 kilometers, and a significant number of drownings are recorded annually, a significant innovation in the Greek education system is that swimming is taught in schools with compulsory attendance in the elementary school.

According to the detailed curriculum in PE for the elementary school, EVZIN (EYZEIN) has been a pioneering program of the Charokopio University of Greece in cooperation with the Ministry of Education, with the entire student population of the country as the final recipient. The program records and evaluates various health parameters of the students over time, while through parallel actions, it intervenes in the everyday life of the Greek family, school, and society. The main objective of the program is to ensure the healthy development of children and adolescents through the adoption of balanced eating habits and physical activity, by evaluation of health parameters, information of students, parents, teachers, and institutions, and intervention in the school, the family, and the whole society (https://eyzhn.edu.gr/).

From the above, one may assume that in recent years, state initiatives aimed at the upgrade of skill development and physical awareness through PE, the results of which begin to be evident.

Dimension 2: Facilities and Norms in PE (FNPE)

PE is compulsory for all levels of school education, 12 years in total. Concerning safety in the PE class, annual inspections are carried out in school complexes, while PE teachers are given appropriate manuals and attend seminars on safety and crisis management. PE teachers are qualified in teaching, as all of them are graduates from university PE departments and are assessed every year in terms of their teaching, pedagogical, and behavioral aspects.

The implementation of the PE curriculum in modern Greek schools requires that certain basic requirements be met regarding the facilities and equipment. Given that the modernization of school facilities did not coincide with the reform of the new PE curriculum, several issues arose when teaching PE – mainly due to the existence of old-school complexes. Still, there are several modern schools in which PE classes can be perfectly implemented. Moreover, in Greece, there are more than 1000 private schools at all levels of education, most of which have modern sports facilities and equipment, giving them a comparative advantage over public educational institutions (www.alfavita.gr/ekpaideysi/).

Sports facilities in public Greek universities vary; some of them have excellent sports facilities, while others have substandard ones. However, the participation rate of students in the non-compulsory sports programs that are offered is low compared to other European universities (Gdonteli & Gavriilidis, 2014).

In addition, children's disabilities, long-term health conditions, and special educational needs can limit meaningful participation in PE unless appropriate support is provided. Approaches are needed that encourage the development of an inclusive educational environment, value diversity, monitor individual functioning, and consider social and emotional states by modifying traditional sports and providing optional activities at appropriate skill levels (Hart et al., 2014; Tant & Watelain, 2016). The purpose of Adapted PE is the same as that of PE in typical education, with the ultimate goal of the full and equal inclusion of students both in the school environment and at all levels of social life.

To this end, the Institute of Educational Policy of the Ministry of Education has a special and inclusive education unit to promote a school for all children so as to reflect an inclusive culture and a learning environment that is differentiated for special educational needs. The unit ensures the continuous processing of relevant programs, educational material, methods, and practices to enhance inclusivity (https://iep.edu.gr/el/special-education).

Additionally, more than 500 Special Education schools operate in preschool, primary, and secondary education that facilitate accessibility. They are staffed with PE teachers specialized in special PE. Regarding the typical schools in which students with non-visible disabilities or mild disabilities attend, the institution of parallel support operates, which has been applied in Greece since 2010 to create "a school for all". Parallel support provides students with disabilities the opportunity to study in the general classroom, and inclusive education is put into practice with effective co-teaching with teachers and PE teachers specializing in Special Education. The aim is to provide equal rights for all students in education (Troupkou & Gdonteli, 2023). This goal has been achieved to a great extent, but not yet completely.

Dimension 3: Quality Teaching of PE (QTPE)

The concept of "quality teaching" includes several parameters that are important during the teaching–learning process. The teaching styles, as well as the strategy that each PE instructor chooses to carry out the educational process, are of fundamental importance. As noted, PE teacher-centered as well as student-centered teaching styles (methods) have been developed to achieve the goals of the course and act for the benefit of the students (van Munster et al., 2019).

Effective teaching depends significantly on the method, the teaching style chosen, and the communication skills (Khan et al., 2017). An important condition for the effectiveness of teaching is the concept of inclusion, in which the flexibility of the teacher facilitates the participation of all (Lieberman et al., 2024).

A recent study in Greece examined teachers' views on effective teaching and implementation of PE for preschool and early school-age children (Garzoni et al., 2023). The study showed that PE and kindergarten teachers, despite their different education and specialization, share a common view of what essentially concerns pedagogical science and its most effective practices. Specifically, they believe that the choice of content in accordance with children's needs, the active participation of children as well as the involvement of teachers in the activities they choose, the intention, the configuration of ways to make the space available to them functional and to make use of materials provided, are high priorities. Similarly, creating a learning environment that facilitates learning, using student-centered teaching methods, supporting and highlighting the importance of communication, and providing feedback on the achievement of their students are reported as central elements in the formation of their practices. Finally, they try to focus on successes, a constant critical attitude towards their work, and an introspective look towards self-improvement. Particular attention needs to be paid to those elements of effective teaching of movement, as recorded in modern literature, which do not appear to be prominent in the average practices of the interviewees of the study, such as nutrition, the complementary use of relevant textbooks regardless of professional experience, the facilitation of students' communication problems as part of teaching, the more methodical assessment of students, and the use of technology (Kelmendi & Dedi, 2024).

All levels of education include intramural sports events, sporting events, and traditional dance performances, while Panhellenic school competitions are held in a large number of sports for high school students.

Greece is a nation with extremely rich folklore and outstanding traditions regarding dance, music, anthropology, ethnochoreology, musicology, and folk song (Koutsouba, 2019). Greek traditional dances are a thematic unit in the levels of education up to the age of 18 to introduce traditional Greek songs, rhythm, melody, dance movement, and the elements of the popular tradition of the country. The purpose is to get to know the body through movement, rhythm, and creativity. According to Masadis et al. (2019), for the final three grades of primary school, the teamwork method is the most appropriate to use when teaching social skills, and traditional dancing is the best option.

Moreover, Olympic Education is a top concern in PE at all levels of education. As the birthplace of the Olympic Games, the Olympic ideals are part of the culture that is imparted through the education system. Olympic Education is a pedagogic program from 2004 in the context of which values are promoted, and knowledge, experiences, and skills are acquired that stem from the Olympic Games and the Sports Tradition and whose purpose is the physical, mental, and spiritual cultivation of students and the creation of attitudes and behaviors socially recipients. The "Olympiψ Week", which takes place at the end of the school year, aims to inspire, sensitize, and mobilize students in the formation of attitudes and skills that emanate from the spirit of Olympism. It is addressed to all Greek school units and specifically to three age categories of students: 6–8 years old (Primary School), 9–12 years old (Primary School), and 13–15 years old (High School).

Dimension 4: Plans for Feasibility and Accessibility of PE (PFAPE)

The Greek Ministry of Education, in collaboration with competent bodies, such as the Regional Educational Planning Centers, is elaborating programs for further education and training of PE teachers at all levels of education. Teacher training in digital technologies is often carried out. In addition, the importance of the role and training of PE teachers is widely recognized in the context of advancing towards the formation of educational systems with a more inclusive orientation.

The Institute of Educational Policy has the overall responsibility of planning, organizing, implementing, and evaluating the training programs for PE teachers, which currently cannot be carried out with foreign bodies.

Although a large number of PE teachers graduate annually from the five University Schools of PE and sports science in Greece, the system does not facilitate their corresponding absorption in schools, resulting in staff shortages in several school units so far. In addition, it seems that existing training programs for PE teachers are insufficient, and the majority need upgrading.

Dimension 5: Social Norms and Cultural Practice (SNCP)

The Olympic Education as a pedagogic program in the school curriculum promotes the social development of students. Specifically, it elaborates on the free development of human personality, interpersonal relationships, sociability, and communication through the game and the transmission of the Olympic Ideals. The program also aims at deepening the knowledge about different cultures and religions and the values of friendship, hospitality, gender equality, cooperation, solidarity, and understanding of people. The Olympic Values through PE are built on four primary pillars (Georgiadis, 2007), as shown in Table 8.1: Personal, Social, Cultural, and Global.

Although Greek society understands the important role of sports in education, the course of PE does not yet have the place it deserves, which is mainly due to the pathologies of the Greek educational system combined with the economic crisis.

Dimension 6: Governmental Input for PE (GIPE)

In 2024, the Ministry of Education formed a working group for the upgrade of PE and school sports. An important action of the working group is the establishment of two sports high schools.

The working group will make recommendations in the context of PE and school sports activities and programs to improve the health indicators of the student population, highlight lifelong exercise and a healthy lifestyle, as well as ensure the equal participation of all male and female students without exclusions and discrimination. It will connect school and university sports and align them with the strategic planning for the development of Greek sports, and also deal with the

Table 8.1 Olympic values through PE in Greece

Personal	Social	Cultural	Global
Harmonious development of body and spirit	Friendship	Respect for cultural values	Coexistence of nations
Self-respect	Equality	Cross-cultural exchanges between individual persons countries and continent	Respect for the environment
Participation	Respect for the other	Equal participation independent of race religion, sex, culture, and socioeconomic conditions	Patriotism
Voluntary services	Understanding		Internationalism
Self-discipline	Solidarity		Altruism
Self-respect	Brotherhood		Peace
Persistence	Fair play		Democracy in athletics
Attempt to succeed in achieving one's highest aims	Equality of opportunities		
Pursuit of excellence	Fellowship		
Well-being and health	Deontology		
	Mutual respect		

upgrading of the competitive and administrative presence of school and university sports abroad.

The working group's task will be to develop a "motivation system" for the participation of young people in competitive sports to further develop Greek sports through the essential competitive and academic support of distinguished student-athletes.

From the above, it seems that governmental input has increased in the field of PE, and significant steps forward have been taken.

Dimension 7: Cognitive Skill Development (CSD)

The Educational Policy Institute of the Ministry of Education has designed the "Aesop" Platform for Digital Teaching Scenarios. It is an innovative integrated tool for the development, design, writing, evaluation, and presentation of digital interactive teaching scenarios in a modern and functional environment. The digital material can be transformed and fully adapted to the structure of digital teaching scenarios by matching them with teaching objectives, thematic taxonomies, implementation phases, etc. (https://aesop.iep.edu.gr/).

In this light, some of the significant proposed scenarios concern interdisciplinary actions that involve PE in education. Some examples are listed here:

1 "Physics of Olympic sports" is a didactic scenario aimed at students in the last grades of elementary school, which includes elements from physics, PE, and ICT of primary education (https://aesop.iep.edu.gr/node/23485).
2 The Eurovelo 6 cycling route: gain knowledge and disseminate it to their classroom community. Students participate as "partners" in the European network of the European Cycling Federation (ECF) and propose, plan, and update. In the context of PE, they are involved with lifelong exercise and behavior change towards a healthier and sportier way of life. In IT, they apply Web 2.0 tools to express and externalize their knowledge and ideas and to challenge others. In the subject of geography, they recognize multiple levels of research through "tourist cycling".

A special mention should be made of the "skills workshops", an innovative educational activity from 2022 included in the curriculum of kindergartens, primary and secondary schools, public and private. "Skill workshops" aim to strengthen the cultivation of students' skills through the development of soft and life skills, science, technology, engineering and mathematics (STEM) skills via participation in activities (https://iep.edu.gr/el/psifiako-apothetirio/skill-labs).

The above actions are very recent, and therefore, the magnitude of the results has not been recorded.

Dimension 8: Habituated Behavior in Physical Activities (HBPA)

According to the Analytical Curriculum (2013), the PE course includes activities that help students develop appropriate knowledge and skills to allow them to design their exercise programs. The contents of the knowledge field include two thematic modules:

1 "Knowledge about exercise and health" includes experiential activities to gain knowledge about exercise and its practical application: (a) types and health benefits of exercise, (b) recommendations of national and international bodies for exercise and ways of integrating them into students' everyday lives, (c) components of physical fitness for health, (d) safe exercise and first aid, and (e) healthy diet and exercise.
2 "Self-regulation skills" include the development of skills that contribute to the achievement of the central goal of lifelong exercise for health and quality of

life: (a) principles governing self-regulation skills and their value in exercise and/or life, (b) practices of integrating self-regulation skills into physical fitness programs in the PE course, and individual or group exercise programs, (c) strategies for transferring self-regulation skills to other subjects and areas of students' lives – tomorrow's adults.

From the monitoring of habituated behavior until now, the goals have been partially achieved (Adamakis & Dania, 2020).

Conclusion

In this chapter, an initial attempt to record the evolution of PE in modern Greece has been made. Overall, it seems that there has been significant progress regarding the quality characteristics of PE at all levels of education, especially in recent years. This progress is in alignment with practices established in the EU. Some of the most important initiatives are the adoption of the concept of Physical Literacy, the development of a large network of special schools and the parallel support to strengthen inclusion, the institutionalized evaluation of PE teachers, the scientific evaluation of students' various health parameters, the establishment of the courses of Greek traditional dances and Olympic Education, the guidance of students in lifelong exercise, and the implementation of interdisciplinary actions for the further cognitive development of students through PE. Deficiencies noted relate to school infrastructure and insufficient training of PE teachers.

References

Adamakis, M., & Dania, A. (2020). Physical education and school sport in Greece. *Research on Physical Education and School Sport in Europe, 155*, 155–189.

Avgerinos, T. (2000). *Didactis and Methodology of PE [Διδακτική και Μεθοδική της Αθλητικής Αγωγής]*. Athens: Salto.

European Commission. (2007). *White Paper on Sport*. https://eurlex.europa.eu/LexUriServ/LexUriServ.do?uri=COM%3A2007%3A0391%3AFIN%3AEN%3APDF

European Commission. (2008). *EU Physical Activity Guidelines*. https://ec.europa.eu/assets/eac/sport/library/policy_documents/eu-physical-activity-guidelines-2008_en.pdf

European Commission, European Education and Culture Executive Agency, Eurydice. (2013). *PE and Sport at School in Europe*. Publications Office. https://data.europa.eu/doi/10.2797/49648

Garzoni, E. M., Derri, V., Filippou, F., & Diggelidis, N. (2023). Teachers' views on effective teaching of movement/PE and its implementation, for preschool and early school-age children. *Sport and Society, 1*, 15–34. http://ojs.staff.duth.gr/ojs/index.php/ExSoc/article/view/484

Gdonteli, K., & Gavriilidis, A. (2014). An explanation on a prediction level of sport commitment from motivation, constraints and service quality in academic sports. *International Journal of Sport Management, 15*(2), 172–192. www.americanpresspublishers.com/IJSMContents2014.html

Georgiadis, K. (2007). *Proceedings. 1st International session for Olympic medalists.*: 23–41. Ancient Olympia.

Hart, S., Drummond, M. J., & McIntyre, D. (2014). Learning without limits: Constructing a pedagogy free from determinist beliefs about ability. *The Sage Handbook of Special Education* (vol. 2, pp. 439–458). SAGE Publication. www.torrossa.com/en/resources/an/5018795#page=498

International Monetary Fund. (2024, January 23). IMF Executive Board Concludes 2023 Article IV Consultation with Greece. *Press Release*, 24/23. www.imf.org/en/News/Articles/2024/01/23/pr2423-imf-concludes-2023-article-iv-consultation-with-greece

Kelmendi, D., & Dedi, T. (2024). Effective Teaching Methods in Physical Education Classes: A pilot study implementing a new survey for teachers. *Journal of Anthropology of Sport and Physical Education, 8*(3), 15–21. https://doi.org/10.26773/jaspe.240703

Khan, A., Khan, S., Zia-Ul-Islam, S., & Khan, M. (2017). Communication skills of a teacher and its role in the development of the students' academic success. *Journal of Education and Practice, 8*(1), 18–21. https://files.eric.ed.gov/fulltext/EJ1131770.pdf

Koutsouba, M. I. (2019). Traditional Dance in Urban Settings:'Snapshots' of Greek dance traditions in Athens. In *The Routledge Companion to Dance Studies* (pp. 285–297). Routledge. ebook ISBN 9781315306551

Lieberman, L. J., Houston-Wilson, C., & Grenier, M. (2024). *Strategies for Inclusion: PE for Everyone*. Human Kinetics.

Masadis, G., Filippou, F., Derri, V., Mavridis, G., & Rokka, S. (2019). Traditional dances as a means of teaching social skills to elementary school students. *International Journal of Instruction, 12*(1), 511–520. https://eric.ed.gov/?id=EJ1201159

Pavlinis, E. (1927). *The History of Gymnastics [Η Ιστορία της Γυμναστικής]*. G. H. Kallergis.

Tant, M., & Watelain, E. (2016). Forty years later, a systematic literature review on inclusion in PE (1975–2015): A teacher perspective. *Educational Research Review, 19*, 1–17. https://doi.org/10.1016/j.edurev.2016.04.002

Troupkou, A., & Gdonteli K. (2023). Exploring teacher's views and perceptions of students with non-visible disabilities. *European Journal of Special Education Research, 9*(2), 122–140. http://dx.doi.org/10.46827/ejse.v9i2.4848

van Munster, M. A., Lieberman, L. J., & Grenier, M. A. (2019). Universal design for learning and differentiated instruction in PE. *Adapted Physical Activity Quarterly, 36*(3), 359–377. https://doi.org/10.1123/apaq.2018-0145

World Health Organization. (2016). *Factsheets on Health Enhancing Physical Activity in the 28 European Union States of the WHO European region*. https://ec.europa.eu/assets/eac/sport/library/factsheets/eu-wide-overview-methods.pdf

Chapter 9

Quality Physical Education in India

Usha Sujit Nair, Kishore Gopinathan, and Sandeep Tiwari

Introduction to India

India, the world's second most populous country with a staggering population of approximately 1.44 billion people as of 2024, commands global attention as a formidable powerhouse. Not only is it the world's fifth-largest economy, but its gross domestic product (GDP) is also approximately $3.55 trillion in 2022 (Knoema, 2022). Despite economic strides, India faces multifaceted challenges, including entrenched gender inequality, highlighted by its 130th rank out of 155 countries on the gender inequality index (World Economic Forum, 2023). Variability in human development indicators across states underscores the need for targeted interventions, with Kerala leading in literacy rates while Bihar lags behind. The nation's rich tapestry of languages and cultures, encompassing 22 regional languages from diverse families, presents policymakers with the intricate task of ensuring inclusive and quality education for all. Furthermore, the persistent influence of the caste system perpetuates systemic inequalities, posing hurdles to equitable educational practices. However, India's role in international development cooperation is increasingly prominent, leveraging its experience as a former aid recipient to actively engage in global assistance programs and regional partnerships, thereby contributing to worldwide economic growth and development.

Education in India

India, with over 1.5 million schools, more than 8.7 million primary and secondary teachers, and over 260 million students enrolled, is home to the largest and most complex education system in the world (British Council, 2019). After gaining independence from British rule in 1947, the Department of Education was established under the Ministry of Human Resource Development (MHRD) with the mandate to improve both access to and the quality of education. This effort led to the first National Policy on Education in 1968. Initially, the expansion of the education sector was limited by India's economic growth but continued steadily until the end of the 20th century. Since committing to the Millennium Development Goals in 2000, India has made significant progress toward achieving universal primary education.

DOI: 10.4324/9781003513582-11

According to the World Bank, elementary school enrolment increased by more than 33 million between 2000 and 2017, rising from 156.6 million in 2000–2001 to 189.9 million in 2017–2018. While achievements vary greatly across India's 29 states and 7 union territories, two-thirds of them have claimed to have achieved universal primary enrolment. Two major initiatives by the Indian government—the Sarva Shiksha Abhiyan (SSA, or "Education for All Campaign") in 2001 and the Right of Children to Free and Compulsory Education (RTE) Act in 2009—have focused on improving access, inclusivity, and quality in education. The mean years of schooling for the working population (those over 25 years old) increased from 4.19 years in 2000 to 6.4 years in 2017 (British Council, 2019). A significant achievement in recent years is the implementation of the National Education Policy (NEP) 2020, and this has transformed the educational landscape in the country.

Physical Education in India

Since gaining independence, the Government of India has launched numerous initiatives to integrate physical education (PE) and sports into the educational system, aiming to promote a culture of sports nationwide. These measures, supported by various policies and commissions, have focused on addressing challenges, nurturing talent at the grassroots level, and fostering widespread physical activity. Notably, the National Education Policies of 1968, 1986, and 2020 have significantly shaped India's educational landscape by emphasizing holistic development, inclusivity, and the integration of sports and PE into the curriculum, reflecting the government's commitment to comprehensive educational reform.

Given the limited research on quality physical education in the country, peer-reviewed literature was obtained from the PubMed database. For grey literature, tailored Google searches were conducted for each dimension, along with specific searches of government and ministry websites, physical activity and health-focused non-profit organizations, school board websites, and national program sites. However, literature specific to Dimension 1: Skill Development and Bodily Awareness (SDBA) was not available. This chapter focuses on the remaining dimensions and expects to assist readers to have some understanding of quality physical education development in India.

Dimension 2: Facilities and Norms in Physical Education (FNPE)

The Central Board of Secondary Education (CBSE) has adopted a comprehensive approach to health and PE, encompassing health education, PE, and yoga—critical components for holistic health. Students are evaluated in four areas: Games and Sports, Health and Fitness, Social Empowerment through Work Education and Action (SEWA), and the Health and Activity Card. For students in grades 1–10 (ages 5–16), a daily 45-minute PE class is mandated across all school boards. For grades 11–12 (ages 16–18), 90–120 minutes of physical activity per week is required. In 2019, CBSE's network included over 22,030 affiliated schools, of which 17,553 were private and 2,727 were government (CBSE, 2019; Times of India, 2018). A daily sports period is compulsory for all classes from grades 1 to 12. A 2017 survey of 16 schools in Delhi found that 15 had playground equipment, 9 had courts for outdoor sports, and 25% had dedicated sports areas. However, most lacked the infrastructure to support physical activity, though 37% had general play spaces (Tarun et al., 2017).

The Annual Status of Education Report (ASER) documented trends in school PE across 16,000 government schools in 2018 and 17,002 in 2022. It showed a slight decrease in the presence of dedicated PE teachers in elementary schools, from 5.8% in 2018 to 4.3% in 2022, but an increase in upper primary schools from 30.8% to 31.3%. Schools with playgrounds increased to 68.9% in 2022 from 66.5% in 2018, and the availability of sports equipment in upper elementary schools rose to 82.7% in 2022, compared to 71.5% in 2018 (ASER, 2023). A 2019 survey in New Delhi found that 80% of primary and 90% of secondary private schools included PE in the curriculum, while 78% of primary and 100% of secondary government schools did the same. Yoga was incorporated in 70% of primary and 60% of secondary private schools and 67% of primary and 78% of secondary government schools (Bassi et al., 2019). In Bangalore, 16% of private and 65% of government schools had playgrounds, but regular access for students was limited (Periyasamy et al., 2019). A national survey involving 1,402 households and 1,531 adolescents revealed that two-thirds of schools offered health education, including PE, with 64.3% of adolescents reporting an average of 16.1 minutes of physical activity at school (Mathur et al., 2021). These findings suggest that while PE is mandated in Indian schools, limited access to PE equipment and areas outside school hours may restrict physical activity opportunities.

Dimension 3: Quality Teaching of Physical Education (QTPE)

Academic institutions under the Ministry of Youth Affairs and Sports, Government of India, such as the National Sports University in Manipur, Lakshmibai National Institute of Physical Education in Gwalior, Netaji Subhas National Institute of Sports in Patiala, Lakshmibai National College of Physical Education in Thiruvananthapuram, and a number of State Sports Universities, offer programs in PE, coaching, and related fields at the masters and doctoral levels. Teacher training courses in PE must be recognized by the National Council for Teacher Education (NCTE), the statutory body responsible for regulating and setting standards for teacher education in India.

Across the nation, there are 166 institutions offering a Diploma in Physical Education program D.P.Ed, 632 offering Bachelors of Physical Education (B.P.Ed), and 181 providing Masters of Physical Education (M.P.Ed) programs accredited by NCTE. Many of these institutions also provide doctoral programs in PE. As of March 31, 2022, the intake approved by the NCTE for all institutions was as follows: D.P.Ed—9,495; B.P.Ed—47,860; M.P.Ed—7,415. However, this number falls significantly short of the annual demand (NCTE, 2020).

Dimension 4: Plans for Feasibility and Accessibility of Physical Education (PFAPE)

A study conducted in rural Mathura, Uttar Pradesh, found that 90.7% of participants engaged in some form of sport, with gender differences in preferences. Boys predominantly played cricket (74.2%), while girls favored "physical exercises" like resistance or muscle-strengthening activities (50%) (Shoor et al., 2021). In urban and rural Pune, primary data from children and youth aged 5–17 indicated that 77.5% participated in organized sports, with 59.1% involved in competitive school activities against other schools. A cross-sectional study in Karnataka involving youth aged 13–16 ($n = 395$) revealed that girls spent an average of 21 minutes daily in active play, compared to 54 minutes for boys. The study also highlighted a significant gender disparity in outdoor playtime, with girls averaging 16 minutes and boys 49 minutes daily (Raskind et al., 2020). In Chennai, a cross-sectional study of youth aged 12–17 ($n = 324$) found that 73.5% did not walk to or from school, and 78.4% did not cycle, indicating a preference for motorized transportation (Kingsly et al., 2020). Conversely, a similar study in Kanpur, Uttar Pradesh, across nine high schools ($n = 1,096$) showed that 35% of adolescents engaged in active transport, with 24.5% of males cycling and 15.4% walking to school, compared to 18% of females walking and 10% cycling. In Punjab, 90% of adolescents from urban and rural government schools reportedly used active transportation (Kaur et al., 2018).

Since its launch in 2019, the Fit India Movement has introduced several initiatives, including the Fit India Week, initially celebrated in schools and later extended to colleges and universities. The Fit India School Week requires participation criteria such as having a trained PE teacher, a playground supporting two or more outdoor games, a PE period for all classes, and students engaging in at least 60 minutes of daily physical activity. In the fourth edition, 5.56 lakh schools participated. The Fit India Quiz has also become a national platform, with the second edition in 2022 involving 61,981 students from 16,702 schools. The Fit India School Certification offers titles like Fit India School, Fit India 3-Star School, and Fit India 5-Star School, with Rajasthan leading in certification requests (Fit India, 2024).

Dimension 5: Social Norms and Cultural Practice (SNCP)

Socio-economic factors such as income, parental education, and demographic setting significantly influence children's physical activity levels. A study of 272 students from government schools in the 12- to 15-year age group revealed that children whose parents regularly encouraged exercise ($n = 138$) engaged in physical activity for an average of 0.455 hours more per day. Gender disparities were notable, with girls ($n = 150$) exercising for an average of 30 minutes less per day than boys ($n = 122$). Furthermore, 66% of girls were unaware of the importance of exercise compared to 52% of boys. Urban children ($n = 140$) exercised an average of 0.396 hours more per day than their rural peers. These findings emphasize the need to promote physical activity among girls and rural students through culturally relevant practices such as indigenous games and daily activities like using stairs, cycling, walking, and participating in household chores. Schools and communities can foster healthier environments by incorporating movement and exercise into the school day (Nandivada & Gurtoo, 2022).

Further research on barriers and enablers of physical activity among school children highlighted gender differences and variations by school type (government vs. private). Involving 174 students aged 12–16 years from Delhi—88 from private schools (47% girls) and 86 from government schools (48% girls)—the study identified several challenges and motivations related to physical activity. Private school girls frequently cited body image concerns as a barrier, while both private and government schoolgirls faced greater social censure compared to boys. A common environmental barrier was the limited opportunity for physical activity within schools. Nevertheless, perceived health benefits were a strong motivator, and active parents and sports role models played a significant role in increasing physical activity. However, few environmental enablers were identified, suggesting the need for further attention (Satija et al., 2018).

A focus group study involving 14- to 15-year-olds ($n = 36$) revealed cultural and environmental contexts affecting physical activity trends. Reported barriers included parental and teacher discouragement, gender-specific deterrents for girls such as appearance concerns, limited participation options, societal reputation issues, and advice to avoid exercise during menstruation. These barriers varied by urban and rural residence and socio-economic status (SES), with rural boys and girls from lower SES families experiencing different barriers compared to their higher SES urban counterparts (Vaz et al., 2015).

Dimension 6: Governmental Input for Physical Education (GIPE)

The *Khelo* India program was introduced to rejuvenate the sports culture in India at the grassroots level by creating a robust framework for all sports played in the country, with the aim of establishing India as a leading sporting nation. The program identifies 12 key areas that impact the entire sports ecosystem, including sports infrastructure, talent identification, coaching for excellence, community sports, competition structure, and the sports economy (Khelo India, 2024).

In August 2023, the Department of School Education and Literacy, under the Ministry of Education (MoE), issued the Revised Guidelines for Sports Grant under the Samagra Shiksha initiative, titled *"Khelen Bhi Aur Khilen Bhi."* These guidelines align with the objectives of the NEP 2020, emphasizing the integration of sports into mainstream education to promote holistic development and cognitive enhancement. Reflecting the goals of NEP 2020, particularly Para 4.8, the guidelines focus on sports-integrated learning to develop essential skills like collaboration and self-discipline, with the aim of fostering lifelong fitness attitudes.

The scheme, introduced as part of the Integrated Scheme on School Education, provides grants for the procurement of sports equipment in government schools, ranging from Rs. 5,000 to Rs. 25,000 based on the school's level. Additional grants are available for schools with medal-winning students in the Khelo India Youth Games. The initiative also mandates Fitness Assessment and Monitoring, requiring schools to follow Khelo India Fitness Assessment protocols. The promotion of *Yogasana* and participation in International Day of Yoga activities are included alongside traditional sports events.

The proposed initiatives ensure that sports equipment is accessible in all schools, emphasize the inclusion of sports in the curriculum, and support the "Khelo India" movement. PE is also listed among the "17 trades" under the Vocationalization of Secondary Education scheme to enhance employability. PE teachers play a critical role in sports management and are responsible for implementing guidelines, talent identification, and injury prevention. They are encouraged to incorporate adaptive sports, parasports, and Paralympic sports to cater to diverse student needs, with a particular emphasis on inclusive opportunities for female students. Schools are urged to prioritize equitable access to sports facilities and ensure the necessary support for girls' participation, fostering a culture of sports and physical fitness within schools (Department of School Education and Literacy, 2024).

Dimension 7: Cognitive Skill Development (CSD)

A study involving 40 school children aged 11–14 years from Tamil Nadu who participated in a structured physical activity program for 20 weeks revealed significant improvements in attention following the intervention (Vishnupriya et al., 2022). In another study conducted at Jawahar Navodaya Vidyalaya, Pondicherry, 439 healthy adolescents aged 12–17 years underwent neuropsychological cognitive tests. Following 24 weeks of intervention, significant cognitive improvements were observed, with notably greater enhancements in attention, concentration, and mental flexibility (Subramanian et al., 2015).

Dimension 8: Habituated Behavior in Physical Activities (HBPA)

Data from 23,34,739 students enrolled in classes 5–10 from 6,010 schools in Kerala revealed that only 14% of the student population met the minimum recommended standards in health-related physical fitness tests, with boys at 16.58% and girls at 11.46% (Kerala State Sports Council, 2010).

According to the 2007 India Global School-Based Student Health Survey (GSHS), 3.5% of students often went hungry due to a lack of food, 10.8% were overweight, 2.1% were obese, 30.2% were physically active for at least 60 minutes daily, and 23.2% spent three or more hours per day sitting (WHO, 2007).

India's 2022 Report Card, covering 27 states with a sample size of 3,808 individuals, found that among 15- to 17-year-olds, 25.2% had insufficient levels of physical activity, with urban residents (38%) and girls (29.3%) particularly affected. Objective data from Chennai adolescents ($n = 324$) showed an average of 25.8 minutes of moderate-to-vigorous physical activity (MVPA) daily. In contrast, studies from Mumbai and Tamil Nadu found that only 38% and 31.7% of youth met the MVPA guidelines of 60 minutes per day, respectively (Active Healthy Kids Global Alliance, 2022; Kumar & Shirley, 2019; Moitra et al., 2021).

Sedentary behavior, defined as less than 2 hours of recreational screen time per day, varied across India's urban centers. For example, urban boys in Thanjavur spent an average of 6.59 hours on screens daily, while girls in Mumbai exceeded 120 minutes of screen time daily, with an average of 218 minutes (Katapally & Muhajarine, 2015; Moitra et al., 2021).

Studies highlighted that urban students were less active than their rural counterparts, with significant gender differences in activity levels (Raskind et al., 2020; Satija et al., 2018). School audits in Delhi revealed that 60% of private and 33.3% of government schools lacked appropriate playgrounds, limiting physical activity opportunities (Tarun et al., 2017). These findings emphasize the need to address sedentary behavior and promote physical activity in Indian schools to improve overall health and well-being (Active Healthy Kids Global Alliance, 2022).

Discussion

The implementation of quality PE programs in Indian schools presents several critical challenges that require urgent attention. A primary issue is the shortage of qualified PE teachers, which impacts the delivery and effectiveness of PE classes. Many primary schools rely on teachers with general education degrees or non-specialists for PE instruction, compromising the quality and effectiveness of PE periods (International Charter of PE and Sports; UNESCO, 2015). Additionally, the poor pupil–teacher ratio contributes to large class sizes, making it difficult to provide personalized attention and meet the diverse needs of students. This exacerbates the challenge of implementing a comprehensive PE program.

Deficiencies in the quality of PE teachers further compound these issues. Challenges include inadequate training, difficulties in planning structured lessons, gender stereotyping, and a low perceived value of PE. These factors hinder effective student engagement and result in suboptimal teaching practices. The complex structure of India's education system, characterized by a mix of centralized and decentralized elements, government initiatives, and private institutions, adds to the difficulty of implementing effective PE programs. The interplay between central and state governments aims to address diverse needs but complicates policy execution.

Addressing these challenges requires a coordinated effort involving multiple stakeholders, including the MoE, the Central Advisory Board of Education (CABE), the University Grants Commission, the National Council of Teacher

Education, Union and State Governments, and various other educational bodies like CBSE, etc. Effective policy execution demands meticulous planning and collaboration. The current research on quality PE in India is limited, highlighting a significant research gap in areas such as policies, facilities, and curriculum allocation. More comprehensive research across regions and school types is essential to inform evidence-based policies and interventions.

Conclusion

The introduction of the NEP 2020 offers promising prospects for the future of PE in India. The policy's emphasis on integrating PE into the educational framework for holistic student development aims to improve sports facilities, increase PE periods, and enhance teacher training (Ministry of Education and Literacy, 2023). This progressive shift has the potential to significantly enhance students' physical well-being, foster essential life skills, and contribute to academic success. By addressing existing challenges and embracing collaborative efforts, India can move towards a future where PE is a cornerstone of education, promoting healthier and well-rounded individuals.

References

Active Healthy Kids Global Alliance. (2022, July 29). *Core physical activity indicators*. www.activehealthykids.org/tools/

Annual Status of Education Report (ASER). (2023, January 18). https://img.asercentre.org/docs/ASER%202022%20report%20pdfs/All%20India%20documents/aserreport2022.pdf

Bassi, S., Gupta, V. K., Park, M., Nazar, G. P., Rawal, T., Bhaumik, S., Khochhar, K. P., & Arora, M. (2019). School policies, built environment and practices for non-communicable disease (NCD) prevention and control in schools of Delhi, India. *PloS One, 14*(4), e0215365. https://doi.org/10.1371/journal.pone.0215365

British Council. (2019). *The school education system in India: An overview*. www.britishcouncil.in/sites/default/files/school_education_system_in_india_report_2019_final_web.pdf

CBSE. (2019). *Mainstreaming health and physical education*. www.cbse.gov.in/cbsenew/documents/CBSE@90-15-11-2019.pdf

Department of School Education and Literacy. (2024). *About School Education & Literacy*. Ministry of Education. https://dsel.education.gov.in/about-us

Fit India. (2024). *Fit India School*. Youth Affairs and Sport. https://fitindia.gov.in/fit-india-school

Katapally, T. R., & Muhajarine, N. (2015). Capturing the interrelationship between objectively measured physical activity and sedentary behaviour in children in the context of diverse environmental exposures. *International Journal of Environmental Research and Public Health, 12*(9), 10995–11011. https://doi.org/10.3390/ijerph120910995/

Kaur, S., Bains, K., & Kaur, H. (2018). Comparative study on sedentary behaviour and physical activity pattern of urban and rural government school children of Punjab (India). *Applied Biological Research, 20*(3), 271–277. https://doi.org/10.5958/0974-4517.2018.00037.X

Kerala State Sports Council. (2010). *2009 Kerala total physical fitness programme test results.* http://doi.org/10.13140/RG.2.1.4131.7605

Khelo India. (2024). *Khelo India – National Program for Development of Sports. Ministry of Youth Affairs and Sports.* https://kheloindia.gov.in/

Kingsly, A., Timperio, A., Veitch, J., Salmon, J., Pradeepa, R., Ranjani, H., & Anjana, R. M. (2020). Individual, social and environmental correlates of active school travel among adolescents in India. *International Journal of Environmental Research and Public Health, 17*(20), 7496. https://doi.org/10.3390/ijerph17207496/

Knoema. (2022). *World GDP ranking 2022.* https://knoema.com/nwnfkne/world-gdp-ranking-2022-gdp-by-country-data-and-charts

Kumar, S. S., & Shirley, S. A. (2019). Association of screen time with physical activity and BMI in middle school children at Tamil Nadu, India. *International Journal of Contemporary Pediatrics, 7*(1), 78–83. https://doi.org/10.18203/2349-3291.ijcp20195730

Mathur, P., Kulothungan, V., Leburu, S., Krishnan, A., Chaturvedi, H. K., Salve, H. R., ... & Shelke, S. C. (2021). Baseline risk factor prevalence among adolescents aged 15–17 years old: Findings from National Non-communicable Disease Monitoring Survey (NNMS) of India. *BMJ Open, 11*(6), e044066. https://doi.org/10.1136/bmjopen-2020-044066

Moitra, P., Madan, J., & Verma, P. (2021). Independent and combined influences of physical activity, screen time, and sleep quality on adiposity indicators in Indian adolescents. *BMC Public Health, 21,* 1–12. https://doi.org/10.1186/s12889-021-12183-9

Nandivada, V., & Gurtoo, A. (2022). Socio-economic and awareness correlates of physical activity of government school children in India. *Journal of Emerging Investigators, 5*(1), 1–8.

NCTE. (2020). *Recognized institutions.* https://ncte.gov.in/Website/PDF/AnnualReport/English-2021-22.pdf

Periyasamy, S., Krishnappa, P. & Renuka, P. (2019). Adherence to components of Health Promoting Schools in schools of Bengaluru, India. *Health Promotion International, 34*(6), 1167–1178. https://doi.org/10.1093/heapro/day082

Raskind, I. G., Patil, S. S., Tandon, N., Thummalapally, S., Kramer, M. R., & Cunningham, S. A. (2020). Household chores or play outdoors? The intersecting influence of gender and school type on physical activity among Indian adolescents. *Health Education & Behavior, 47*(5), 682–691. https://doi.org/10.1177/1090198120931040/

Satija, A., Khandpur, N., Satija, S., Gaiha, S. M., Prabhakaran, D., Reddy, K. S., Arora, M., & Narayan, K. M. V. (2018). Physical activity among adolescents in India: A qualitative study of barriers and enablers. *Health Education & Behavior, 45*(6), 926–934. https://www.jstor.org/stable/48615193

Shoor, P., Chauhan, A. K., Kaur, G. D., & Ankur, M. (2021). Prevalence and factors influencing sports participation among adolescents residing in rural field practice area of medical college, Mathura. *International Journal Dental and Medical Sciences Research, 3*(3), 446–456. http://doi.org/10.35629/5252-0303446456/

Subramanian, S. K., Sharma, V. K., Arunachalam, V., Radhakrishnan, K., & Ramamurthy, S. (2015). Effect of structured and unstructured physical activity training on cognitive functions in adolescents—a randomized control trial. *Journal of Clinical and Diagnostic Research, 9*(11), CC04–CC9. https://doi.org/10.7860/JCDR/2015/14881.6818

Tarun, S., Arora, M., Rawal, T., & Benjamin Neelon, S. E. (2017). An evaluation of outdoor school environments to promote physical activity in Delhi, India. *BMC Public Health, 17,* 1–9. https://doi.org/10.1186/s12889-016-3987-8

Times of India. (2018). *CBSE makes health physical education a must for Std IX to XII*. https://timesofindia.indiatimes.com/education/news/cbse-makes-health-physical-education-must-for-std-ix-to-xii/articleshow/63873756.cms

United Nations Educational, Scientific and Cultural Organization (UNESCO). (2015). *International Charter of Physical Education, Physical Activity and Sport*. UNESCO. https://unesdoc.unesco.org/ark:/48223/pf0000235409/PDF/235409eng.pdf.multi

Vaz, M., Swaminathan, S., Rajaraman, D., & Kuriyan, R. (2015). *Overweight and obesity in Asian Indian children in India and Canada: Multi-level determinants, functional consequences and novel mechanisms*. Report. Ref No. 58/4/2/ ICMR-CIHR/2009/NCD-II (IRIS No: 2009-09540).

Vishnupriya, R., Srividya, G., & Kannan, D. (2022). Effects of structured physical activity in improving attention among school going children. *International Journal of Medical and Exercise Science*, 8(1), 1172–1180. 10.36678/IJMAES.2022.V08I01.002

WHO. (2007, January 01). *GSHS Fact Sheet India*. www.who.int/publications/m/item/2007-gshs-fact-sheet-india

World Economic Forum (2023). *Global Gender Gap Report 2023*. World Economic Forum. www3.weforum.org/docs/WEF_GGGR_2023.pdf

Chapter 10

Quality Physical Education and Development in Japan

Naoki Suzuki, Yutaka Sato, Seiji Hirosawa, and Yu Furuta

Introduction

Japan is an island country located in the North-West of the Pacific Ocean with neighbours of Korea and China on the West and Philippines in the South. The country consists of five main islands stretching from Hokkaido in the north, Honshu, Shikoku, Kyushu, and Okinawa in the south. Tokyo is the capital and the largest city in the country. The population in Japan was around 124 million people in 2024 (Statistics Bureau of Japan, 2024). The ancient Japan had a long period of ruling by warlords and unified in 1603 by the Tokugawa Shogunate government. The Tokugawa government enacted an isolation policy for the country. Such policy lasted for almost 300 years and ended after the arrival of the United States fleet in 1854. The open trade to the West and changing government during the Meiji period initiated drastic reform works towards industrialization and modernization. There were two major transformation processes modelling from Western experiences (Hata & Sekine, 2010; Terayama & Yagi, 2021; Ohkuma, 2001). The first transformation took place during the Meiji period, and the other happened after World War II. These two transformations shaped the country from a feudal state to a modern society with democratic legislative structure to support the country's growth (Schoppa, 2002).

Education reform performed with a significant role in these transformation works. The first transformation enacted the policies of universal primary education and a meritocratic system to educate the general citizens into workforces and development of talented elites for Japanese society (Schoppa, 2002). In 1910, there was the record of almost 98% of primary school-aged children received 4 years compulsory education which was much earlier than in the Western countries (Sakurai, 2016). The second transformation aimed to develop a more egalitarian and democratic education system for the training of skilled workers and professionals for post-war recovery. The talented and creative workforce created by the education system and a lifelong learning culture seemed to be the important aspect to support the changing demands of the fast-growing science and technology industries and international business for world trade (Schoppa, 2002).

DOI: 10.4324/9781003513582-12

Physical Education Development in Japan

Physical education (*taiiku*) in Japan was firstly initiated during the early Meiji period under the appellation of "*taijutsu* (i.e., physical-technique)," and subsequently transformed into "*taiso* (i.e., gymnastics)." Even evolving the name over time, it has become a compulsory subject and an integral component of school education. This subject was placed with special functions and initially served with purpose to associate with war, with a focus on physical and military training (Ho, 2009; Ohkuma, 2001). Such attitudes in physical education experienced drastic change after World War II. Takahashi (2000) summarized the physical education development into three stages after the end of World War II. The first phase was "goals of new physical education" based on experiential education positioned as part of democratic human development influenced by American physical education under the supervision of the General Headquarters (GHQ). In the first phase, a significant challenge emerged in dispelling the influence of pre-war militaristic physical education, and the vision was transformed from "education of physical" to "education through physical activities." The second phase was the shift from "empiricist education" to "systematic education" was implemented, emphasizing the improvement of basic motor skills and athletic abilities. These fundamental policies in physical education were further modified according to social transitions, such as independence, economic revival, the Tokyo Olympics, and intellectual ability problems in educational circles from the late 1950s to the 1960s (Takahashi, 2000). The third phase was transformed from "education through physical activities" to "education in movement; education in sport." In the third phase, the aim was focused on "joy" or "fun" under the concept of lifelong sport. This was influenced by the philosophy of "sport for all." Further, in addition to joy and fun, in the current course of study, competency-based learning is emphasized and accounted into three components: (1) ensure that knowledge and skills are acquired; (2) develop the students' abilities to think, make judgements, and express themselves; and (3) cultivate the motivation to learn and humanity (Ministry of Education, Culture, Sports, Science and Technology (MEXT), 2017). There is no doubt that these works enabled the development of good foundation for physical education in schools, and with the advanced development of scientific works, the country can move on with the adoption of latest technology in computer science, artificial intelligence and virtual reality in teaching physical education.

In Japan, the Basic Act on Education was revised in 2006 for the first time in 60 years, emphasizing 21st-century skills (MEXT, 2006, 2012). These skills include the basic knowledge and abilities needed to adapt to a rapidly changing society, the capacity to independently identify, learn, think, judge, and act on issues, as well as "zest for life" which encompasses cooperation, empathy, health, and physical fitness. This philosophy aligns with the key competencies defined by the Organisation for Economic Co-operation and Development (OECD). In physical education, the 2007 revision already promoted the integration of teaching and assessment. Given the 2017 curriculum revision that integrated teaching and assessment across all subjects, it can be said that physical education had been ahead in terms of integrating competency-based content with assessment.

The current curriculum emphasizes that exercise is closely related to mental health as well as physical health, focusing on the promotion of lifelong physical and mental well-being and the realization of a rich sports life (MEXT, 2017). Physical education constructs its curriculum based on the perspective of nurturing the following three components: (1) knowledge and skills related to exercise; (2) thinking skills, judgement, and expression abilities for identifying and solving exercise-related issues; and (3) attitudes for proactive learning, learning motivation, and humanity. A study by Dismore et al. (2006) compared the Japanese and English students' views on physical education. The study suggested that Japanese students were more likely to state that physical education was as important as other subjects than their English counterparts. Dismore et al. (2006)'s study helped to identify the importance of sports in life among Japanese students. There is no doubt that sports have the special value in the normal life of Japanese students. In fact, nowadays, the number of physical education teaching hours is the highest among other core subjects (Nakayasu, 2016). Such facts may indicate a healthy and optimistic development for the teaching of physical education in Japanese schools.

The country operates a unified curriculum and expects schools to attain the required teaching quality of physical education. Nevertheless, the educational arrangement operates under the prefectural practices (Koyama, 2008; National Center on Education and the Economy (NCEE, 2021)). The Ministry of Education in Japan provides the standard for schools and students are expected to achieve similar developmental outcomes in education. While in actual practice, each prefecture can have its own policy for its implementation and schools will have the autonomy in designing the curriculum. The works of the schools and policy of physical education are then influenced by the economic situation of individual prefectures and the availability of professionals in the teaching field. Central and local governments share the responsibility of providing budget support for the educational development in each city or prefecture. The educational budget from the local governments is then influenced by the city's economic revenue or local gross domestic product (GDP). As such, the tax revenue in cities such as Tokyo will have the better financial support than cities with poorer revenue or income (Mayger & Dormido, 2017).

This chapter expects to focus on the various dimensions which are essential behind the construction of quality physical education program in schools. The discussion covers aspects such as teacher training, curriculum design, latest use of technology in teaching, policies for physical education, support for lifelong learning in sports, exercises and physical activities, extra-curriculum activities, and research in physical education. The authors would like to indicate a message that the development of a quality program in physical education requires the proper developmental targets of different dimensions and holistic management concept for these dimensions seems to be the essential strategy for success.

Dimension 1: Skill Development and Bodily Awareness (SDBA)

Since 1964, physical fitness tests have been conducted in Japanese schools. At that time, health-related physical fitness and skill-related physical fitness were measured separately. However, in 1998, they were integrated and reorganized into the new physical fitness test. Furthermore, surveys on exercise habits have been conducted in conjunction with the physical fitness tests. These surveys will be utilized to elucidate the status of elementary and junior high school students in relation to the quality physical education.

Although the physical fitness of Japanese children is on a downward trend compared to the 1980s, there is no significant difference compared to children in the 1960s, except for certain disciplines (MEXT, 2014). Furthermore, a 2020 survey of health-related fitness in junior high school students in eight Asian cities revealed that students from Tokyo had better performance in the two items of total body endurance (maximal oxygen uptake) and muscular endurance (number of upper body raises for 60 seconds) (Hui et al., 2020). According to Suzuki (2020), children in Tokyo spent more time exercising and playing sports than children in other cities, and this was supported by club activities. In other words, he states that this high record is because opportunities for sports are provided in the public sphere of school education.

Dimension 2: Facilities and Norms in Physical Education (FNPE)

Status of Physical Education Facilities

The establishment of physical education facilities is based on the Standards for the Establishment of Schools (Elementary, Middle, and High Schools), (1) which states that school buildings, playgrounds and gymnasiums shall be provided (Article 10). In principle, all schools are required to have playgrounds and gymnasiums. Consequently, all public schools are equipped with outdoor playgrounds and gymnasiums. Furthermore, the Guidelines for the Development of Facilities in Junior High Schools Where Budo Is to Begin (2014), published by the Education Facilities Planning Department of the Minister's Secretariat at the Ministry of Education, Culture, Sports, Science and Technology; (2) stipulates that consideration must be given to the content of activities, the number of users, the availability of martial arts grounds, and the school's openness, among other factors. Although not mandatory, the status of swimming pools and martial arts facilities are encouraged to establish in each school.

Positioning of Physical Education

In Japan, physical education is a combined subject of health and physical activities. In elementary schools, classroom teachers are primarily responsible for all subjects, while in junior high and high schools, health and physical education teachers are in charge. In accordance with the Japanese educational system, students aged 6–17 are required to engage in physical education for a minimum of 2–3 hours per week. Additionally, students aged 8–16 are required to participate in health education. In elementary schools, students aged 8.9 years old receive 4 hours of physical education, while those aged 10 and 11 years old receive 8 hours, and those aged 12–15 years old receive 16 hours of combined physical education and health education. In high schools, students aged 15 and 16 years old receive 2–3 hours of physical education per week and 1 hour of health education per week (35 times per year). With regard to competencies, the content is structured around three principal pillars: knowledge and skills, the capacity to think, judge, and express oneself, the capacity to learn, and humanity. As a foundation for the physical education facilities previously outlined, the athletic events to be conducted are delineated, and the requisite facilities are secured.

Dimension 3: Quality Teaching of Physical Education (QTPE)

Quality physical education is defined as the right to participate in physical education, physical activity, and sports without discrimination based on race, gender, sexual orientation, language, religion, political or other opinion, national or social origin, property, or any other reason. From this, it can be seen that girls are more likely to report disliking physical education than boys, and that there has been no significant change in the percentage of girls who do not like physical education. This may indicate that there are gender differences in learning experiences in physical education.

It is similarly held that physical education should be taught by instructors who are qualified and possess a high level of expertise. In Japanese elementary schools, classroom teachers are typically responsible for all subjects, and physical education is often taught by the homeroom teacher. It is evident that elementary school teachers are qualified to teach all subjects. However, there are also subject teachers who possess a higher level of expertise. In recent years, the percentage has been on the rise, yet it remains below 30% (MEXT, 2024).

Dimension 4: Plans for Feasibility and Accessibility of Physical Education (PFAPE)

International Cooperation

While international cooperation is active, mainly through the National Institute for Educational Policy Research, universities, etc., exchange at the school level is mainly through opportunities such as exchange schools and school trips. There is an undeniable language barrier in terms of day-to-day collaboration.

Domestic Cooperation

Domestic physical education research encompasses a range of subject-specific studies conducted by academic institutions, such as the Japan Society of Physical

Education and the Japan Society of Sports Education. Additionally, government-sponsored training, public research initiatives, such as the National School Physical Education Research Federation research conferences, class study groups held within each prefecture and municipality, and in-school training are also part of the landscape. Private-level research groups are also conducted.

As a result of the limited scope of public research groups, which often exchange information only with teachers from a specific school type, the physical education class study group conducted by the author holds wide-area study groups in 20 prefectures per year in various parts of Japan. These groups facilitate the exchange of ideas among universities, students, teachers, administrators, and school board personnel, transcending their respective positions https://kyushunet.com/sns/pages/katudou/k-keikaku.php.

Dimension 5: Social Norms and Cultural Practice (SNCP)

First, as a peculiarity of Japan, the current situation is that people live their lives incorporating various religious rituals. These include Shinto rituals for New Year and Setsubun, celebrations of Halloween and Christmas, and funerals conducted in Buddhist ceremonies.

This is because Shintoism is a culture of belief in 8 million (yayorozu) deities, and the idea that all things have a deity is commonplace. Furthermore, animist belief is fundamental to the culture. Against the backdrop of cultural ideas that are not monotheistic, which are found in many other countries in historical circumstances such as the Shinto–Buddhist syncretism, 62% of respondents in the ISSP International Comparative Survey (2018) identified as "Mujinshinkyo."

While there is considerable debate about the interpretation of this trend, it is clear that the lack of major conflicts due to religious differences and the high level of civility and often reported social norms are the defining characteristics of Japanese society. These values are shaped by a comprehensive body of family and community education outside of school education.

In physical education, the Course of Study provides specific guidance on attitudes such as fairness, cooperation, responsibility, participation, coexistence, health and safety, etc. However, the curriculum as a whole is structured with a special subject, "morality," and clean-up activities are routinely conducted outside the curriculum. It can be inferred that ethical values are naturally instilled in children from an early age through the interaction of these activities www.nhk.or.jp/bunken/research/yoron/pdf/20190401_7.pdf.

Dimension 6: Governmental Input for Physical Education (GIPE)

Inclusive Education System

In accordance with the Convention on the Rights of Persons with Disabilities (signed in 2007, ratified in 2014), the Basic Law for Persons with Disabilities

(2011), and the partial revision of the School Education Law (2013), the revision of the Courses of Study in 2018 has enhanced instruction from the perspective of reasonable accommodation in each subject and improved procedures for students who require special support. The revision of the Courses of Study has a history of being implemented in the past.

Physical Education Initiatives

In the subjects of Physical Education and Health and Physical Education, the statement that "it is important to devise instructional content and methods in a planned and organized manner to meet the difficulties that arise when conducting learning activities" for students with disabilities, etc. has been expanded to include the following: Nevertheless, disparities based on geographical location, such as the delivery of gender-based lessons in the classroom, continue to be observed. Nevertheless, disparities by region persist, such as the continued practice of gender-segregated lessons in the classroom. Furthermore, the company disseminates information regarding the teaching and evaluation of "coexistence" in the National Institute for Educational Policy Research's reference materials for evaluation, as well as specific teaching and evaluation of "respect for diversity" in physical education classes.

Furthermore, the author's research in the field of education is contributing to the development of teaching materials that promote inclusiveness in teacher training classes. The National Institute for Educational Policy Research has published reference materials on the assessment of learning for the integration of instruction and evaluation. The case study on health and physical education (physical education) can be found on page 82 www.nier.go.jp/kaihatsu/pdf/hyouka/r020326_mid_hok ent.pdf. The objective of this class is to examine the potential for devising rules that transcend differences in ability, such as difficulty in movement, to facilitate participation in a fun and inclusive manner. To this end, the class will engage in a series of activities where each student will play for a specified amount of time. One student will play in a wheelchair. The class will then discuss the implications of these activities for the design of inclusive rules.

Dimension 7: Cognitive Skill Development (CSD)

One notable aspect of Japanese schools is the prevalence of discussion scenes. As the following question illustrates, a significant number of teachers incorporate discussion scenes in their classes. Similarly, it is evident that they prioritize having students reflect on their learning at the conclusion of each class period.

A significant proportion of teachers are utilizing Information and Communication Technology (ICT) in their classroom practice, which is often employed as a tool for thinking and decision-making. In both elementary and junior high schools, the percentage of teachers who indicate that they do not utilize ICT is approximately 3% (MEXT, 2024), which is a relatively small percentage. This exemplifies the fact that in Japanese school physical education, the teaching of physical education places a strong emphasis on the development of critical thinking and decision-making abilities.

Dimension 8: Habituated Behaviour in Physical Activities (HBPA)

It is evident that the quantity and quality of physical activity in a child's daily life not only affect their health during childhood but also influence their physical activity and health as an adult. This physical activity encompasses not only exercise and sports, but also daily activities such as attending school and shopping.

MEXT (2024) has presented the results of the question, "Outside of physical and health education classes at school, how much time in total do you spend in physical activity (including physical play) and sports per day?" The World Health Organization (WHO) Guidelines for Physical Activity and Sedentary Behavior (WHO, 2020) stipulate that children should engage in moderate-to-vigorous physical activity (MVPA) for at least 60 minutes per day. Accordingly, 50% of elementary school boys and less than 30% of girls meet this requirement, while less than 80% of middle school boys and less than 60% of girls do so. This result can be interpreted as indicating that they are not fully active (MEXT, 2024).

In comparison to other countries, elementary and junior high schools in Japan frequently utilize walking or bicycling as the primary mode of transportation for students, and cleaning time is often an active physical activity. In addition, elementary schools typically have two long recess periods per day, while junior high schools have one. The fact that these results were obtained despite the limited time does not indicate that the physical activities learned in physical education are being incorporated into daily life and enjoyed in physical activity. It can be argued that in order to enhance the integration of physical education into daily life, it is not sufficient to merely increase the frequency of physical education classes and the number of students participating. Rather, it is also necessary to enhance the quality of the learning experience in physical education.

Conclusion

The development of physical education in Japan has been significantly influenced by its historical background and the transitions over different eras. Beginning as "Tai-jutsu" in the early Meiji period, transitioning to the "New Physical Education" aimed at fostering democracy and holistic human development post-World War II under American influence, and evolving into the current emphasis on "Lifetime Sports," Japan's physical education curriculum has become comprehensive. It now emphasizes not only the enhancement of physical abilities but also the cultivation of critical thinking, decision-making, and human qualities.

Moreover, based on the revised Fundamental Law of Education in 2006, the acquisition of 21st-century skills has been emphasized, and the 2017 revision of the National Curriculum Guidelines promoted the integration of instruction and evaluation across all subjects. Consequently, advanced educational content and evaluation methods have been incorporated into physical education, fostering both mental and physical health and a rich sports life.

Furthermore, Japan's physical education focuses on enhancing facilities and improving the quality of teachers. Based on the National Curriculum Guidelines, each school creatively develops its own curriculum, ensuring quality assurance. However, actual educational environments vary due to differences in regional economic conditions and educational policies.

This chapter has highlighted essential elements for building high-quality physical education programs, including teacher training, curriculum design, the introduction of advanced technology, support for lifelong learning, enrichment of extracurricular activities, and research in physical education. Managing and developing these elements comprehensively is considered the key to the success of high-quality physical education.

References

Dismore, H., Bailey, R., & Izaki, T. (2006). Japanese and English school students' views of physical education: a comparative study. *International Journal of Sport and Health Science, 4*, 74–85. https://doi.org/10.5432/ijshs.4.74

Hata, T., & Sekine, M. (2010). Philosophy of sport and physical education in Japan: its history, characteristics and prospects. *Journal of the Philosophy of Sport, 37*(2), 215–224. https://doi.org/10.1080/00948705.2010.9714777

Ho, W. (2009). *Social perspectives in physical education – Foundations and experiences in Chinese soil*. Berlin: Logos Verlag.

Hui, S.S.C., Zhang, R., & Suzuki, K. (2020). Physical activity and health-related fitness in Asian adolescents: the Asia-fit study. *Journal of Sports Sciences, 38*(3), 273–279. https://pubmed.ncbi.nlm.nih.gov/31774367/

Koyama, N. (2008). *Education administration in Japan and the role of local governments*. Council of Local Authorities for International Relations (CLAIR). www.jlgc.org.uk/en/pdfs/BunyabetsuNo9en.pdf

Mayger, J., & Dormido, H. (2017, December 13). The rich are getting richer in Abe's Japan. *Bloomberg*. www.bloomberg.com/graphics/2017-japan-inequality/

Ministry of Education, Culture, Sports, Science and Technology (MEXT). (2006). *The fundamental law of education [教育基本法について]* www.mext.go.jp/b_menu/kihon/houan.htm

Ministry of Education, Culture, Sports, Science and Technology (MEXT). (2012). *1st Study on educational goals, content, and evaluation methods in the qualities and abilities development [育成すべき資質・能力を踏まえた教育目標・内容と評価の在り方に関する検討会（第1回）]* www.mext.go.jp/b_menu/shingi/chousa/shotou/095/shiryo/1329013.htm

Ministry of Education, Culture, Sports, Science and Technology (MEXT). (2014, October 12). *Results of the 2013 physical fitness and athletic performance survey [平成25年度体力・運動能力調査の結果について]*. www.mext.go.jp/b_menu/houdou/26/10/__icsFiles/afieldfile/2014/10/14/1352498_01.pdf

Ministry of Education, Culture, Sports, Science and Technology (MEXT). (2017). *Curriculum guide for primary education (2017) [小学校学習指導要領（平成 29 年告示）解説]*. www.mext.go.jp/component/a_menu/education/micro_detail/__icsFiles/afieldfile/2019/03/18/1387017_010.pdf

Ministry of Education, Culture, Sports, Science and Technology (MEXT). (2024). *Results of the 2023 physical fitness and athletic performance survey [令和5年度体力・運動能力調査の結果について]* www.mext.go.jp/sports/b_menu/toukei/kodomo/zencyo/1411922_00007.html

Nakayasu, C. (2016). School curriculum in Japan. *The Curriculum Journal*, 27(1), 134–150. https://doi.org/10.1080/09585176.2016.1144518

National Center on Education and the Economy. (2021). *Japan: Governance and Accountability*. NCEE. https://ncee.org/center-on-international-education-benchmarking/top-performing-countries/japan-overview/japan-system-and-school-organization/

Ohkuma, H. (2001). The significance of adopting the military gymnastics and drill at the formation and reorganization of physical education system, especially in the Meiji and Taisho Era. *Bulletin of Institute of Health and Sport Sciences, University of Tsukuba*, 24(3), 57–70. https://core.ac.uk/download/pdf/56631929.pdf

Sakurai, R. (2016). Impacts of recent education reforms in Japan: voices from junior high schools in Japan. *Journal of International Cooperation in Education*, 18(2), 55–65. https://ir.lib.hiroshima-u.ac.jp/journals/JICE/v/18/i/2/item/43797

Schoppa, L. J. (2002). *Education reform in Japan: a case of immobilist politics*. London: Routledge.

Statistics Bureau of Japan. (2024). *Preliminary count of population in Japan*. Statistics Bureau of Japan. www.stat.go.jp/english/index.html

Suzuki, K. (2020, December 21). Physical fitness in early childhood determines lifelong health: supporting children's physical fitness improvement through remote exercise play. *Good Health Journal*. https://goodhealth.juntendo.ac.jp/social/000204.html

Takahashi, T. (2000). Perspectives of school physical education curriculum in Japan: analyzing changes in the Japanese education ministry's course of study after World War II. *Japanese Journal of Sport Education Studies*, 20(2), 91–98. https://cir.nii.ac.jp/crid/1520290884947945216

Terayama, Y., & Yagi, A. (2021). Turing point for Japanese women and sports: from moon to the sun. In D. L. D'Amico, M. K. Jahromi, & M. L. Guinto (Eds.), *Women and Sport in Asia* (pp. 99–100). London: Routledge

World Health Organization (WHO). (2020). *Guidelines on physical activity and sedentary behaviour*. www.who.int/publications/i/item/9789240015128

Chapter 11

Quality Physical Education in Jordan

Challenges and Evolutions

Eid Mohammed Kanaan and Md. Dilsad Ahmed

Introduction

Situated in the heart of the Middle East, Jordan, officially known as the Hashemite Kingdom of Jordan, is bordered by Palestine, Syria, Iraq, and Saudi Arabia. Since gaining independence from the British mandate in 1946, Jordan has gained international recognition. The population is predominantly Muslim, with Christians constituting about 4%. Islam significantly influences Jordan's culture and education system. In education, Islamic teachings advocate gender segregation in schools, resulting in physical education (PE) classes for women being conducted in private settings with female instructors (United Nations, 2024).

Jordan's educational system, overseen by the Ministry of Education, is divided into three tiers: Preschool education (a non-mandatory 2-year phase without government support), Basic education (a government-funded program for children aged 6–16 with a common core curriculum and mandatory PE), and Secondary education (which includes applied and comprehensive secondary programs, ending with a general secondary education examination) (World Bank Group, 2010). PE is an elective in secondary school and does not have the same weight as other subjects in the examination (Ministry of Education, 1988). Jordan's education system has undergone three major reforms. The first, beginning in 1987, revised the entire system and curriculum to address issues such as a lack of books, qualified teachers, and facilities. While PE was included, it was not prioritized. The second reform, from 2003 to 2013, focused on enhancing knowledge, developing skills, integrating educational technology, and improving the learning environment, with funding from large companies, international donors, and government agencies. The third reform, Jordan's National Strategy for Human Resource Development (2016–2025), aimed to revitalize vocational and professional education, establishing a national development center in 2017 to improve curricula and textbooks.

This chapter explores Jordan's PE program, detailing its evolution, current practices, and challenges. Despite reforms, PE's low status and its exclusion from major examinations have limited its impact. In response to rising childhood obesity, the Ministry of Education and the Royal Health Awareness Society have implemented initiatives to promote physical activity (PA) and healthy lifestyle habits among students (Royal Health Awareness Society, 2011).

Physical Education in Jordan

Over the centuries, Jordan's culture and people have been shaped by various influences, with two significant factors being the introduction of Islam in Arabia over 1,400 years ago and the arrival of the Prophet Muhammad (PBUH). Islam, with its comprehensive teachings on health, fitness, and life, emphasizes the importance of PA for maintaining good health and strength. The Prophet Muhammad (PBUH) conveyed the message that "The believer who is strong in body is more loved by Allah than a believer who is weak in body" (Al-Khatib, 1984). During his time, activities like horseback riding, wrestling, running, and shooting were popular, and Islam supported sports participation for both genders as long as they were segregated. Arab medical philosophers underscored the significance of exercise for overall health, with Ibn Hubal and ibn (1122-1213) describing sport as "the fundamental principle of protecting health" (p. 25). Similarly, Ibn Al-Abas emphasized that engaging in sports "is the best means to protect health and offers significant benefits for strengthening the body's limbs" (Ibn Sina, 1593). The influence of British rule also impacted Jordanian sports, particularly among the affluent, who favored activities like football, polo, and hockey (*Al-Sha'ar*, 2018). Initially, after independence, PE was not formally taught in schools but served as a recreational activity. The recognition of the health benefits of PA emerged in 1964. As education levels increased and PE became a mandatory subject in the curriculum, certified PE teachers began to be employed by various organizations. The First National Conference for Education Reform (FNCER) in 1987 introduced a 10-year plan advocating for stronger links between mainstream Jordanian school PE programs and the sports and health sectors. To facilitate this integration, an extracurricular period was introduced at the end of the school day, allowing interested students to participate in an activity of their choice (Ministry of Education, 1988). Initially, PE in Jordan focused on gender-specific activities suited to local terrain, such as football for boys and dancing for girls, using minimal equipment. Over time, the quality of PE improved with local sports centers providing equipment and facilities. The scope expanded to include diverse activities and competitions for both genders, with tournaments organized within and between schools. In 2017 PE was considered a holistic subject, where emphasis was placed on health promotion, healthy lifestyle, education about obesity, and other conditions linked with sedentary lifestyles, as well as the activities themselves. PE sessions in schools are given twice a week; however, the subject itself is not given priority by students, parents, or teachers as it does not hold grades in the GCSE certificate and is often overlooked due to pressure from more academic subjects.

Quality Teaching of Physical Education

Although PE is a mandatory part of the curriculum, it faces a lack of interest from both parents and students, particularly because it is not included in the GCSE certificate. The Ministry of Education's activities are often restricted to newly built or privately owned facilities with sufficient resources. Oudat (2016) found that 82.60% of PE teachers view a lack of abilities, equipment, and resources as major challenges, while 84.40% cited large class sizes as a significant obstacle to effective PE instruction and new teaching methods. Despite various initiatives, challenges remain. Approximately 20% of schools lack qualified PE teachers, and rural areas often face shortages of certified teachers and have limited access to equipment. Effective PE teaching should incorporate both cognitive skill development and practical activities, as outlined in textbooks and educational plans.

Dimension 1: Skill Development and Bodily Awareness (SDBA)

In Jordanian schools, PE teachers are responsible for planning and implementing in-class and after-school programs. The initial educational reform encouraged schools to establish clubs and operate during the summer to expand activity options and provide more opportunities for students to develop their PE skills. The reform also emphasized the need for specialized PE teachers to form school teams for various sports competitions (Ministry of Education, 1988). Specialized PE teachers coordinate interschool activities, allowing students to explore diverse PE interests (Ministry of Education, 2009). After-school activities are organized by the educational governorate and include competitions with other schools. These activities, seen as extensions of the school curriculum, are optional for students, and schools are not required to offer them. According to Rowe and Champion (2000), students' engagement in sports during their free time outside school hours better reflects their commitment and enthusiasm compared to participation in mandatory school lessons. A study by Haddad et al. (2009) revealed that around 50% of students did not participate in school activities, and 67.2% refrained from extracurricular activities.

The "Health Competent" Project

The Health Competent Project in Jordan (2010–2011) aimed to promote health through an instructional "tool kit" covering eight topics for students from kindergarten to seventh grade. School staff were trained to use the kits, which addressed PAs, nutrition, dental care, hygiene, anti-smoking education, psychological issues, adolescent health, and healthy lifestyle habits. The program included competitive sports like basketball and football, interschool competitions, and after-school classes in volleyball and basketball (World Health Organization, 2023).

Dimension 2: Facilities and Norms in Physical Education (FNPE)

Jordan's current PE curriculum offers a range of activities including individual sports (badminton, table tennis, gymnastics, athletics) and team games (football, basketball, volleyball, handball), influenced by weather conditions favoring outdoor activities in warmer months. Gender disparity poses a significant challenge to PE implementation, with studies indicating lower participation among female students due to cultural norms, family responsibilities, and societal expectations (Nassar et al., 2018). The exclusion of PE from the General Secondary Certificate Examination further exacerbates this issue, as it is often viewed as less important than academic subjects. Additionally, variations in PE curriculum content exist due to factors such as allocated time, student age, school location, staff qualifications, and gender biases, hindering adequate PE provision, particularly for girls. The recent development in PE in Jordan presents a mix of challenges and opportunities, with significant disparities in facilities and teaching standards across institutions. The University of Jordan is recognized for maintaining high standards in physical fitness tests and sports facilities, crucial for assessing students' readiness for sports excellence (Abudari et al., 2022). However, other universities like Yarmouk, Muta, and Hashmite face recommendations to close their PE colleges due to outdated methods and inadequate facilities (Al-Rabadi, 2013). Despite these challenges, PE plays a vital role in fostering national values and enhancing students' physical, psychological, and social well-being, underscoring the evolving responsibilities of PE teachers (D'Oum & Anannza, 2012). In the northern governorates, the implementation of Jordanian PE curricula is at a medium level, with experienced teachers demonstrating better adherence to standards (Al-Atoom & Hussein, 2020). Nevertheless, the lack of essential resources like gyms and science labs in some schools continues to impact the overall quality of PE in the country (Ufheil-Somers, 2010).

Dimension 3: Quality Teaching of Physical Education (QTPE)

In 2009, the Ministry of Education introduced guidelines to enhance PE teaching in Jordanian schools, covering objectives, curriculum, methods, assessments, and extracurricular activities. The guidelines emphasize regular PE sessions to build healthy habits, critical thinking, and teamwork, although PE is less prioritized compared to core subjects like math and English. PE is mandatory for students aged 6–16 for 90 minutes per week and optional for those aged 17–18 for 45 minutes. Despite its importance, PE is not a core subject in the general secondary education exam and lacks textbooks and theoretical instruction. The PE teaching guidelines outline specific activities for different educational stages (elementary, basic, and secondary) to help teachers deliver theoretical, practical, social, and emotional aspects effectively. These guidelines aim to build students' personalities from all aspects in the early stages, forming a foundation for future motor skills, play rules, personality development, and cognitive learning. The process begins with basic individual skills, builds confidence and coordination, progresses to more complex skills and teamwork in small groups, and ultimately develops complex activity-related skills and teamwork. However, the theoretical part of PE has been neglected, with the focus primarily on practical aspects. The lack of textbooks adversely affects students' theoretical knowledge. The National Center for Curriculum Development (2020) identified that PE is the only school subject without a textbook, which impacts students' learning. Consequently, the MoE created textbooks for grades 1, 4, 7, and 10 to cover all theoretical knowledge in the subject (Massad, 2021).

Dimension 4: Plans for Feasibility and Accessibility of Physical Education (PFAPE)

Jordan's PE framework is based on nine principles, with the first seven focusing on outcomes and life skills as defined by the standards. These principles emphasize the evaluation of knowledge, motor skills, and behavioral aspects to ensure students are well-equipped. The eighth principle highlights integrating PE with technology, suggesting using social media to boost student participation (National Center for Curriculum Development, 2020).

The Nashatati Program, a collaboration between Jordan's education sector plan and UNICEF, aims to enhance life skills and relationships among students (UNICEF, 2019). It covers 12 core life skills in 4 categories: active citizenship, cognitive skills, personal empowerment, and employability. Launched in 2017–2018, it initially targeted 100 public schools and 10,000 students aged 12–15. By 2018–2019, it expanded to 100 more schools, impacting 18,013 students. The program integrates learning, life skills, citizenship education, and social cohesion through sports-based games. In 2019, the Ministry of Education incorporated the program into the regular curriculum, dedicating 20% of the school day to these activities (UNICEF, 2019–2030). The Madrasati (My School) initiative, launched by Queen Rania in 2008, collaborates with the Ministry of Education to enhance schools. It provides additional training for PE teachers, necessary equipment, and support for extracurricular activities, and implements the "Life Skills through Sports" program. This program teaches fundamental life skills through team sports like volleyball, football, handball, basketball, and Frisbee. Despite progress, 20% of Jordanian schools still lack qualified PE teachers. The Madrasati initiative offers stipends for after-school sessions to boost student engagement in PA. Challenges in rural areas include teacher shortages and limited sports resources. The "Sports for Development" project, involving 30 schools and 70 teachers, aims to enhance life skills and health for 4,000 students, with a focus on empowering girls. Collaborating with Action Aid Denmark and the Greater Amman Municipality, Madrasati has improved attendance, distributed sports supplies, and enhanced PE instruction quality. The program emphasizes self-awareness and communication skills through team sports.

Dimension 5: Social Norms and Cultural Practice (SNCP)

In the past decade, obesity rates among adults and children in Jordan have steadily increased. Significant lifestyle changes have occurred, with approximately half of the Jordanian population engaging in no physical exercise. Contributing factors include the widespread use of motor transport, household machinery, and advancements in agricultural practices, all leading to decreased PA levels. For children, obesity is often linked to energy-dense foods and sedentary lifestyles, exacerbated by motorized transport and gender disparities. Cultural norms, family responsibilities, and societal expectations significantly hinder female students' participation in PE (Nassar et al., 2018). The exclusion of PE from the General Secondary Certificate Examination further devalues its importance compared to academic subjects. Additionally, PE curriculum content varies due to factors such as allocated time, student age, school location, staff qualifications, and gender biases, particularly impacting girls' access to adequate PE. Promoting healthy lifestyles and PA for both genders is crucial. Addressing unhealthy habits, such as excessive screen time, is vital, especially given parents' lack of education and their tendency to prioritize recreational devices over sports equipment. Moreover, parents often show little interest in non-academic subjects (Kanan & Al-Karasneh, 2009). Misinterpreted religious norms, like the belief that sports can cause loss of virginity, also pose obstacles for female participation. Government programs aim to address these social norms by fostering confidence and a desire among female students to participate in sports through education and health promotion initiatives.

Dimension 6: Governmental Input for Physical Education (GIPE)

In 2008, the WHO and Jordan's Ministry of Health aimed to create 100 health-promoting schools nationwide, focusing on health education and services. Despite efforts to provide equal PE opportunities for all students, challenges remain due to limited resources, unemployment, and refugee influxes. Initiatives like Right to Play and collaborations with United Nations Relief and Works Agency for Palestinian Refugees in the Near East (UNRWA) use sports to foster positive interactions among Jordanian and refugee students, promoting peace through themed play days and tournaments (Koss, 2023). The 2019 curriculum revision by the National Center for Curriculum Development integrated PE, forming committees to align with global standards and digital advancements. The new framework emphasizes PE's role in developing essential knowledge, values, and skills, and encourages students to engage in sports at all levels (Ministry of Health et al., 2019). Jordan's PE curriculum framework is organized into four domains (National Center for Curriculum Development, 2020):

- Psychomotor: It enhances physical, mental, cognitive, social, and emotional development through diverse motor and sports experiences.
- Cognitive: It develops an understanding of motor skills, athletic concepts, and recreational strategies.

- Emotional/Social: It builds positive relational skills and emotional well-being through sports and activities.
- Health: It teaches health and fitness knowledge to promote physical fitness and healthy lifestyle habits.

Following these guidelines (Massad, 2021), a PE textbook for grades 1, 4, 7, and 10 was to be introduced by the 2023–2024 academic year, covering sports skills, knowledge, laws, health, and behavioral aspects. Despite mandatory PE and defined goals, PE lacks status in Jordanian society, leading to poor collaboration between staff and administrators, disinterest from parents and students, and facilities inadequacies.

The Ministry of Youth manages 65 youth centers, and the Jordanian Olympic Committee (JOC), with 34 federations, promotes sports nationwide. Improved communication among these institutions could enhance facilities, equipment, expert tuition, and public interest in PE.

Jordanian society is recognizing the importance of PA for a healthy lifestyle. The Ministry of Education has initiated programs to promote PA among children, addressing modern life challenges.

Founded in 2005, the Rania Health Awareness Society promotes healthy habits in schools, focusing on safety, health, and hygiene. The Ministry of Education's 2009 guidelines support PE instruction by providing objectives, curriculum adjustments, instructional methods, and extracurricular guidance. In 2008, the WHO and Jordan's Ministry of Health aimed to establish 100 health-promoting schools nationwide. Initiatives like "Right to Play" and partnerships with UNRWA use sports to foster positive behavior among students. The 2019 curriculum framework highlights the importance of PE in developing essential skills and encouraging regular sports participation. In Jordan, several organizations focus on sports and physical exercise. The Ministry of Youth manages 65 youth centers, and the JOC promotes sports across the country. The King Abdullah II Award for Physical Fitness encourages exercise among youth aged 9–17. The Nashatati Programme, a joint effort with UNICEF, enhances life skills through sports. The Madrasati initiative, launched by Queen Rania in 2008, provides PE teachers with training, equipment, and support for extracurricular activities (World Health Organization, 2024).

Dimension 7: Cognitive Skill Development (CSD)

The broader concept of "well-being" includes factors such as physical fitness, maintaining a healthy body weight, overall health, cognitive development, and satisfactory academic performance. However, the health and well-being of children in Jordan are currently at risk. Recent data from a study involving 1,163 students aged 6–12 show that over one-quarter of school-age children in this group are overweight or obese, with 12% classified as obese and 16% as overweight (Ministry of Health et al., 2019). This is a matter of concern as obesity is a significant risk factor for non-communicable diseases such as diabetes, high blood pressure, heart disease, and certain cancers (Pinhas-Hamiel & Zeitler, 2005). Urgent action is needed to address obesity in Jordan, as emphasized by the National Institutes of Health in 2013. Jordan has experienced a rise in obesity due to significant lifestyle changes over the past three decades, including decreased PA. Widespread access to tap water, electricity, motorized transport, and mechanized agriculture has affected both adults and children, who often adopt their parents' behaviors. Globally, youth are engaging in less PA, spending more time on computers, video games, and TV, and walking or biking to school less frequently (World Health Organization, 2017). In Jordan, about half of adults report no PA, and 81% consume insufficient fruits and vegetables (Behavioral Risk Factor Survey for Jordan).

According to World Health Organization (2014), primary factors contributing to childhood or adolescent obesity include increased consumption of energy-dense foods, reduced PA, sedentary lifestyles, changes in transportation methods, urbanization, and other societal factors. Obesity rates among Jordanian youth are notably high, with a gender disparity observed. Urbanization may exacerbate this trend by shifting traditional diets to calorie- and fat-rich ones while lacking vegetables and fiber. Sedentary lifestyles and stressful social environments also contribute to higher overweight and obesity rates among young women, increasing the risk of maternal mortality and morbidity during pregnancy, labor, and delivery. Another survey in Jordan revealed that 14.3% of 13- to 15-year-olds were overweight or at risk, with 83% not engaging in sufficient PA, and only 14.3% reporting being physically active (Hamaideh et al., 2010). Engaging in PA offers many health benefits, including better academic performance and increased self-esteem. From 2000 to 2016, overweight rates in Jordan rose from 60.6% to 69.6% among adults and from 22.8% to 31% among children and adolescents. By 2019, obesity had become the leading risk factor for disability-adjusted life years (DALYs) in Jordan, with rates increasing from 26.4% to 35.5%. Jordan now has the second-highest adult obesity rate in the region, after Kuwait. Barriers to sports participation, particularly for young girls, include social and religious norms, such as concerns about delayed menarche and virginity. A study showed only 15.6% of young females prioritize PA compared to 58.5% of males. The Royal Health Awareness Society, established by Queen Rania in 2005, promotes healthy lifestyles through initiatives like the Healthy Schools Programme to address these issues.

Dimension 8: Habituated Behavior in Physical Activities (HBPA)

As part of a nationwide initiative to promote regular exercise among youth aged 9–17 years and encourage a healthy lifestyle, this award was established during the 2005–2006 academic year. The program, a joint effort by the Jordanian Association for School Sport, the Ministry of Education, and the Royal Health Awareness Society, involved structured 6-week programs in participating schools, with daily 1-hour sessions. At the end of the program, students underwent fitness assessments, including push-ups, sit-ups, flexibility tests, shuttle runs, and endurance runs. The award criteria were divided into three levels: school level, where participants receive a certificate for their involvement but score below 50%; directorate level, where a certificate of excellence is awarded along with a certificate of participation; and ministry level, where participants receive both a certificate of excellence and a certificate of participation. Winners in this category are honored with medals. Schools are further ranked based on student participation and achievement, with the top 10 schools receiving plaques in acknowledgment of their accomplishments. The Ministry of Education (MoE) in Jordan emphasizes the importance of PE in the school timetable. PE is mandatory for students aged 6–16 for 90 minutes per week and optional for students aged 17–18 for 45 minutes per week. The guidelines specify that PE lessons should consist of four parts: warm-up, theoretical knowledge related to the activity, practical application, and cooling down with feedback. Despite its importance, PE is not considered a core subject in the general secondary education examination and lacks textbooks and theoretical instruction.

Future Vision

Inspired by King Abdullah and Queen Rania, Jordan aims to ensure children thrive physically, mentally, and emotionally. However, challenges remain in advancing PE and health. The Ministry of Education needs to overhaul its strategy and work with the Ministry of Health, the School Sport Federation, and the Royal Health Awareness Society. This collaboration should focus on improving health education, refining PE teaching methods, utilizing sports facilities, and enhancing school-external organization communication. Schools should emphasize a PE curriculum that integrates knowledge, skills, and attitudes to promote physical competence, health literacy, and enjoyable participation. Using new technologies, such as tracking participation and showcasing exercise videos, can boost children's PA and health education. Jordan needs to revamp its PE curriculum and assessment, potentially offering PE as an elective in the General Secondary Certificate Examinations to clarify its importance. Shifting societal views on PA through weekend events, competitions, and holiday clubs can enhance health education. Specialized PE teachers currently instruct students in grades 10–18, while class teachers handle grades 6–9. Workshops and training are crucial to make PE engaging. Increasing the number of teachers could enable more extracurricular activities, with one teacher managing classes and another organizing events. However, this requires additional time, funding, and resources.

Conclusion

This chapter provides an overview of Jordan's PE program, highlighting its history, improvements, current practices, and challenges. Key issues include PE's low status in the curriculum and its exclusion from the General Certificate Secondary Examination (GCSE), which hampers student engagement and physical well-being. The Ministry of Education and the Royal Health Awareness Society have introduced initiatives to link PE with healthy lifestyles. Addressing the rise in childhood obesity requires more resources and collaboration with community sports organizations to enhance extracurricular activities and student performance. In conclusion, the necessity for adopting healthy lifestyle choices and embracing lifelong PA becomes increasingly apparent amid rapidly changing lifestyles. Over the past three decades, Jordan's educational system has seen heightened efforts and reforms to integrate PE and improve its instructional quality. However, challenges persist, given Jordan's central location in the dynamic Middle East and current geopolitical instability, which may hinder immediate educational system changes. Nevertheless, Jordan must persevere in its pursuit of success and improvement, aiming to enhance the health of its population and alleviate the burden of associated chronic diseases in an increasingly sedentary society.

References

Abudari, A. S., Al dababseh, M. F., & Al Fattah, O. A. (2022). Standard levels of physical fitness components as one of the admission indicators for students of sports excellence. *International Journal of Health Sciences*, 11641–11650. https://doi.org/10.53730/ijhs.v6ns5.12013

Al-Atoom, J. F. M., & Hussein, A. S. J. (2020). The degree of the application of the Jordanian physical education curricula in light of the relevant Jordanian standards from the viewpoint of the teachers in the northern governorates of Jordan. *Journal of Education and Practice, 11*(4), 81–89. www.iiste.org/Journals/index.php/JEP/article/view/51644

Al-Khatib, M. (1984). *The history of physical education*. Baghdad, Iraq: Ministry of Higher Education and Scientific Research.

Al-Rabadi, K. (2013). The concept of total quality management in the faculty of physical education in the Hashemite Kingdom of Jordan. *Dirasat: Educational Sciences, 38*. Retrieved from https://archives.ju.edu.jo/index.php/edu/article/view/3804

Al-Sha'ar, A. (2018). The history of Jordanians' sport movement from the evolution of the state to the independence of the kingdom. *Dirasat: Human and Social Sciences, 45*(4), 225–239.

D'Oum, H., & Anannza, J. (2012). The extent of carrying out the physical education curriculum by physical education for the basic stage teachers according to world measurement criteria from the perspective of school principals in Jordan. *Journal of Physical Education and Sport, 12*(1), 55–64.

Haddad, L., Owies, A., & Mansour, A.(2009).Wellness appraisal among adolescents in Jordan: A Model from Developing Country: A Cross-Sectional Questionnaire Survey. *Health Promotion International*, 24(2), 130-139. https://doi.org/10.1093/heapro/dap013

Hamaideh, S., Reham, R. Y., & Al-Rawashdeh, A. B. (2010). Overweight and obesity and their correlates among Jordanian adolescents. *Journal of Nursing Scholarship, 42*, 387–394. http://dx.doi.org/10.1111/j.1547-5069.2010.01367.x

Ibn Hubal, ., &'A. ibn A. (1122–1213). *The book of choice in medicine*. India: Ottoman Circle of Knowledge Publishing.

Ibn Sina, A. (1593). *The book of the canon of medicine*. Saab Medical Library, American University of Beirut. https://en.wikipedia.org/wiki/The_Canon_of_Medicine

Kanan, E., & Al-Karasneh, S. (2009). The impact of parental social support on promoting children's physical activities. *African Journal for Physical, Health Education, Recreation & Dance, 15*(2), 331–355.

Koss, J. (2023). *The right to play in Jordan*. https://righttoplay.nl/nl/countries/jordan/

Massad, M. (2021). A textbook for physical education next year. *Al Rai Newspaper*, Amman, Jordan. https://alrai.com/article/10606655/

Ministry of Education. (1988). The first national conference of educational development. *Message for Teachers, 3*(4), Issue 29 (in Arabic). Jordan: MoE.

Ministry of Education.(2009).Physical Education Guides. General Directorate of Physical Education at the Ministry of Education, Jordan: MoE (in Arabic).

Ministry of Health, UNICEF, WFP, Jordan Health Aid Society International, Department of Statistics, Biolab, Groundwork. (2019). *Jordan national micronutrient and nutritional survey*. Amman, Jordan. www.moh.gov.jo/ebv4.0/root_storage/ar/eb_list_page/jnmns19_report_220207_printable.pdf

Nassar, O., Shaheen, A. M., Jarrah, S. S., Norton, M. E., Khalaf, I. A., & Hamdan, K. M. (2018). Jordanian adolescents' health behavior and school climate. *Journal of Research in Nursing, 23*(1), 58–73.

National Center for Curriculum Development. (2020). *Physical education standards and performance indicators framework for Jordanian learners (K-12)*. Amman, Jordan. https://nccd.gov.jo/AR/ListDetails/%D8%A7%D9%84%D8%A5%D8%B9%D9%84%D8%A7%D9%86%D8%A7%D8%AA/15/2

Oudat, M. (2016). Challenges facing physical education teachers in Jordan from the perspective of the teachers themselves. *Advances in Physical Education, 6*, 43–51. https://doi.org/10.4236/ape.2016.62005

Pinhas-Hamiel, O., & Zeitler, P. (2005). The global spread of type 2 diabetes mellitus in children and adolescents. *The Journal of Pediatrics, 146*, 693–700.

Rowe, N., & Champion, R. (2000). *Young people and sport: National survey 1999*. London: Sport England Research.

Royal Health Awareness Society. (2011). *Royal Health Awareness Society: A year in review*. Amman, Jordan. https://rhas.org.jo/Photos/Files/1c8c32b0-1e14-4aa4-be07-7c6ad09c73fe.pdf

Ufheil-Somers, A. (2010, September 20). The Politics of Aid to Iraqi Refugees in Jordan. *MERIP*. https://merip.org/2010/09/the-politics-of-aid-to-iraqi-refugees-in-jordan/

UNICEF. (2019). *Learning, life skills and citizenship education and social cohesion through game-based sports – Nashatati Programme*. Jordan: Every Child Learns: UNICEF Education Strategy 2019–2030.

United Nations. (2024). *World population prospects*. www.macrotrends.net/global-metrics/countries/JOR/jordan/population

World Bank Group. (2010). *Jordan – Education reform for knowledge economy program project*. Washington, DC: World Bank Group. http://documents.worldbank.org/curated/en/239641468774926089/Jordan-Education-Reform-for-Knowledge-Economy-Program-Project

World Health Organization. (2014). *Children obesity causes global strategy on diet physical activity and health*. www.who.int/publications/i/item/9241592222

World Health Organization. (2017). *Global health observatory indicator views*. Geneva. http://apps.who.int/gho/data/node.imr

World Health Organization. (2023). *Nutrition country profile: Jordan*. https://iris.who.int/handle/10665/367696

World Health Organization. (2024). *King Abdullah II Prize for fitness. Jordan*. www.emro.who.int/health-education/physical-activity-case-studies/king-abdullah-ii-prize-for-fitness-jordan.html

Chapter 12

Understanding and Advancement of Quality Physical Education in Madagascar

Klaudia Rafael, Walter Ho, Jennie Yang Yang Xie, Patrice Ranaivason, Harison P. Andrianarivao, Laurent Rabarivelo, and Min Liu

Introduction

Madagascar is an island country in the Indian Ocean off the south-eastern coast of Africa. The United Nations Office for the Coordination of Humanitarian Affairs (OCHA, 2024) reported a population of 30.3 million in Madagascar. Antananarivo and Toamasina are the cities with the largest population (City Population, 2018). The recent poverty rates and difficulties faced in its economic growth indicate a different challenge toward the need for social, economic, and educational reform in Madagascar (The World Bank, 2021). Currently, Madagascar has to deal with serious problems such as poverty, violence, and issues related to education (Ferguson, 2018) and the extra burden of natural disasters every year, resulting in loss of life and infrastructure damage; this has a tremendous influence on the development of school facilities (Education Development Trust, 2016). On the contrary, the country followed the French system in educational development from 1896 when France was the colonizer of the country. During the colonial period, the French built a public school system in Madagascar. This system appeared to be unfair to the indigenous society, as it aimed to provide practical and vocational education while neglecting leadership training. After its independence in 1960, Madagascar had an education system almost identical to that in France (Metz, 1994).

Education Development and Problems Encountered

When reviewing the educational development of Madagascar, the country has adopted the French system with an identical public school system since 1896 (Metz, 1994) and when the country became independent in 1960, the French education system was prevalent. This system consists of five educational stages for students. Children at the age of 4–5 years will be enrolled in the preschool level. When they are in the age of 6 to 11 years, they are included in the primary education. Four years of lower secondary education is followed and another 4 years in upper secondary education. After upper secondary school, students are prepared for baccalaureate education (Ministere De L` Education Nationale, 2020). The education at public primary schools is free. Higher education is steered by the Ministry

DOI: 10.4324/9781003513582-14

of Technical Education and Vocational Training and overseen by another higher education sub-sector of the Ministry of Higher Education and Scientific Research (The World Bank, 2017).

The schooling for students is structured with different developmental steps from general education to elite training. UNICEF (2015) noted the differences in educational arrangement in Madagascar with more investment in primary education but significantly less in secondary or higher education. Such uneven educational input also appeared in regions, and the cost per child in school varies with regional differences (UNICEF, 2015). The reason for the differences is complex but relates to challenges that are interconnected with the geographical location, and its political, economic, and social situation (African Development Bank, 2006; BTI Transformation Index, 2024). Apart from these problems, the country is immersed in the crisis of child labor and gender inequality issues. Although there has been a significant increase in gross enrolment from 2000 to 2019 (The World Bank, 2020), high school enrolment is at a record low due to the child labor problem (Beuchner, 2019).

Development of Physical Education (PE) and the Desire of Reform

Although the French education system was followed, PE seemed not to be the priority in development. In 2019, the Conference of Experts hosted in Madagascar, on the Implementation of Quality Physical Education (QPE) in Africa for sports officers, highlighted the desire for educational improvement in PE (UNESCO, 2019). The conference participants agreed on the *Antananarivo Recommendations* to indicate the required actions in completing the works on QPE, and recommendations in building necessary capacities for such development (UNESCO, 2019). In response to such an initiative, the Ministre De L'Education Nationale in Madagascar (2022a, 2022b) started to introduce the national curriculum in PE to cover various issues in health maintenance, talent identification, extracurricular activities and literacy development in values, competition, and group responsibility. Although there was such an initiative to improve PE development in the country, there was no substantial research on PE development in the country. There was no specific knowledge of the support for its growth and policy establishment.

Quality Physical Education

Madagascar's Ministry of Youth & Sport decided to participate in recent international research on QPE and is expected to establish a comprehensive understanding of PE development in the country in 2020. The ministry adopted the questionnaire "*Global Index of Quality Physical Education (GIQPE)*" established by the research team from the International Society for Comparative Physical Education and Sport (ISCPES) and the 48 items in 8 dimensions were designed to

Table 12.1 Number and percentage of participants by gender, city, position, years of work experience, and school system

Gender		Male	Female	Totals	
Cities	Antananarivo	48 (60%)	32 (40%)	80 (50%)	160
	Toamasina	43 (53.8%)	37 (46.3%)	80 (50%)	
Position	Primary T	20 (33.3%)	40 (66.7%)	60 (37.5%)	160
	Secondary T	41 (69.5%)	18 (30.5%)	59 (36.9%)	
	Others	30 (73.2%)	11 (26.8%)	41 (25.6%)	
Years of work experience	1–5 years	26 (59.1%)	18 (40.9%)	44 (28.5%)	154
	6–10 years	17 (47.2%)	19 (52.8%)	36 (23.4%)	
	11–16 years	16 (50%)	16 (50%)	32 (20.8%)	
	16 and above	26 (61.9%)	16 (38.1%)	42 (27.3%)	
School system	Public	33 (44.6%)	41 (55.4%)	74 (57.4%)	129
	Private	33 (62.3%)	20 (37.7%)	53 (41.1%)	
	Others	2		2 (1.5%)	

investigate the overall development of QPE development in the country (Ho et al., 2021, 2023). PE professionals (160) from the two cities of Antananarivo (80) and Toamasina (80) were invited to answer the QPE questionnaire and their feedback helped to outline what was happening for the development of physical education in the country. The distribution of participants in numbers and percentages is shown in Table 12.1. The participants were assigned to groups, according to gender, city, position, years of work experience, and school system. The number and percentage of participants in each group are presented in Table 12.1.

Research Tool

The questionnaire *GIQPE* contained two parts. The first part invited professionals to offer their perceptual understanding of the situation in PE in the city they work in. The questionnaire consisted of 48 items in 8 dimensions: S*kill Development and Bodily Awareness* (SDBA), *Facilities and Norms in PE* (FNPE), *Quality Teaching of PE* (QTPE), *Plans for Feasibility and Accessibility of PE* (PFAPE), *Social Norms and Cultural Practice* (SNCP), *Governmental Input for PE* (GIPE), *Cognitive Skill Development* (CSD), and *Habituated Behavior in Physical Activities* (HBPA). The research team added one item to distinguish PE as a compulsory subject at primary and secondary schools, increasing the number of items to 49 in total. A Likert scale ranging from 0 to 10 was employed, where 0 indicated *Totally Not Achieved* and 10 indicated *Totally Achieved*. The initial questionnaire was in English, and a French translation was produced by using the services of a professional agency. The second part of the questionnaire contains questions about participants' demographic information, including gender, work position, years of work experience, and school types.

GIQPE and Dimensional Analysis

The study expects to explore and understand the QPE development in Madagascar. Table 12.2 contains the descriptive statistics for overall QPE development in different dimensions.

An overall mean score of 5.01 points of all dimensions is recorded, which could be interpreted as marginal success for quality in PE. More work is needed to improve the current situation and what to do seems to be the immediate question for QPE development in Madagascar.

In the case of Madagascar, studies and research exploring the QPE are insufficient. When the national PE curriculum introduced by Ministère De l'Éducation Nationale (2022a, 2022b) with the Guidelines for QPE by UNESCO (2015), it can be seen that the national PE curriculum lacks focus on a safe environment during PE classes, social interactions with classmates, enjoyment and fun during PE classes, conditions related to facilities and equipment, sport-attitudes and values, theoretical foundations of PE such as prevention, drinking regime, lifestyle and lifelong participation in PE and sport, proper explanation of the relationship between health and sport. The importance of health and PE is emphasized in the study by Chikafu and Chimbari's (2020), who have presented insufficient daily physical activity as a problem in Southern African countries. The authors have also recommended applying health education interventions. These health education interventions could be a part of the PE curriculum like it is in QPE by UNESCO (2015) and it is in the national curriculums of different countries (Štatny Tatny Pedagogicky Ustav, 2022). Numerous organizations have demonstrated the necessity of studying PE and supporting physical activity and sports in African countries (African Union, 2021; Ministère de l'Éducation Nationale, 2016, 2017; UNICEF, 2009). This has also been echoed by several researchers (Tomaz et al., 2019; Venart and Reuter, 2014) that there are similar findings on the QPE development in Madagascar and Southern African countries.

Table 12.2 Descriptive statistics, Cronbach's alpha by dimension and overall score

Dimensions	Range	Mean	SD	95% CI Lower	95% CI Upper	Skewness	Kurtosis	A
SDBA	0–10	5.74	2.10	5.42	6.07	0.37	−0.86	0.912
CSD	0–10	5.43	2.34	5.06	5.79	0.46	−0.60	0.913
HBPA	0–10	5.42	2.50	5.03	5.80	0.32	−0.97	0.939
QTPE	0–10	5.26	2.40	4.88	5.63	0.53	−0.88	0.894
FNPE	0–10	4.86	1.74	4.59	5.13	0.38	−0.71	0.891
GIPE	0–10	4.38	2.27	4.03	4.73	0.54	−0.70	0.835
PFAPE	0–10	3.98	2.39	3.60	4.35	0.45	−0.46	0.626
SNCP	0–10	3.50	2.25	3.15	3.85	0.60	−0.13	0.699
QPE	0–10	5.01	1.99	4.70	5.32	0.40	−1.02	0.980

Social Norms and Cultural Practice (SNCP) and Plans for Feasibility and Accessibility of Physical Education (PFAPE)

The order of the dimensions in Table 12.2 seems to indicate the areas with the most serious problems and where urgent improvements are needed. The lowest-ranked dimensions were SNCP (3.50 ± 2.25) and the dimensions of PFAPE (3.98 ± 2.39). The two dimensions covered issues in equality, gender, religion, the country's economic situation, and possibilities for international and inter-state collaboration in PE development. It seems that a negative image was outlined with low scoring to indicate dissatisfaction. Members of both the QPE team and the Ministry of Youth and Sport acknowledge the need for improvement in the provision of support to the social environment, and PE classes that consist of physical activities that improve moral and social values. It seems that these actions may carry positive effects in decreasing inequality among participants (OECD, 2012; UNESCO, 2017).

Although the national curriculum in Madagascar regards the promotion of social adaptability and skills of communication as priorities in development, apparently there has been a failure in materializing them. Intervention activities might again be a good solution to support this dimension. In this context, a recently published study suggests the delivery of intervention activities with a focus on students' interests that may be found suitable for PE classes (Munoz-Lienera et al., 2022). The PE curriculum in Madagascar offers the promotion of three sports at the primary level, namely swimming, athletics, and judo with priority. Members of the team acknowledge such a good strategy and the expansion to cover sports such as football, dodgeball, and basketball; it may have beneficial effects in improving the learning of PE in class. The evidence of the positive association between participation in team sports and improving the social environment has been already proven in different studies (Lee and Lim, 2019; Maslen, 2015). Nevertheless, the selection of intervention activities for supporting social change in PE classes needs to be carefully considered. For example, soccer is a popular activity but also contains elements such as stereotyping and unproportional funding between genders (Bredtmann et al., 2016). Sports are also religiously bound. Although Christianity is the major religion on the island, the Muslim population is another group in Madagascar that needs to be attended to (U.S. Department of State, 2022). Nevertheless, lower scores in the SNCP dimension highlighted existing gender inequality, and based on the reviewed background, females are at a much higher risk of, for example, not attending school or failing to complete secondary school than males (Ferguson, 2019; Ralavita, 2019).

Facilities and Norms in Physical Education (FNPE) and Government Input for Physical Education (GIPE)

The dimensions of FNPE (4.86 ± 1.74) and GIPE (4.38 ± 2.27) had a mean score below five points. These dimensions incorporate insufficient facilities for PE lessons, adequate qualified teachers, PE as a compulsory subject, space, and opportunities for practicing sports after school, all of which are related to governmental input. Related to facilities and their improvement, a good solution can be to construct open spaces for practicing PE classes with a roof as protection against sun and rain. This simple model of construction can benefit from easier maintenance as natural disasters are common in Madagascar (Education Development Trust, 2016) and destroy school facilities (Siddiqui, 2014).

Skill Development and Bodily Awareness (SDBA), Cognitive Skill Development (CSD), Habituated Behavior in Physical Activities (HBPA), and Quality Teaching of Physical Education (QTPE)

Dimensions that received the highest score were SDBA (5.74 ± 2.10), followed by CSD (5.43 ± 2.34), which was very closely followed by HBPA (5.42 ± 2.50), and then QTPE (5.26 ± 2.40). The best-evaluated dimension of success was SDBA. This dimension covers issues such as whether PE lessons can enhance students' physical skills; their knowledge of sports and related terms, as well as the importance of physical activity; and interaction with classmates. The remaining dimensions explore whether the teaching of PE encourages the development of critical, innovative thinking and problem-solving skills. They also include whether students demonstrate regular exercise habits, develop the skills to participate in school and out-of-school sports programs, and understand the importance of physical activities and health development in Madagascar (Ho et al., 2021). Positively, it seems that PE content with respect to skills, knowledge, and understanding, is better evaluated than facilities, equipment, social norms, and government input for PE. The reason for this developmental pattern may reflect the choice of development of the Madagascar government. Madagascar seems to have a focus on sports skill development and bodily awareness of health and physical aspects as the way to tackle the health problems of students.

The health problem and physical inactivity level in the population seems to be the agenda and it is positively associated with the Human Development Index (HDI) ranking (Dumith et al., 2011; Atkinson et al., 2016; Jayasinghe, 2021). Although Madagascar belongs to the low-income group, a higher HDI is probable in the future when there is an improvement in the economic situation. The increasing number of inactive populations is a foreseeable problem. To prevent physical inactivity from increasing, accessibility to PE in schools for children and youth and the inclusion of sports learning in school education play an essential role. The current investigation of QPE in Madagascar is expected to be an essential step toward developing a strategic plan for improving sports and physical activity situations through strengthening QPE development. Current research on QPE in Madagascar intends to help authorities understand the current PE situation from local PE professionals' perspectives. These professionals provided feedback and an initial understanding of QPE by participating in the questionnaire survey.

Conclusion

While reviewing the education development in Madagascar, Venart and Reuter (2014) discussed the many obstacles that students, teachers, and policymakers encountered, and questioned the practical relevance of the curriculum in meeting the needs of students. The lack of resources and the need for in-service training to upgrade the qualification of teachers were the challenges to the educational development in Madagascar (Government of Madagascar et al., 2015).

The UNESCO Office for Africa (2022) wrote with this concern about 'Quality of education in Madagascar: a system that struggles to support the implementation of its policy' in their official web page on education planning in Madagascar. Although there is the initiative to improve the educational work in schools, are teachers ready and able to catch up with the changes? The UNESCO Office for Africa (2022) further discusses the issue and answers the following comment:

> The majority of teachers and trainers feel that this is an unfavourable factor. The actors say that these frequent changes do not make their task any easier and that they have to adapt to a new approach even before they have mastered the previous one.

In fact, the teachers' quality in Madagascar is the real threat to achieving the desired changes.

DHL (2019) had a report on their website on the sustainability of education in Madagascar and provided this figure of 'the low literacy rate is also a result of a dearth of qualified educators – more than 80 percent of teachers, or about 80,000 of them, have no formal training'. The educational situation in Madagascar may indicate the facts of the implementation of the national curriculum in many of the subjects, the ability to attain the desired quality is encroached by the teachers' quality and differences in practice between cities and regions; with worse practice in rural areas (Venart and Reuter, 2014). Such curriculum initiatives request qualified professionals in physical education to achieve the change. Nevertheless, the lack of concrete evidence and information on QPE enhances the doubt in moving forward with the improvement to achieve the desired changes.

References

African Development Bank. (2006). *African Economic Outlook*. African Development Bank. www.oecd.org/en/publications/2006/05/african-economic-outlook-2006_g1gh69c6.html

African Union (AU). (2021). *Education, Science & Technology*. https://au.int/en/education-science-technology

Atkinson, K., Lowe, S., & Moore, S. (2016). Human development, occupational structure and physical inactivity among 47 low and middle income countries. *Preventive Medicine Reports*, *3*, 40–45. https://doi.org/10.1016/j.pmedr.2015.11.009

Beuchner, M. (2019). *How UNICEF Supports Families to Prevent Child Labor in Madagascar.* www.unicefusa.org/stories/how-unicef-supports-families-prevent-child-labor-madagascar/36676

Bredtmann, J., Crede, C.J., & Otten, S. (2016). The effects of gender equality on International Soccer Performance. *International Journal of Sport Finance, 11*, 288–309. https://discovery.ucl.ac.uk/id/eprint/1543103/7/Otten_document.pdf

BTI Transformation Index. (2024). The transformation index – Madagascar. *Bertelsmann Stiftung.* https://bti-project.org/en/?&cb=00000

Chikafu, H., & Chimbari, M.J. (2020). Levels and correlates of physical activity in rural Ingwavuma community, uMkhanyakude District, KwaZulu-Natal, South Africa. *International Journal of Environmental Research and Public Health, 17*(18), 6739. https://doi.org/10.3390/ijerph17186739

City Population. (2018). *Madagascar, Republic of Madagascar.* City Population. www.citypopulation.de/en/madagascar/cities/

DHL (2019) *Sustainability - Education in Madagascar a work in progress.* DHL. https://lot.dhl.com/education-in-madagascar-a-work-in-progress/

Dumith, S.C., Hallal, P.C., Reis, R.S., & Kohk, III, H.W. (2011). Worldwide prevalence of physical inactivity and its association with human development index in 76 countries. *Preventive Medicine, 53*(1–2), 24–28. https://doi.org/10.1016/j.ypmed.2011.02.017

Education Development Trust. (2016). *A Study on Children with Disabilities and Their Right to Education: Madagascar.* www.unicef.org/esa/media/1696/file/UNICEF-EDT-Madagascar-2016-children-with-disabilities.pdf

Ferguson, S. (2018). *Fighting Poverty and Violence to Educate Girls in Madagascar.* www.unicefusa.org/stories/fighting-poverty-and-violence-educate-girls-madagascar/34940

Ferguson, S. (2019). *Keeping Girls in School in Madagascar.* www.unicefusa.org/stories/keeping-girls-school-madagascar/36813

Government of Madagascar. (2015). *Madagascar 2014 Public Expenditure Review Education and Health.* www.unicef.org/esa/sites/unicef.org.esa/files/2019-04/PER-of-Education-and-Health-in-Madagascar-Policy-Note-%282016%29.pdf

Ho, W., Ahmed, D., & Rafael, K. (2021). Development and validation of an instrument to assess Quality Physical Education. *Cogent Education, 8*(1), https://doi.org/10.1080/2331186X.2020.1864082

Ho, W., Ahmed, D., Rafeal, K., de D'Amico, R.L., Antala, B., Liu, M., Dong, X.X., & Xie, Y.Y. (2023). Quality Physical Education (QPE) measuring tool development. *International Sports Studies, 45*(2), 6–27. https://doi.org/10.30819/iss.45-2.02

Jayasinghe, S., Byrne, N.M., Patterson, K.A.E., Ahuja, K.D.K., & Hills, A.P. (2021). The current global state of movement and physical activity – the health and economic costs of the inactive phenotype. *Progress in Cardiovascular Diseases, 64*, 9–16. https://doi.org/10.1016/j.pcad.2020.10.006

Lee, Y., & Lim, S. (2019). Effects of sports activity on sustainable social environment and Juvenile Aggression. *Sustainability, 11*(8), 2279. https://doi.org/10.3390/su11082279

Maslen, P. (2015). *The Social and Academic Benefits of Team Sports.* www.edutopia.org/discussion/social-and-academic-benefits-team-sports

Metz, H.C. (1994). *Madagascar: A Country Study.* Washington: GPO for the library of congress.

Ministere de L Education Nationale. (2016). *Education Physique sportive – La Fédération Malagasy de Basket Ball Á La Rescousse de deux écoles publiques.* Ministere de l'Education Nationale. www.education.gov.mg/education-sportive-la-federation-malagasy-de-basket-ball-a-la-rescousse-de-deux-ecoles-publiques/

Ministere de L Education Nationale. (2017). *Championnats Nationax du sport scolaire 2017 á Mahajanga: une épreuve D`urban cross S`affichera dans la discipline D`Athlétisme.* www.education.gov.mg/championnats-nationaux-sport-scolaire-2017-a-mahajanga-epreuve-durban-cross-saffichera-discipline-dathletisme/

Ministere de L Education Nationale. (2020). *Lycée.* www.education.gov.mg/systeme-educatif/lycee/

Ministere de L Education Nationale. (2022a). *Direction des curricula at des intrants DCI, Programmes Scolaires, Classe de 11eme a partir de l'annee scolaire 2015–2016.* www.education.gov.mg/wp-content/uploads/2016/10/PROGRAMMES-SCOLAIRES-11eme.pdf

Ministere de L Education Nationale. (2022b). *Direction des curricula at des intrants DCI, Programmes Scolaires, Classe de 6eme a partir de l'Annee Scolaire 2015–2016.* www.education.gov.mg/wp-content/uploads/2016/10/Programme-scolaire-6eme.pdf

Munoz-Llerena, A., Nunez Pedrero, M., Flores-Aguilar, G., & Lopez-Meneses, E. (2022). Design of a methodological intervention for developing respect, inclusion and equality in physical education. *Sustainability*, *14*(1), 390. https://doi.org/10.3390/su14010390

United Nations Office for the Coordination of Humanitarian Affairs (OCHA) (2024). *Overview of humanitarian response in Madagascar.* OCHA. www.unocha.org/madagascar

OECD. (2012). *Equity and Quality in Education: Supporting Disadvantaged Students and Schools.* OECD Publishing. http://dx.doi.org/10.1787/9789264130852-en

Ralavita, A. (2019). *I Don't Have to Wait for the Help of Boys to Solve Small Problems.* www.unicef.org/madagascar/en/stories/«-i-dont-have-wait-help-boys-solve-small-problems-»

Siddiqui, N. (2014). *Education in Madagascar.* www.borgenmagazine.com/education-madagascar/

Štatny Tatny Pedagogicky Ustav. (2022). *Telesná a športová výchova.* www.statpedu.sk/files/articles/dokumenty/inovovany-statny-vzdelavaci-program/telesna-a-sportova-vychova_nsv_2014.pdf

The World Bank. (2017). *Madagascar Basic Education Support Project (P160442).* http://documents1.worldbank.org/curated/en/169021516793508504/pdf/ITM00194-P160442-01-24-2018-1516793506238.pdf

The World Bank. (2020). *School Enrolment, Primary (%Gross) – Madagascar.* https://data.worldbank.org/indicator/SE.PRM.ENRR?end=2019&locations=MG&start=1971&view=chart

The World Bank. (2021). *Data Low Income.* https://data.worldbank.org/income-level/low-income?view=chart

Tomaz, S.A., Jones, R.A., Hinkley, T., Twine, R., Kahn, S.A.N., & Draper, C.E. (2019). Physical activity in early childhood education and care settings in low-income, rural South African community: an observational study. *Rural Remote Health*, *19*(4), 5249. https://doi.org/10.22605/RRH5249

UNESCO. (2015). *Quality Physical Education (QPE). Guidelines for Policy-Makers.* UNESCO Publishing. Paris, France: UNESCO. https://unesdoc.unesco.org/ark:/48223/pf0000231101

UNESCO. (2017). *A Guide for Ensuring Inclusion and Equity in Education.* https://unesdoc.unesco.org/ark:/48223/pf0000248254

UNESCO. (2019). *The Antananarivo Recommendations.* https://unesdoc.unesco.org/ark:/48223/pf0000370641. Retrieved 26 September 2022.

UNESCO Office for Africa (2022). *Quality of education in Madagascar.* UNESCO. https://dakar.iiep.unesco.org/en/news/quality-education-madagascar-system-struggles-support-implementation-its-policy

UNICEF. (2009). *Going for the Goal.* www.unicefusa.org/stories/going-goal/6555. Retrieved 19 April 2021.

UNICEF. (2015). *Madagascar Public Expenditure Review 2015 Education.* www.unicef.org/esa/sites/unicef.org.esa/files/2019-04/PER-of-Education-in-Madagascar-%282015%29.pdf. Retrieved 29 April 2021.

U.S. Department of State. (2022). *2022 Report on International Religious Freedom: Madagascar.* www.state.gov/reports/2022-report-on-international-religious-freedom/madagascar/#:~:text=The%20U.S.%20government%20estimates%20the,6.9%20percent%20have%20no%20affiliation. Retrieved 1 August 2023.

Venart, L.C., & Reuter, K.E. (2014). Education in Madagascar: A guide on the state of the educational system, needed reforms and strategies for improvement. *University of Mauritius Research Journal, 20,* 196–235. www.ajol.info/index.php/umrj/article/view/134617

Chapter 13

Towards Quality Physical Education in Malaysia

Selina Khoo and Thariq Khan Bin Azizuddin Khan

Background to the Country

Malaysia, a country in Southeast Asia, is made up of Peninsular Malaysia on the Malay Peninsula and East Malaysia on the island of Borneo. It has a land area of 330.35 thousand square kilometres and comprises 13 states and 3 federal territories. A former British colony that gained independence in 1957, Malaysia is a federal constitutional monarchy with the Prime Minister as the head of government. Malaysia is a multi-cultural, multi-ethnic, and multi-religious upper-middle-income country with an estimated population of 32.78 million, of which 30.24 million are citizens, according to Ministry of Economy (Malaysia) (2022a). Nearly a quarter (23.3%) of the population is under 15 years and 7.4% over 65 years. Females constitute 48.5% of the population. The three main ethnic groups are Malays, Chinese, and Indians. Although Islam is the official religion of Malaysia, other religions are practised. In Malaysia, ethnicity and religion are closely related. Malays practise Islam, the Chinese mainly practise Buddhism or Christianity, and Indians practise Hinduism or Christianity.

The country's gross domestic product in 2022 was USD235.4 billion (Ministry of Economy (Malaysia), 2022a). The manufacturing and service sectors contribute the most to the economy. The mean monthly household gross income for 2022 was approximately USD1,800 (Ministry of Economy (Malaysia), 2022b).

Physical Education at School

Free public schooling is provided at primary (7–12 years old) and secondary levels (13–17 years old), although only primary education is compulsory. Physical and health education is a compulsory subject in primary and secondary schools. The time allocated for physical education (PE) is more than for health education. There are 42 weeks in the school year, and the minimum allocation for PE is 32 hours a year for primary school and 48 hours a year for secondary school (Ministry of Education (Malaysia), 2019). This is compared to a minimum of 16 hours of health education in both primary and secondary schools. The objectives of the PE component include improving the physical development, fitness, and health of students as well as teaching them basic movement skills and sports (Ministry of Education (Malaysia), 2015b). The curriculum includes basic gymnastics, rhythmic movement, athletics, aquatics, team sports, as well as leisure and recreation.

There have been changes in Malaysian education, including in physical and health education for primary and secondary schools. The New Primary School Curriculum was adopted in 1983, and Integrated Secondary School Curriculum in 1989. There was a transformation in the curriculum from a knowledge-based curriculum to a standard-based curriculum (Ministry of Education (Malaysia), 2019). The Standard Primary School Curriculum was adopted in 2011, and the Standard Secondary School Curriculum in 2017. This new curriculum was planned based on Malaysia's sports policy and is in line with recommendations by international bodies, namely the United Nations Educational, Scientific and Cultural Organization (UNESCO), World Health Organization (WHO), and International Council for Health, Physical Education, Recreation – Sports and Dance (ICHPER-SD). In summary, the Malaysia Physical and Health Education Curriculum transformation was based on the National Education Philosophy that emphasised the intellectual, spiritual, emotional, and physical development of students. The following sections discuss the development and current state of the quality of PE in Malaysia according to eight dimensions.

Dimension 1: Skill Development and Bodily Awareness

With regard to skill development and body awareness, an important element in teaching PE in Malaysia is the progress in developing student motor skills from primary to secondary school. Clear information and guidance regarding the development of students' motor skills are provided, and PE teachers in Malaysia are trained according to the Curriculum and Assessment Standard Document (Ministry of Education (Malaysia), 2015b).

The Psychomotor Domain is emphasised when teaching PE, where students are introduced to various movements and motor skills. Teaching is conducted according to the progression and individualized principles to cater to primary and secondary students. Within the cognitive domain, students are expected to acquire and be able to apply the knowledge and sports skills they learnt in PE class during co-curricular activities. A complete development of physical, emotional, and spiritual effects on students has become a key performance index in PE. Malaysian students are provided with opportunities to take part in different sports and physical activities. For example, in primary school, students are taught fundamentals of gymnastics and rhythmic movements as well as basic athletics, aquatics, and various sports skills (Ministry of Education (Malaysia), 2015c). In secondary school, students are progressively taught different physical elements to explore the fundamentals of gymnastics and rhythmic movements. They are also taught attacking, netting, batting, and fielding for basketball, hockey, table tennis, tennis and softball. During PE, teaching and learning of sport and physical activities are taught to all the students systematically according to the level of student maturity and knowledge. PE sessions in primary and secondary school provide ample opportunities for schoolchildren to learn and interact with their classmates (Ghani et al., 2014). Particularly, group activities provide students with opportunities to discuss and interact. Furthermore, basic knowledge regarding health, fitness, and body composition is included in PE activities in school, as health education is also taught as part of the same subject.

Students are encouraged to participate in sports activities after school and also to represent their school in structured recreational and competitive inter-school competitions. One of the objectives of PE is to encourage participation in sports at both competitive and recreational levels (Kilue & Muhamad, 2017). In other words, schoolchildren in Malaysia have the opportunity to participate in sports either for leisure or competition. Sports competitions at inter-school, inter-district, and inter-state levels are organised by the Malaysian School Sports Council.

Dimension 2: Facilities and Norms in Physical Education

The Malaysian school PE curriculum and its implementation strategy were planned strategically, systematically, and updated to meet future student requirements. Various education departments and universities, including experienced education administrators and academicians, were involved in the development of the curriculum based on education reviews. As the main outcome would be measured on the optimum development of students, aspects of facilities and norms in PE education should be the benchmark and periodically monitored. The Malaysian government has allocated billions of ringgit (Malaysian currency) annually for education, including PE. The aim is to provide every school in Malaysia with a conducive environment and sufficient facilities or equipment for PE subjects to be delivered effectively. However, not all schools have sufficient facilities and equipment. This is because PE is not a priority, and funding is given to other subjects (Ghani et al., 2014).

There are a few issues related to PE in schools. One of the main challenges is in providing facilities equally throughout the country as demand increases in tandem with the Malaysian population. Urban schools face constraints in terms of space, and some schools do not have fields. In parts of Malaysia, PE could not be implemented effectively among the indigenous population due to the lack of facilities (Kilue & Muhamad, 2017).

Another challenge is the perception among some school administrators and parents that PE is not important compared to other examination subjects such as Mathematics and Science. Other challenges include a limited budget for PE, qualified PE teachers not teaching PE, and non-PE specialists teaching PE. This might reduce the teaching quality of PE.

Under the Standard School Curriculum for Physical and Health Education, all students in Malaysia should be provided with equal opportunity in PE. Thus, all children, whatever their ability, gender, age, ethnicity, and socioeconomic status, are included in PE activities. There is a separate PE curriculum for children with disabilities in special schools where teaching and learning are more flexible and adapted to individual ability (Ministry of Education (Malaysia), 2015a). However, the main constraint for children with disabilities was the lack of accessible equipment and facilities, with only 50% of PE teachers specialised in teaching children with disabilities in Malaysia (Bari & Ali, 2005). In summary, although PE was designed and implemented to develop a balanced individual in terms of physical, spiritual, cognitive, and emotional development, there needs to be adequate facilities for students with and without disabilities.

There have also been incidents where students were injured during PE and sports in schools. As a result, the Director General of Education (Malaysia) (2000) issued a circular on safety guidelines when teaching physical and health education as well as co-curricular activities and sports. However, injuries still occur.

Dimension 3: Quality Teaching of Physical Education

To ensure quality teaching of PE in Malaysia, state and district education departments under the Ministry of Education monitor the teaching of PE in schools. The school inspectorate under the state and district education departments periodically visits schools and provides PE teachers with documents, information, and teaching guides There are teacher training institutions in all states in Malaysia that train PE teachers for primary school. An education university, the Sultan Idris Education University, produces more than half of the new PE teachers in Malaysia, with others graduating from education faculties in other universities. Moreover, PE refresher courses and teaching practice sessions are planned and conducted for PE teaching to maintain the quality of teaching. These programmes are conducted to ensure that PE is taught according to the standard school curriculum. Although physical and health education in primary and secondary schools is a non-examination subject, there is a National Physical Fitness Standard Test for Malaysian School Students to evaluate basic physical skills and general fitness (Ministry of Education (Malaysia), 2019). This test is taken by students from Primary 4 to 6 and Secondary 1 to 5.

An integrated approach in the PE syllabus in Malaysia adopts other fields of knowledge to enhance students' decision-making, communication, and other soft skills. PE teachers also conduct soft skill evaluation assessments (e.g., communication and problem-solving) during the PE subject. In terms of enhancing holistic knowledge of physical health among school children, an interactive teaching style that is student-centred and prioritises meaningful and enjoyable sessions was introduced. This teaching style, teaching games for understanding (TGfU), was implemented so students could communicate among themselves, express their ideas and feelings, and be involved in problem-solving activities during PE teaching and learning activities (Ministry of Education (Malaysia), 2019; Salimin et al., 2022). Teachers were encouraged to blend other teaching styles to avoid monotonous teaching and to cater to students' levels of ability and different sports skills. There is online monitoring of daily teaching plans, which are uploaded by PE teachers. State and district education department staff can monitor and provide guidance.

Overall, a comprehensive and holistic plan based on the standard school curriculum for PE might support the aim of developing holistic and harmonious students. However, continuous discussion, research, and two-way communication among the various stakeholders, including the education department, teachers, teachers training institutes, and universities, must be conducted regularly to ensure this idealistic PE teaching plan can be applied effectively.

Dimension 4: Plans for Feasibility and Accessibility of Physical Education

The PE syllabus has undergone many changes and reforms to accommodate the need of the nation's aspiration to develop a holistic and dynamic future generation. Moreover, to ensure that the PE standard school curriculum caters to current development, continuous research, and international education collaboration are needed. Important factors, particularly the support system for students with disabilities to get better PE, should be highlighted as a national education agenda (Mokmin & Ridzua, 2022). The planning and implementation of a pragmatic PE syllabus must go hand in hand with the development of high-quality teaching among PE teachers (Salimin et al., 2022). Thus, the Malaysian government has provided more opportunities for teachers to further their studies until the doctorate level in local and international universities. Various scholarships for PE teachers and university lecturers are offered every year. There have been knowledge enhancement opportunities for the academic community who are directly or indirectly involved in teaching PE in school. However, how far research on PE has been applied in the PE teaching process in schools to improve the PE teaching process is questionable. This could be due to rapid changes in the teaching and learning process in school and a lack of collaboration among universities, education department staff, and schoolteachers. Therefore, collaboration among education departments, universities, and teachers should be increased in future, especially when developing PE syllabi or standard education curricula.

Dimension 5: Social Norms and Cultural Practice

Various factors influence participation in physical activity, including gender, ethnicity, and social environment. In terms of gender, a review by Mohammadi et al. (2019) reported that Malaysian male adolescents were generally more physically active compared to female adolescents. The 2012 Global School-based Student Health Survey also showed that compared to boys, a lower percentage of Malaysian girls aged 13–17 years were physically active for at least 60 minutes per day on 5 or more days during the past 7 days and attended PE class on 3 or more days each week during the school year (World Health Organization, 2012). In terms of ethnicity, Malay adolescents were the most active, and Chinese adolescents were the least active. Larger household size increased physical activity in adolescents. Family and peers had a positive influence on adolescent physical activity.

Cheah et al. (2016) found that adolescents whose mothers had a tertiary education were more active compared to those with mothers with lower education levels. Adolescents who self-rated their academic performance as excellent or good spent more time on physical activity. An additional day of PE also increased physical activity participation.

Girls have been reported to face various barriers to participation in physical activity. Barriers may be related to minimal support from parents or guardians and gender role expectations, which makes them feel that sport somehow makes them less ladylike or too masculine. In addition to these, the emphasis on academic achievement in schools makes it difficult for some students to balance sports and studies (Khoo & Abidin, 2021). Cheah et al. (2016) also reported that safety might be another reason for lower participation rates among female adolescents.

Dimension 6: Governmental Input for Physical Education

The Malaysian government recognises the importance of PE. This is evident from the National Education Philosophy for Malaysia (published in 1988 and revised in 1996), which states that the country's school curriculum aims to develop the child holistically (Ministry of Education (Malaysia), 2017).

The aim of the PE curriculum is to ensure that students are fit and healthy as well as practice values through physical activity in achieving well-being (Ministry of Education (Malaysia), 2015b, 2017). There is funding for school sports to ensure effective and systematic sports activities are conducted in schools (Ministry of Education (Malaysia), 2017). Funding is based on the total enrolment of students in the school.

Students are required to participate in co-curricular activities, including one sport. Participation is recorded based on the participation and achievement of students according to the Assessment of Physical Activity, Sports, and Co-Curriculum (Ministry of Education (Malaysia), 2017).

Another government policy, the "One Student, One Sport" policy, was introduced in 2011. This was an initiative to get schoolchildren involved in at least one sport (Ministry of Education (Malaysia), 2011). This is in line with the National Education Philosophy, which stresses the holistic development of the child. It is hoped that the policy would inculcate a sporting culture among students, leading to a healthy lifestyle. It is compulsory for students from Year 4 to Year 6 (primary school) and Secondary 1 to Secondary 6 to participate in at least one sport. These sports programmes are conducted year-round.

Dimension 7: Cognitive Skill Development

The Primary School Physical Education Curriculum aims to build students to be fit and healthy individuals who are skilled, knowledgeable, and practice good values through physical activity towards achieving well-being in life (Ministry of Education (Malaysia), 2015c). The drafting of the Primary School Physical

Education Standard Curriculum aims to fulfil the wishes of the National Education Philosophy to produce balanced and harmonious people intellectually, spiritually, emotionally, and physically. This curriculum prepares students for building a healthy and fit human capital. However, this can only be achieved if students participate in physical activity as part of their daily lives.

Dimension 8: Habituated Behaviour in Physical Activities

Malaysia published recommendations for physical activity for various populations in 2015 in the National Strategic Plan for Active Living (Ministry of Health (Malaysia), 2015). It follows the WHO's physical activity recommendation. Children and adolescents aged 5–17 years should participate in at least 60 minutes of moderate to vigorous-intensity physical activity daily and activities that strengthen muscles and bones at least three times per week.

Participation in physical activity among Malaysian adolescents is low. The Adolescent Health Survey 2022 (Institute for Public Health, 2022) reported that 21.4% of adolescents (13–17 years) were active for at least 60 minutes daily for 5 days or more in the past 7 days. Although this was a slight improvement from 2017 (which was 19.8%), sitting behaviour has increased from 47.3% in 2012 to 50.1% in 2017 to 66.7% in 2022.

The Malaysian Sports Culture Index (Institute for Youth Research (Malaysia), 2021) reported that adolescents aged 13–14 years had moderate sporting spirit (volunteering, dedication, expenditure, and contribution). Despite government initiatives to encourage physical activity, participation rates remain relatively low.

Conclusion

Malaysia has mixed results in terms of the quality of PE dimensions. Although there are policies and programmes in place to ensure that quality PE is achieved, their implementation should be improved. PE and sports programmes in schools should be more targeted to ensure that all students gain the benefits of a physically active lifestyle. For example, based on the Malaysian national education plan, dimensions of skill development and bodily awareness were included during PE sessions for primary and secondary students. However, various challenges, including a syllabus that is too idealistic and compact to be implemented in PE classes, might have impacted the effectiveness of PE in achieving these dimensions. Not all schools have the same facilities and access to PE. The financial support provided by the government for education in Malaysia can be considered adequate to provide basic PE facilities; however, more funding should be provided to schools in rural areas that do not have enough fundamental equipment to conduct PE classes. In terms of PE teaching quality, most PE teachers graduated from universities or teacher training colleges specialising in PE. This should provide enough qualified PE teachers in the school system if all these PE teachers were to be given the opportunity to teach PE. Dynamic and holistic education plans that involve PE should provide national and international collaboration learning opportunities to teachers in Malaysia. Currently, this opportunity is limited. Finally, independent expert and specialised committees can be set up to provide input and suggestions to education departments in terms of best practices in PE. These should be consistent with the education plan and dynamic education revolution for the implementation of PE to be relevant to current local and international norms and behaviours.

References

Bari, S., & Ali, H. M. (2005). *Aktiviti Pendidikan Jasmani Suaian Pelajar Berkeperluan Khas [Adapted Physical Education Activities for Students with Special Needs]*. Unpublished manuscript, Universiti Kebangsaan Malaysia, Bangi, Malaysia.

Cheah, Y. K., Lim, H. K., Kee, C. C., & Ghazali, S. M. (2016). Factors associated with participation in physical activity among adolescents in Malaysia. *International Journal of Adolescent Medicine and Health*, 28(4), 419–427.

Director General of Education (Malaysia). (2000). *Student personal safety guide during teaching physical education and health and co-curricular activities and sports inside and outside the school area*. (Special circular letter no. 9/2000).

Ghani, M. F. A., Elham, F., & Awang, Z. (2014). Pengajaran mata pelajaran Pendidikan Jasmani di sekolah menengah kawasan bandar dan luar bandar: Perspektif murid [Teaching Physical Education in urban and rural secondary schools: Pupils' perspectives]. *JuPiDi: Jurnal Kepimpinan Pendidikan*, 1(3), 54–76.

Institute for Public Health. (2022). *Technical Report National Health and Morbidity Survey (NHMS) 2022*. Adolescent Health Survey, Malaysia.

Institute for Youth Research (Malaysia). (2021). *Malaysian Sports Culture Index 2021*. Ministry of Youth and Sports Malaysia

Khoo, S., & Abidin, N. E. Z. (2021). Sport in Malaysia: Towards gender equality. In *Women and Sport in Asia* (pp. 124–135). Routledge, London.

Kilue, D., & Muhamad, T. A. (2017). Cabaran pengajaran subjek pendidikan jasmani di sekolah menengah di Malaysia [Challenges in the teaching of physical education subject in Malaysian secondary schools]. *Journal of Nusantara Studies (JONUS)*, 2(2), 53–65.

Ministry of Economy (Malaysia). (2022a). *The Malaysian Economy in Figures 2022*. www.ekonomi.gov.my/sites/default/files/2023-01/MEIF_2022.pdf

Ministry of Economy (Malaysia). (2022b). *Mean of Monthly Household Gross Income by Ethnic Group of Head of Household, Strata and State, Malaysia, 1970–2022*. www.ekonomi.gov.my/sites/default/files/2023-12/Jadual3-Pendapatan-Isi-Rumah-Kasar-Bulanan-Purata-Mengikut-Kumpulan-Etnik-Ketua-Isi-Rumah-%20Strata-dan-Negeri-Malaysia-1970-2022.pdf

Ministry of Education (Malaysia). (2011). *Guide to the Implementation of the One Student One Sport Policy*. Putrajaya: Curriculum Development Section, Ministry of Education (Malaysia).

Ministry of Education (Malaysia). (2015a). *Kurikulum Standard Sekolah Menengah Pendidikan Khas: Pendidikan Jasmani dan Pendidikan Kesihatan Tingkatan 1 [Secondary School Standard Curriculum: Special Education Physical Education and Health Education Secondary 1]*. Putrajaya: Curriculum Development Section, Ministry of Education (Malaysia).

Ministry of Education (Malaysia). (2015b). *Kurikulum Standard Sekolah Menengah: Pendidikan Jasmani dan Pendidikan Kesihatan Tingkatan 1 [Secondary School Standard Curriculum: Physical Education and Health Education Secondary 1]*. Putrajaya: Curriculum Development Section, Ministry of Education (Malaysia).

Ministry of Education (Malaysia). (2015c). *Kurikulum Standard Sekolah Rendah: Pendidikan Jasmani Tahun 6 [Primary School Standard Curriculum: Physical Education Year 6]*. Putrajaya: Curriculum Development Section, Ministry of Education (Malaysia).

Ministry of Education (Malaysia). (2017). *National Education Policy*. Putrajaya: Curriculum Development Section, Ministry of Education (Malaysia).

Ministry of Education (Malaysia). (2019). *Buku panduan pengurusan mata pelajaran Pendidikan Jasmani dan Kesihatan [Handbook for the Management of Physical Education and Health]*. Putrajaya: Curriculum Development Section, Ministry of Education (Malaysia).

Ministry of Health (Malaysia). (2015). *National Strategic Plan for Active Living 2016–2025*. Putrajaya: Curriculum Development Section, Ministry of Education (Malaysia).

Mohammadi, S., Jalaludin, M. Y., Su, T. T., Dahlui, M., Azmi Mohamed, M. N., & Abdul Majid, H. (2019). Determinants of diet and physical activity in Malaysian adolescents: A systematic review. *International Journal of Environmental Research and Public Health*, *16*(4), 603.

Mokmin, N. A. M., & Ridzua, N. N. I. B. (2022). Immersive technologies in Physical Education in Malaysia for students with learning disabilities. *IAFOR Journal of Education*, *10*(2), 91–110.

Salimin, N., Jani, J., Shahril, M. I., & Muszali, R. (2022). *Buku Pedagogi dalam Pendidikan Jasmani Berdasarkan Stail Pengajaran [Pedagogy in Physical Education Based on Teaching Style]*. Tanjung Malim: Universiti Pendidikan Sultan Idris (UPSI) Press.

World Health Organization. (2012). *Global School-based Student Health Survey*. https://extranet.who.int/ncdsmicrodata/index.php/catalog/194/get-microdata

Chapter 14

Analysis of Quality Physical Education in Mexico

Oswaldo Ceballos Gurrola, Rosa Elena Medina Rodríguez, Oswaldo Ceballos Medina, and Ernesto Ceballos Gurrola

Background to the Country

Mexico is a country located in North America, bordered to the north by the United States, to the south and west by the Pacific Ocean, to the southeast by Belize and Guatemala, and to the east by the Gulf of Mexico and the Caribbean Sea. It is the third largest country in Latin America in terms of land area and has a great geographic diversity that includes mountains, jungles, deserts, coasts, and plains. It is the 11th most populous country in the world, with a population of approximately 118 million inhabitants. The native language is Spanish, which coexists with 67 indigenous languages (Secretaría de Relaciones Exteriores, 2024). According to data from Mexico's National Institute of Statistics and Geography (Instituto Nacional de Estadística y Geografía/INEGI, 2020), the country's total population is estimated at around 126 million people. In terms of political information, Mexico is a democratic federal republic, divided into 32 federative entities, including 31 states and Mexico City, which is the capital of the country and is also considered a federative entity, there are three branches of the federation: the Legislative, the Executive and the Judiciary. Mexico has a diversified economy and is one of the leading economies in Latin America; however, it faces several challenges, such as income inequality, poverty, corruption, and insecurity. In addition, Mexico's economy is closely linked to that of the United States, which makes it vulnerable to changes in the trade and economic policy of its northern neighbor.

The Mexican education system is divided into three levels: basic, middle, and higher education. These include preschool, primary, secondary, high school, bachelor's, master's, and doctoral studies, as well as diplomas and other forms of higher education and continuing education. Article 3 of the Political Constitution of the United Mexican States establishes that education provided by the state shall be compulsory, universal, inclusive, public, free, and secular. In May 2019, a reform of the article stipulated the compulsory nature of education from preschool to high school and recognized the right of children to early childhood education (Secretaría de Gobernación, 2019). The New Mexican School is an educational project with a critical, humanistic, and community approach to form students with a comprehensive vision. It seeks equity, excellence, and continuous improvement in education, placing the maximum learning achievement of children and adolescents at the center of public action (Secretaría de Educación Pública, 2023). The development of education in Mexico has been a complex process that has evolved throughout the country's history, with educational reforms to improve quality and equity, as well as challenges that require continuous attention from educational authorities and society in general, such as low educational quality, lack of infrastructure in some rural areas and inequality in access to education (Colín-Mercado et al., 2020). The challenge is to ensure that all children have access to quality education, remain in it, and complete it with the expected learning for their age and educational level, especially the most vulnerable children and adolescents (Ramos, 2024).

Physical Education in Mexico

To conduct this research in Mexico, it is necessary to make a brief description of the context of physical education. The development of physical education in Mexico has depended on the social, economic, and political advances of the country (Ceballos-Gurrola et al., 2013). The first antecedents of physical education focused on hygiene and gymnastic exercises at the end of the 19th century. The first physical education program in basic education had a military approach in 1940, then sports in 1960, psychomotor in 1974, organo-functional in 1988, the motor of dynamic integration in 1993, global motor skills in 2011, and building motor competence in 2018, the latter with the purpose of pedagogical intervention in physical education, the interaction of capacities, abilities and skills promoted by physical education, planning and evaluation of physical education, and health (Secretaría de Educación Pública, 2017). Physical education classes offered in public schools are once or twice a week, with a duration of 30 minutes for preschool, 40 in elementary, and 50 in high school. The Mexican Report Card on Physical Activity of Children and Youth shows some problems with the scope of physical education in basic education, as in Mexico there are 207,682 public schools of basic education for 96,000 physical education teachers; in rural, indigenous areas and the peripheries of large cities, there are few or almost none hired teachers (Galavíz et al., 2018). It is important to note that physical education teacher training in Mexico is historically developed in public and private universities, as well as in teacher training colleges. The curricula are developed by the government, and the current approach is the new Mexican school, it aims that students are able to develop their physical competencies, that they have knowledge about the movements they perform, and that they learn to develop activities related to a healthy lifestyle.

The Development of Eight Dimensions in Quality Physical Education

The author Walter Ho is one of the authors who has studied QPE the most (Ho et al., 2018); for his analysis, he proposed a questionnaire containing 48 items and 8 dimensions to establish a holistic understanding of the development of QPE through physical education teachers. In Mexico, there is a study (Rodríguez Rodríguez et al., 2021) where they examined the psychometric properties and factor structure of the quality physical education (QPE) scale from the perspective of teaching practice, translated and adapted to the Spanish and Mexican context. A quantitative study with an instrumental design is presented. The participants were 763 physical education teachers from Mexico with an age range of 19–71 years old (M = 37.89 ± 11.18), where 31.7% were women and 68.3% were men. Of the total, 59.4% work in schools that belong to the federal system, 33.9% to the state system, and 6.7% work in private schools. The translation and adaptation to Spanish and the Mexican context of the QPE survey was carried out. It is composed of 50 items that are answered on a scale that goes from 0 "not totally achieved" to 10 "completely achieved". It was carried out the exploratory factorial analysis (EFA) using the Kaiser-Meyer Olkin KMO correlation matrix (.97) and Bartlett's sphericity test ($x22$ $x2$= 30645.936 y gl = 990), obtaining 6 factors and the reduction to 46 items. Confirmatory factor analysis (CFA) showed good internal consistency and inter-factor correlations (x^2/gl = 2.98, Non-Normal Fit Index (NNFI) = .98, CFI = .98, and Root Mean Square Error of Approximation (RMSEA) = .07, as well as when divided by gender, level, and educational system. The instrument shows good psychometric properties to evaluate QPE from the perspective of teaching practice in the Mexican context. Due to its characteristics, it could be used in other Spanish-speaking countries as its writing, terminology, and contents are adapted to the context.

The following is a description of the studies carried out in Mexico on the dimensions that comprise the QPE survey.

Dimension 1: Skill Development and Bodily Awareness

The New Mexican School includes concepts of physical education, sport, physical activity, physical exercise, recreation, leisure and free time, health, and nutrition, which are developed within the formative field of the human and the community-oriented to health, education, psychosocial behaviors, and sports performance (Juárez Lozano et al., 2023). The development of basic motor skills is characteristic of the natural motor skills of individuals, and the best known that are part of the contents of physical education programs are running, jumping, throwing, catching, carrying, driving, pushing, pulling, and their combinations (Roa Gonzalez et al., 2019).

The authors Pérez Hernández et al. (2022) make a didactic proposal through motor experiences at the elementary school level that contribute to the development of basic motor skills through the implementation of playful motor skills and the game-based teaching strategy. They highlight the importance for the physical education teacher to master the contents found in the key learning program for physical education of the Mexican educational system, as well as specific didactic strategies related to the competency-based model to achieve a varied, broad and inclusive practice during physical education sessions at different educational levels or in the area in which he/she works professionally.

In another study conducted in northern Mexico (Juárez Lozano et al., 2020), a multidisciplinary physical activity and sports program based on the development of life skills from a multiple intelligences perspective was implemented in elementary and high school students. The results point to differentiation in terms of gender when choosing to join the program, as well as a strong influence of family culture in the decision to practice sports. The most developed skills in the participants were the physical-motor ones, and they presented a high development of their kinesthetic-corporal skills. The implications of such results are discussed as an alternative measure to favor corporeality in the student during vacation periods.

Dimension 2: Facilities and Norms in Physical Education

Most public elementary schools in Mexico have sports facilities for physical education classes. However, these facilities are mostly outdoors, and there is no recent study to validate whether they are adequate and sufficient to offer QPE. One area of opportunity would be to maintain the sports facilities of the schools in optimal conditions of use and maintenance according to the regulations, equipping them with each and every one of the material elements necessary for the practice of each specialty, having cutting-edge infrastructure and technological advances (González-Rivas et al., 2021).

Regarding material resources, it has been found that they are not sufficient, and the budget for their acquisition is limited. For this reason, teachers have been forced to buy materials with their own money or use recycled materials. Furthermore, it is important to consider the socioeconomic differences in the country, which are reflected in the infrastructure for physical activity. Localities with fewer economic resources are the most affected, so it is pertinent to consider support from the private sector (Venegas, 2019). The authors Flores-Allende et al. (2021) report that in Mexico, between 2010 and 2019, there were 40 cases of people, mainly minors, who lost their lives while playing soccer and basketball due to the fall of a goalpost and/or a basketball hoop.

The Mexican Federal Government's proposal "Towards a National Strategy for the Provision of Physical Education (EFC) in the Mexican Educational System" mentions the establishment of minimum infrastructure standards, the review of operational rules for the management of material resources, and the establishment of agreements with local and community government agencies to use their material resources and sports facilities (Jauregui de la Mota et al., 2018).

Dimension 3: Quality Teaching of Physical Education

The quality of teaching in physical education could be considered as follows: being a reflective and open-minded teacher who is willing to share his or her practice, making the most of class time and minimizing transition or waiting times, providing necessary feedback during activities, planning lessons in advance, avoiding punishment or favoritism, possessing technical and didactic knowledge of the content to be taught and providing clear and correct explanations and demonstrations in class, using more active roles for students in class, helping students develop intrinsic motivation towards the subject through a motivational climate aimed at autonomy, quality interpersonal relationships, and providing many opportunities for success (Pereira et al., 2021).

In the educational intervention of physical education classes in Mexico, it has been found that there is an implementation of unmotivating and repetitive didactic strategies, mainly using a sports approach, which negatively affects the satisfaction of physical education classes (Baños, 2020). There is a tendency for teachers to use traditional teaching methodologies and, in some cases, improvisation of classes (González-Rivas et al., 2021). Additionally, the study by Baños et al. (2021) found that Mexican schoolgirls tend to get bored more in physical education classes compared to boys. The results of Hall-López (2020) follow this line, finding that Mexican girls perform the activities with less intensity. Flores et al. (2017) identified that a lot of time is wasted in physical education classes receiving instructions, reducing the duration of activities. Added to this, the motivational climate of the sessions does not seem to be the most adequate, which means that students do not develop a taste for physical activity, approaching the acquisition of sedentary behaviors (Vílchez & Ruiz-Juan, 2016). These findings are a reflection of obsolete pedagogical plans, and they show opportunities for improvement in the planning and intervention of the teacher.

Dimension 4: Plans for Feasibility and Accessibility of Physical Education

Plans for feasibility and accessibility require economic and material resources, as well as adequate technical support, to guarantee access to physical education for all students, including those with disabilities and those with specific religious needs (UNESCO, 2015).

Several authors, such as Considine et al. (2017), indicate that transitioning to this new paradigm requires a profound transformation of the educational system, where the community must assume the responsibility and the challenge of critically reflecting on those practices that limit student success. In this sense, cooperative teaching and learning methodologies stand out as a means to favor interaction, collaboration, and inclusive attitudes among students (Velázquez et al., 2014).

Studies have been conducted on elementary school students in Mexico on hearing impairment (Ochoa-Martínez et al., 2019), intellectual (Ogarrio Perkinson et al., 2021), and motor (Martínez Díaz, 2017) with intervention programs that show improvements in their integration into the physical education class and daily life.

UNESCO (2015) indicated that QPE is a planned, progressive, and inclusive learning experience that is part of the curriculum in early childhood and primary and secondary education. In this regard, it serves as the starting point for a lifespan commitment to physical activity and sport.

Dimension 5: Social Norms and Cultural Practice

School is the only space where Mexican students exercise regularly and mandatorily; therefore, QPE classes become more important, as when students are satisfied with the classes, they are more likely to develop a taste for physical activity in their free time. This indicates the importance of QPE in the prevention of obesity and non-communicable degenerative diseases, but also the positive impact it can have on solving social problems facing the country (Ceballos et al., 2021).

At present, stereotypes related to physical education and sports persist in basic education students, specifically in primary and secondary schools, where the teacher who teaches the physical education class still continues to carry out activities that maintain a binary vision of the female and male body, preserving a cultural, symbolic and unequal burden by considering the disproportionate body image according to the gender of people (Hernández Ramírez, 2020).

Dimension 6: Governmental Input for Physical Education

Public policies and programs related to the provision of physical education in Mexico depend on three government sectors: the Ministry of Public Education, the National Commission for Physical Culture and Sports, and the Ministry of Health (Jauregui de la Mota et al., 2018).

The interest of the Federal Government in Mexico in improving the quality of physical education is evident; however, according to various studies, the work carried out so far has not been reflected in the reality of schools, perhaps it is too early to clearly visualize the progress. On the other hand, the COVID-19 pandemic was an educational challenge that could have substantially influenced the development and application of government strategies (González Rivas et al., 2023).

The main strength identified for the provision of QPE in Mexico is the institutional capacity of the Ministry of Public Education, which has pre-established mechanisms for ensuring the provision of infrastructure, materials, human resources, monitoring the assurance and quality of physical education sessions, as well as experience at the federal level in establishing partnerships with other sectors, such as Health and through the National Sports Commission (Jauregui de la Mota et al., 2018).

Dimension 7: Cognitive Skill Development

Cognitive skills refer to the ability to identify and acquire information from the environment to integrate it with existing knowledge. In physical education classes, concentration, visual attention, visual tracking, and quick decision-making are developed through games and sports practice; these skills are then transferred to daily life activities (Childrens Health, 2024).

The learning experience offered to children and youth through physical education classes should be appropriate for helping them acquire psychomotor skills, cognitive development, and social and emotional skills needed to lead physically active lives (UNESCO, 2021).

Another purpose of physical education in Mexico is the development of sociomotor skills, which are characterized by interaction and the possibility of communicating, expressing, and relating with others through motor play. Within the activities that physical education deploys, these interactions become important in situations associated with cooperation among peers, antagonism with opponents, and the possibility of generating divergent, creative, and innovative motor responses that allow children and adolescents to implement strategic thinking and action, from simple games in preschool, sports initiation in primary school and then educational sport in secondary school (Secretaría de Educación Pública, 2017).

Dimension 8: Habituated Behavior in Physical Activities

The physical education program has as a cross-cutting theme, the promotion of health-related to prevention and self-care to encourage a taste for the systematic practice of physical activities, which is complemented by assuming healthy habits, such as healthy eating, drinking water, dental hygiene, good sleep, controlled use of social networks and physical exercise, which represent alternatives to deal with overweight and obesity (Secretaría de Educación Pública, 2017).

In Mexico, there is a prevalence of overweight and obesity of 37% in children and 41% in adolescents, with high consumption of ultra-processed foods, for example, 80% consume sugary drinks; 17% of adolescents use tobacco. It is proposed to analyze interrelated risk factors such as tobacco, alcohol, and teenage pregnancy (Lazcano-Ponce & Shamah-Levy, 2023). Data from Instituto Nacional de Salud Pública (2016) show that 22.7% of children (10–14 years) and 21.4% of youth (15–19 years) spend 2 hours or less per day in front of a screen; among the children, more girls (24.4%) than boys (21.0%) met the screen time recommendation, while among the youth, more boys (25.3%) than girls (17.4%) met it; shows more screen time in urban areas than in rural ones, and in children with obesity than in those with normal weight.

Conclusion

The eight dimensions provide valuable information for developing QPE in Mexico. Their analysis allows for the identification of areas for improvement that require effort from the teacher, school, and government authorities for their fulfillment. The important thing is the physical education literacy of children and young people through concerted, collaborative, and participatory action to support the rounded development of every individual. As it has been observed, factors associated with QPE are complex and interwoven with the learning situation designed to build an active and healthy society. In the school environment, the physical education class is a fundamental axis of the promotion of physical activity levels in school-going children, with the physical education teacher playing an important role in planning content in programs that are inclusive.

References

Baños, R. (2020). Intención de práctica, satisfacción con la educación física y con la vida en función del género en estudiantes mexicanos y españoles. *Retos: Nuevas Tendencias en Educación Física, Deporte y Recreación, 37*, 412–418. https://doi.org/10.47197/retos.v37i37.73019

Baños, R., Barretos-Ruvalcaba, M., Baena-Extremera, A., & Fuentesal-García, J. (2021). Análisis de los niveles de actividad física en el tiempo libre, IMC, satisfacción y apoyo a la autonomía en educación física en una muestra mexicana. *Retos: Nuevas Tendencias en Educación Física, Deporte y Recreación, 42*, 549–556. https://doi.org/10.47197/retos.v42i0.87088

Ceballos, O., Pérez, T., Medina, R., Espino, F., & Ceballos, E. (2021). Propósitos y contenidos del programa de educación física en países de latinoamérica. *Acción Motriz, 26*, 102–112. www.accionmotriz.com/index.php/accionmotriz/article/view/168

Ceballos-Gurrola, O., Alfonso-García, M.R., Medina-Rodríguez, R.E., Muela-Meza, Z., Enríquez-Martínez, M., & Ceballos-Gurrola, E. (2013). Enfoque historico de la Educación Física en México. *Revista Electrónica Actividad Física y Ciencias, 5*(1), 1–30. 2244–7318. www.actividadfisicayciencias.com/volumen5numero1.html

Childrens Health. (2024). La importancia de las habilidades cognitivas en los deportes. *Children's Health*. https://es.childrens.com/health-wellness/the-importance-of-cognitive-skills-in-sports#:~:text=%C2%BFQu%C3%A9%20son%20las%20habilidades%20cognitivas,integrarla%20con%20el%20conocimiento%20existente

Colín-Mercado, N.A., Llanes-Sorolla, L., & Iglesias-Piña, D. (2020). El sistema educativo en México, ¿visión sustentable?. *Revista Copala. Construyendo Paz latinoamericana, 9*, 155–170. www.redalyc.org/pdf/6681/668170996005.pdf

Considine, J., Mihalick, J., Mogi-Hein, Y., Penick-Parks, M., & Van Auken, P. (2017). How do you achieve inclusive excellence in the classroom?. *New Directions for Teaching and Learning, 151*, 171–187. https://doi.org/10.1002/tl.20255

Flores, P.J., Margarita, C., Gómez, J.A., Barreto, Y., Valdovinos, O., Vicente, J.U., & Del Río, J.E. (2017). Medición del tiempo efectivo de la clase de educación física y su impacto en el gasto calórico en escolares de nivel primaria del municipio de Colima, México. *Sportis, 3*(1), 34–49. https://doi.org/10.17979/sportis.2017.3.1.1766

Flores-Allende, G., Velarde Martínez, O., Cuevas Vázquez, F.E., & García-Tascón, M. (2021). Compliance with the Spanish standard (UNE-EN) for basketball hoops and soccer goals inmunicipal sports facilities in the Metropolitan Area of Guadalajara, Mexico. *Retos: Nuevas Tendencias en Educación Física, Deporte y Recreación, 39*, 769–779. https://doi.org/10.47197/retos.v0i39.82592

Galavíz, K.I., Argumedo, G., Medina, C., Gaytán-González, A., González-Casanova, I., Villalobos, M.F., ... Pelayo, R.A. (2018). *¡Es hora de hacer la tarea! Por una educación física de calidad en México. Boleta de Calificaciones Mexicana sobre la Actividad Física de Niños y Jóvenes*. www.activehealthykids.org/wp-content/uploads/2018/11/mexico-report-card-short-form-2018.pdf

González-Rivas, R.A., del Carmen Zueck Enríquez, M., Baena-Extremera, A., Soto Valenzuela, M.C., & Gastélum Cuadras, G. (2021). El Programa de formación pedagógica para docentes universitarios. *Revista Publicando, 8*(29), 21–34. https://doi.org/10.51528/rp.vol8.id2186

González Rivas, R.A., Laguna Celia, A., & Nuñez Enriquez, O. (2023). Factors that influence in Physical Education in Mexico. *Retos: Nuevas Tendencias en Educación Física, Deporte y Recreación, 48,* 349–357. https://doi.org/10.47197/retos.v48.96752

Hall-López, J.A. (2020). Secondary physical education, participation by sex in moderate to vigorous physical activity. *Retos: Nuevas Tendencias en Educación Física, Deporte y Recreación, 38,* 543–546. https://doi.org/10.47197/retos.v38i38.77152

Hernández Ramírez, C.I. (2020). La perspectiva de género en las prácticas deportivas: hacia una visión coeducativa en educación física. *Diálogos Sobre Educación. Temas Actuales en Investigación Educativa, 11*(20), 1–3. https://doi.org/10.32870/dse.v0i20.592

Ho, W., Ahmed, D., Lopez de D'Amico, R., Ramos, A., Lucia, F.E., Rocha Ferreira, M.B., … Wong, B. (2018). Measuring the perception of quality physical education in Latin American professionals. *Revista Brasileira de Ciências do Esporte, 40*(4), 361–369. https://doi.org/10.1016/j.rbce.2018.05.006

Instituto Nacional de Estadística y Geografía/INEGI. (2020). *Consulta de indicadores sociodemográficos y económicos por área geográfica.* www.inegi.org.mx/

Instituto Nacional de Salud Pública. (2016). *Encuesta Nacional de Salud y Nutrición de Medio Camino 2016.* www.gob.mx/cms/uploads/attachment/file/209093/ENSANUT.pdf

Jauregui de la Mota, A., Salinas, A., Sánchez, A., Rivera Villafuerte, A., & Juárez, O. (2018). *Hacia una estrategia nacional para la prestación de Educación Física de calidad en el nivel básico del Sistema Educativo Mexicano.* Instituto Nacional de Salud Pública. www.insp.mx/resources/images/stories/2019/Docs/190607_978-607-511-173-5.pdf.

Juárez Lozano, R., Lara Rodriguez, L.M., & Medrano Donlucas, G. (2020). La corporeidad como estrategia para el desarrollo de habilidades y preservación de la salud en escolares en la nueva normalidad. *Recie. Revista Electrónica Científica de Investigación Educativa, 5*(1), 227–236. https://doi.org/10.33010/recie.v5i1.1053

Juárez Lozano, R., Medrano Don Lucas, G., & Mendoza López, D. (2023). Education and corporeality: an exploration of Physical Culture in the New Mexican School (NMS). *Latam Revista Latinoamericana de Ciencias Sociales y Humanidades, 4*(5), 850–868. https://doi.org/10.56712/latam.v4i5.1360

Lazcano-Ponce, E.C., & Shamah-Levy, T. (2023). Mexican National Health and Nutrition ContinuousSurvey 2022: public policy recommendations. *Salud Publica Mexico, 65*(1), S268–S274. https://doi.org/10.21149/15168

Martínez Díaz, C. (2017). La corporeidad de niños y niñas con discapacidad motora: cuerpos, deseos y sueños. *Ponencia XIV Congreso Nacional de Investigación Educativa.* COMIE, San Luis Potosí, México. www.comie.org.mx/congreso/memoriaelectronica/v14/doc/1074.pdf

Ochoa-Martínez, P.Y., Hall-López, J.A., Carmona López, A., Morales Ramírez, M., Alarcón Meza, E., & Sáenz-López, P. (2019). Efecto de un programa adaptado de educación física en niños con discapacidad auditiva sobre la coordinación motora. *Mhsalud: Revista en Ciencias del Movimiento Humano y Salud, 16* (2), 1–11. www.revistas.una.ac.cr/index.php/mhsalud/article/view/11980/16847

Ogarrio Perkinson, C.E., Bautista Jacobo, A., Barahona Herrejón, N.C., Chávez Valenzuela, M.E., & Hoyos Ruiz, G. (2021). Efecto de un programa de Educación Física con actividades motrices para desarrollar el área motora en niños con discapacidad intelectual. *Ciencias de la Actividad Física UCM*, 22(2), 1–12. https://doi.org/10.29035/rcaf.22.2.3

Pereira, P., Marinho, D.A., & Santos, F. (2021). Positive motivational climates, physical activity and sport participation through self-determination theory: striving for Quality Physical Education. *Journal of Physical Education, Recreation and Dance, 92*(6), 42–47. https://doi.org/10.1080/07303084.2021.1936307

Pérez Hernández, H.J., Simoni Rosas, C., Fuentes-Rubio, M., & Castillo-Paredes, A. (2022). Ludomotricity and basic locomotion motor skills (walk, running and jump). A didactic proposal for Physical Education in Mexico. *Retos: Nuevas Tendencias en Educación Física, Deporte y Recreación, 44*, 1141–1146. https://doi.org/10.47197/retos.v44i0.91338

Ramos, M. (2024). *Educación y Aprendizaje*. UNICEF, México. www.unicef.org/mexico/educaci%C3%B3n-y-aprendizaje

Roa Gonzalez, S.V., Hernandez Garay, A., & Valero Inerarity, A (2019). Actividades físicas para desarrollar las habilidades motrices básicas en niños del programa Educa a tu Hijo. *Conrado, 15*(69), 386–393. https://conrado.ucf.edu.cu/index.php/conrado/article/view/1088

Rodríguez Rodríguez, J., Ceballos-Gurrola, O., Zamarripa Rivera, J.I., Medina RodrRodríguez Rodríguez, R.E., Ho, W., & López D´Amico, R. (2021). Quality Physical Education from the perspective of teaching practice: psychometric properties of an instrument for it. *Retos: Nuevas Tendencias en Educación Física, Deportes y Recreación, 41*, 373–379. https://doi.org/10.47197/retos.v0i41.86253

Secretaría de Educación Pública. (2017). *Aprendizajes clave hacia una educación integral.* www.imageneseducativas.com/wp-content/uploads/2018/01/Educaci%C3%B3n-F%C3%ADsica.-Educaci%C3%B3n-b%C3%A1sica.pdf

Secretaría de Educación Pública. (2023). *La Nueva Escuela Mexicana (NEM): orientaciones para padres y comunidad en general.* https://educacionmediasuperior.sep.gob.mx/work/models/sems/Resource/13634/1/images/030623_La%20Nueva%20Escuela%20Mexicana_orientaciones%20para%20padres%20y%20comunidad%20en%20general_COSFAC.pdf

Secretaría de Gobernación. (2019). *DECRETO por el que se reforman, adicionan y derogan diversas disposiciones de los artículos 3o., 31 y 73 de la Constitución Política de los Estados Unidos Mexicanos, en materia educativa.* Diario Oficial de la Federación. www.dof.gob.mx/nota_detalle.php?codigo=5560457&fecha=15/05/2019#gsc.tab=0

Secretaría de Relaciones Exteriores. (2024). *Información general sobre México.* https://acortar.link/8FjSk4

UNESCO. (2015). *Educación Física de Calidad. Guía para los responsables políticos.* http://unesdoc.unesco.org/images/0023/002313/231340s.pdf.

UNESCO. (2021). *How to influence the development of Quality Physical Education policy: a policy advocacy toolkit for youth.* UNESCO, París. https://unesdoc.unesco.org/ark:/48223/pf0000375423

Velázquez, C., Fraile, A., & López, V. (2014). Aprendizaje Cooperativo en Educación física. *Revista Movimento, 20*(1), 239–259. https://seer.ufrgs.br/Movimento/article/view/40518

Venegas, S. (2019). El derecho fundamental a la cultura física y al deporte: un derecho económico, social y cultural de reciente constitucionalización en México. *Cuestiones Constitucionales, 41*, 151–180. https://doi.org/10.22201/iij.24484881e.2019.4 1.13944

Vílchez, P., & Ruiz-Juan, F. (2016). Clima motivacional en Educación Física y actividad físico-deportiva en el tiempo libre en alumnado de España, Costa Rica y México. *Retos: Nuevas Tendencias en Educación Física, Deporte y Recreación, 29*, 195–200. https://doi.org/10.47197/retos.v0i29.42448

Chapter 15

Quality Physical Education Development in New Zealand

Francisco Serrano Romero

Introduction

New Zealand is an island country located in the southwestern corner of the Pacific Ocean, and Australia is the neighbouring country on the western side of the island. New Zealand became a dominion under the British in 1907 and gained full statutory independence in 1947. The country retains the monarch as the head of the state. New Zealand consists of two major lands – the North Island and the South Island, and Wellington is the capital. The country has a population of around 5.30 million in 2023 (Stats New Zealand, 2024), and the Europeans remain the largest descents in the country. The second largest population group is the Māori. Due to this specific population profile, the official languages of the country are English and Māori.

Physical Education in New Zealand

Physical education in New Zealand has a rich history, deeply intertwined with the nation's culture and sporting identity. The country's emphasis on outdoor activities, sports, and a healthy lifestyle has significantly influenced physical education within the New Zealand Curriculum, the framework guiding education across the country, which outlines physical education as a core subject, emphasizing its importance for students' physical, social, emotional, and intellectual development.

The New Zealand Curriculum and Physical Education

The New Zealand Curriculum provides a framework for health and physical education, outlining key learning areas and expectations. It emphasizes "the well-being of the students themselves, of other people, and of society through learning in health-related and movement contexts" (Ministry of Education, 2014b). The New Zealand Health and Physical Education Curriculum is designed to foster this comprehensive student development, encompassing the following concepts of Hauora (Durie, 1998), attitudes and values, a socio-ecological perspective, and health promotion.

The subject of health and physical education in schools plays a vital role in the development of students and their well-being, and health and physical education is a compulsory subject from year 1 to year 10 (The National Curriculum, n.d.). In 2024, the New Zealand Curriculum has set a weekly minimum time requirement for reading, writing, and maths (Stanford, 2023), yet a minimum requirement for physical activity has not been set for health and physical education and is therefore dependent on each school and level. The guiding document for this purpose is the New Zealand Physical Activity Guidelines for 5- to 17-year-olds, which states, "an accumulation of at least 1 hour a day of moderate to vigorous physical activity (incorporating vigorous physical activities and activities that strengthen muscles and bones, at least 3 days a week)" (Health New Zealand, 2018).

The health and physical education curriculum focuses on having students become increasingly capable of taking care of themselves and making positive contributions to their communities through the development of resilience, self-awareness, and a sense of social responsibility through physical activity. They learn to appreciate the importance of physical activity for both mental and physical health, and they develop the skills necessary to lead healthy and active lifestyles.

From a socio-ecological perspective, the curriculum can foster a deep connection to the environment. By engaging in outdoor activities and learning about environmental issues, students develop a greater appreciation for the natural world and develop a sense of stewardship for their planet, taking action to protect and preserve the environment for future generations. Thus, connecting health and physical education to other learning areas.

The way health and physical education curriculum has been structured entails a comprehensive framework that integrates four interconnected strands and seven key areas of learning. This framework provides a robust foundation for student development, ensuring that they acquire the knowledge, skills, and attitudes necessary for personal well-being, effective movement, positive relationships, and responsible citizenship (Ministry of Education, 2014a).

The four strands – personal health and physical development, movement concepts and motor skills, relationships with other people, and healthy communities and environments – guide students in developing a holistic understanding of health and well-being. These strands are supported by seven key areas of learning: mental health, sexuality education, food and nutrition, body care and physical safety, physical activity, sport studies, and outdoor education. Each area contributes to different aspects of student development, with a strong focus on health education (Ministry of Education, 2014b).

The New Zealand Health and Physical Education Curriculum offers a comprehensive framework for student development and well-being. By integrating Hauora, attitudes and values, a socio-ecological perspective, and health promotion, the curriculum empowers students to care for themselves, contribute to their communities, and connect with the environment. Through physical activity, resilience, self-awareness, and social responsibility, students are equipped to lead healthy, active lives. The curriculum's focus on student well-being ensures that health and physical education is not just about fitness but also about developing the skills and attitudes necessary for responsible citizenship and a sustainable future.

Sport New Zealand and Balance Is Better

Sport New Zealand plays a crucial role in supporting sport and physical education in New Zealand. As the National Sports Organization, Sport New Zealand provides resources, training, and guidance to schools and communities. Their initiatives focus on promoting participation, well-being, skill development, and inclusivity by creating sustainable sports environments.

Balance Is Better (Sport New Zealand, n.d.) is a philosophy behind Sport New Zealand that promotes a balanced approach to youth sport in New Zealand. It emphasizes the importance of providing quality sport experiences for all young people, regardless of ability, needs, or motivations. The initiative aims to encourage lifelong participation in sport and help young people have a meaningful engagement with sport. Schools are invited to integrate the Balance Is Better philosophy into their sport and physical education delivery by collaborating with local sports clubs to deliver sport and physical education and support coaches in implementing the philosophy.

Sport New Zealand supports the delivery of play, active recreation, and sport activities at schools for children and young people (5–18 years) through a fund called Tū Manawa. According to the March 2024 Insights Report (Sport New Zealand, 2024b), the fund has impacted over 1.7 million children and youth, and it has helped improve their access to play, active recreation, and sport opportunities. Additionally, the fund has supported youth to have an improved sense of belonging and connectedness through sport, play, and recreation.

Key Drivers for Physical Education and Post-Pandemic Impacts

The COVID-19 pandemic has had a profound effect on physical education in New Zealand. While schools faced challenges such as closures and restrictions, there have also been opportunities for innovation and adaptation.

Key Drivers Influencing Physical Education Post Pandemic

- **Increased focus on mental health:** The pandemic highlighted the importance of physical activity for mental well-being. Schools in line with the New Zealand Curriculum have incorporated mindfulness, stress management, and emotional resilience into their health and physical education programmes.
- **Digital technologies:** Online health and fitness resources have become valuable tools for physical education since the pandemic. However, a recent government ban on mobile phones in schools limits their use in the classroom (Ministry of Education, 2023). This restriction hinders the potential of digital tools to enhance learning experiences and offer personalized approaches.

- **Outdoor education:** Outdoor education is an important element that schools look to incorporate in their delivery yearly. This approach aims to connect students with the outdoors, fostering a deeper appreciation for nature and promoting physical activity in a unique and engaging way through camps, tramp biking, orienteering, and other activities.
- **Inclusive practices:** Inclusive practices in physical education supported by Balance Is Better and Tū Manawa funding have been essential for ensuring that all students have equal access to physical activity, regardless of their abilities or backgrounds. A proactive approach has helped students develop their physical skills, build confidence, and improve their overall well-being, thus enabling all students to access the benefits of physical activity.
- **Community partnerships:** Schools have forged stronger connections with local sports clubs, community organizations, and health providers. These partnerships offer students access to additional resources, expertise, and opportunities, such as coaching, equipment, and facilities. An articulated approach between the New Zealand Curriculum and Sport New Zealand to achieve a connection between schools and community sport organizations has created a more vibrant and inclusive physical activity environment for all students.

Physical education in New Zealand continues to evolve in response to the changing needs of students and the broader community. The New Zealand Curriculum, Sport New Zealand, and Balance Is Better provide essential frameworks and support for health and physical education programmes in schools. The pandemic presented challenges that have led to opportunities for innovation and growth in key areas. By focusing on mental health, digital technologies, outdoor education, inclusive practices, and community partnerships, schools are ensuring that physical education remains a valuable and impactful part of the New Zealand education system.

Dimensions of Quality Physical Education in New Zealand

Skill Development and Bodily Awareness (SDBA)

New Zealand's major National Sporting Organizations (NSOs) have recognized the pivotal role of skill development in nurturing young athletes. This approach emphasizes the acquisition of fundamental motor skills as a foundation of sport development and lifelong participation in physical activity.

Rugby New Zealand, for instance, has implemented a comprehensive skill development programme that focuses on teaching core skills such as passing, kicking, tackling, and running. The programme emphasizes a fun and engaging learning environment, encouraging children to develop their skills through games and activities (New Zealand Rugby Union, 2019). Similarly, Netball New Zealand has developed a curriculum that prioritizes skill development, with a focus on ball handling, shooting, defending, and teamwork (Netball New Zealand, 2024).

Football New Zealand (Northern Football Region, 2024) and New Zealand Cricket (New Zealand Cricket, 2024) have also adopted a skill-based approach to coaching. These organizations provide resources and training for teachers and coaches to help them deliver effective skill development sessions. The emphasis is on providing children with a solid foundation of skills that can be built upon as they progress in their sporting journeys.

The community partnerships that support the delivery of physical education in New Zealand schools are closely aligned with the skill development approach of the NSOs. These partnerships often involve NSO coaches or representatives who work with school teachers to provide specialized coaching and resources. By focusing on skill development, these partnerships help to ensure that children have access to quality physical education programmes that support their overall sporting development.

Sport New Zealand's philosophy of Balance Is Better further reinforces the importance of skill development in New Zealand's sporting landscape. This philosophy emphasizes the value of providing quality sport experiences for all children, regardless of their ability or motivation. By focusing on skill development and creating inclusive environments, NSOs and community partners can help to ensure that all young people have the opportunity to develop their skills and enhance their bodily awareness through sport.

The skill development approach adopted by New Zealand's major NSOs has become a cornerstone of youth sport development in the country. By emphasizing the acquisition of fundamental skills and providing quality coaching and resources, these organizations are helping to create skilled and physically confident students. The community partnerships that support physical education in schools and Sport New Zealand's philosophy of Balance Is Better further reinforce the importance of skill development in ensuring that all children have the opportunity to benefit from the positive experiences and outcomes associated with sport.

Facilities and Norms in Physical Education (FNPE)

New Zealand's geography, with its abundance of natural landscapes and outdoor spaces, has naturally shaped its approach to physical education. The country's rural landscapes, mountainous terrain, coastlines, and vast open spaces provide ample opportunities for outdoor activities, fostering a strong connection between physical education and the natural environment.

While the country's climate, with its frequent rainfall and high UV exposure, necessitates covered outdoor spaces for physical education and sports, the overall emphasis remains on outdoor activities. This is reflected in the national curriculum, which places a strong emphasis on outdoor education as a key component of the formation of young New Zealanders. Yearly, outdoor education programmes and modules are expected to be part of every school's health and physical education curriculum.

New Zealand schools' facilities often include covered courts, sports fields, and gymnasiums, providing a safe and conducive environment for physical education activities, especially during inclement weather.

Sport New Zealand, through its Tū Manawa funding, plays a crucial role in facilitating resources and partnerships with community sport organizations. This enables schools to deliver high-quality physical education and sporting activities at purpose-built facilities and by experts in the field. These partnerships not only enhance the quality of physical education programmes but also foster a strong connection between schools and local communities.

In terms of norms and expectations, the health and physical education curriculum focuses on inclusivity, safety, and well-being. Schools have implemented strategies to promote a positive and supportive learning environment, ensuring that all students feel valued and included. Safety measures are in place to minimize risks and ensure that students participate in activities that are appropriate for their age and abilities.

Overall, New Zealand's approach to physical education is characterized by a strong emphasis on outdoor activities, a commitment to having access to appropriate facilities, and a focus on creating inclusive and supportive learning environments. These factors contribute to the development of well-rounded individuals who are physically active, connected to their natural environment, and equipped to lead healthy and active lives.

Quality Teaching of Physical Education (QTPE)

New Zealand has made substantial strides in providing quality physical education teaching, focusing on developing fundamental movement skills, promoting bodily awareness, fostering positive attitudes towards physical education, and integrating physical education with other subjects. These efforts have resulted in a more comprehensive and effective approach to physical education instruction.

To develop fundamental movement skills, schools have implemented strategies in conjunction with the resources and expertise of national sport organizations to deliver skill-based learning, movement exploration, and targeted feedback. These approaches help students acquire a strong foundation in basic movement patterns, improve their coordination, and develop a deeper understanding of their bodies whilst playing different games and sports.

Promoting bodily awareness is another key aspect of health and physical education teaching in New Zealand. Schools have incorporated activities that foster the mind-body connection through a focus on Hauora. These practices help students develop and understanding of body and self while also promoting holistic well-being that encompasses mental, physical, spiritual, and social well-being.

Fostering positive attitudes towards physical education is an essential part of encouraging lifelong participation in physical activity. Schools have implemented inclusive practices to ensure that all students feel welcome and valued, regardless of their abilities or backgrounds. Additionally, inquiry-based learning and community engagement initiatives have helped to make physical education more enjoyable and relevant for students.

Integrating health and physical education with other subjects has been another important strategy for enhancing the learning experience. By connecting health and physical education activities to real-world scenarios and incorporating them into interdisciplinary projects, schools help students see the relevance of physical activity in their daily lives and develop a broader understanding of the world around them.

Plans to Make Physical Education Feasible and Accessible (PFAPE)

New Zealand has made significant strides in making physical education more accessible and feasible for students. The delivery of the curriculum can integrate the learning of health and physical education with other subjects, ensuring that all students, regardless of their abilities, have access to quality physical education experiences. Additionally, a strong emphasis has been placed on outdoor education, leveraging the country's natural resources.

Community partnerships have played a crucial role in enhancing the accessibility of physical education. Schools collaborate with local sports organizations to provide students with a wider range of activities and facilities. Moreover, community-based initiatives have emerged, offering additional opportunities for students to participate in physical activity. These partnerships have facilitated resource sharing and reduced costs, making physical education programmes more accessible to a broader range of students.

Sport New Zealand actively supports physical education delivery through funding (Tū Manawa), resource allocation, and professional development initiatives. These efforts have ensured that schools have the necessary equipment, facilities, and teacher training to deliver high-quality physical education and sport programmes. Furthermore, initiatives have been implemented to make physical education more accessible for students with disabilities, including providing adaptive equipment and specialized training.

Furthermore, New Zealand has recognized the importance of promoting physical activity beyond the school setting. Initiatives have been launched to encourage physical activity in the community, such as creating safe and accessible walking and cycling paths, promoting active transportation, and organizing community sports events. These efforts help to reinforce the positive values and habits associated with physical activity that students learn in health and physical education.

New Zealand has made significant progress in making health and physical education more feasible and accessible for students. By combining curriculum delivery, community partnerships, government support, and innovative strategies, the country has created a supportive environment that encourages students to participate in physical activity and reap the benefits of a healthy and active lifestyle. These efforts have helped to ensure that health and physical education remains a vital component of the New Zealand education system.

Social Norms and Cultural Practices (SNCP)

Social norms and cultural practices have significantly influenced the development and delivery of health and physical education in New Zealand. These factors have shaped the values, attitudes, and behaviours associated with health and physical education, as well as the types of activities and programmes offered.

Hauora is an integral concept in the health and physical education curriculum, which stems from Māori culture, that encompasses the holistic well-being of an individual, which goes beyond physical health to include mental, emotional, spiritual, and social aspects. The learning of Hauora promotes balance and harmony in all areas of life. The embedded cultural understanding of this concept is broader than just being "healthy" and encompasses the interconnectedness of a person's mind, body, and spirit.

Cultural Influences

Māori and Pacific Island cultures have made significant contributions to health and physical education in New Zealand. Māori values such as whanaungatanga (kinship), manaakitanga (hospitality), and kaitiakitanga (guardianship) are often incorporated into health and physical education programmes. Māori games and activities, such as ti rakau (Māori stick fighting) and haka (Māori war dance), are popular in schools and communities.

Similarly, the cultural heritage of Pacific Island communities has influenced health and physical education in New Zealand. Popular sports amongst Pacific Islanders are rugby, rugby league, and netball, which are widely played in schools and communities. These sports often reflect the values and traditions of Pacific Island cultures, and students are strongly supported in their experiences by their families.

Social Norms

Social norms encourage children to play sports, driven by perceived benefits like fitness, social development, and academic achievement. However, gender stereotypes persist, influencing programme design, student participation, and student experiences. While progress has been made, stereotypes can still impact opportunities. Recently, female participation in traditionally male-dominated sports has increased, reflecting growing recognition of female athletic abilities. Body image and self-esteem issues connected to sporting experiences affect students' experiences. Thus, creating a positive and inclusive environment that promotes body positivity and challenging negative stereotypes remains an ongoing challenge for teachers and coaches.

Impact on Physical Education Programmes

Social norms and cultural practices can influence the types of activities offered in physical education programmes, as well as the teaching approaches and assessment practices used. For example, schools can prioritize sports that are popular in the local community or that align with cultural traditions. Teachers also adapt their teaching styles to reflect the cultural background of their students, incorporating culturally relevant activities and language.

Assessment practices can also be influenced by social norms. Assessments based on physical performance of students in a particular sport or physical activity are discouraged as they do not contribute to lifelong participation in physical activity. Educators are encouraged to consider alternative forms of assessment that reflect the diverse needs and abilities of their students.

Social norms and cultural practices play a significant role in shaping health and physical education in New Zealand. The delivery structure of health and physical education promotes a more inclusive and culturally relevant curriculum that meets the needs of all students.

Government Input for Physical Education (GIPE)

Sport New Zealand's Strategic Plan 2024–2028 (2024a) outlines four key goals that shape the organization's direction and significantly influence the delivery of sport, recreation, and physical activity in New Zealand, which impacts schools and the delivery of the health and physical education curriculum.

The first goal is to create a New Zealand where everyone has the opportunity to play sports and be active. This inclusive approach aims to break down barriers and ensure that all individuals, regardless of their background, ability, or socioeconomic status, can participate in sports and physical activities. Teachers are expected to adopt an inclusive mindset, creating welcoming and supportive environments that cater to diverse student needs.

The second goal focuses on promoting the value of sport and physical activity in society. Sport New Zealand aims to raise awareness of the positive health, social, and economic benefits associated with sport and physical activity. Teachers contribute to this goal by highlighting these benefits to students, emphasizing the importance of lifelong participation in sports and physical activities.

The third goal is to ensure that sport and physical activity are well-governed and well-resourced. Sport New Zealand aims to create a sustainable and efficient sporting system by providing adequate funding, supporting good governance practices, and fostering partnerships between various stakeholders. This goal has implications for health and physical education delivery, as it ensures that schools have the necessary resources and support to implement effective sport and physical education activities.

The fourth goal is to utilize sport and physical activity as a force for good. Sport NZ aims to promote positive social change through sport, emphasizing values such as fairness, respect, and inclusivity. Teachers contribute to this goal by incorporating social and emotional learning into their health and physical education delivery, fostering a positive and inclusive school culture, and teaching students about the role of sport in promoting social justice and cultural connectedness.

By aligning with these four goals, teachers play a crucial role in helping to create a New Zealand where everyone has the opportunity to play sports and be active. They can promote the value of sport and physical activity, ensure that health and physical education programmes are well-resourced and effective, and utilize physical education as a tool for positive social change.

Cognitive Skills Development (CSD)

New Zealand has made significant strides in integrating cognitive skill development into its health and physical education delivery. This focus has been driven by a recognition that physical education is not solely about physical fitness but also provides health and opportunities for intellectual growth.

One key approach has been to emphasize the cognitive aspects of movement. This includes teaching students about movement concepts, such as body parts, spatial relationships, and force. By understanding these concepts, students can make informed decisions about their movements and develop problem-solving skills. Additionally, health and physical education programmes often incorporate activities that require strategic thinking and decision-making, such as game strategies or analysing performance data at the high school level.

Another strategy has been to integrate health and physical education with other subjects, such as science and mathematics. This allows students to apply their knowledge and skills from other subjects to physical education activities, reinforcing their learning and demonstrating the interconnectedness of different disciplines. For example, students might use mathematical concepts to calculate their heart rate during a workout or apply scientific principles to understand the mechanics of a particular movement.

Furthermore, health and physical education programmes in New Zealand focus on developing critical thinking and problem-solving skills. This involves encouraging students to analyse their own performance, identify areas for improvement, and develop strategies to overcome challenges. Teachers use questioning techniques, peer feedback, and self-assessment to foster these skills.

In addition to cognitive skills, health and physical education programmes in New Zealand also aim to develop social and emotional skills. These skills are essential for success in both academic and personal life. Health and physical education provides opportunities for students to work collaboratively, communicate effectively, and develop self-esteem. Through team sports, games, and activities that require cooperation, students learn valuable social and emotional skills.

New Zealand has made significant progress in integrating cognitive skill development into its health and physical education programmes. By focusing on movement concepts, problem-solving, critical thinking, and social-emotional skills, health and physical education provides students with a well-rounded education that goes beyond physical fitness. These efforts provide a holistic development that helps equip students with the knowledge, skills, and values to live an active life.

Habituated Behaviour in Physical Activities (HBPA)

Habituated behaviours in physical activities have been achieved in New Zealand through a multifaceted approach that has involved both school-based and community-based initiatives. Schools have played a crucial role in fostering a culture of physical activity by integrating sport, health and physical education into their deliveries, providing opportunities for students to engage in physical activity beyond the classroom, and creating supportive environments that encourage participation.

Curriculum delivery integration has been a key strategy for promoting physical activity in schools. By incorporating physical education into the daily schedule, schools ensure that students have regular opportunities to engage in physical activity. This has involved developing creative and engaging physical education lessons that cater to diverse interests and abilities, making physical activity more enjoyable and relevant to students' lives.

Extracurricular activities have also been instrumental in promoting physical activity among students. Schools have implemented a variety of after-school sports programmes, walking clubs, fitness challenges, and other initiatives that provide opportunities for students to participate in physical activity outside of regular school hours. These programmes help to reinforce the habit of being active and make physical activity a more enjoyable and social experience.

Creating supportive environments is another essential component of fostering habituated behaviours in physical education. Schools have focused on providing safe and accessible facilities, promoting positive attitudes towards physical activity, and encouraging students to set personal fitness and sporting goals. By creating a welcoming and supportive atmosphere, schools help to motivate students to participate in physical activity and develop a lifelong appreciation for its benefits.

Community partnerships have also played a role in promoting physical activity in schools. Schools have collaborated with local sports clubs, community organizations, and government agencies to provide students with additional opportunities to participate in physical activity.

Conclusion and Future Vision of Physical Education in New Zealand

New Zealand's health and physical education programmes have been significantly shaped by a focus on four key dimensions: skill development, habituated behaviours, social norms and cultural practices, and cognitive skill development. These dimensions have collectively contributed to a comprehensive and effective approach to physical education delivery in the country.

The Balance is Is Better philosophy, as a cornerstone of New Zealand's approach to physical education, also provides a strong foundation for future development. As outlined in the Sport New Zealand Strategic Plan 2024–2028 (2024a), sport, recreation, and physical activity can play a pivotal role in achieving a New Zealand where everyone has the opportunity to play sport and be active.

Future development areas include increased inclusivity, personalized and digital learning, enhanced cognitive skills development, further integration with other subjects, ongoing emphasis on mental health, and furthering community partnerships. By incorporating these elements, health and physical education programmes can become more inclusive, engaging, and effective.

By embracing these areas of development, health and physical education delivery in New Zealand can align with the goals of the Sport New Zealand's Strategic Plan (2024a) and create a more inclusive, engaging, and effective learning experience for all students. This will contribute to the physical and mental health of young people but also help to develop a more active and engaged society.

References

Durie, M. (1998). *Whaiora: Māori Health Development* (2nd ed.). Oxford University Press.

Health New Zealand. (2018). *Physical Activity*. Te Whatu Ora; Health New Zealand. www.tewhatuora.govt.nz/for-new-zealanders/support-for-families-and-children/physical-activity#children-and-young-people-5 17-years

Ministry of Education. (2014a, April 2). Learning area structure / Health and physical education / The New Zealand Curriculum / Kia ora – NZ Curriculum Online. *Nzcurriculum.tki.org.nz.* https://nzcurriculum.tki.org.nz/The-New-Zealand-Curriculum/Health-and-physical-education/Learning-area-structure

Ministry of Education. (2014b, April 14). Health and physical education / The New Zealand Curriculum / Kia ora – NZ Curriculum Online. *Nzcurriculum.tki.org.nz.* http://nzcurriculum.tki.org.nz/The-New-Zealand-Curriculum/Health-and-physical-education

Ministry of Education. (2023, December 5). *Phones away for the Day*. Education in New Zealand. www.education.wa.edu.au/web/policies/-/student-mobile-phones-in-public-schools-policy

Netball New Zealand. (2024). *Community Coach Starter Resource*. Netball New Zealand. www.netballcentral.co.nz/images/zones/central/community-netball/NNZ_Community_Coach_Starter_Resource.pdf

New Zealand Cricket. (2024). *NZC Development Coaching Course*. New Zealand Cricket. https://play.nzc.nz/sites/default/files/2022-09/Development%20Coaching%20Course%20E-Manual.pdf

New Zealand Rugby Union. (2019). *Foundation of Rugby Coaching*. New Zealand Rugby Union.

Northern Football Region. (2024). *NRF Junior Football Handbook*. Northern Football Region. https://ecbafc.nz/media/1764/nrf-junior-handbook-2023.pdf

Sport New Zealand. (n.d.). *About Balance Is Better*. Sport New Zealand. https://balanceisbetter.org.nz/about/

Sport New Zealand. (2024a). *Sport New Zealand Strategic Plan 2024–2028*. Sport New Zealand. https://sportnz.org.nz/media/pywhcqw5/sport-nz-2024-28-strategic-plan.pdf

Sport New Zealand. (2024b). *Tū Manawa Insights Report 2024*. Sport New Zealand. https://sportnz.org.nz/media/ngtke1pb/tu-manawa-active-aotearoa-infographic-3_8-final.pdf

Stanford, E. (2023, December 19). Foundation Curriculum Policy Statements and National Curriculum Statements / Ngā Kaupapa Here Tauākī Tūāpapa Marautanga me ngā Tauākī Marautanga ā-Motu – 2023-go5904 – New Zealand Gazette. *Gazette.govt.nz*. https://gazette.govt.nz/notice/id/2023-go5904

Stats New Zealand. (2024). *Population*. www.stats.govt.nz/topics/population

The National Curriculum. (n.d.). *Community Law*. https://communitylaw.org.nz/community-law-manual/schools-kura-chapter-2-enrolment-attendance-and-the-school-system/enrolment-attendance-and-the-school-system/the-national-curriculum/

Chapter 16

Quality Physical Education in Nigeria

Franz U. Atare and Bello Odunola

Background to the Country

Nigeria is a patchwork of distinctive regions, including deserts, plains, swamps, mountains, and steamy jungles. It has one of the largest river systems in the world, including the Niger Delta, the third-largest delta on earth. Nigeria covers an area of approximately 923,768 sq. km, much of which is covered with plains and savannas. Nigeria is often called the Giant of Africa owing to its large population with over 230 million people across the 36 states and the Federal Capital Territory (FCT). For administrative and geographic convenience, the states are further grouped into six geopolitical zones (North-West, North-East, North-Central, South-West, South-East, and South-South). Nigeria has a diverse society encompassing over 371 ethnic groups and cultures. Nigeria is one of Africa's largest economies, with its approximately $395 billion GDP among the top three in the continent. The nation's wealth is largely attributed to its extensive oil and gas reserves, making it one of the world's leading oil exporters.

The World Bank (2023) reported that 30,455,582 pupils were in primary school as of 2021 and by 2023 the number rose to over 47,000,000 in 171,027 primary schools (Public 77,027; Private 94,000). As of 2019, 5.2 million students enrolled in 27,042 secondary schools (Private 9,589; Public 17,453). As of February 2024, there are 274 universities in Nigeria (Private 149; State 63; Public 62). This increase can be attributed to government efforts to improve access to education and reduce the gender gap, family income, and parents' level of education, and the quality and availability of education to improve life (UN, 2021, World Bank, 2023; Universal Basic Education Commission (UBEC), 2023). In 2022 the World Economic Forum ranked Nigeria 120th out of 136 countries concerning the quality of primary education as more than 11 million out-of-school children between the ages of 6 and 15 represent 1 in 12 out-of-school children globally. This is the highest number of out-of-school children globally (World Bank, 2022; UNICEF 2023).

The UBEC (2023) reported that Nigeria has about 1.68 million Teachers. Its 2022 national personnel audit breakup showed 1,686,535 teachers for 47,010,008 million students in 171,027 schools. The statistics show that there are acute shortages of teachers generally including physical education (PE).

Physical Education/Sport Education/Learning Activities at School

Historically, formal education was generally introduced into Nigeria by the missionaries/colonial masters in the course of evangelism and imperialism. In the Southern part of Nigeria, the introduction of Western-oriented education was exclusively due to the efforts of the Christian missionaries as they were evangelists first and educationists second, while in the north Muslim jihadists (Adejare, 2018).

With the establishment of the College of Arts, Science and Technology in Zaria now Ahmadu Bello University, PE was introduced in 1957 as a course leading to the award of a diploma. In 1960 when the University of Nigeria Nsukka was established, a Department of Physical Education in the Faculty of Education was included in the discipline of the university. In 1969, the University of Ife became the second university in Nigeria to offer PE as a degree course. In 1975, the University of Ibadan established a full Department of Physical Education. This led to the training of PE specialists in Nigeria (Omoruan & Eboh, 2016). The current Nigeria Education structure is based on a 9-3-4 system commonly referred to as the Universal Basic Education (UBE). Emphasis is placed on improvements in movement and manipulation skills and fitness levels, a better understanding of the functioning of the human body, and an increasing capacity to care for the body.

Physical Education Teacher Preparation

The goals of teacher preparation as spelt out by the National Policy on Education (Federal Ministry of Education (FME) 2020) include the need to graduate educated individuals who are prepared and committed to teaching to influence not only the intellectual life of students but also the emotional and ethical aspects of their professional careers and to acquaint prospective teachers with the rights and responsibilities of potential service. In Nigeria, the training of PE teachers is currently based on two modes. Either through a three-year training course in Physical and Health Education in a College of Education or similar institution leading to the award of the Nigeria Certificate in Education (NCE) based on the standard set by the National Commission for Colleges of Education (NCCE) Minimum Standards (2012) or a four-year degree program in PE offered by a university or a degree-awarding institution at the end of which a Bachelor of Science (B.Sc.Ed) degree or Bachelor of Education (B.Ed) is awarded. Those with NCE are admitted into three-year degree programmes in a university. All these modes of training are designed to promote quality in service delivery.

Dimensions of Quality Physical Education

In the Nigerian school system, PE is a vital component of a well-rounded education, focusing on developing physical fitness, coordination, and overall health. Recently, Physical and Health Education in Nigeria has shifted to more scientific aspects of sports performance, physical fitness, and healthful living. At the same time, it ensures quality that equips the students with the knowledge, skills, and confidence to be physically active for a lifetime. The discussions on the following sub-themes provide insight on measures for quality PE.

Skill Development and Bodily Awareness (SDBA)

The current PE curriculum has provision for learners to develop fine and gross motor skills. These include running, jumping, throwing, and catching, which improve coordination and agility. The curriculum promotes critical thinking, problem-solving, and decision-making skills as students learn to strategize in computer games and individual and team sports. Team sports and group activities in PE foster cooperation, communication, and leadership skills, helping students develop positive social interactions (Atare, 2023). Sufficient time is provided in the timetable as 120 minutes are allocated for the subject each week. Most schools run non-boarding systems so opportunities for extra periods for sporting activities are limited, but for those in boarding schools, 160 minutes are allocated. This creates ample opportunity for the students to learn and interact with classmates and also improve their knowledge of a variety of physical activities, sports, and games. (Oluwasanu & Oladepo, 2017; Ogundele & Ojo, 2019). The curriculum is very rich in content as regards the contribution of PE to overall human growth and development. Theme three borders on basic human anatomy and physiology about physical activities. The aspect of recreation and leisure helps students to develop the habit of using physical activities and sports during their spare time. The application is seen when students return to the playing field after normal school hours while waiting for their parents.

Facilities and Norms in Physical Education (FNPE)

Studies (Oluwasani et al, 2021; Bichi, 2018) have shown that most schools in Nigeria lack adequate facilities and equipment to meet the needs as stipulated by the curriculum. Maintaining the few that are available to ensure the safety of students is another serious problem in Nigerian schools (Sanni et al, 2018; Manjo, 2024). In the southern part of Nigeria, schools are relatively safe and have suitable environments for PE lessons, but in the northern part, the situation is different. This has led to the Safe School Initiative (SSI) launched by the Nigerian Government in collaboration with the UN Special Envoy for Education – Gordon Brown in 2014. The initiative aimed to ensure that every child is offered a safe place to learn, play, and realize their full potential, especially for children in emergencies and conflict (Chester, 2015). Regardless, in a majority of schools, students are given opportunities for active learning in confined spaces and well-secured environments, and this has resulted in positive sport-related attitudes and values and shown in the number willing to participate in school sports festivals. In each level of the curriculum, personal health, hygiene, care of the human body parts, and school and community health are incorporated as major learning content for the students and it is linked to the variety of sporting and games activities.

The students always look forward to PE and sports sessions as these activities serve as an outlet for fun, enjoyment, and relaxation from classroom academic activities. In Nigeria, PE is compulsory at the basic school but optional at the senior school, and as such opportunities for extracurricular and co-curricular activities are not well enforced or promoted. However, every school must organize an annual intramural sports competition.

Due to the scarcity of PE teachers, not all teachers are qualified; in some schools, former sportsmen and other subject teachers are employed as game masters who teach PE as well. The curriculum promotes inclusivity and ensures that all learners, regardless of ability, gender, or background, are given equal access and opportunity (Jona & Atare, 2019). In some instances, special schools are established to cater for the needs of those who could not benefit from regular inclusive PE activities.

Quality Teaching of Physical Education (QTPE)

The primary and secondary school curriculum for PE is general across the country as developed by the National Education and Research Development Council (NERDC) and approved by the National Council of Education. At this level, a variety of activities from fundamental movements and rhythmic activities to athletics, games, and sports provide ample opportunities for the student to develop basic skills in different physical activities and sports. First aid and safety education, personal, school and community health, pathogens, diseases and prevention, physical fitness, and body conditioning lessons assist the students in demonstrating a basic understanding of the importance of physical activities and health. Recreation, dance events, and martial arts provide opportunities for students to interact, and share ideas and feelings with the teachers when the lessons are going on (Idowu et al, 2012; Gankun et al, 2016). Gymnastics, locomotor, non-locomotor, and swimming activities are included in the curriculum basically for students to demonstrate motor skills within the context of appropriate physical activities and sports. At senior school, emphasis is placed on promoting physical fitness, motor skills, knowledge of physical activities, and understanding of health and wellness (Udomiaye & Umar, 2010). Other related topics are sports and society, human trafficking, sports law, a career in PHE, accident and safety, posture, consumer health, and non-communicable diseases. All these are designed to make the learners develop and demonstrate basic decision-making skills, and communication and set goals toward active sports participation for healthy living.

Plan for Feasibility and Accessibility of Physical Education (PFAPE)

Very few opportunities exist for international collaboration and learning opportunities for PE teachers in Nigeria. Although the British Council, UNICEF, World

Bank, UNESCO, and some NGOs do sometimes provide training, it is not holistic. In terms of a national plan for training PE teachers, there is a regular programme from UBEC and the Ministry of Education for teachers in basic public schools, not much can be said at the senior and tertiary levels. However, there have been consistent annual conferences and workshops organized by the Nigeria Association for Physical, Health Education, Recreation, Sports and Dance (NAPHERSD) and the Science Teachers Association of Nigeria (STAN) for up-to-date training and retraining of PE teachers in Nigeria.

Social Norms and Cultural Practice (SNCP)

Social norms and cultural practices significantly influence the quality of PE lessons in Nigeria. In the northern part of the country dominated by Muslims, there are specific expectations about which sports or physical activities are appropriate for different genders. This has limited participation, especially among girls, in certain activities or sports, considered "masculine" (Hamafyelto et al, 2015; Oluwasanu et al, 2021; Azzez et al, 2024) and has prohibited them from putting on sportswear that exposes any part of their body including their faces creating an unequal learning opportunity. But in other parts of the country, gender disparities do not exist.

The harsh economic conditions have influenced the resources available for PE. In most city schools, there are limited sports facilities or equipment not to mention rural areas. This hurts the development of PE and the range of activities that can be offered in PE lessons. In some areas, parents cannot afford the basic materials to support their children participating in PE lessons as students do sport on bare feet without canvas shoes or boots (Adebusoye et al, 2022).

Governmental Input for Physical Education (GIPE)

The Nigerian Government does not support research to improve the effectiveness and quality of PE. Although there is a PE desk in The FME in Nigeria indicating that the subject is recognized as part of balanced education, it has failed in the aspect of realizing its importance in the overall human development. Currently, the subject is merged with basic science at the basic school level, undermining its potential for the health and well-being of its citizens. There is no partnership with international financial institutions for PE as part of their aid programme in education. The Government has neglected the employment of quality teachers as those dying and retiring are not replaced. Even with the few available, no provision is made for training rather emphasis is placed on Science Technology Engineering, and Mathematics (STEM).

Governments have supported the development of PE policies that ensure all have equal access to PE such as making PE and Sports compulsory at all levels and provision of basic sports facilities for approval to be given to run a private school, yet not implemented.

Cognitive Skill Development (CSD)

PE lessons in Nigerian schools play a significant role in promoting CSD in several ways. The activities assist the students in performing critical thinking skills like planning, organizing, strategizing, and managing time are learnt from lessons taught in schools which often involve games and activities that require students to use these skills, such as setting goals, following rules, and making quick decisions (Coimbra et al, 2021). For instance, football and basketball often involve developing strategies, working as a team, and adapting to changing situations and also promote social and emotional learning, which is linked to cognitive development. Through group activities and team sports, students learn conflict-resolution skills. Activities like dance, gymnastics, and certain sports that are found in the curriculum encourage creativity and the exploration of new ways to move and solve problems (Kryshtanovych et al, 2020). This can translate into innovative thinking and independent thoughts that can be transferred to other aspects of life. In the end, the students can develop socially acceptable moral thinking and behaviour.

Habituated Behaviour in Physical Activities (HBPA)

The knowledge gained in PE lessons that regular physical activity reduces the risk of various health issues such as obesity, cardiovascular diseases, diabetes, and mental health disorders assists the students in making decisions for maintaining a healthy life (Hagger, 2019). An average Nigerian school child can engage in regular physical activities without supervision with their mates/peers demonstrating to an extent an understanding of the relationship between physical and sports activities to personal and social development. During sports and other community events, students are highly enthusiastic to take up suitable responsibilities of service such as cleaning, setting canopies, marking fields and courts, and other activities that may require physical strength. In Nigeria looking for students with advanced proficiency in different physical activities and sport is not an issue as these skills abound in every community. This is a result of skills developed during PE activities in school as can be seen in interschool sports competitions, community sports meets, and Nigeria's participation in international sporting activities which is sustainable for many as lifetime participation.

Barriers and the Ways Forward to Physical Education in Nigeria

Numerous factors are working against quality PE in Nigeria such as a shortage of qualified PE teachers in the school system, inadequate provision of infrastructure and equipment and facilities in schools, religious and cultural interference; and poor economic situation in the country. Also, poor implementation of educational policies, absence of international aid partners for the PE programme, and ineffective monitoring and evaluation mechanisms.

The Ways Forward

Government support is essential for creating a qualitative, comprehensive, and effective PE programme that can enhance students' physical health, mental well-being, and overall academic performance.

- There should be massive recruitment and continuous professional development for teachers to stay updated with the latest trends.
- All students should equally have access to the necessary resources to participate fully in PE activities.
- The government should take an active interest in sourcing funding to promote PE and sports.
- There should be regular intramural and extramural events that encourage active participation from everyone.
- The PE program must offer a variety of activities so that all students can find something to enjoy, which will increase life-long participation.
- Policies promoting mass participation in PE and sports should be implemented and strictly adhered to.

Conclusion

Improving the quality of PE requires a multidimensional approach. Skill development and body awareness must be given topmost priority. Adequate facilities that conform with the norms of the community should be provided for use by well-trained teachers to meet the needs of the learners. All should be given equal opportunity to access easily PE programmes irrespective of their diversity and ability status. Cultural practices and religious norms that tend to interfere with quality service delivery should be discarded and there should be a renewed commitment from the Government and other significant stakeholders to fund sports and PE programmes in school to promote both CSD and habituated learning for life-long experience. This can best be achieved when PE is made compulsory at all levels.

References

Adebusoye, B., Leonardi-Bee, J., Phalkey, R., & Chattopadhyay, K. (2022). Barriers and facilitators of physical activity among school attending adolescents in Lagos state, Nigeria: A qualitative study exploring views and experiences of decision-makers in secondary schools. *Health Science Report.* 6(2), e997. DOI: 10.1002/hsr2.997

Adejare, B. (2018). Influence of missionary and colonization on educational development in Nigeria. *International Journal of Educational Research and Management Technology.* 3(2), 12–19.

Atare, F. U. (2023). The Power of Extracurricular Sport Activities: Reminiscing on the Nigerian School Situation. In Fadoju, et al (Eds). *A Life Time in Human Kinetics: A Festschrift in Honour of Prof. B. O. Asagba.* Ibadan: Department of Human Kinetics, University of Ibadan. pp 1–8.

Azzez, F. A., Osiesi, M. P., Aribamikan, C. G., Doh-Nubia, W,m Odinko, M. N., Blignaut, S., & Oderinwale, T. A. (2024). Exclusion of the female child from primary education: exploring the perceptions and experiences of female learners in northern Nigeria. *International Journal of Primary, Elementary and Early Years Education.* 3(13), 1–20. www.tandfonline.com/doi/epdf/10.1080/03004279.2024.2308307?needAccess=true

Bichi, S. M. (2018). Constraint to teaching and learning physical education and sports in Nigeria. *FUDMA Journal of Sciences.* 2(1), 139–142.

Chester, S. (2015). *Introducing the Safe School initiative in Nigeria.* https://pie.pascalobservatory.org/pascalnow/blogentry/associate-features/introducing-safe-schools-initiative-ssi-nigeria

Coimbra, M., Cody, R., Kreppke, J., & Gerber, M. (2021). Impact of physical education based behavioural skill training program on cognitive antecedents of exercise and sport behaviour among adolescents: a cluster randomized control trial. *Physical Education and Sport Pedagogy.* 26(1), 16–35. DOI:10.1080/17408989.2020.1799966

Federal Ministry of Education (FME) (2020). *National Policy on Education.* Abuja: Federal Ministry of Education.

Gankon, B., Udo, E., Anchau, I. Y., Udoudoh, F. A., Atare, F. U., Jatau, A. A., Usman, B., & Oladeji, F. (2016). *STAN Basic Science and Technology for Primary Schools.* [UBE Edition]. Ibadan: University Press Plc.

Hagger, M. S. (2019). Habit and physical activity, theoretical advances, practical implications and agenda for future research. *Psychology of Sports and Exercise.* 42, 118–129.

Hamafyelto, S. S., Nahshon, l. H., & Ndahi, M. P. (2015). Personal, social and environmental correlates of sports participation among varsity student-athletes in insurgency ridden areas of northern Nigeria. *Case Study Journal.* 4(8), 59–65.

Idowu, B., Jimoh, A., & Gbagi, L. (2012). *Physical and Health Education for Primary Schools.* [UBE edition]. Ibadan: University Press Plc.

Jona, I., & Atare, F. U. (2019). Promoting inclusive education in adapted physical education, recreation, and sport. *International Journal of Educational Research and Development.* 7:143–147.

Kryshtanovych, S., Bilostotska, O., Lilianova, V., & Tkachova, T. (2020). Experience in the application of cognitive techniques in the field of physical education and sport. *BRAIN: Broad Research in Artificial Intelligence and Neuroscience.* 11(2), 147–159.

Manjo, Y. G. (2024). Examining the administrative structure and implementation approach of a safe school initiative in Nigeria. *Journal of Political Discourse.* 2(1), 212–220

National Commission for Colleges of Education (NCCE) (2012). *Nigeria Certificate in Education Minimum Standards for General Education.* NCCE. www.ncceonline.edu.ng/NCCE-Digitization/minstandard/new_cul_pdf/general_edu.pdf

Ogundele, B. O., & Ojo, O. R. (2019). Impact of physical fitness activities on students' basic science achievement in selected Nigerian secondary schools. *Annual Journal of Technical University, Varna. Bulgaria.* 3(2), 21–31.

Oluwasanu, M. M., & Oladepo, O. (2017). Qualitative views of Nigerian school principals and teachers on the barrier and opportunities for promoting students' physical activity behaviours within the school setting. *BMC Public Health.* 21, 1–12

Oluwasanu, M. M., Oladepo, O., & Ibitoye, S. E. (2021). Effects of a multi-level intervention on the pattern of physical activity among in-school adolescents in Oyo state Nigeria: a cluster randomised trial. *BMC Public Health.* 17, 1–11

Omoruan, J. C., & Eboh, L. O. (2016). *A Handbook on Physical Education and Sports*. (2nd Edition). Benin-City: Justice-Jeco Printing and Publishing Global.

Sanni, D. M., Ede, C., & Fashina, A. A. (2018). A study on the effects of inadequate sports equipment and facilities on sports development and academic performance in primary schools: a case study of Bwari Area council of Abuja-Nigeria. *SPC Journal of Education*. 1(1), 4–8

Udomiaye, M., & Umar, Z. (2010). *Understanding Physical and Health Education for Junior Secondary School*. Benin-City: Waka Fast Publishers.

UNICEF (2023). *The Challenge: One in Every Five in the World Out-of-School Is in Nigeria*. Abuja: UNICEF Nigeria.

United Nations (2021). *United Nations Country Annual Results Reports in Nigeria*. https://nigeria.un.org/en/203764-un-country-annual-results-report-nigeria-2021

Universal Basic Education Commission (UBEC) (2023). *Reports: Universal Basic Education Commission*. Abuja: Universal Basic Education Commission. www.ubec.gov.ng

World Bank (2023). *Education Statistics: Country at a Glance – Nigeria*. World Bank Group.

World Bank (2022). *Nigeria Development Update*. World Bank Group.

Chapter 17

Quality Physical Education in the Philippines

Challenges and Opportunities

Marvin Luis C. Sabado, Zyra Ruth T. Brebante, Marie Eloisa D. Ulanday, Henry C. Daut, Mila A. Gallardo, Atreju Mikhail Sam A. Gallardo, Michelle Layao, and Abdulrasid T. Lucman

Introduction

Physical education (PE) is an integral part of the educational process and plays a significant role in schools. It is the only subject that focuses on the total development of an individual – physical, mental, social, and moral and contributes to values learning, knowledge, and skills acquisition in health, fitness, sports, recreation, and dance among others. It aims to promote awareness, appreciation, and active participation in sports and physical activity for a healthy and active lifestyle among individuals.

The Declaration of Berlin 2013 recognized that "Physical education is the most effective means of providing all children and youth with the skills, attitudes, values, knowledge, and understanding for lifelong participation in society" (UNESCO, 2015). PE plays a multifaceted and vital role in the educational system. It helps students develop and maintain their physical health by engaging in regular physical activity. Engaging in physical activities promotes student's mental and emotional well-being, relieves stress, and boosts self-esteem and confidence. Participation in physical activities has been shown to enhance cognitive development by improving memory and concentration. It also promotes problem-solving skills as well as critical thinking and decision-making.

Furthermore, PE provides opportunities for social and behavioral development by promoting teamwork, cooperation, communication, and important life skills such as discipline, perseverance, and resilience. Sports and physical activities have been shown to promote inclusivity and diversity by providing opportunities for students of all backgrounds and abilities to participate, enjoy, and excel, thereby contributing to long-term health benefits for students. Scientific evidence supporting the significant role of physical activity in the health and well-being of individuals has been extensively documented and PE plays an important role in public health (Pate, Corbin, Simons-Morton, & Ross, 1987; Sallis & McKenzie, 1991).

The growing concern for the well-being of future generations worldwide highlighted the important role of PE beyond the academic requirements in schools. PE is often given less priority in many countries around the world characterized by poor implementation, limited funding, inadequate time allotment, lack of facilities and equipment, and lack of well-trained professionals among others. The alarming levels of physical inactivity resulting in increasing rates of obesity and other non-communicable diseases around the world highlighted the impact of physical activity participation and focused attention on the quality of PE in schools.

Quality PE represents the best opportunity to provide all children with physical activity experiences that promote physical activity now and for a lifetime (Masurier & Corbin, 2006). Enhancing the quality of PE in schools worldwide can significantly contribute to developing future generations of healthy, more resilient, socially responsible, and citizens. There is an urgent need to reassess the status of PE as a profession, highlight its significance in schools, and promote quality PE as an instrument for healthy, strong, and productive students, communities, and societies.

Quality Physical Education in the Philippines

The 1987 Philippine Constitution affirms the significant role of PE in the total development of an individual as stipulated in Article XIV, Section 19 of the Constitution which states that

> The State shall promote PE and encourage sports programs, league competitions, and amateur sports, including training for international competitions, to foster self-discipline, teamwork, and excellence for the development of a healthy and alert citizenry. All educational institutions shall undertake regular sports activities throughout the country in cooperation with athletic clubs and other sectors.
> (Official Gazette, 1987)

Republic Act No. 5708 known as The Schools Physical Education and Sports Development Act of 1969 provided for:

> An integrated physical education and sports development program in all schools in the Philippines (Section 2) ... to instill in young citizens a proper appreciation of the importance of physical development hand in hand with the mental development in individual and social activities; ... provide opportunities for the athletic development of children and youth who have the competitive spirit as well as grace, coordination, stamina, and strength; and provision for a well-rounded PE program must be addressed to physical growth, social training, and personal discipline for all pupils and students, as well as superior athletic achievement for those who are psychologically inclined and physically gifted.
> (Supreme Court E-Library, 2019)

Every school in the Philippines is mandated to offer PE programs to provide opportunities to all children and teach them the knowledge and skills needed to establish and sustain an active healthy lifestyle and promote alert citizenry.

In response to the need of the changing times, the present PE curriculum for basic education in the Philippines shifted from the previous sport-dominated PE curriculum to a health and movement-related curriculum anchored on the tenet "Move to Learn, Learn to Move." The core of the K to 12 PE Curriculum is fitness and movement education including value, knowledge, skills, and experiences in physical activity participation to achieve and maintain health-related fitness (HRF) and optimize health. It hopes to instill an understanding of why HRF is important so that the learner can translate this knowledge into action. Time allotment for PE in the Philippines consists of 40 minutes/week for Grades 1–6; 60 minutes/week for Grades 7–10; and 129 minutes/week for Grades 11–12, while at Kindergarten, it is integrated with other subject areas (Department of Education (DepEd), 2016).

Implementing quality PE in the Philippines poses a big challenge considering the many issues and concerns that need to be addressed. Limited government support, inadequate facilities and equipment, lack of qualified PE teachers in many schools, time allotment, resource materials, and the long-standing problem of undervaluing PE among others. The review and revision of the PE curriculum in basic education brought a lot of promise for quality PE in schools. Efforts are being exerted to enhance the quality of PE in the country through curricular revisions, infrastructure development, teacher training, and funding support.

Despite efforts to make education a key priority in the country, the Philippine education system continues to face significant challenges that prevent many Filipinos from accessing education. Major challenges include poverty, armed conflicts, and lack of resources and infrastructure. In addition, teachers are overworked and receive low salaries compared to other countries (Chalk & Bai, 2023). There is an urgent need to elevate the status of PE in the Philippines as an important subject in schools from a perceived status of a "second-class" profession to a "first-class" status by providing evidence of quality PE and its link to the outcomes of physical activity participation to individuals.

The Eight Dimensions of Quality Physical Education in the Philippines

Skill Development and Bodily Awareness

The present PE curriculum under the K-12 basic education of the DepEd provides students with a progressive development in physical literacy. It helps students acquire knowledge, understanding, and skills in body management, movement skills, rhythms and dance, games and sports, and physical fitness for Grades 1–3. It allows students to participate in diverse physical activities, interact with others, and encourage physical activity participation beyond PE classes and after school. Grades 4–10 focus on physical fitness, games and sports (individual and dual sports, Team sports), and rhythms and dance. Grades 11 and 12 center on fitness and sports, and dance and recreation (aquatics and mountaineering), respectively (DepEd, 2016). The revised PE curriculum and its content are on point in achieving skill development and bodily awareness among students while enhancing skills acquisition in sports for after-school physical activities.

The PE curriculum focuses on developing fitness, movement skills, and healthy behaviors. It consists of five learning strands including body management, movement skills, games and sports, rhythm and dance, and physical fitness. The health curriculum aims to develop students' health literacy and promote lifelong wellness. It covers various health content areas such as injury prevention, nutrition, growth and development, and substance abuse. Both curricula emphasize a learner-centered approach and developing students' knowledge, attitudes, and skills for active and healthy living (DepEd, 2023a, 2023b, 2023c).

In line with the revised PE curriculum, the DepEd conducted trainings, seminars, and workshops to prepare and equip physical educators on the new curriculum. Training on the MATATAG Curriculum for teachers and school leaders was conducted in various regions in the Philippines to provide professional development and support for teachers and school leaders, ensuring an in-depth understanding of the curriculum (DepEd RIII, 2024). A series of School-Based Training of Teachers on the MATATAG Curriculum (Professional Regulation Commission, 2024) was held in schools nationwide (DepEd DM 251, s. 2024). The training helps ensure that the physical educators are well prepared to deliver quality PE to students in the schools by equipping them with the knowledge and skills to achieve the program's goals.

PE and health assessment are aligned with national standards and established grade-level outcomes and is included in the written PE and health curriculum, along with the different department orders, i.e., DO 8, s. 2015 and DO 31, s. 2020, and assessment practices set in the general assessment guidelines. It utilizes different assessment practices relevant to P E and health, like developmental and age-appropriate assessment. It includes evidence-based practices that measure student achievement in all areas of instruction, including physical fitness (DepEd, 2023c).

Facilities and Norms in Physical Education

Facilities and equipment are vital components in effective teaching and learning in PE and sports. The DepEd through its *Revised Education Facilities Manual* outlined the facility requirements for schools to include facilities for PE and sports as part of the learning environment for educational growth. Guidelines for the planning, design, construction, management, maintenance, and supervision are specified not only for the sole purpose of an improved PE program but also for the use of pupils/students and teachers in all other educational activities (DepEd, 2010).

Facilities, equipment, resources, and curriculum flexibility were considered significant factors in assessing the quality of PE in schools (Panganiban, 2019). Many schools in rural areas lack the necessary PE facilities and equipment to provide quality physical education. Studies conducted showed the lack of facilities, spaces, and equipment as one of the major challenges of PE in schools.

PE is a required subject in schools in the Philippines. However, provisions for differently abled students or those with handicaps are not emphasized in elementary and secondary physical education. There are very few differently abled students enrolled in the schools. Participation in physical activities is limited. In tertiary schools, adaptive PE subjects are offered to cater to differentially abled students.

In helping students extend their learning experiences after school, the DepEd through Memorandum No. 005, s. 2013 encourages all schools to establish a Sports Club Program where students can participate in sports to enhance physical literacy, optimize health, strengthen character development, and create pathways for long-term development and success. This after-school sports program allows students to extend their learning experiences, and further develop their skills in sports as well as values and attitudes to help them succeed in sports and more significantly in life (DepEd, 2023c).

The institutionalization of the Palarong Pambansa (National Games) as the premier sporting event for basic and secondary education students in both public and private schools provides opportunities for highly skilled athletes to compete. The program promotes PE and sports as an integral part of the basic education curriculum for holistic youth development. It further inculcates the values of discipline, solidarity, sportsmanship, teamwork, excellence, and fair play, as well as promoting and achieving peace through sports (Supreme Court E-Library, 2013).

Quality Teaching of Physical Education

The MATATAG Physical Education and Health curriculum of the DepEd is geared toward the development and attainment of physical and health literacy as well as 21st-century skills that contribute to the well-being of the individual, family, community, improve the quality of life in society, and motivate them to take responsibility for their lifelong holistic health and well-being in a varied and rapidly changing society (DepEd, 2023c).

The PE curriculum in schools is designed for students to acquire knowledge and skills in physical activities and sports. The conduct of PE classes in schools consists of theoretical and practical applications of the knowledge and skills learned. Students are taught the foundation of the activity by introducing its history, values, safety, terminologies, fundamental skills, basic rules, and scoring among others. The practical aspect of PE class includes the introduction and demonstration of the skills to be learned, practice of the skills, identification of errors and corrections, and the formation of groups or teams where students can participate in a team. During practice, various approaches are utilized to enhance learning and performance. While the traditional approach is commonly used, the infusion of the teaching game for understanding and the games-based approach is incorporated. These methods allow students to develop not only the technical aspect of learning the skill but also the ability to develop critical thinking and decision-making.

The lack of professionally prepared PE teachers in many schools, particularly in rural areas of the country is a major concern. The low supply of PE graduates creates a gap filled by those with little or no background in physical education. Many teachers whose areas of specialization are not in PE are assigned to teach PE subjects. The recent changes in the PE curriculum require learning and unlearning to meet the demands of the changes in the content of the curriculum. Imbalanced teacher-to-student ratios, shortages in classrooms, and large class sizes have perennially plagued the education sector in the Philippines including PE (Filoteo, 2021).

The DepEd in its efforts to strengthen the competencies of physical educators in implementing the revised curriculum in PE conducts the annual School-Based Training of Teachers in Physical Education (SBTT). The objective of the training is to provide professional development support to teachers in implementing the revised curriculum by acquiring the necessary knowledge, skills, and competencies to provide quality PE (Philippine Regulation Commission, 2024).

Plans for Feasibility and Accessibility of Physical Education (PFAPE)

International collaboration and learning opportunities for PE teachers in the Philippines are aplenty. PE teachers are encouraged to attend international and local conferences, seminars, congresses, and training. It allows PE professionals to present their research work at the global level, thereby opening opportunities for possible linkages and collaboration. It also allows them to gain new insights and generate new ideas apart from learning new and best practices in instructional delivery. Hosting international conferences and seminars in the Philippines enables more PE practitioners to access and benefit from attending at a minimal cost. Funding from each academic institution's Research and Dissemination (R and D) unit is available for participants.

In 1985, the National Educator Academy of the Philippines (NEAP) was established to ensure a more effective and efficient implementation of DepEd's professional enhancement programs for its teachers and administrators. NEAP is tasked to tap various stakeholders to provide quality education, thus promoting greater accountability and smooth delivery of DepEd's curriculum (DepEd Region VIII, 2020).

The increase in the number of national organizations or associations in PE resulted in a more vibrant promotion and development of the profession. In recent years, numerous seminars have been held to upgrade the skills and know-how of PE teachers nationwide. In 2021, while the world was still reeling from the effects of the COVID-19 pandemic, the 1st International Physical Education Conference was launched to provide PE academics and academicians a platform to highlight trends and issues in the field. This was followed by the National Physical Education Teachers' Convention in 2022 (1Physed.Ph, n.d.). The 2023 and 2024 National Physical Education Convention convened to give clear direction and provide a richer perspective of the salient role of PE teachers in promoting and facilitating lifetime fitness and wellness and sports participation amongst the students (DepEd

Region VIII, 2022). Likewise, PE teachers participate in teaching enhancement seminars, trainings, and clinics conducted by other government agencies like the Philippine Sports Commission (PSC), the Philippine Olympic Committee (POC), and the National Sports Associations (NSA).

The DepEd is steadfast in improving the K-12 Basic Education Program in the Philippines including its service delivery to all its stakeholders. To realize these, the DepEd established partnerships and linkages (DepEd, 2013).

The MATATAG Curriculum was launched on August 10, 2023, with partial implementation in different grade levels this School Year 2024–2025. It aims to enhance Filipino student's competencies in reading, mathematics, and life skills. The MATATAG Curriculum implementation envisions an academic environment that is conducive to producing competent, job-ready, active, responsible, and patriotic citizens. Before the start of the school year, intensive training for teachers was laid out to fully implement the desired transformative goals of the MATATAG Curriculum by learning innovative strategies for curriculum delivery, assessment, and support mechanisms (ICT, n.d.).

Social Norms and Cultural Practice

The Philippines is a multi-ethnic country consisting of more than 100 ethnolinguistic tribes inhabiting various regions of the archipelago. Filipino, the national language, and English are used as the medium of instruction and communication in schools and offices. In 2012, the DepEd adopted the "Mother Tongue-Based Multilingual Education" program as a medium of instruction in schools. The aim is to enhance the learning of students using language used at home.

Studies on the application of mother tongue in other subject areas were made with favorable results; however, no research was conducted on the effectiveness of mother tongue in the teaching of physical education. In Southern Philippines, specifically Mindanao, the population is a mixture of Muslims, Christians, and Indigenous People or "Lumad." Cultural sensitivity is observed in the teaching of PE with consideration to the cultural and religious practices of the students including attire, body contact, and separation of male and female students.

Furthermore, traditional and indigenous sports and games are incorporated into PE activities to safeguard, preserve, promote, and propagate the rich cultural heritage of Filipinos. This promotes cultural awareness, cultural pride, and identity and contributes to understanding, unity, and peace.

Most classes in Philippine schools consist of boys and girls with a few exclusive schools for boys or girls in urban centers. PE classes in basic education are coeducational and require teachers to be culture- and gender-sensitive. An analysis of gender issues in teaching PE revealed that PE teachers need to work on delivering subject matter, planning lessons, and developing didactics in a way that is more gender sensitive. Furthermore, PE teachers lacked the preparation to discuss gender concepts, regulations, standards, and development approaches in instructing PE (Mortejo, 2023).

Governmental Input for Physical Education

The government plays a vital role in promoting quality PE and physical activity through policy. PE is recognized as a significant component in the total educational development of an individual while contributing to the realization of human potential and the well-being of people in society. An evaluation of existing policies promoting physical activity among Filipino youth identified 17 policies that cover promoting physical activity mainly through sports participation and active transport among students, student-athletes, physical education, physical activities, persons with disabilities, and the general population in school and community settings (Palad et al., 2023).

Other government agencies involved in the promotion of physical activity, physical education, and sports include the PSC, the Commission on Higher Education (CHED), and the Department of Interior and Local Government Unit (DILG). The PSC is the sole policy-making and coordinating body of all amateur sports development programs and institutions in the Philippines and is mandated "to provide the leadership, formulate the policies, and set the priorities and directions of all national sports promotion and development, particularly giving emphasis on grassroots participation" (PSC, 2021). PSC has partnered with the DepEd, the CHED, and the DILG in all programs related to sports, physical education, and grassroots development.

The PSC through the Philippine Sports Institute (PSI) conducts sports clinics, seminars, and training for PE teachers, coaches, and sports leaders. The National Coaching Certification Program of the PSI caters to coaches from the schools providing a multi-level certification course to improve coaching in the schools and the country, particularly at the grassroots level. PSC also provides funding and technical assistance to various programs of DepEd, CHED, and DILG (PSC, 2023). The above-mentioned government agencies assist in the training and enhancement of knowledge and skills of coaches and physical educators in schools.

Cognitive Skill Development

The present PE under the MATATAG Curriculum combines PE and health. It provides a more comprehensive educational experience for the learners by teaching practical skills for exercise and sports and learning how to make appropriate healthy choices in their daily lives (DepEd, 2023c). Through game-like practices and actual competitions, students can develop the ability to read situations, evaluate tactical knowledge, and make appropriate decisions during practices and competitions. PE activities, likewise, provide opportunities to make socially acceptable moral judgments during sports and physical activity and help develop critical thinking, moral judgments, values of fair play, integrity, sportsmanship, and camaraderie.

Habituated Behavior in Physical Activities

The DepEd instituted programs to encourage physical activity participation to promote and develop healthy habits among students during school and beyond.

It issued Memorandum Order no. 060 s. 2021 providing guidelines on Galaw Pilipinas (Move Philippines) as DepEd's National Calisthenics Exercise Program. Its aim is to promote an active lifestyle for Filipinos that will benefit both their physical and socio-emotional well-being, improve health and wellness, enhance cultural awareness by integrating Philippine cultures in the exercise, and inculcate nationalism, unity, and discipline among student-learners.

Likewise, the sports club program was instituted with the purpose of enhancing physical literacy through engagement in various physical activities in key stages of learning, formation of character through values-based approached, and creation of pathways for long-term development and success (Miranda, 2023). These programs aim to encourage regular participation in sports and physical activities not only to promote health and well-being but also to develop skills to engage in sports within and outside of the school programs for recreation or competition.

Challenges and Opportunities of Quality Physical Education

PE in the Philippines has struggled to establish itself as an important part of the school curriculum. The challenges facing PE in the country are many covering both as a profession and as a subject area in the school curriculum. Among the major challenges include: (1) perception of PE as a subject area; (2) budgetary constraints; (3) inadequate facilities and equipment for physical education; (4) a crowded curriculum; (5) lack of professional development; and (6) inadequate time allotment.

Compared to other subject areas, PE is perceived and treated as a "second class" subject area by administrators and students. Elevating the status of PE as an important component of the total educational development of students in the school is a major challenge that needs to be addressed by the practitioners. The limited funding for physical education, the crowded curriculum in schools where PE is combined with Music, Arts, and Health (MAPEH), the lack of facilities and equipment, and the lack of professional development indicate how PE is valued and treated in schools.

Providing quality PE in schools is vital in elevating the status of PE in the school curriculum. It provides a strong justification for the need to address the issues and concerns of PE and highlights its vital role in the total development of students. It promotes lifelong participation in sports and physical activities contributing to the development of a healthier, stronger, more resilient, and productive citizenry.

Conclusion

The Philippines is working toward quality PE in schools with the recent revision of the PE curriculum under the MATATAG program. Despite the challenges faced by

PE as a subject area and PE professionals, there are indicators of PE practices that can be enhanced based on the dimensions of quality physical education. There is a need for PE professionals to be organized into a strong force to lobby and work for the interest of the profession. Training programs in delivering quality PE are necessary to equip physical educators with the knowledge and skills to provide quality service to students. The significance of quality PE goes beyond its role as a subject in schools but to its impact on the health and well-being of the people in the country and the world.

References

Chalk, B., & Bai, N. (2023 August 5). *Philippine Institute for Development Studies. Educational Challenges in the Philippines.* PIDS. https://pids.gov.ph/details/news/in-the-news/educational-challenges-in-the-philippines

Department of Education (DepEd). (2010). *Educational Facilities Manual.* DepEd. www.teacherph.com/deped-educational-facilities-manual/

Department of Education (DepEd). (2013, February 13). *February 13, 2013 DO 8, s. 2013 – Policy Guidelines on Regulating the Issuance of DepEd Advisories.* www.deped.gov.ph/2013/02/13/do-8-s-2013-policy-guidelines-on-regulating-the-issuance-of-deped-advisories/?fbclid=IwY2xjawFcRMlleHRuA2FlbQIxMAABHZlITXBT0Qlw4QuyO6ky-ZV1Z44BSYgKxB9VCh9DQ7iDcTS0EYwuaZATGw_aem_XVNuScAIPQyKRQ51TQ7n5w

Department of Education (DepEd). (2016, May). *K–12 Curriculum Guide Physical Education.* www.deped.gov.ph/wp-content/uploads/2019/01/PE-CG.pdf

Department of Education (DepEd). (2023a). *K to 12 Curriculum Guide: Physical Education.* www.deped.gov.ph/wp-content/uploads/2019/01/PE-CG.pdf

Department of Education (DepEd). (2023b). *MATATAG Curriculum Physical Education and Health Grades 4–7.* www.deped.gov.ph/wp-content/uploads/PE-and-HEALTH_CG-2023_Grade-4-and-7.pdf

Department of Education (DepEd). (2023c). *MATATAG Curriculum | Department of Education.* (2023). www.deped.gov.ph/matatag-curriculum/

Department of Education (DepEd). (2024). *Conduct of School-Based Training of Teachers (SBTT) on the Matatag Curriculum.* www.depedsdo1pangasinan.com/post/conduct-of-school-based-training-of-teachers-sbtt-on-the-matatag-curriculum

DepEd DM 251, s. 2024 (2024). Submission of district/eddis consolidated report on the learning camp volunteers assessment and selection for the 2024 national learning camp. *Department of Education.* https://bulacandeped.com.ph/division-memorandum-no-251-s-2024-submission-of-district-eddis-consolidated-report-on-the-learning-camp-volunteers-assessment-and-selection-for-the-2024-national-learning-camp/

DepEd Region VIII. (2020, May 5). *APRIL 29, 2020 DO 006, S. 2020 – Adoption of the National Educators Academy of the Philippines (NEAP) Interim Structure.* https://region8.deped.gov.ph/2020/05/05/april-29-2020-do-006-s-2020-adoption-of-the-national-educators-academy-of-the-philippines-neap-interim-structure/?fbclid=IwY2xjawFcS9xleHRuA2FlbQIxMAABHfZ6blKs7BynCG5Gbh_Ev0Nhps6fvjiV8TjiDjytOqjKO4Ulf9DBHiAQww_aem_IWDLpHIH7Fegaqirchfr CA

DepEd Region VIII. (2022, September 16). *SEPTEMBER 15, 2022 RA 150, S. 2022–2022 National Physical Education Teachers' Convention.* https://region8.deped.gov.ph/2022/09/16/september-15-2022-ra-150-s-2022-2022-national-physical-education-teachers-convention/

DepEd RIII. (2024). *RM 10, s. 2024 Training on the Matatag Curriculum for Teachers and School Leaders.* www.scribd.com/document/698925583/Rm-No-010-s-2024-Training-on-the-Matatag-Curriculum-for-Teachers-and-School-Leaders

Filoteo, M. (2021). *The Philippine Education System in Crisis, Philippine Institute for Development Studies.* https://pidswebs.pids.gov.ph/CDN/NEWS/09_26_medium.pdf

ICT. (n.d.). *CPDAS | Professional Regulation Commission.* https://cpdas.prc.gov.ph/public/nameOfProvider.aspx?id=qAuzfW%2BUljX0yjl0b2hSOQ%3D%3D#:~:text=The%20Division%20Training%20of%20Trainers,in%20schools%20across%20the%20division

Masurier, G. L., & Corbin, C. (2006). Top 10 reasons for quality physical education. *Journal of Physical Education, Recreation & Dance, 77*(6), 1–58. DOI:10.1080/07303084.2006.10597894

Miranda, R. (2023). *DepEd Sports Manual Overview.* Slideshare. www.slideshare.net/slideshow/depedsportsmanualoverviewpptx/255925523

Mortejo, A. L. (2023). A descriptive analysis on the gender issues in teaching physical education. *International Journal of Multidisciplinary Educational Research and Innovation. 1*(2). 155–161. doi: 10.5281/zenodo.7947463

Official Gazette. (1987). *The Constitution of the Republic of the Philippines.* www.officialgazette.gov.ph/constitutions/1987-constitution/

Palad, Y. Y., Guisihan, R. M., Aguila, M. E. R., Ramos, R. A. A., & Cagas, J. Y. (2023). An evaluation of policies promoting physical activity among Filipino youth. *International Journal of Environmental Research & Public Health 20*(4), 13pp. https://doi.org/10.3390/ijerph20042865

Panganiban, T. D. C. (2019). Quality assessment of physical education program of state universities in the Philippines. *Jurnal SPORTIF : Jurnal Penelitian Pembelajaran. 5*(2), 166–174. https://doi.org/10.29407/js_unpgri.v5i2.12983

Pate, R. R., Corbin, C. B., Simons-Morton, B. G., & Ross, J. G. (1987). Physical education and its role in school health promotion. *Journal of School Health, 57*(10), 445–450.

Philippine Regulation Commission. (2024). *Examination and Registration Service.* Philippine Regulation Commission. www.prc.gov.ph/

Philippine Sports Commission (PSC). (2021). *Republic Act No. 6847 An Act Creating and Establishing the Philippine Sports Commission, Defining Its Powers, Functions and Responsibilities, Appropriating Funds Therefor, and for Other Purposes.* www.psc.gov.ph/images/vitaldocuments2021v9_spread_compressed.pdf

Philippine Sports Commission (PSC). (2023). *PSC Programs and Projects 2023–2028.* https://psc.gov.ph/psc_site/wp-content/uploads/2023/12/ProgramsandProjects.pdf

Professional Regulation Commission. (2024). *School-Based Training of Teachers on the Matatag Curriculum.* https://cpdas.prc.gov.ph/public/nameOfProvider.aspx?id=7nF51j%2BJTR7Hsj24rOF9Zg%3D%3D

1Physed.Ph. (n.d.). *Programs & Activities.* www.1physedph.com/programs-activities/

Sallis, J. F., & McKenzie, T. L. (1991). Physical education's role in public health. *Research Quarterly for Exercise and Sport, 62*(2), 124–137.

Supreme Court E-Library (2013). Memorandum Circular No. 49, July 04, 2013 (Authorizing all government agencies and instrumentalities to extend support and participate in the

"Laro'T Saya Sa Parke" Project. Supreme Court. https://elibrary.judiciary.gov.ph/thebookshelf/showdocs/11/59173

Supreme Court E-Library. (2019). *An Act Providing for the Promotion and Financing of an Integrated Physical Education and Sports Development Program for the Schools in the Philippines*. Republic Act No. 5708, June 21, 1969. https://elibrary.judiciary.gov.ph/thebookshelf/showdocs/2/7676

UNESCO. (2015). *Quality Physical Education (QPE): Guidelines for Policymakers*. https://unesdoc.unesco.org/ark:/48223/pf0000231101

Chapter 18

Quality Physical Education in Puerto Rico

Luisa Velez

History of Puerto Rico

Archipelago of Puerto Rico is located between the Caribbean Sea and the Atlantic Ocean, East of the Dominican Republic, west of the British Virgin Islands, and northwest of the U.S. Virgin Islands. The Island is 110 miles long from east to west and 40 miles from north to south. Puerto Rico's strategic location has played a fundamental role in its historical, socioeconomic, and political development. Its geostrategic (logistical) value as a bastion of war and its potential as a center of exchange and dialogue in the region has lent the two powers that have colonized Puerto Rico (in the little more than 520 years to the present) to maintain its presence (Flores Ortiz, 2016).

The history of Puerto Rico is traced to an indigenous people between 3000 and 2000 B.C. Evidence of ball games and ballparks where games took place suggests Tainos enjoyed structured physical activity. The arrival of Christopher Columbus in 1493 challenged the dominant indigenous culture of the natives. The Spanish Crown ruled the Island from 1493 until the Treaty of Paris in 1898. The Treaty of Paris provided for the succession of Puerto Rico from Spain to the United States of America. It is at this moment in history and as a result of the Spanish–American War that Puerto Rico became a territory of the United States later negotiating a commonwealth-type government.

To appreciate the present situation of Puerto Rico's public education system and its physical education (PE) program, it is imperative to understand the history of the educational system and its challenges in the Department of Education.

Early Formal Education in Puerto Rico

Colonizations, at different times in history, brought changes in language, religion, and education. Spanish educational efforts were aimed at reading and writing Spanish and Christianity. In 1512, the first School of Grammar, for secondary education in Caparra, Puerto Rico, was established when the soldiers of Juan Ponce de León were authorized to bring their families to the Island. Education was offered by the Spaniards to indigenous people, and to the black population arriving on the

DOI: 10.4324/9781003513582-20

Island (López Borrero, 2005). During this time the church acted as the entity that qualified teachers. Early education included studies in Latin, history, and mathematics, among others. PE did not yet exist in the education program.

The succession of Puerto Rico from Spain to the United States of America brought the English language to the Island, thus bringing a dual language status. The requirement of American education on the Island taught in English was supported by the Caroll Commission (García Martínez,1976) with the intention to Americanize the population through the school system (Carroll, 1975). Through a series of decrees of the military government, public education was reorganized on the Island in the style of the existing systems in the United States. The Department of Public Instruction was created, and the Puerto Rican education system was designed according to the following trends.

The public school became totally independent of ecclesiastical tutelage, according to the principles of separation of Church and State instituted by the United States Constitution. Both primary and secondary schools were opened to all socioeconomic classes and any discrimination based on sex was eliminated. The educational system was organized according to the guidelines of the one that governed the United States. An administrative system with almost absolute centralization was developed. During the early years of the U.S. administration, the Commissioner of Instruction not only directed public schools but simultaneously presided over the University of Puerto Rico and the Board of Trustees (Helvia Quintero, 2021).

The Industrial Normal School was established with the purpose of preparing the teachers for public schools. In 1903 it was moved to the town of San Juan and renamed the University of Puerto Rico. Soon after, the United States extended Morill Nelson's benefits to the University of Puerto Rico, thus becoming a Land Grant University eligible for financial aid. It was then that the University of Puerto Rico became and continues to be the flagship University of Puerto Rico. The University of Puerto Rico goes through a change of curricular style separating itself from the European style and modeling that of the United States. The College of Pedagogy was established in 1925 and in 1942 the legislature of Puerto Rico created the Superior Council of Education, later known as the Council of Higher Education.

During this time, the first governor elected by the people, Luis Muñoz Marin, managed to have greater control over the development of the public and university education system. Great emphasis was placed on educating the population although the number of teachers fell short of the demand. The decade of the 1960s was declared the Decade of Education (Helvia Quintero, 2021). Changes in government power (an opposition political party winning elections) have been the Achilles heel of the educational progress and stability in Puerto Rico. There is a pattern of a complete overhaul when the opposing party has handed over power due to election results. Until the 1960s public education was a centralized system. Toward the end of the decade, a movement toward decentralization was in the air. The 1970s and 1980s experienced a setback due to an increase in hiring thus channeling economic resources to support the spending plan. The 1980s brought a curriculum review and changes in policy due to a change in power right before the elections of 2000, in an effort to force the decentralization of the public education system, public schools were declared community schools which meant each school had autonomy and the authority to make its own decisions. Later, in the decade of the 2000s, the role of superintendents emerged to support and stabilize the school system. This however was short-lived due to changes in government (Helvia Quintero, 2021). The come-and-go of leadership and initiatives within the education system continues the stall learning progress of the student body.

Physical Education Development and the Program in Learning

PE in Puerto Rico has experienced significant changes; it is not exempt from the come-and-go leadership of the system. Until the 1940s, PE, as an academic discipline, was led by doctors. This changed with the creation of a university Baccalaureate in PE for the training of teachers. Studies related to sports and/or physical activity have increased and specialized, for example: PE and Adapted Physical Education (APE) Baccalaureate, Master's Degree in Physical Education Curriculum and Instruction; and Exercise Sciences, Baccalaureate and Master's Degree. The aforementioned specialties were incorporating Health and Recreation topics as supplementary areas. Puerto Rico's growth was happening at an accelerated rate. In the same way, the university environment; specifically in educational training to meet the emerging needs for the development of the Island.

Department of Education

Public Education in Puerto Rico is administered by the Department of Education and directed by the governor-appointed Secretary of Education. The Department of Education of Puerto Rico (DEPR) is committed to developing students' attitudes, skills, and knowledge necessary for success in a global labor market (Plan Estratégico 2021–2026). Its mission is to develop independent lifelong learners respectful of the law and their environment, effective communicators, ethical citizens, entrepreneurs, and participants of different communities (Carta Circular Num.: 9-2016-2017).

The DEPR had an active enrollment of 276,413 students for the 2020–2021 school year. Of these, 16,272 students began their educational process by entering kindergarten. According to a report published by the DEPR (2020), approximately 19,976 students will earn their high school diploma, a potential increase of 2.1%. However, it is important to note that enrollment in public schools has decreased by 41% over the past 30 years. The decline in birth rates and the immigration Puerto Rico has experienced has contributed to the decline in the student population (Ponencia 2020). A decline in the number of teachers has emerged as a problem because of immigration, low wages, and scarce resources.

Physical Education

The PE program in Puerto Rico offers a variety of experiences to promote corporal movement as part of a healthy lifestyle for the development and personal integration of each learner. The goal is to develop students who will become physically educated with knowledge, skill, and confidence to enjoy a healthy and active lifestyle throughout their entire lives (Estandares de Contenido, 2020). This, however, was not always the case. Until 1990, PE was not a required academic subject and sometimes was not offered in public schools. PE became a mandatory subject within the public education curriculum in 1990 (Ley Organica de Puerto Rico 68 de 1990). Law 68 required all students to take PE class three times per week (3 hours). With this mandate, PE teachers were assigned permanent classrooms and facilities appropriate for the offering of PE; previous to Law 68, PE teachers would have to find any available space within the school campus to offer their class. Furthermore, every school in Puerto Rico must have at least one specialized PE teacher. If enrollment in a school passed 250 students, an additional PE teacher would be assigned, and for every 250 students thereafter.

As a result, the number of PE programs grew exponentially. The need for PE teachers was a pressing matter resulting in more colleges and universities offering PE programs both bachelors and masters. The presence of PE programs and their initiatives became increasingly visible during the decade of the 1990s. However, the positive effects of Law 68 were short-lived. Just 10 years after PE became a mandatory subject in public schools, a new law (Ley 146 August 10, 2000) was passed allowing for the substitution of PE for other elective courses. Lack of consistency and continuity like the one mentioned has plagued the progress of the education and the education system on the Island.

Academic Requirements for Physical Education Teachers

There are various paths to obtain a teacher's certification and teach in the public school system. The traditional route to a teacher certification includes a Bachelors Degree in Education with a concentration in PE (K-12), and a course of Clinical experiences (practicum) – in the area to be certified or its equivalent, Methodology in the K-12 discipline and, in addition, pass the Teacher Certification Test (PCMAS). Also, the completion of the following courses is required:

1 Introduction to the Exceptional Child course that includes technological assistance and inclusion
2 Special Education Course – intervention for the regular stream
3 Course on Integration of Technology in Education
4 Distance Education Course or Distance Learning
5 Evaluation and Assessment Course
6 Puerto Rican History Course
7 U.S. History Course

The alternate route to a teacher's certification in PE requires:

1 A Bachelor's, Master's or Doctorate degree and passing the following requirements:
2 A concentration (21 cr) at Baccalaureate level or a specialty (18 cr) at the Masters level or a combination of both levels (21 cr) in PE.

In addition, the following courses are available for people who want to have a career in PE:

1 (9) core credits in education that include philosophical, sociological, and psychological foundations
2 a course in Clinical Experience (practical) or its equivalent (1 year of experience as a teacher at the level and category in school full-time public or private).
3 Introduction to the Exceptional Child course that includes technological assistance and inclusion
4 Special Education Course – intervention for the regular stream
5 Course on Integration of Technology in Education
6 Distance Education Course or Distance Learning
7 Evaluation and Assessment Course
8 Puerto Rican History Course, and
9 pass the Teacher Certification Test (PCMAS) (Reglamento de Certificación, 2012).

Curricular Model

PE in the public education system of Puerto Rico contributes to the development of individuals to become physically educated citizens, possess the skills, knowledge, and attitudes necessary to move in a variety of ways, and live in harmony with their physical environment, and their peers. They must be able to select the movement activity in accordance with their personal purposes and interests, making it part of their lifestyle. The PE program aims at promoting leadership, teamwork, integration, and training of the person–student–citizen through the development of competencies in terms of knowledge, skills, and values (Carta Circular Num.: 9-2016-2017).

The curricular model of the PE program in Puerto Rico is based upon the concept of personal meaning, organized in two dimensions: process and purpose. Jewett and Mullan's (1977) Personal Meaning curricular model is a structure that works upon reasons or motivation for which people participate in physical activity. The basis of this curricular model views the students as holistic beings in a continuous process of development, correspondingly the PE class is responsible for creating meaning in movement and teaching the student to value movement and facilitate the search for meaning in movement; and requires a future-oriented approach. The goals of PE are individual development, environmental management, and interpersonal relationships (Carta Circular Num.: 9-2016-2017).

Standards of Physical Education Program

The PE program established five standards upon which the teacher must develop the course.

Standard 1: Mastery of movement. It demonstrates competency in a variety of motor skills and movement patterns.
Standard 2: Movement comprehension. It applies concepts, principles, strategies, and tactics related to motor skills and movement.
Standard 3: Personal Physical Fitness. It demonstrates an understanding of skills to reach and maintain an appropriate level of physical fitness.
Standard 4: Responsible Behavior. It exhibits behavior that is personally and socially responsible toward himself and others
Standard 5: Healthy and Active Lifestyle. It recognizes the value of physical activity for health, enjoyment, self-expression, and social interaction (Estandares 2015; Carta Circular Num.: 9-2016-2017).

The Longitudinal Strategic Plan of the Department of Education establishes three basic premises with regard to the role of the PE teacher:

A. The student is the focus of the educational system, and the teacher is its main facilitator.
B. The interaction between students and teachers is the main task of the school. Other school activities should be aimed at facilitating teaching, improving educational management, and strengthening the school's services to the community.
C. Schools belong to the communities they serve, and they must participate in the management of school governance.

Implementation of the Longitudinal Strategic Plan will be measured through: Performance, Satisfaction, and Effectiveness. The structure of the PE program allows for the teacher to select the physical activities that are most appropriate to study the curricular concept and develop the skills, acquire the knowledge, and obtain the experience required for the intended activity. Corporal movements selected by the teacher may include fitness, fundamental motor skills, sports or modified sports, games, invasions, goals and nets, fielding and striking, target or marksmanship, cooperative, creative, pre-sports games, nature activities, aquatics, individual activities, lifetime activities, and cultural activities, dances and rhythms among others (Appendix 1. page 221–222, Estándares 2015).

Attention to Specific Populations

Overweight and Obese Students

The secretary of education and the secretary of sports and recreation have the responsibility to offer strategies to guarantee all students and the community at large to implement activities that improve the quality of life including those who are overweight and obese (Carta Circular Num.: 9-2016-2017).

Disabilities

Children with disabilities are protected by The Individuals with Disabilities Education Act (IDEA) (1990 and reauthorized in 1997). IDEA is a federal law designed to protect the rights of students with disabilities by ensuring that everyone receives a free and appropriate public education regardless of ability. Under IDEA, special education services are personalized to meet the needs of the student in the least restrictive environment. Services are offered according to the established Individual Educational Plan (IEP) (Carta Circular Num.: 9-2016-2017).

Dimension for Quality Physical Education

The PE program in Puerto Rico has undergone many administrative changes resulting in directional changes and programmatic instability. To this end, the Association for Physical Activity, Physical Education, and Dance of Puerto Rico (AEFR PUR) has the main focus to act as an organization of support and continuity for PE and its teachers around the Island. Furthermore, it is imperative to understand the current state of PE programs and their teachers to efficiently and effectively assist its output and provide a quality PE program pertinent to the population being served. With this intention, eight dimensions have been identified and will be used to assess PE teachers and PE programs. The identified eight dimensions have emerged as necessary for a quality PE program.

Dimension 1 addresses skill development and bodily awareness. Standard one of the PE programs in Puerto Rico addresses competency in a variety of motor skills and movement patterns. The curriculum expects teachers to provide a variety of opportunities for students to develop their skills and explore the navigation of the space around them.

Dimension 2 evaluates facilities and norms in the PE classroom. This dimension may find itself deficient as Puerto Rico was gravely affected by Hurricane Maria in 2017 wreaking havoc on many educational facilities; particularly vulnerable were recreational facilities, with many made with zinc roofs being severely damaged. Today, 6 years after Hurricane Maria, there are still teachers without appropriate facilities to teach the PE class. Two major factors that impeded the restoration of these facilities are the lack of federal funds assigned to restore these spaces and the mass closing of public schools by then Secretary of Education Julia Keleher under the Administration of Ricardo Rosello. Stating "someone had to be the responsible adult", Keleher announced she would close 225 schools in Puerto Rico; yet another administrative decision causing instability and losing focus of what is needed (Primera Hora, 6 de abril de 2019). This mass closing of schools in a short period of time caused a lack of trust in the system, resulting in a number of negative outcomes including teachers opting for a career change, early retirement, or moving to mainland USA.

Quality teaching of PE is measured in the third dimension. The first item of the third dimension addresses student learning, understanding, communication, and decision-making skills. These may vary depending on the teacher and environment. Learning opportunities for teachers, however, are more easily measured. AEFR PUR offers an annual conference specifically for teachers to improve their practice and get updated on new trends, class strategies, and the like. Although it is a national congress, frequently there are international speakers on the program.

Dimension 4 measures the plan for feasibility and accessibility of PE. AEFR PUR, a chapter of the Association for Activity, Physical Education and Recreation, offers a yearly congress for all professionals in areas related to health and human movement such as PE, recreation and any other activity that is physical. Furthermore, the Department of Education has regional offices that support these professionals according to their geographic location.

Social norms and cultural practice, under dimension 5, have traditionally been a barrier to the practice of physical activity. Nonetheless, those barriers with regard to the athlete, or the students, have been less and less upheld. At present, there is fair access and participation in sport and physical activity regardless of gender. Furthermore, female PE teachers are strongly represented in terms of numbers and visibility. This accomplishment, however, cannot be extrapolated to the elite sports coaching or training world. Government input for physical seems to be severely lacking in Puerto Rico.

Dimension 6 addresses government support and effectiveness in quality PE. The most fundamental basis for this perception of lack of government support is the decommissioning of Law 68 of 1990 which made PE a non-required course. The domino effect of this decommissioning was fewer funds for the programs, fewer placement opportunities for teachers, and a message that PE was not as important. PE is an effective tool for the development of cognitive skills and critical thinking.

Dimension 7 is challenging to measure due to the autonomy of each teacher in how they will conduct their classes while following the curricular model. A survey, like the one to be used in this study, will provide a much-needed and clearer understanding of how teachers develop cognitive skills through their PE class.

The final dimension seeks to measure the habituated behavior of physical activity. At present, Puerto Rico's behavior regarding physical activity seems to be conflicting. Sports clubs/leagues are growing faster than ever before. More and more children are participating in organized sports like soccer/football, volleyball, basketball, tennis, and track and field being the disciplines with greatest growth and participation. Table tennis has experienced a burst in participation in the past 10 years. Baseball has traditionally always had strong participation because of what is locally referred to as the "pampers or diapers" level (3- and 4-year-olds) through professional leagues. Without a deep analysis of participation in sports and physical activity, it would appear that the population is very active. However, some concerns must be addressed. The most pressing concern is the 61.6% rate of obesity in the adult population (BRFDFS, 2002-Estadisticas, P.R.). The causes for the alarming rate of obesity in adults need to be understood in depth and addressed, as they relate to quality PE.

Challenges

The PE program in Puerto Rico faces an issue of lack of teachers. The removal of PE as a mandatory subject in the public system has weakened the need for teachers as there are fewer and fewer students taking the class. Furthermore, school grounds have become less available than in the past due to hurricane damage and the lack of government initiative to repair facilities. These unused and unrepaired facilities have become abandoned and dangerous to the surrounding communities. In the past 2 years, heat waves have become a reason for discouraging PE from taking place opting for more passive in-classroom options.

With regard to APE, a teacher and facilitator of the Associate Secretary of Special Education said, "The APE program in 2022–2023 has 226 APE specialist teachers around Puerto Rico to serve an enrollment of 5,116 students". Furthermore, the director of the Department of Adapted Physical Education at the University of Puerto Rico, Bayamón Campus, denounced that "the Department of Education has placed Adapted Physical Education in a kind of limbo, (without its own place). Where they have difficulty differentiating between a Special Education teacher, a Regular Physical Education teacher, and an APE teacher" (Metro Puerto Rico, 2023). In the past 30 years, the Department of Education has experienced drastic changes: school closures, relocating students and teachers, constant changes in leadership, and the move to outsource a significant number of services. Meanwhile, obesity rates, sedentarism, and mental health struggles continue to rise among the student population. Action must be taken at all levels to ameliorate this situation for students and teachers.

References

Carroll, Henry K. (1975). *Report on the Island of Porto Rico; Its Population, Civil Government, Productions, Roads, Tariff, and Currency*. New York: Arno Press.
Carta Circular Num.: 9-2016-2017 (22 de julio de 2016). *Estado Libre Asociado de Puerto Rico*. Departamento de Educación. https://transicion2016.pr.gov/agencias/081/Info rme%20de%20Cartas%20Circulares/09-%202016-2017%20Pol%C3%ADtica%20 P%C3%BAblica%20sobre%20la%20organizaci%C3%B3n%20del%20Programa%20 de%20Educaci%C3%B3n%20Especial.pdf

Estandares de Contenido. (2020). https://dedigital.dde.pr/pluginfile.php/145096/mod_resou rce/content/7/Est%C3%A1ndares%20y%20Expectativas%20Programa%20de%20Educ aci%C3%B3n%20F%C3%ADsica.pdf

Estándares de Contenido y Expectativas de Grado. (2022). *Programa de Educación Física.* Departamento de Educación. https://dedigital.dde.pr/pluginfile.php/145096/mod_resou rce/content/7/Est%C3%A1ndares%20y%20Expectativas%20Programa%20de%20Educ aci%C3%B3n%20F%C3%ADsica.pdf

Flores Ortiz, H. (21 de febrero de 2016). *La Geografía de Puerto Rico. Enclyclopedia PR.* http://enciclopediapr.org/content/la-geografia-de-puerto-rico/

García Martínez, A. L. (1976). *Idioma y política: El papel desempeñado por los idiomas español e inglés en la relación política Puerto Rico–Estados Unidos.* San Juan, PR: Editorial Cordillera.

Helvia Quintero, A. (17 de septiembre de 2021). *Breve historia de la educación publica preuniversitaria y universitaria en Puerto Rico.* Encyclopedia PR. http://enciclopediapr. org/content/historia-educacion-en-puerto-rico/

Jewett, A., and Mullan, M. (1977). *Curriculum Design: Purpose and Processes in Physical Education Teaching-Learning.* AAPHERD Publications.

Ley Organica de Puerto Rico 68 de 1990 (1990). *Num. 68 Aprobada en 28 de agosto de 1990.* Gobierno de Puerto Rico. https://bvirtualogp.pr.gov/ogp/Bvirtual/leyesreferencia/ PDF/2/0068-1990.pdf

López Borrero, A. (2005). *Mi escuelita: Educación y arquitectura en Puerto Rico.* Editorial Universidad de Puerto Rico. 197 p.

Metro Puerto Rico. (05 de junio 2023). *Urgen mayor cantidad de maestros y recursos para programa de Educación Física Adaptada.* www.metro.pr/noticias/2023/06/05/urgen-mayor-cantidad-de-maestros-y-recursos-para-programa-de-educacion-fisica-adaptada/

Plan Estratégico 2021–2026. (2024). Documento de trabajo n° 35. Departamento de Educación. https://www.indec.gob.ar/ftp/cuadros/menusuperior/documentos-auxiliares/ plan_estrategico_INDEC_2021_2026.pdf

Ponencia del Departamento de Educación para el Proceso de Transición de Gobierno 2020. (2020). Departamento de Educación. Oficina del Secretario. https://transicion2020. pr.gov/Agencias/081/Ponencias/Ponencia%20DEPR%20.pdf

Primera Hora (6 de abril de 2019). Keleher sobre el cierre de escuelas: "Alguien tenia que ser el adulto responsable". *Noticias Gobierno y política Primera Hora.* www.primerah ora.com/noticias/gobierno-politica/notas/keleher-sobre-el-cierre-de-escuelas-alguien-tenia-que-ser-el-adulto-responsable/

Reglamento de Certificación del Personal Docente de Puerto Rico. (2012). https://de.pr.gov/ wp-content/uploads/2022/02/reglamento-de-certificacion-de-personal-docente-de-pue rto-rico.pdf

Chapter 19

Nurturing Holistic Development through Quality Physical Education in Saudi Arabia

A Dialectical Approach Considering Gender and Cultural Diversity

Md. Dilsad Ahmed

Introduction

Saudi Arabia, officially known as the Kingdom of Saudi Arabia (KSA), is located in the Middle East and occupies most of the Arabian Peninsula, spanning approximately 2,150,000 square kilometers. This makes it the fifth largest country in Asia and the largest in the Middle East. Known for its rich cultural and historical heritage, Saudi Arabia is a sovereign nation governed as an absolute monarchy, with Islam as its official religion. Riyadh, the capital city, is the central hub for political, economic, and cultural activities (General Authority of Statistics, 2021). As the birthplace of Islam in the seventh century, KSA holds significant religious importance, housing Islam's holiest cities, Makkah and Madinah. The country has historically played a crucial role in the global spread of Islamic civilization, featuring vast deserts, ancient cities, and revered religious sites such as Mecca and Medina (World Civilization, 2023). As a major global oil producer with the second largest proven hydrocarbon reserves (20%), KSA is pivotal to the world economy. The Gross Domestic Product (GDP) per capita reached Saudi Arabian Riyal (SAR) 29,820 in Q2 2022, showing a substantial increase. Homelessness is reportedly nonexistent in Saudi Arabia (Saudi Arabia—OHCHR, 2015). The latest demographic data indicates that Saudi Arabia's population is 37,427,215. Currently, 83.5% of the population is urban, with a median age of 30.6 years (Worldometer, 2024; Monshat, 2024). The gender distribution is 49.8% women and 50.2% men, with the non-Saudi population numbering 13,382,962, comprising 23.5% women and 76.5% men.

Historical Background on the Incorporation of Physical Education (PE) in the Saudi Arabia's Education

Contemporary sports and PE in Saudi Arabia began in the 1950s with the establishment of a national education system, making sports integral to the curriculum. This integration helped spread sports activities nationwide. The First Development Plan in the early 1970s further boosted sports development, creating a national network of public sports facilities and youth clubs. In 1974, the

General Presidency of Youth Welfare (GPYW) was established to promote public involvement in sports, supporting the Ministry of Education's PE and the Ministry of Higher Education's sports initiatives. GPYW aimed to engage Saudi youth in sports, recreation, and cultural events by providing facilities and opportunities nationwide. It implemented a three-tier program after assessing regional needs and population density. The first tier involved constructing large sports complexes in densely populated areas, known as "Sports Cities," featuring Olympic-sized swimming pools, courts, playgrounds, cafeterias, conference halls, and multi-purpose stadiums (Saudi Embassy, 2024). PE has always been a part of boys' education in Saudi Arabia. However, in 2017, Saudi's Ministry of Education made a historic decision to allow girls to participate as well (Arab News, 2017). Primary schools now allocate 112 minutes per week to PE for girls, whereas secondary schools allocate only 45 minutes (Clark et al., 2012; UNESCO, 2013). However, with the advent of the Saudi Vision 2030 plan, more progressive practices have been introduced (Chowdhury et al., 2021; Rahman & Qattan, 2021; Alhammad et al., 2023). This plan emphasizes community engagement in physical activities (PAs) and advocates for at least 30 minutes of exercise per week as part of the Vision 2030 Quality of Life Program, aiming to enhance overall quality of life. PE has become mandatory in Saudi schools, though the allocated time varies by educational level. For instance, middle school students typically receive 45 minutes of PE per week, taught by qualified specialists (Aljuhani & Sandercock, 2019). Universities, such as Prince Mohammed Bin Fahd University, have also made PE compulsory for all students, regardless of their major, requiring them to pass the course. PE teachers in Saudi Arabia are trained through specialized programs at institutions like King Saud University, Princess Nourah Bint Abdulrahman University, and Jeddah University, ensuring they are well equipped to promote students' health and fitness.

Advancing Physical Activity and Health through Quality Physical Education (QPE)

While Saudi Arabia maintains the interpretation of Islamic law, current discussions and initiatives are aiming to drive societal changes, particularly concerning gender roles and women's participation in various life aspects. Cultural and social practices in Saudi Arabia significantly shape attitudes and behaviors related to women's involvement in sports, PE, and other PAs. The country's landscape of gender equality and women's empowerment reflects a complex interaction of tradition, religion, and evolving societal norms.

This chapter explores the findings of an extensive study that investigates the impact of QPE on skill development, bodily awareness, facilities and norms, teaching quality, cognitive skill development, and habitual behavior in PAs among male and female students in KSA. QPE stands as a cornerstone in this progressive educational philosophy, transcending the boundaries of conventional classrooms to embrace the physical, mental, and social dimensions of learning.

In recent years, the discourse on education has expanded beyond textbooks and lectures, recognizing the pivotal role played by extracurricular activities, particularly QPE, in shaping well-rounded individuals. This study, a meticulous exploration of QPE's influence on students, serves as a beacon guiding us through the nuanced terrain of PE's impact on their overall development. By scrutinizing various dimensions—ranging from skill development and bodily awareness to cognitive skill enhancement and habituated behavior—this research aims to unravel the intricate tapestry of benefits woven by a robust QPE curriculum. Research on QPE in Saudi Arabia is scarce. Ahmed and Salim (2024) used Ho et al.'s (2021) questionnaire to explore various aspects of QPE, including skill development, PE facilities, teaching quality, cognitive skill development, governmental inputs, and habitual PA behavior. The study involved 610 students (467 males and 143 females) from different university departments, participating in over 27 sports. This chapter discusses these eight factors to provide insights into the state of PA engagement among students in KSA.

Skill Development and Bodily Awareness (SDBA)

The journey begins with examining the impact of QPE on skill development and bodily awareness, dissecting the nuanced interplay between PAs and the cognitive understanding of one's body. As the findings unfold, we traverse the landscapes of enhanced physical skills, a deepened knowledge of sports-related terminology, and a heightened understanding of how the human body functions. The study unveils the universal benefits of transcending gender disparities, and underscores the program's efficacy in fostering physical prowess and a sense of responsibility among students (Table 19.1).

Facilities and Norms in Physical Education (FNPE)

Transitioning into the realm of facilities and norms, the study encapsulates the perceptions of students regarding the conducive environments for PE. As the mean scores weave a narrative of positive attitudes towards safety, suitable equipment, and inclusive norms, we unravel the fabric of an education system that not only imparts knowledge but also cultivates positive values and attitudes. This section emphasizes the collective voice of students advocating for enjoyable, inclusive, and accessible PE, irrespective of individual backgrounds (Table 19.2).

The table highlighted Saudi male and female responses regarding the importance of various aspects of FNPE in university and highlighted no significant differences between genders (t = 0.410, Sig. = 0.682, MD = 0.518, η^2 = 0.03). Overall, the data suggest that both male and female respondents similarly value safe, inclusive, and comprehensive PE environments and practices. This means that students of both genders in Saudi universities hold comparable views on the importance of various aspects of PE. They agree on the necessity for schools to provide a safe environment, appropriate equipment, and facilities for PE classes.

200 Quality Physical Education

Table 19.1 Skills development and bodily awareness (SDBA)

QPE	Male Mean	SD	Female Mean	SD
Enhances your physical skills.	4.88	1.29	4.79	1.46
Enhances students' knowledge of sport-related terms.	4.90	1.23	4.77	1.40
Enhances students' knowledge of different activities.	4.88	1.23	4.86	1.38
Gives students chances to learn and interact with classmates	4.81	1.27	4.76	1.36
Teaches students how important activity is to the process of growth.	4.85	1.20	4.74	1.43
Helps students understand how their bodies work.	4.85	1.31	4.82	1.40
Helps students to develop a habit of attending sports activities after School and use their spare time in sports wisely.	4.67	1.37	4.78	1.36
Total	33.88	7.04	33.54	8.26

Source: Ahmed and Salim (2024).
The SDBA items did not report significant differences between the sexes' perception (t = 0.481, p = 0.631, MD = 0.337), which signifies their equal consensus to the enhancement of all the QPE items.

They also concur on the importance of offering opportunities for active learning, promoting positive sports-related attitudes and values, including health education in the curriculum, and making PE enjoyable and accessible to all students (Ahmed & Salim, 2024).

Quality Teaching of Physical Education (QTPE)

As the chapter progresses, the spotlight shifts towards the quality of teaching in PE. The study delves into students' perspectives on the effectiveness of teaching methodologies, unraveling how QPE contributes to their learning experiences. From the development of basic skills to effective communication, the findings underscore the program's pivotal role in not only shaping physically adept individuals but also fostering cognitive skills such as critical thinking and problem solving (Table 19.3).

The table presents mean scores and standard deviations (mean ± SD) for male and female students on various QPE items. QTPE shows no significant difference between genders, as indicated by a non-significant t-value (t = 0.863, p = 0.388, MD = 0.525, η^2 = 0.08). For other items, mean scores are provided separately for males and females, but no statistical comparison is presented. Despite this, both genders generally demonstrate similar mean scores across these QPE items, suggesting comparable perceptions and experiences in various aspects of PE.

Table 19.2 Facilities and norms in physical education (FNPE)

Schools	Male Mean	SD	Female Mean	SD
Should provide a safe and appropriate environment for PE classes.	5.03	1.31	5.05	1.31
Ensure they have safe and appropriate equipment for PE classes.	5.02	1.33	5.07	1.28
Maintain safe and appropriate facilities for physical education classes.	5.04	1.30	4.99	1.35
Give students opportunities for active learning during PE classes.	4.94	1.29	4.96	1.26
Focus on promoting positive sports-related attitudes and values.	4.89	1.27	4.76	1.41
Consider health education as a major area of learning.	4.85	1.32	4.70	1.43
Include various types of PAs and related knowledge in the curriculum.	4.85	1.23	4.80	1.28
Make PE instruction enjoyable and fun.	4.97	1.19	5.06	1.27
Make PE a mandatory subject for all children.	4.76	1.35	4.69	1.41
Extend PA opportunities through after-school or extra-curricular/co-curricular activities to enhance students' learning experiences in sports and PAs.	4.66	1.30	4.67	1.39
Ensure that teachers are properly qualified to teach PE.	4.92	1.31	4.93	1.37
Make PE accessible to all children, regardless of their abilities, Disabilities, gender, age, culture, race/ethnicity, religion, or socioeconomic background.	4.95	1.29	4.80	1.51
Recognize that PE is the most effective means of equipping children with the skills, attitudes, values, knowledge, and understanding necessary for lifelong PA and sport participation.	4.88	1.28	4.76	1.32
Total	63.83	12.81	63.31	14.45

Source: Ahmed and Salim (2024).

Habituated Behavior in Physical Activities (HBPA)

The journey concludes by unraveling the long-term impact of QPE on students' behaviors and choices. The study exposes how QPE goes beyond the confines of the school years, shaping individuals who maintain healthy lifestyles, engage in regular exercise, and understand the profound relationship between PAs and personal development. This section serves as a testament to the enduring influence of QPE on shaping lifelong habits, fostering a sense of responsibility towards sports clubs, communities, and out-of-school programs (Table 19.4).

Table 19.3 Quality teaching of physical education (QTPE)

QPE	Male Mean	SD	Female Mean	SD
Learn and develop basic skills in different physical and sports activities.	4.91	1.27	4.94	1.32
Demonstrate a basic understanding of the importance of physical activities and health.	4.88	1.28	4.77	1.46
Communicate ideas, and feelings effectively with others.	4.76	1.34	4.72	1.31
Basic motor skills within the context of appropriate physical activities of a low organization.	4.57	1.37	4.49	1.38
Demonstrate basic skills in decision-making, communication, etc.	4.76	1.26	4.63	1.32
At the middle-class level, developing appropriate health and fitness understanding that includes setting and achieving personal goals for healthy living.	4.77	1.32	4.59	1.48
Total	28.68	6.18	28.15	6.92

Source: Ahmed and Salim (2024).

Table 19.4 Habituated behavior in physical activities

QPE	Male Mean	SD	Female Mean	SD
Demonstrate suitable decisions on actions for maintaining healthy living.	4.77	1.29	4.73	1.31
Demonstrate a habit of regular exercise.	4.82	1.29	4.79	1.36
Understand the relationship between physical and sports activities and personal and social development.	4.82	1.27	4.70	1.30
Take up suitable responsibilities to serve sports clubs or other related activities in school or the community.	4.59	1.30	4.56	1.30
Develop advanced proficiency in different physical and sports activities.	4.77	1.28	4.63	1.36
Develop necessary skills of participation in and out-of-school programs available within the community and which have the potential for lifelong long involvement and participation	4.71	1.32	4.65	1.40
Total	28.50	6.13	18.08	6.48

Source: Ahmed and Salim (2024).
The HBPA analysis reveals a non-significant difference between male and female students (t = 0.689, p = 0.491, MD = 0.415, with a small effect size η^2 = 0.06). In other words, both male and female students exhibit similar mean scores for HBPA, suggesting comparable levels of HBPAs between genders.

Ahmed and Salim (2024) found that male students in Saudi Arabia outperformed female students in all levels of PA, including strenuous, moderate, and mild exercises. This raises the question of why, despite the availability of QPE at universities, gender disparities in PA levels persist. This trend aligns with previous studies, such as Alqahtani et al. (2020), which reported that only 28.30% of males engaged in PA compared with 8.90% of females. Cultural factors, including restricted access to PA opportunities for women and a focus on home-based activities, contribute to this disparity. Additionally, technological advancements have led to increased screen time and sedentary behavior, further impacting PA levels (Al-Hazzaa, 2004a; 2018).

Cognitive Skill Development (CSD)

Cognitive Skill Development is a crucial factor that intersects with the challenges faced by female university students in Saudi Arabia regarding PA. Aljehani et al. (2022) found that 62% of female students did not engage in adequate vigorous activity, and 70% fell short on moderate activity. Academic pressures and cognitive demands often lead students to prioritize studies and rest over PA. Heavy workloads, gender roles, cultural norms, and additional barriers like extreme heat, and cultural dress codes further limit PA. Parental safety concerns also restrict outdoor activity. Despite these obstacles, students motivated by body image and family support are more likely to engage in PA. Historically, Saudis led active lives, but economic and technological changes have led to more sedentary behavior and unhealthy diets, increasing non-communicable diseases (Al-Hazzaa, 2004b). Enhancing cognitive skills could help students' better balance academics and PA, fostering a healthier lifestyle.

Plans for Feasibility and Accessibility of Physical Education (PFAPE)

Saudi Vision 2030 emphasizes sports and PE at all educational levels, from primary schools to universities. It aims to increase participation in sports and PA across all age groups, promoting healthy lifestyles. Significant investments are being made in sports infrastructure, such as building and renovating facilities and establishing sports academies. PE is being integrated into the curriculum to ensure students receive high-quality PE regularly. Programs encourage youth participation in sports, fostering a culture of health and fitness. It also positions Saudi Arabia as a hub for national and international competitions. Special focus is given to enhancing facilities and programs for disabled students and females, ensuring inclusivity. Public awareness campaigns further encourage daily PA, contributing to a healthier society (Saudi Vision 2030, 2022a).

Social Norms and Cultural Practice (SNCP)

In Saudi Arabia, traditional social norms have historically emphasized male participation in sports. However, recent reforms under Saudi Vision 2030 are promoting gender inclusivity in PE programs. Significant progress has been made in including girls in sports, with new facilities and programs established to support female participation and improve access. This shift fosters a more inclusive environment, benefiting girls' health and well-being (Arab News, 2017; Alahmadi & Almasoud, 2022). Traditional Saudi games are also being integrated into PE curricula to preserve cultural heritage and boost engagement. Evolving community attitudes and supportive PE programs are crucial for advancing the goals of Saudi Vision 2030 (2022b).

Governmental Input for Physical Education (GIPE)

Students in Saudi Arabia have a consistently positive perception of sports facilities due to their variety and quality. The Kingdom offers an array of options, from large sports complexes to local clubs. Major population centers feature sports cities with amenities like stadiums seating 10,000 to 60,000 people, Olympic-sized pools, courts, playgrounds, conference rooms, and sports medicine clinics. In larger urban areas, smaller neighborhood facilities and playgrounds allow young Saudis to engage in sports like basketball and volleyball near their homes. Local sports clubs in every town provide playgrounds, swimming pools, tennis courts, soccer fields, and accommodations for youth camps, organizing community activities year round (Saudi Embassy, 2024). Furthermore, the study of Sayyd et al. (2022) examines how the availability of sports facilities and equipment at universities in Saudi Arabia impacts student participation in PAs, based on a study of 643 undergraduates from 25 universities. Findings indicate that the quality and availability of these facilities significantly influence student engagement in sports. There is a strong consensus among students on the need for improvements in sports infrastructure. The study concludes that investing in better facilities and equipment is crucial for enhancing student participation in PAs, which benefits their physical and mental well-being.

Conclusion

Alarabia News (2021) revealed that over 25,000 individuals in Saudi Arabia succumbed to cancer and diabetes that year alone, with projections suggesting this figure could double to 50,000 by 2025. These conditions predominantly affect adults aged 20 to 39 years, with physical inactivity, sedentary behavior, and unhealthy dietary habits identified as primary contributors. The exponential rise in non-communicable diseases (NCDs) in Saudi Arabia highlights the critical need for effective strategies to combat this escalating trend. In response to this health crisis, promoting a healthy and active lifestyle has been firmly integrated into the

Saudi Vision 2030 initiative, which aims to "encourage widespread and regular participation in sports and athletic activities." However, there are significant challenges to overcome. According to a 2013 UNESCO report, Saudi children receive about 120 minutes of PA per week at the primary level, declining to just 45 minutes per week at the secondary level—substantially lower than children in neighboring countries. This places Saudi Arabia's PA levels on the lower end of the middle average range of 40–160 minutes per week, as reported by UNESCO.

In Saudi Arabia, the perception and prioritization of QPE have undergone significant changes in recent years, particularly with the introduction of gender-specific requirements and the broader reforms under the Saudi Vision 2030 initiative. Historically, PE was not uniformly prioritized, especially for girls, who were often excluded from such programs. This historical exclusion highlighted a significant gender disparity in the education system. Saudi Vision 2030 has made progress but still faces challenges. Despite increased opportunities for female sports participation, traditional gender norms can limit involvement. Overcoming these barriers and promoting equal participation is essential. Raising awareness about the benefits of physical fitness and developing an inclusive PE curriculum aligned with international standards are key tasks. Effective policy implementation and ongoing professional development for PE teachers are also crucial. Creating engaging PE programs tailored to students' interests can boost participation. Achieving these goals requires collaboration among government bodies, educational institutions, and communities to support a healthier, more active population. With the implementation of Saudi Vision 2030, there has been a significant shift toward more progressive practices that emphasize the importance of PE for all students. The Vision 2030 plan, particularly through its Quality of Life Program, advocates for integrating PA into daily life, including in schools. This reflects an increasing recognition of QPE as essential to the education system, contributing to both students' physical health and overall well-being. PE is now mandatory across Saudi schools, with time allocations varying by educational level, highlighting QPE's growing importance in creating a well-rounded education. This evolving emphasis aligns with Saudi Vision 2030's broader goals of promoting a healthier, more active society.

References

Ahmed, M. D., & Al Salim, Z. A. (2024). Provision of quality physical education to enhance the motive of physical activity and its underlying behavior among university students. *Heliyon*, *10*(3), e25152–e25152. https://doi.org/10.1016/j.heliyon.2024.e25152

Alahmadi, M., & Almasoud, K. (2022). Saudi Arabia's first female physical education teachers: a study of health-related physical fitness. *The International Scientific Journal of Physical Education and Sport Sciences*, 11(1), 52–59. https://doi.org/10.21608/isjpes.2022.87787.1062

Alarabia News. (2021, May 20). Alarming number of young people in UAE, Saudi Arabia diagnosed with cancer: Study. *Al Arabiya English*. https://ara.tv/jccd6

Alhammad, S. A., Almutairi, F. M., Bajsair, A. S., Alghamdi, A. S., Algarni, F. S., Aldaihan, M. M., Alshehri, W. M., & Alwadeai, K. S. (2023). Physical activity levels among undergraduate students at the College of Applied Medical Sciences, King Saud University, Riyadh: a prevalence study. *Medicine, 102*(48), e36386. https://doi.org/10.1097/MD.00000000000363866

Al-Hazzaa, H. M. (2004a). Prevalence of physical inactivity in Saudi Arabia: a brief review. *Eastern Mediterranean Health Journal, 10*(4–5), 663–670. https://doi.org/10.26719/2004.10.4-5.663

Al-Hazzaa, H. M. (2004b). The public health burden of physical inactivity in Saudi Arabia. *Journal of Family & Community Medicine, 11*(2), 45–51. www.ncbi.nlm.nih.gov/pmc/articles/PMC3410089/

Al-Hazzaa, H. M. (2018). Physical inactivity in Saudi Arabia revisited: a systematic review of inactivity prevalence and perceived barriers to active living. *JMIR Preprints,* 9883. https://doi.org/10.2196/preprints.9883

Aljehani, A. M., Banjar, S. A., Alshehri, G. A., Alnojaidi, T. F., Alkhammash, S. M., Almomen, F. A., Alolayan, O. K., Bagazi, G. A., & Bamhair, A. S. (2022). Association of Academic Performance with Obesity and Unhealthy Lifestyle among female university students. *Cureus, 14*(1), e21561. https://doi.org/10.7759/cureus.21561

Aljuhani, O., & Sandercock, G. (2019). Contribution of physical education to the daily physical activity of schoolchildren in Saudi Arabia. *International Journal of Environmental Research and Public Health, 16*(13), 2397. https://doi.org/10.3390/ijerph16132397

Alqahtania, B., Alenazia, A., Alhowimela, A., & Elnaggar, R. (2020). The descriptive pattern of physical activity in Saudi Arabia: analysis of national survey data. *International Health, 13,* 232–239. https://doi.org/10.1093/inthealth/ihaa027

Arab News. (2017). *Saudi Arabia approves physical education programs in girls' schools.* www.arabnews.com/node/1127811/saudi-arabia

Chowdhury, S., Mok, D., & Leenen, L. (2021). Transformation of healthcare and the new model of care in Saudi Arabia: Kingdom's Vision 2030. *Journal of Medicine and Life, 14,* 347–354. https://doi.org/10.25122/jml-2021-0045

Clark, V. L., Ekelund, U., Hardman, K., Bull, F. C., Andersen, L. B., Haskell, W., Azevedo, M., & Hallal, P. C. (2012). A look into physical education curriculum time requirements around the world. Unpublished paper.

General Authority of Statistics. (2021). *General information about the Kingdom of Saudi Arabia.* www.stats.gov.sa/en/page/259

Ho, W. K. Y., Ahmed, D. M., & Klaudia, K. (2021). Development and validation of an instrument to assess QPE among Asian professionals. *Cogent Education, 8*(1), 1864082. https://doi.org/10.1080/2331186X.2020.1864082

Monshat. (2024). *Business Atlas.* Retrieved May 31, 2024, https://atlas.monshaat.gov.sa/en/profile/country/saudi-arabia

Rahman, R., & Qattan, A. (2021). Vision 2030 and sustainable development: state capacity to revitalize the healthcare system in Saudi Arabia. *Inquiry, 58,* 46958020984682. https://doi.org/10.1177/0046958020984682

Saudi Arabia—OHCHR. (2015). *The office of the high commissioner of human rights.* www.ohchr.org/sites/default/files/Documents/Issues/Housing/Homelessness/SaudiArabia.pdf

Saudi Embassy. (2024). www.saudiembassy.net/sports-and-recreation

Saudi Vision 2030. (2022a). *Developments in Saudi sports following Saudi Vision 2030.* www.google.com/search?q=https%2F%2Fwww.tamimi.com%2Flaw-update-articles%2Fdevelopments-in-saudi-sports

Saudi Vision 2030. (2022b). *Quality of life program.* www.tamimi.com/law-update-articles/developments-in-saudi-sports-following-saudi-vision-2030

Saudi Vision 2030. (2024). *Saudi Vision 2030*. www.vision2030.gov.sa/

Sayyd, S. M., Asnaldi, A., Zainuddin, Z. A. B., & Nahary, A. M. (2022). Management of sports facilities and equipment in physical activities according to Saudi Vision 2030. *Journal MensSana: Jurnal Ilmiah Bidang Pendidikan Olahraga, 7*(2), 118–125. https://doi.org/10.24036/MensSana.07022022.15

UNESCO. (2013). *UNESCO-NWCPEA: World-wide survey of school physical education—Final report 2013*. https://unesdoc.unesco.org/ark:/48223/pf0000229335

World Civilization. (2023). *Ch. 7 The rise and spread of Islam*. https://courses.lumenlearning.com/suny-hccc-worldcivilization/chapter/arabian-cities/#:~:text=Sarah's%20handmaiden%20Hagar.-,Kaaba,of%20Islam's%20most%20sacred%20mosque

Worldometer. (2024). Elaboration of data by United Nations, Department of Economic and Social Affairs, Population Division. In *World Population Prospects: The 2022 Revision*. www.worldometers.info/world-population/saudi-arabia-population/

Chapter 20

Quality Physical Education in Slovakia and Its Challenges

Klaudia Rafael and Branislav Antala

Country Background

Slovak Republic (SR) became an independent state on January 1, 1993; its capital is Bratislava. It has a population of approximately 5,400,000, and the official language is Slovak It is a state system and has a democratic parliament (150 members elected for 4 years). It is a member of the European Union (EU) (since May 1, 2004), NATO, UN, UNESCO, OECD, OBSE, WHO, etc.

Short History of Physical Education (PE) Development in Slovak Territory

The development of school PE on the territory of Slovakia can be divided into the following stages (Antala, 2021):

1 School PE from its beginning to 1918
2 School PE between two world wars in the years 1918–1939
3 School PE during Second World War in the years 1939–1945
4 School PE in the years 1945–1992
5 School PE from the creation of the independent SR in 1993 until today.

In this chapter, we will focus mainly on PE during the last stage, specifically on the last 20 years. Since 2008, PE has been taught at all levels of primary and secondary schools as a compulsory subject with 2 hours per week to all grades divided between two separate lessons, each of 45 minutes, and also as a form of additional courses (swimming, skiing, and a course on human and health protection) organized in additionally teaching time out of the compulsory two lessons. The schools can willingly increase the weekly number of hours of PE as part of the educational programs; however, this option was implemented only to a minimal extent. Since 2015, the name of the teaching subject in all school levels has changed to "physical and sports education" (for convenience we will be using the abbreviation PE).

To support the subject of PE in schools, the Association of Physical and Sports Education Teachers was established in 2012, which represents the professional organization of PE teachers. The Committee of Physical and Sports Education Subject at the State Pedagogical Institute, which in 2021 was transformed into the Central Committee for the Educational Area Health and Movement, also carries out its supporting and coordination activities. The commission approves all professional materials related to physical and sports education in schools and is also the highest professional body in this field. In 2012, the Ministry of Education, Science, Research, and Sport of the Slovak Republic (MSVVS SR) also established the Curriculum Council. Member of this council was also the chair of the Committee for Physical and Sports Education Subject. The Council was the highest advisory body of the MVSVVS SR in the field of curricular issues of education. Several electronic portals were also created to help the management of PE, such as the school sports information portal of the MVSVVS SR www.skolskysport.sk.

In 2015, the *Sports Act No. 440/2015* was adopted. The Sports Support Fund, which regularly issues calls for building sports infrastructure, was created in 2019. From 2020 the positions of the *state secretary for sports* and *assistant state secretary for physical and sports education* in schools were created. The participation of a representative from the ranks of school principals with approval for physical and sports education in the Council for Sport MVSVVS SR, which also includes care for school sport and physical activities in the school environment, was also a benefit. Currently, attention is also paid to the system of selecting talented youth in sports. Since 2017, the project of *testing the physical abilities of first- and third-year elementary school pupils* has been implemented on a regular basis every year. The aim of the project is to find out the level of physical performance of children in Slovakia, to bring children to sports and at the same time to increase the probability of identifying sports talents in children (www.testovanieziakov.sk).

A number of civil associations, national sports associations, national sports organizations, and private companies are also active in the supporting the schools, which coordinate various types of projects and activities aimed at increasing the physical activity of children and youth in school and extra-curricular environments, such as the Slovak Tennis Association project "Tennis in schools"; the project of the Slovak Olympic and Sports Committee "Olympic Badge of Versatility"; the project of the Slovak Government Responsible for Sports "Coaches at School"; "McDonald's Cup" of McDonald's in cooperation with the Slovak Football Association, and so on.

The pandemic years 2020 to 2022 brought several restrictions for PE and physical activities to children and youth at school, which affected the entire school population. Primary schools continued to teach most of the time at the first level face-to-face, including PE. However, PE could only be taught in open outdoor spaces, while the use of such physical activities was recommended, during which the pupils came into the smallest possible personal contact. In the second grade of elementary schools and in secondary schools, during the pandemic, all subjects were taught only online, including PE.

Dimensions of Quality Physical Education (GIQPE)

In 2021, research on quality physical education (QPE) was finalized in Slovakia. The questionnaire utilized in this study was adapted from the international research project: GIQPE (Ho et al., 2021). Comprising 49 items, the questionnaire was structured into eight dimensions, each delineating various areas of PE. A total of 54 PE and sport professionals participated in the questionnaire, consisting of 25 males and 29 females. The overall result for GIQPE questionnaire was 5.86 with a standard deviation of .64. Considering that the maximum achievable score is 10, it can be inferred that QPE in Slovakia exhibits significant disparities between the actual implementation of PE practices and the desired standards or expectations as outlined in the UNESCO – Quality Physical Education Guidelines for Policy Makers (UNESCO, 2015), which served as a major basis for the development of the GIQPE questionnaire (Ho et al., 2021, 2023). The items of the questionnaire are distributed across eight dimensions, which facilitate a comprehensive understanding of the QPE situation. Thirteen of 29 female respondents, worked at primary schools, while among the male participants, only three held similar positions. Here, a notable issue arises in Slovakia, there is a prevailing cultural perception that primary school teaching is predominantly a profession for women. However, a more critical challenge pertaining to primary schools directly impacts physical education; specifically, teachers at the primary level are tasked with instructing all subjects, including PE, despite often lacking a robust educational background in this field. Consequently, the quality of PE instruction at the primary level may be compromised. To address this issue, a solution was devised, inspired by a project originated in the Czech Republic named "*Coaches at school*" and subsequently implemented in Slovakia. Secondary PE teacher during collecting the data were working 18 males and 12 females. The third groups of respondents were working at the university level, only eight individuals working at the university level. After analysis (average mean, standard deviation) of the overall GIQPE results, those who worked at secondary school scored the highest, then those in the primary school 5.75; and the lowest scored respondents from universities 5.13.

Dimensions of QPE

Below are listed the results in each dimension of QPE in descending order based on their respective scores, from highest to lowest based on the respondents in PE and Sport profession from Slovakia.

The highest score based on the 54 PE and sport professionals' perceptions on QPE from Slovakia achieved the dimension *Facilities and Norms in Physical Education* (FNPE), with an average mean of 6.93, and a standard deviation of .75. It is noteworthy that the maximum attainable score was 10. This dimension encompasses aspects such as the environmental situation, availability of suitable equipment and facilities for PE classes, fostering positive sport-related attitudes, inclusion of PE as a compulsory subject in school curricula, qualification of PE teachers, and provision of opportunities for learning physical activities, emphasizing accessibility, fun, and enjoyment. The items receiving the highest rankings were associated with the compulsory inclusion of PE as a subject in primary and secondary schools, scoring 8.98 and 8.91, respectively. To enhance this dimension, attention should be directed toward addressing the item with the greatest disparity between respondent perceptions and expectation. Consequently, priority should be given to addressing concerns related to the provision of equipment for PE classes, which scored 5.61, and the efficacy of equipping children with the necessary skills, attitudes, values, knowledge, and understanding for lifelong participation in physical activity and sports, which scored 5.24. In 2014, the MSVVS SR assessed PE facilities in primary and secondary schools and found unsatisfactory results. Of all Slovak schools, 784 (64%) lacked their own gymnasiums, depending instead on municipal, city, sports club, or other school facilities (MSVVS SR, 2017). However, in 2017, MVSSV SR allocated €4,900,000 to support physical education development. Many schools applied for these funds, earmarked for capital expenditures, and thus improved their facilities.

The dimension *Skill Development and Bodily Awareness* (SDBA) achieved the second highest score, with average mean of 6.38 and a standard deviation of .71. The dimension focusing on the area of PE related to enhancing physical skills, improving students' knowledge of the sport-related terms, provides students chances to learn with classmates, helps students to understand how their body works and develops a habit of attending sport activities in their spare time. Notably, respondents from this study identified significant gaps in providing students with opportunities to interact with classmates (scored at 5.52), a concern that could be addressed by incorporating more group activities into the PE curriculum. Developing a lifelong habit of engaging in sports activities (scored at 4.50) emerged as the lowest-ranked item. However, it is imperative to recognize that cultivating this habit is pivotal for fostering an active society. Addressing these gaps is paramount for bringing about necessary changes in this dimension. Recently, as mentioned in the first part of the article, Slovak authorities have been continuously improving and updating the PE curriculum. One of the suggestions that did not pass as a mandatory requirement was to increase compulsory PE classes to three sessions per week, and, as a result, schools are required to have a minimum of two PE classes per week, but they have the option to increase this number to three if they choose (MVSSV SR, 2023).

Follows the dimension *Quality Teaching of Physical Education* (QTPE), scored with average mean of 6.09 and a standard deviation of .84. The dimension refers to the areas in PE as are: the development of fundamental skills across different physical and sport activities within appropriate contexts, fostering an understanding of the significance of physical activity for health and fitness, as well as the ability to set and achieve personal goals, and demonstrating proficiency in decision-making and communication skills. Remarkably, the lowest score of 3.61 was attributed to an item similar to one found in the SDBA dimension. This item pertains to effectively enhancing students' physical skill development through the PE program.

Next is the dimension *Social Norms and Cultural Practise* (SNCP), with average mean of 5.74 and a standard deviation of .83. The dimension comprises three items, all pertaining to the establishment and adherence to clear policies ensuring equal learning opportunities regardless of gender or religious and economic issues. Items related to economic issues and religion scored lower (4.46 and 4.07, respectively) while the item related to gender equality in PE environment scored the highest 8.69. This suggests that gender disparity is not a significant concern within the realm of PE. Integration and inclusion are gradually becoming one of the central topics in research on PE. The training program for future PE teachers includes several subjects where students learn how to conduct and teach PE classes for both healthy students and those with health impairments. For example, a number of studies have been conducted to examine how able-bodied students perceive PE classes that include students with health impairments, such as intellectual disabilities (Nemček, 2024) or hearing impairments (Kyselová & Nemček, 2024).

The dimension *Cognitive Skill Development* (CSD) ranked fifth, garnering an average mean of 5.32 and a standard deviation of 1.46. This dimension consists of the items related to cultivation of critical thinking skills, problem-solving abilities, innovative thinking skills, independent thinking, and moral thinking developed through PE classes. Notably, the item focusing on critical thinking received the lowest score (3.98), while problem-solving achieved the highest score (6.26) with other items scoring around 5 points.

Habituated Behavior in Physical Activities (HBPA) is the dimension that focuses on demonstrating appropriate decisions and actions to maintain a healthy lifestyle, cultivating a habit of regular exercise, actively participating in sports clubs or at school sport activities, and understanding the relationship between personal needs, health, and physical activity. The dimension achieved an average mean of 4.98 and a standard deviation of .84. All items within this dimension scored within the range of 4.5 to 5.4. Only the item related to participation in extracurricular school activities with the potential for lifelong involvement in sports received a higher score (5.81). These activities are privately organized, but parents and schools partially receive donations from the government.

The dimension *Governmental Input for Physical Education* (GIPE) received lower score, with an average mean of 4.42 and a standard deviation of .90. GIPE comprises five items all pertaining to governmental support and involvement in PE. These include supporting research, recognizing the distinctive role of PE as a part of balanced education system, providing financial support, establishing norms regarding to qualification of PE instructors, and implementing PE as a fundamental human right issue for all children. The respondents from this study identified the largest gap related to the recognition of PE as an integral part of a balanced educational system, scoring the lowest at 3.26. The remaining items scored similarly, ranging from 4.5 to 5.1. This suggests a need for greater emphasis on the integration of PE within educational frameworks and increased governmental support to address the identified gaps in this dimension.

The lowest scored dimension *Plans for Feasibility and Accessibility of Physical Education* (PFAPE) with an average mean of 3.33, and a standard deviation of 1.31. PFAPE comprises only two items, both centered around collaborative efforts for creating opportunities for teachers at national and international levels to enhance the feasibility and accessibility of physical education. Our explanation for why this dimension scored the lowest is that teachers often have almost no cooperation and collaboration with other school on international level and few on national level. However, this dimension might improve soon, as many schools are starting to participate in larger international programs such as the International Baccalaureate Diploma Programme (IB).

Following from GIQPE research, it remains a challenge to focus on providing national and international opportunities to make physical education more effective for teachers; also, to provide continuous lifelong education for PE teachers. An important challenge is to recognize the subject of physical and sports education as equally important as other subjects and to pay sufficient attention to it, especially at the government level. Another challenge is in the real fulfilment of the competences arising from the field of *Health and Movement*, and through PE lessons to provide pupils with knowledge about health, the benefits of regular physical activity, but also to support individual personal needs. On the other hand, physical and sport education in Slovakia is more positively evaluated in terms of material equipment, teachers' qualifications, and the provision of exercise opportunities for pupils.

Many of the mentioned challenges from GIOPE research were taken into account during preparation of new curriculum in physical education that was part of the general curricular reform in primary school in Slovakia started in 2021.

PE Curriculum in the Most Recent Curricular Reform of 2021

The most important points of PE area as were established in the recent curriculum reform:

Changing of the Primary School Education Structure

Curricular reform should ensure the creation of a harmonized and integrated curriculum in both vertical and horizontal lines. A curriculum will be prepared for primary schools structured into three cycles, i.e., first to third grades is the first cycle; the fourth and fifth grades is the second cycle, and the sixth to ninth grades is the third cycle.

Placing More Emphasis on Educational Areas Than on the Subjects Themselves

Educational areas should be the basis of the curriculum. The construction of new curricula should be based on the development of educational areas, a higher degree of harmonization of individual programs within which it will be possible to better integrate knowledge from individual subjects and avoid repetition of knowledge in individual subjects. The framework curriculum will not contain a breakdown of the number of hours by grades and individual subjects, but by educational areas and cycles. The school will have great autonomy in how it creates school programs through educational areas and subjects within individual cycles.

Educational Area "Health and Movement"

At the end of 2021, the newly established Central Committee for the Educational Area Health and Movement in the MSVVS prepared a proposal of a new Health and Movement educational area curriculum, including curriculum for the subject of PE in primary schools (Vzdelávacia oblasť Zdravie a pohyb, 2021). We selected from the document basic ideas that are mentioned as follows:

Emphasis on the Educational Area Health and Movement, Its Aim and Goals

The area creates space for the pupils to develop physical literacy, including the development of lifelong physical competence, with a focus on the acquisition of knowledge and skills related to a healthy lifestyle, physical, and sports activity. The goal of the area for pupils is to understand the importance of physical and sports activity in strengthening physical and mental health and to recognize the effect of the performed exercises on the body. The educational area develops the social, emotional, intellectual, and ethical aspects of the students. When implementing the content of the educational area, it is important to respect the pupils' individual dispositions in accordance with the basic principles of inclusion. An important part is the pupils' motivation to achieve individual improvements in their general motor performance, while accepting their own movement possibilities and their limitation. The educational area is implemented in accordance with the philosophy of an active school through the teaching subject PE, daily compulsory physical activities, course forms of teaching, as well as physical activities performed within the schoolchildren's club. An important mission of the educational area is to create a positive relationship of students to regular physical and sports activities as a necessary basis for active use of free time.

Components of the Educational Area

The basic components of the Health and Movement area are as follows:

Health and lifestyle – topics related to healthy nutrition, hygiene, prevention of addictive substances, hardening, and mental balance. Supporting a healthy lifestyle in the school environment should be a daily part of education and training, not only in PE classes. Nowadays, lifestyle is often associated with the concept of well-being, which includes many different dimensions. Well-being represents the ability to create a long-term feeling of fulfilment and satisfaction in one's life, which can be achieved and built in different ways. Sport and physical activity are one of the ways that can be proven to contribute to well-being and mental balance, and in the future, it can form an important component of relaxation and life balance for male and female pupils.

A prerequisite for an active lifestyle is basic *movement competences*, which can be considered a key component of this educational field. We understand movement competences as a set of movement abilities and skills that a person possesses to move economically and with confidence in various movement situations. In general, movement competences can be perceived as a common movement framework for participation in movement and sports activities, but, on the other hand, movement competences are part of our everyday life, such as in walking, running, catching, throwing, or maintaining balance. The development of the movement competences themselves is necessarily related to the culture and environment where the individual moves.

Another important component is *physical fitness and motor performance,* which are related to the overall resistance of the organism and its ability to adapt to the load, both physical and mental. Currently, it is observed as a decline in physical fitness and motor performance among students of all age categories, which can later significantly affect their health in adulthood. The purpose is to motivate students to improve their own level of physical fitness and motor performance, as well as appreciate their individual progress, the ability to achieve appropriately set goals, and to support the pleasant positive emotions of a sense of success that are associated with it.

Sport and physical activity is another component aimed at motivating pupils to use exercise in their free time, whether in an organized or unorganized form. Education and training through sport consist of the integration and implementation of elements of sport so that they can be used for educational purposes and build the pupils' personal and social competences. It is during PE that there is room to develop emotional skills and empathy, to be aware of one's strengths and weaknesses, to learn cooperation and effective communication with people, or to constructively solve potential conflict situations. Naturally, it is possible to develop the self-development competencies of male and female pupils during sports, such as the ability to achieve an appropriately set goal, to motivate oneself to achieve a result, or to find creative solutions to situations. The development of mutual respect, solidarity, and understanding are educational goals that sport should fulfill through specific sports or movement tasks. Motor performance should not be of primary importance in this case, although it plays an important role. The goal is for all children to gain experience in sports and be able to actively participate in it.

The purpose of the component *protection and safety of life and health of the population* is to guide pupils to protect their health and life, as well as the health and life of other people through theoretical and practical knowledge, skills in self-protection, providing assistance to others in case of threats to safety, health, and life. At an age-appropriate level, it integrates the attitudes, knowledge, and skills of pupils aimed at their own and society-wide safety and the protection of life and health in crisis situations.

Conclusions (Challenges in PE and QPE in Slovakia)

PE in Slovakia is a compulsory subject in primary and secondary schools, which is taught twice a week for 45 minutes. Schools can voluntarily increase the number of hours through the available hours, but this option is not too much used by schools. In the curriculum, the subject falls into the area of Health and Movement, which has the following components: healthy lifestyle, movement competencies, physical fitness and motor performance, sport and physical activity, protection and safety of life, and health of population.

Important challenges for future of PE teaching praxis and physical and sport activities in Slovak schools are:

- Implementation of the "Active school" project in praxis;
- Increasing of quality PE in primary and secondary schools together with increasing of number of PE classes per week;
- Acceptance of physical literacy as basic aim of PE teaching, especially in primary schools;
- Focusing on lifelong movement competencies development of children and youth;
- Implementation of tandem teaching in PE in first grade in all primary schools.

References

Antala, B., Balga, T., Šmela, P., Pačesová, P., Luptáková, M., Luptáková, G., & Popluhárová, M. (2021). *Didaktika telesnej a športovej výchovy pre vzdelávaciu oblast Zdravie a pohyb – vybrané kapitoly [Didactics of Physical and sport Education for the educational area Health and Movement]*. Bratislava, SVŠ TŠV.

Ho, W., Ahmed, D., Rafael, K., López de D`Amico, R.L., Antala, B., Liu, M., Dong, X., & Xie, Y.Y. (2023). Quality physical education (QPE) measurement tool development. *International Sports Studies*, 45(2), 6–27. https://doi.org/10.30819/iss.45-2.02

Ho, W.K.Y., Ahmed M.D., & Kukurova, K. (2021). Development and validation of an instrument to assess quality physical education. *Cogent Education*, 8(1). www.tandfonline.com/doi/epdf/10.1080/2331186X.2020.1864082?needAccess=true

Kyselová, B., & Nemček, D. (2024). Postoje žiakov športových a nešportových tried k inklúzii žiakov so sluchovým postihnutím do telesnej a športovej výchovy [Attitudes of students from sports and non-sports classes towards the inclusion of students with hearing impairments in physical education and sports activities]. *Telesná výchova & šport*, 34(1), 93–106.

Ministry of Education, Science, Research and Sport of the Slovak Republic (MSVVS SR). (2017). *Analýza stavu telocviční v základných a stredných školách v Slovenskej republike*

[Analysis of the state of gymnasiums in primary and secondary schools in the Slovak Republic]. www.minedu.sk/data/att/ca0/11913.0a3d3a.pdf

Ministry of Education, Science, Research and Sport of the Slovak Republic (MSVVS SR). (2023). *Rezort školstva pripravil usmernenia pre ZŠ a SŠ k tretej hodine telesnej výchovy od školského roku 2023/2024 [The Department of Education has prepared guidelines for primary and secondary schools for the third hour of physical education from the 2023/2024 school year]*. www.minedu.sk/rezort-skolstva-pripravil-usmernenia-pre-zs-a-ss-k-tretej-hodine-telesnej-vychovy-od-skolskeho-roku-20232024/

Nemček, D. 2024. How would able-bodied children perceive a student with an intellectual disability in inclusive physical education? *Specijalna edukacija i rehabilitacija*, 23(1), pp. 1–20. https://doi.org/10.5937/specedreh23-45047

UNESCO. (2015). *Quality Physical Education Guidelines and Police Markers*. France, UNESCO. https://unesdoc.unesco.org/ark:/48223/pf0000231101.

Vzdelávacia oblasť Zdravie a pohyb. (2021). *[Educational area Health and Movement] Ústredná predmetová komisia pre vzdelávaciu oblasť Zdravie a pohyb, rukopis*. MSVVS

Chapter 21

Quality Physical Education in South Africa

Aphiwe Jadezweni and Rudolph Leon van Niekerk

Introduction

In the past two decades, physical education (PE) in school curricula worldwide has seen a decline and deterioration (du Toit et al., 2007). Factors contributing to this trend include a crowded curriculum, reduced time allocation, diminished perceived importance of PE, and inadequate resources (du Toit et al., 2007). Notably, PE is absent from the South African curriculum, mirroring challenges in European countries (Hardman, 2010; Morgan & Bourke, 2008), where inadequate teacher training affects PE quality significantly.

According to the South African Curriculum and Assessment Policy Statement (CAPS), the primary goal of the South African PE curriculum is to cultivate an appreciation for regular physical activity through various activities (Department of Basic Education, 2015:10). Regular physical activity supports and promotes physical and social well-being (Van Sluijs et al., 2007; Mcveigh et al., 2004:982).

Studies on children's physical activity levels in South Africa yield mixed results. Toriola and Monyeki (2012:802) found gender disparities in fitness levels and activity rates, with some adolescents exhibiting low activity (Toriola & Monyeki, 2012:803). As such, physical activity tends to decline with age (Mamabolo et al., 2007:1047; Shirinde et al., 2012:236). However, rural children may show higher activity levels (Themane et al., 2006:53), while disadvantaged communities may exhibit lower to moderate activity levels (Lennox et al., 2008:68), influenced by school proximity.

Historic Context of Physical Education in South African Schools

South Africa, as an emerging market and middle-income country in the post-Apartheid era (1948–1994), grapples with significant challenges concerning anti-social behaviors and health risks among its impoverished youth. The Medical Research Council (Malan, 2014) reported that 61% of South Africa's population is at risk for cardiovascular disease, osteoarthritis, chronic kidney disease, cancer, and diabetes. Insufficient levels of health-enhancing physical activity are widespread across all age groups, with a noticeable decline observed during early adolescence. Inactivity rates remain high, with 43% of adolescents and 74.6% of adults leading sedentary lives (Strydom, 2013). Numerous factors contribute to their inactivity, including compromised PE in school curricula, low levels of motor proficiency, excessive screen time, high technology use (particularly social media), limited access to recreation facilities, safety concerns, and transportation issues related to school attendance (Pienaar et al., 2015).

Historically, prior to 1994, during the Apartheid Government's reign over education, PE was segregated by gender, with separate syllabi for boys and girls (Stroebel et al., 2016a). Although acknowledged as part of the school curriculum, the teaching of PE varied across Provincial Departments of Education. The government mandated two PE periods per week for all grades, yet many schools either incompletely implemented it or gradually phased it out due to staffing constraints, inadequate equipment and facilities, or prioritization of "more crucial subjects" such as Mathematics and Science (Stroebel et al., 2016a).

Following the 1994 election and the establishment of the new Democratic Government in 1995, the South African Schools Act was revised, ushering in curriculum reform in 1996. The first National Curriculum Statement (Curriculum 2005 (C2005)), in 1997, introduced a shift from "subjects" to "learning areas" based on the principles of Outcomes-based Education (OBE). This reform redefined PE as one of eight learning outcomes of a new learning area called Life Orientation (LO) (Van Deventer & Van Niekerk, 2008). However, challenges emerged as teachers were often inadequately qualified to teach PE, leading to a neglect of practical aspects, compromising the overall quality of PE (Van Deventer & Van Niekerk, 2008).

The implementation of LO took place incrementally, starting with the General Education and Training Band for Grades R to 9. Specific outcomes focusing on human movement and development were integrated into LO, which became compulsory for all learners from Grade R to Grade 12. LO's human movement and development-specific outcome aimed to engage students in activities demonstrating effective human movement and development. Additionally, the recreation and physical activity component within LO aimed to impart an understanding of the relationship between health and physical activities, as well as how the environment can enhance the quality of life and well-being of all learners (Department of Education, 2002).

Physical Education in South African Schools

Delivering quality education to learners facing socioeconomic hardships is a significant challenge in South Africa's public school system. All learners have the right to education (Department of Basic Education, 2015) and PE plays a vital role in promoting holistic development and encouraging physical activity among young learners (Carse et al., 2018). As such, PE aims to cultivate physically educated individuals capable of lifelong physical activity (World Health Organization,

2007). Quality physical education (QPE) enhances skills, reduces sedentary behaviors, and increases physical activity levels (Morano et al., 2016; Dale & Corbin, 2000:240; Pate et al., 2005:1582). UNESCO's concept of QPE emphasizes active, inclusive, peer-led learning to develop students' physical, social, and emotional skills (2016:1).

Despite the global increase in children's inactivity, PE was reintroduced in South Africa among children due to low physical activity levels (Du Toit et al., 2007:245) as part of LO, with insufficient practical sessions to improve fitness (Bayles, 2023; Department of Basic Education, 2015:7; World Health Organization, 2009, 2016; American College of Sports Medicine, 2013). Many South African schools struggle to implement PE according to national guidelines due to a shortage of qualified teachers (Sherman et al., 2010:2). Generalist instructors often deliver PE, necessitating careful consideration of teaching methods, especially in primary schools (Du Toit, 2019). Effective PE delivery requires comprehensive instruction to develop both theoretical and practical movement knowledge and abilities (Lundvall, 2015).

Pedagogical approaches to PE in South Africa vary, including sport-focused, health-focused, life skills education, and non-teaching approaches (Burnett, 2018:8). Schools often prioritize academic subjects over PE despite student interest in physical activity (Ishee, 2004). The content of PE programs should match students' abilities and motivate physical activity participation. Different approaches contribute to the diversity of PE practices, with sport-focused and health-focused approaches prevalent in higher quintile schools. Some schools outsource PE to non-governmental organizations (NGOs) specializing in sport-for-development programs, while others adopt non-teaching or self-learning approaches (Burnett, 2018). These diverse approaches reflect the complex landscape of PE delivery in South African schools.

Dimensional Studies of Quality Physical Education in South Africa

A recent study on teachers' perceptions and attitudes toward PE (Jadezweni, 2023) in the Eastern Cape raised concerns about the compromised and sometimes neglected state of QPE in South African schools. Despite PE being part of LO in schools, there remains a lack of understanding regarding teachers' perceptions and factors influencing PE quality in South Africa. This study explored teachers' perspectives and the factors influencing QPE in schools within the Raymond Mhlaba Local Municipality of the Eastern Cape, South Africa.

The study by Jadezweni (2023) adopted a quantitative research paradigm with a cross-sectional design to examine factors influencing QPE among primary and secondary school teachers and coaches in the Raymond Mhlaba Local Municipality, Eastern Cape. This municipality was chosen for its proactive stance toward PE, offering a diverse representation of schools across the region. A stratified random sampling method was employed to ensure a comprehensive representation of teachers and coaches from quintile 1 to 5 schools. The sample included a wide range of professionals responsible for delivering QPE, such as LO teachers, life skills teachers, physical educators, and sports coaches. Stratification was based on both district and school type (primary or secondary) to reflect the broader landscape of PE in the region. Data collection was facilitated through the Quality Physical Education Development Questionnaire (QPEDQ), developed by Ho et al. (2019), consisting of 50 items rated on a 10-point Likert scale. The questionnaire, adapted for the South African context and pilot-tested for clarity, demonstrated high reliability with Cronbach's alpha coefficients ranging from 0.85 to 0.93. Factor analysis, specifically principal component analysis with Varimax rotation, was applied to explore the factors influencing QPE. Only items with a factor loading of 0.45 or higher were retained, ensuring robust and meaningful interpretation.

The statistical analysis revealed a well-distributed sample of participants, comprising both male ($n = 46$; 39.3%) and female ($n = 67$; 57.3%) teachers and coaches. Most respondents were from public schools ($n = 113$; 96.6%), while a smaller proportion represented private schools ($n = 4$; 3.4%). The majority (85.5%) reported that PE was integrated into the LO program, while a smaller fraction (7.7%) indicated that PE was offered as a standalone subject. A minority (6.8%) reported that no PE program was available at their schools. Regarding professional roles, a majority of the participants identified as teachers ($n = 91$; 77.8%), with others serving as coaches (n = 19; 16.2%) or holding professional or administrative positions ($n = 7$; 6%). These statistics provide insight into the demographic composition and educational contexts of the sample, highlighting the diversity of roles and settings within which QPE is delivered.

In Jadezweni's (2023) study, six dimensions of quality physical activity were identified, focusing on the educational value, knowledge and skills development, holistic development, compulsory nature, policy and collaboration, and safety in physical activity. Similarly, Ho et al. (2021) developed and validated an instrument that identifies eight dimensions of QPE, which also emphasizes educational outcomes, skills development, and the importance of policy, but adds dimensions like inclusivity and teaching approaches. This discussion compares these two models of QPE, with a focus on contextualizing the findings in the South African environment using relevant local studies.

A descriptive analysis of the six factors identified by Jadezweni (2023) is presented in Table 21.1, showing how these factors align with the eight dimensions identified by Ho et al. (2021). The factors from the South African study are ranked from highest to lowest based on their mean scores.

Educational Value

In both Jadezweni (2023) and Ho et al. (2021), the educational value of PE is highly emphasized. The UNESCO International Paper on Physical Education (2015) and studies like Burnett (2001) highlight how PE (PE) contributes to literacy, well-being, and holistic development. Jadezweni reported that participants regarded educational value as the most significant factor, which aligns with international

Table 21.1 Comparison between 6-factor and 8-dimension models

Eight Dimensions (Ho et al., 2021)	Six-factor Solution (Jadezweni, 2023)						
Dimension	Factor	Mean	Standard Deviation	Eigenvalue	% of Variance	Alpha
3: Quality Teaching of Physical Education	4: Educational Value	7.83	1.83	1.99	9.62	.891
1: Skill Development and Bodily Awareness	3: Knowledge and Skills Development	7.34	1.97	2.32	12.90	.930
4: Plans for Feasibility and Accessibility of Physical Education 5: Social Norms and Cultural Practice 7: Cognitive Skill Development 8: Habituated Behavior in Physical Activities	1: Holistic Development	7.24	1.89	24.56	21.19	.927
2: Facilities and Norms in Physical Education	6: Compulsory School Subject 5: Safety and Suitable Environment	7.01 5.85	2.44 2.35	1.29 1.54	7.86 8.94	.888 .921
6: Governmental Input for Physical Education	2: Policy and Collaboration	6.48	2.32	2.44	13.72	.919

perspectives that advocate for meaningful instruction in PE that transcends mere physical activity. Burnett (2001) similarly notes that in South Africa, PE's potential for holistic education is often underutilized due to weak policy implementation, highlighting the need for a more robust curriculum that integrates educational outcomes.

South African educators' perception of PE's educational value, as shown in Stroebel et al.'s (2016b) study, echoes this need, with teachers recognizing the importance of QPE but often constrained by limited resources. These insights underline the importance of structured, well-resourced QPE programs that focus on educational development, as advocated by both Jadezweni and Ho et al. (2021).

Knowledge and Skills Development

Both frameworks underscore the role of knowledge and skills development in promoting QPE. Ho et al. (2021) identified this as one of the eight dimensions, with high reliability, and stressed that QPE should provide students with both cognitive and physical skills. Similarly, Jadezweni (2023) found that participants viewed knowledge and skills development as crucial to promoting lifelong physical activity.

In the South African context, Van Deventer (2012) emphasizes the critical role of QPE in developing knowledge and skills, especially within the socioeconomic and resource limitations in the country's schools. He stresses that the absence of qualified teachers and poor curriculum integration hinders the ability to impart essential skills to students. In line with Ho et al. (2021), South African schools could benefit from adopting pedagogical approaches like the Sport Education Model (SEM) to deliver richer, more educationally valuable PE experiences, as discussed by Pritchard et al. (2008).

Holistic Development

Jadezweni (2023) identified holistic development as a key factor of QPE, which aligns with Ho et al.'s (2021) dimension of fostering social and emotional learning through PE. The recognition that physical activity impacts not only physical health but also social, emotional, and cognitive development is central to both frameworks. Studies like that of Mahar et al. (2006) and local research by Govender and Naidoo (2015) show that well-rounded PE programs contribute to developing key life skills, such as cooperation, problem-solving, and communication, which are vital for children's overall development.

In South Africa, Govender and Naidoo (2015) further found that socioeconomic challenges create disparities in access to QPE and sports activities, which can limit holistic development opportunities for students. This is particularly concerning in underprivileged areas where facilities and qualified staff are scarce. Thus, implementing programs that prioritize holistic development in QPE, as emphasized by

Jadezweni and Ho et al., is essential for addressing these inequalities in South Africa.

The Compulsory Nature of Physical Education

Both Jadezweni (2023) and Ho et al. (2021) stress the importance of making PE compulsory in schools. Jadezweni's study reflects participants' perceptions that compulsory QPE is vital to ensuring consistent engagement and learning. Similarly, Ho et al. (2021) highlight the value of mandatory QPE programs in promoting prosocial behaviors and fostering lifelong physical activity habits.

Stroebel et al. (2016b) provide a South African perspective, noting that although PE was compulsory before 1994, many schools have phased it out due to resource and policy implementation challenges. Their research aligns with the findings from both Jadezweni and Ho et al., underscoring the need for reintegrating compulsory PE into the curriculum to ensure all students benefit from its educational and developmental advantages.

Policy and Collaboration

Jadezweni (2023) and Ho et al. (2021) both recognize the role of policy and collaboration in fostering QPE. Ho et al. (2021) highlight the need for policies that support teacher training, resource allocation, and curriculum development. Similarly, Jadezweni's findings suggest that policy-related issues, including the lack of collaboration among stakeholders, hinder the implementation of QPE programs in South Africa.

Burnett (2001) and Pillay and Parker (2019) found that South African PE policy is often poorly implemented, with insufficient support for schools to execute QPE programs effectively. Pillay and Parker (2019) argue that clearer policies and better teacher training are essential for improving PE quality, aligning with Ho et al.'s emphasis on effective policies that support QPE. Furthermore, international organizations like UNESCO (2015) have called for improved policy collaboration to enhance physical activity and well-being globally, a goal that remains relevant to the South African context.

Safety and a Conducive Environment

Both Jadezweni (2023) and Ho et al. (2021) identified safety and a conducive environment as critical to QPE. Creating a safe and supportive space for physical activity enables students to engage fully and benefit from PE programs. Ho et al. (2021) emphasized the need for secure environments and appropriate equipment, echoing findings from Jadezweni's study, where participants indicated that the environment and safety are often neglected in South African schools.

Govender and Naidoo (2015) and Van Deventer (2012) pointed out that many South African schools lack the facilities and resources needed to provide safe and engaging QPE experiences. As highlighted by Fuller and Drawer (2004), risk management strategies, such as adherence to safety guidelines, are crucial in PE, particularly in resource-constrained contexts like South Africa. Therefore, efforts to improve safety and provide adequate facilities would enhance the overall quality of PE, a recommendation that resonates with both Jadezweni and Ho et al.'s findings.

Conclusion

The comparison between the six dimensions identified by Jadezweni (2023) and the eight dimensions from Ho et al. (2021) reveals a strong alignment in emphasizing educational value, skills development, holistic growth, policy support, compulsory QPE, and safety. Other South African studies, similarly, highlight the challenges and opportunities in implementing QPE. Collectively, these studies emphasize the importance of comprehensive policies, well-trained educators, and safe, conducive environments for enhancing QPE in South Africa and beyond. Addressing the challenges faced in the Eastern Cape district and providing policy recommendations, the study contributes to the transformation and development of QPE within the broader South African education system. Ultimately, the study concluded that QPE plays a pivotal role in advancing the transformative agenda of the South African education system.

References

American College of Sports Medicine. (2013). *ACSM's guidelines for exercise testing and prescription*. Philadelphia, USA: Lippincott Williams & Wilkins.

Bayles, M. P. (2023). *ACSM's exercise testing and prescription*. Philadelphia, USA: Lippincott Williams & Wilkins.

Burnett, C. (2001). Whose game is it anyway? Power, play and sport. *Sport Education and Society*, 6(1), 37–55.

Burnett, C. (2018). *National research: State and status of physical education in public schools of South Africa*. Pretoria, RSA: UNICEF South Africa.

Carse, N., Jess, M., & Keay, J. (2018). Primary physical education: Shifting perspectives to move forwards. *European Physical Education Review*, 24(4), 487–502. doi: 10.4324/9781315545257-17

Dale, D., & Corbin, C. B. (2000). Physical activity participation of high school graduates following exposure to conceptual or traditional physical education. *Research Quarterly for Exercise and Sport*, 71(1), 61–68. doi: 10.1080/02701367.2000.10608881.

Department of Basic Education (DBE). (2015). *Policy on the South African Standard for Principalship*. Pretoria: Department of Basic Education.

Department of Education. (2002). *National Curriculum statement: Grades 10–12 (schools), overview (draft)*. Pretoria: Published Department of Education.

Du Toit, D. (2019). Service-learning within field experience of physical education teacher education in South Africa: Experiences of pre-service and in-service teachers. *South African Journal for Research in Sport, Physical Education and Recreation*, 41(1), 13–29. https://hdl.handle.net/10520/EJC-14fdd49772

Du Toit, D., Van der Merwe, N., & Rossouw, J. P. (2007). Return of physical education to the curriculum: Problems and challenges facing schools in South African communities: Physical education. *African Journal for Physical Health Education, Recreation and Dance, 13*(3), 241–253. https://hdl.handle.net/10520/EJC19499

Fuller, C., & Drawer, S. (2004). The application of risk management in sport. *Sports Medicine, 34*, 349–356. doi: 10.2165/00007256-200434060-00001

Govender, K., & Naidoo, D. (2015). An investigation into perceptions of sport and physical activity in a selected urban community: A South African study. *African Journal for Physical, Health Education, Recreation and Dance, 21*(1), 107–122.

Hardman, K. (2010). *PE: The future ain"t what it used to be*. Keynote presented at the International Congress, Youth Sport 2010. Knowledge for Sport, Ljubljana, Slovenia, 2–4 December.

Ho, W. K. Y., Ahmed, M. D., Khoo, S., Tan, C. H., Dehkordi, M. R., Gallardo, M., & Shu, C. (2019). Towards developing and validating Quality Physical Education in schools—The Asian physical education professionals' voice. *PloS One, 14*(8), e0218158. doi: 10.1371/journal.pone.0218158. eCollection 2019.

Ho, W. K. Y., Ahmed, M. D., & Kukurova, K. (2021). Development and validation of an instrument to assess quality physical education. *Cogent Education*, 8(1), 1864082.

Ho, W. K. Y., Md. Ahmed, D., Carvalho, P. G., Branislav, A., Makszin, I., Valeiro, M. G., Kougioumtzis, K., Cazzoli, S., Van Niekerk, R. L., Morris, T., Huang, F., & Wong, B. (2019). Development of an instrument to assess perception of quality physical education (QPE) among European professionals. *South African Journal for Research in Sport, Physical Education and Recreation, 41*(1), 31–49. https://hdl.handle.net/10520/EJC-14fdd81ac8

Ishee, J. H. (2004). Are physical education classes encouraging students to be physically active?. *Journal of Physical Education, Recreation & Dance, 75*(2), 6. doi: 10.1080/07303084.2004.10608548

Jadezweni, A. (2023). *Factors contributing to quality physical education in schools in the Raymond Mhlaba Local Municipality, Eastern Cape, South Africa*. Master's dissertation, University of Fort Hare, Alice, Eastern Cape, South Africa.

Lennox, A., Pienaar, A. E., & Wilders, C. (2008). Physical fitness and the physical activity status of 15-year-old adolescents in a semi-urban community. *South African Journal for Research in Sport, Physical Education and Recreation, 30*(1), 59–73. https://hdl.handle.net/10520/EJC108868

Lundvall, S. (2015). Physical literacy in the field of physical education—A challenge and a possibility. *Journal of Sport and Health Science, 4*(2), 113–118. doi: 10.1016/j.jshs.2015.02.001

Mahar, M. T., Murphy, S. K., Rowe, D. A., Golden, J., Shields, A. T., & Raedeke, T. D. (2006). Effects of a classroom-based program on physical activity and on-task behavior. *Medicine and Science in Sports and Exercise, 38*(12), 2086. doi: 10.1249/01.mss.0000235359.16685.a3.

Malan, M. (2014). *SA's the fattest sub-Saharan African nation–study*. Bhekisisa Centre for Health Journalism. http://bhekisisa.org/article/2014-05-29-00-sa-has-the-fattest-subsaharan-african-nation-study [Accessed: 12 August 2020].

Mamabolo, R. L., Kruger, H. S., Lennox, A., Monyeki, M. A., Pienaar, A. E., Underhay, C., & Czlapka-Matyasik, M. (2007). Habitual physical activity and body composition of black township adolescents residing in the North West Province, South Africa. *Public Health Nutrition, 10*(10), 1047–1056. doi: 10.1017/S1368980007668724.

McVeigh, J., Norris, S., & Wet, T. D. (2004). The relationship between socio-economic status and physical activity patterns in South African children. *Acta Paediatrica*, 93(7), 982–988. doi: 10.1111/j.1651-2227.2004.tb02699.x.

Morano, M., Rutigliano, I., Rago, A., Pettoello-Mantovani, M., & Campanozzi, A. (2016). A multicomponent, school-initiated obesity intervention to promote healthy lifestyles in children. *Nutrition*, *32*, 1075–1080. doi: 10.1016/j.nut.2016.03.007.

Morgan, P., & Bourke, S. (2008). Non-specialist teachers' confidence to teach PE: the nature and influence of personal school experiences in PE. *Physical Education and Sport Pedagogy*, *13*(1), 1–29. doi: 10.1016/j.nut.2016.03.007.

Pate, R. R., Ward, D. S., Saunders, R. P., Felton, G., Dishman, R. K., & Dowda, M. (2005). Promotion of physical activity among high-school girls: a randomized controlled trial. *American Journal of Public Health*, *95*(9), 1582–1587. doi: 10.2105/AJPH.2004.045807

Pienaar, A.E., Visagie, M., & Leonard, A. (2015). Proficiency at object control skills by nine- to ten-year-old children in South Africa: The NW-Child Study. *Perceptual and Motor Skills*, *121*(1), 309–332. doi: 10.2466/10.PMS.121c15x8.

Pillay, L., & Parker, M. (2019). The integration of physical education in the South African school curriculum: Pedagogical challenges. *South African Journal of Education*, *39*(2), 1–11.

Pritchard, T., Hawkins, A., Wiegand, R., & Metzler, J. (2008). Effects of two instructional approaches on skill development, knowledge, and game performance. *Measurement in Physical Education and Exercise Science*, 12, 219–236. doi: 10.1080/10913670802349774

Sherman, C. P., Tran, C., & Alves, Y. (2010). Elementary school classroom teacher delivered physical education: Costs, benefits and barriers. *Physical Educator*, *67*(1), 2. doi: 10.47544/johsk.2021.2.2.17

Shirinde, K. S., Monyeki, M. A., Pienaar, A. E., & Toriola, A. L. (2012). Perceived barriers and benefits of participating in physical activity and the levels of physical activity of children attending farm schools. *African Journal for Physical Health Education, Recreation and Dance*, *18*(2), 228–240. https://hdl.handle.net/10520/EJC123255

Stroebel, L. C., Hay, J., & Bloemhoff, H. J. (2016a). Physical education in South Africa: Have we come full circle? *South African Journal for Research in Sport, Physical Education and Recreation*, *38*(3), 215–228.

Stroebel, L. C., Hay, J., & Bloemhoff, H. J. (2016b). Past and present physical education policies in South African schools: A retrospective overview. *South African Journal for Research in Sport, Physical Education and Recreation*, *38*(3), 171–190.

Strydom, G. L. (2013). Physical activity, health and well-being: A strategic objective of the National Sport and Recreation Plan (NSRP) of South Africa. *African Journal for Physical, Health Education, Recreation and Dance*, 19(4/2), 980–992. https://hdl.handle.net/10520/EJC199881

Themane, M. J., Koppes, L. W., Kemper, H. C. G., & Monyeki, K. D. (2006). The relationship between physical fitness, physical activity in rural South African children. *Journal of Physical Education and Recreation*, 12(1), 48–54. doi: 10.24112/ajper.121310.

Toriola, O. M., & Monyeki, M. A. (2012). Health-related fitness, body composition and physical activity status among adolescent learners: The PAHL study. *African Journal for Physical, Health Education, Recreation and Dance*, *18*(4:1), 795–811. https://hdl.handle.net/10520/EJC128341

UNESCO (United Nations Educational, Scientific and Cultural Organization). (2015). Quality Physical Education (QPE): Guidelines for policy makers. https://unesdoc.unesco.org/ark:/48223/pf0000231101

UNESCO (United Nations Educational, *Scientific and Cultural Organization*). (2016). Quality Physical Education. http://unesco.go.ke/social-sciences/36-csr/260-quality-physical-education.html

Van Deventer, K. J. (2012). School physical education in crisis: The need for a new pedagogy for the teaching of physical education in the curriculum. *South African Journal for Research in Sport, Physical Education and Recreation, 34*(1), 123–144.

Van Deventer, K. J., & Van Niekerk, E. (2008). *Life Orientation: Grades R-11: Teacher's perspectives on the implementation of Life Orientation in selected Western Cape Schools.* Unpublished research report. Stellenbosch: Stellenbosch University.

Van Sluijs, E. M., McMinn, A. M., & Griffin, S. J. (2007). Effectiveness of interventions to promote physical activity in children and adolescents: systematic review of controlled trials. *BMJ*, 335 (7622), 703. doi: 10.1136/bmj.39320.843947.BE.

World Health Organization. (2007). *WHO information series on school health, document 12: promoting physical activity in schools: an important element of a health promoting school*. Geneva: WHO.

World Health Organization. (2009). *Obesity and physical activity*. Geneva: Switzerland. (Technical Report Series).

World Health Organization. (2016). *Report of the Commission on Ending Childhood Obesity*. Geneva. www.who.int/end-childhood-obesity/publications/echo-report/en/

Chapter 22

The Development of Quality Physical Education in South Korea

Hyun-joo Cho and Su-jin Kim

From Humble Beginnings to Prosperous Initiatives: QPE in Korea

Background of the Country: Geographical, Political, Economic, and Demographic Information

According to Statistics Korea, the total population of South Korea in 2024 will be 51.75 million, of which 10.6% will be children aged 0 to 14, 70.2% will be people of working age (15- to 64-year-olds), and 19.2% will be the elderly aged 65 and over, indicating a rapidly aging society. Korea's low fertility rate has become a serious social issue. In 2023, the total fertility rate (the average number of children a woman is expected to have during her childbearing years) is expected to be 0.72 and the number of live births to be 190,000, both record lows. On the other hand, the life expectancy of Koreans is 83.5 years (as of 2023) for both men and women, which is higher than the average life expectancy of 80.3 years (as of 2023) for Organisation for Economic Co-operation and Development (OECD) member countries (Office for National Statistics, 2024).

South Korea's economy was estimated to be the 13th largest in the world in 2023, with a GDP of $1.673 trillion. It is down three places from its top 10 ranking in 2022. Politics is centered on a presidential system with a five-year term elected by direct popular vote, with Yoon Seok-yul taking office as the 20th president on 10 May 2022. While South Korea and North Korea are divided under international law, including their simultaneous membership in the United Nations, the Korean Peninsula has a dual legal system, with each country recognizing the other as a state.

South Korea speaks its own language (Korean) and uses Hangul, a unique script created by King Sejong the Great (1397–1450) of the Joseon Dynasty. Every year, UNESCO awards the King Sejong Literacy Prize to someone who has made a significant contribution to literacy in the world. All citizens receive compulsory education up to middle school. Since 2013, the government has subsidized childcare for children aged 0 to 5 years (Ministry of Education, 2024). According to the Programme for International Student Assessment (PISA), South Korean students

DOI: 10.4324/9781003513582-24

perform at a high academic level in math, science, and reading. In PISA 2018, South Korea ranked among the highest-performing OECD countries in reading (second to seventh), math (first to fourth), and science (third to fifth).

Development of a Quality Program for Physical Education

Physical education has played an important role in the history of education in South Korea. With the introduction of modern schools in the late 19th century, physical education began to take hold and has been continuously maintained and developed based on the educational epistemology of 'human-centeredness and harmony of virtues'. From the time of liberation until the Fourth Republic in 1981, school physical education was mainly overseen by the Physical Education Department within the Ministry of Education and Culture. Then, from the Fifth Republic in 1982 to the civilian government in 1993, school physical education was transferred to the Ministry of Physical Education and Sports, and under the civilian government in 1994, the Ministry of Education ('20 'Teaching and Learning Evaluation Division') and the Ministry of Culture, Sports and Tourism ('20 'Physical Education Promotion Division') formed a 'bi-ministerial cooperation period' to oversee school physical education. Under this governance, school sports are supported and managed by local education offices and education support offices, and sports federations and sports organizations are also involved in school sports as part of their business (Ministry of Culture, Sports and Tourism, 2022, 2024).

Physical Education or Sport Education or Learning of Physical Activities at School – a general description of the historical development, methods in dealing with equity issues, teaching quality, professional training, curriculum arrangement, and opportunities for extended learning for physical activities.

The governance system of school sports aims to promote and systematically support school sports in close cooperation at the central government level. Under this governance, we are supporting programs to promote students 'health and fitness' under the policy of internalizing school physical education classes, promoting school sports clubs and leagues, further developing school sports departments, and protecting the learning rights and human rights of student-athletes.

Primary school physical education specialists are teachers who are solely responsible for teaching physical education in primary schools, and as of 2021, there are 5,363 of them in 6,157 schools. Priority is given to teachers with expertise in physical education (e.g., completion of an advanced course in substitute physical education, a university or postgraduate degree in physical education, or previous experience as a physical education director or physical education teacher), who are encouraged to complete a physical education training course to improve their expertise and are provided with a dedicated physical education teacher training course.

Physical education and curriculum at the national level in Korea have been changing in response to social needs. After the establishment of the Korean government and until 1954, there was no systematic curriculum due to chaotic social conditions, but physical education was made a compulsory subject from elementary school to high school during the teaching and learning period (1946–1954). On 4 May 2016, Article 13(2) of the School Sports Promotion Act was amended to read:

> The Minister of Education shall establish basic guidelines necessary for the activation of girls' physical education activities and notify the superintendent of education and the principal of the school, and the principal of the school shall formulate and implement a plan for the activation of girls' physical education activities every year in accordance with the basic guidelines.

The main amendments include the mandatory operation of sports clubs preferred by girls, the establishment of a plan for the activation of girls' physical education activities, the institutionalization of dedicated school physical education facilities, and the establishment of the proportion of female participation in school sports promotion committees (Ministry of Education, 2023).

To begin the discussion on QPE, the 2022 Revised Curriculum for Physical Education and Sports introduced 'physical activity forms', leaving behind the value-based curriculum pursued since the 2007 Revised Curriculum for Physical Education and Sports can be the best start of the discussion. The physical activity forms are presented as 'exercise', 'sport', and 'expression' and are expressed in the domain names. The existing 'Safety' domain has been integrated into each domain. In addition, the four curricular competencies have been transformed into three: movement performance competencies, health management competencies, and physical activity culture competencies. The content elements are presented in three categories: 'Knowledge and Understanding', 'Processes and Skills', and 'Values and Attitudes' according to the core ideas of each domain, in accordance with the 2022 revised curriculum outline.

While on the way for QPE development, the online and offline sports activities utilizing VR and apps for students to engage in physical activities always are listed as with priority for skill learning in sports education. Such initiatives are supported by the building of suitable facilities with gymnasiums, auditoriums, swimming pools, sports fields, and other facilities (tennis courts, etc.) for learning. In addition, the government has expanded the policies to include initiatives such as the Artificial Turf Sports Field Construction Plan (2006–2010), the Various School Sports Fields Project (2009–2012), the Open Multi-Purpose School Gymnasium Construction Project, and the Expanded Changing Room Project in supporting the development of a modern and safe environment for sports learning. Thus, with the introduction of these plans, the capacities and opportunities for physical activity improved in leading active and creative living, healthy and proactive lifestyle development, enjoyable culture of physical activity, and a desirable and shared life of success in society. To this end, the training of specialized personnel in elementary, middle, and high schools helps to extend the potential and even beyond reaching the needs of developing countries.

Socio-culturally speaking, physical education has been established as a basic education for fostering global citizenship in connection with global citizenship education. The government's support for physical education is mainly in terms of school sports governance, and the actual impact is centered on local education departments. The Physical Activity Promotion System is conducted once a year at the beginning of the school year for students in grades 5 and 6, middle school, and high school, and at least once a year for students in grades 4 and 5 after health and physical education classes to minimize the percentage of students with low physical fitness. Finally, in terms of physical activity habituation development, Article 10 of the School Sports Promotion Act mandates the operation of school sports clubs to provide students with various physical activity opportunities. The following section further discusses this QPE concept by means of the eight dimensions as described in Ho et al.'s (2021, 2023) study, and thus offers a comprehensive picture of what is to be done for QPE development.

The 8-Dimensional Development in QPE and the Latest Research

Dimension 1: Skill Development and Bodily Awareness (SDBA)

The 2015 revised physical education curriculum has since been reorganized into a 'competency-based curriculum' for future human resources. Accordingly, the nature of physical education has been divided into 'the nature and role of physical education', 'competence in physical education', and 'areas of physical education'. A distinctive feature of this curriculum is that the concept of physical education competencies is presented according to the 2015 revised curriculum outline. Competencies in physical education are a holistic set of knowledge, skills, and attitudes acquired through the process of experiencing physical activity and internalizing its values, and consist of health management skills, physical discipline skills, competition performance skills, and physical expression skills that are formed based on physical movement. To develop these competencies, the content of physical education is organized into the areas of health, challenge, competition, expression, and safety.

The 2022 Revised Curriculum for Physical Education and Sports, which was announced in 2022, will be implemented in stages, starting with grades 3 and 4 of elementary schools and grades 1 of junior and senior high schools in 2025. The 2022 Revised Curriculum for Physical Education and Sports has left behind the value-based curriculum that has been pursued since the 2007 Revised Curriculum for Physical Education and Sports and introduced physical activity forms. The physical activity forms are presented as 'exercise', 'sport', and 'expression' and are expressed in the domain names. The existing 'Safety' domain has been integrated into each of these domains. In addition, the four curriculum competencies have been transformed into three: movement performance competencies, health management competencies, and physical activity cultural competencies. The content elements are presented in three categories: 'knowledge and understanding', 'processes and skills', and 'values and attitudes' according to the core ideas of each domain, in accordance with the 2022 revised curriculum outline (Ministry of Culture, Sports and Tourism, 2024).

Dimension 2: Facilities and Norms in Physical Education (FNPE)

School sports facilities are facilities that are used continuously by students for classroom and non-classroom physical education activities, and can be generally categorized into gymnasiums, auditoriums, swimming pools, sports fields, and other facilities (such as tennis courts). To expand the infrastructure of school sports facilities, the Korean government has carried out various projects, including the Artificial Turf Sports Fields Construction Plan (2006–2010), Various School Sports Fields Project (2009–2012), Open Multi-Purpose School Gymnasium Construction Project, and the Expansion of Changing Room Facilities Project.

The "Artificial Sports Fields Creation Plan" was launched in 2005, and as of 2009, 986 (8.7%) of the 11,310 schools had artificial sports fields and 337 (3.0%) had natural grass sports fields. This project ended in 2008, and under the "Plan to Revitalize Culture, Arts, and Sports Education", the flooring of sports grounds was replaced with high-tech materials, and school sports grounds were divided into the grass (natural and artificial), urethane facilities (multi-purpose fields, tracks, etc.), and dirt (loess, masato, etc.), depending on school conditions.

The 'Open Multi-Purpose School Gymnasiums' project aimed to build indoor gymnasiums on school grounds, expanding physical education spaces for students and local residents to use together, contributing to the revitalization of physical education and the improvement of people's health. Funding for the project is shared by the Ministry of Education (50%), the Education Agency (20%), local governments (20%), and the Ministry of Culture, Sports and Tourism (30%).

In 2022, to improve the health and fitness of students, whose fitness had been reduced due to COVID-19, early implementation of student health and fitness assessments in the first half of the year was encouraged, and the 'Tailored Programme for Low-Fitness Students' was continued. The five components of physical fitness – cardiorespiratory endurance, flexibility, muscular strength and muscular endurance, quickness, and obesity – were measured, with variation based on school conditions. In addition, we wanted to develop and utilize student-specific fitness improvement programs.

Dimension 3: Quality Teaching of Physical Education (QTPE)

To develop school sports, the Republic of Korea has internalized physical education classes, strengthened teacher leadership capacities and supported physical education professionals, provided practical survival swimming education for elementary schools, promoted girls' physical education activities, distributed virtual reality sports rooms in elementary schools, and operated Saturday sports instruction.

In response to the COVID-19 pandemic, several measures were put in place to support virtual school physical education classes and physical activities. In addition, the government strengthened support for virtual and face-to-face sports activities by shifting from face-to-face to virtual school sports club celebrations and expanding the popularity of one-student-one-sports through intramural leagues at each level and village and regional leagues.

In recent years, to internalize school sports management, we have operated futuristic physical education classes and strengthened health and physical fitness promotion activities; to systematize and improve the quality of school sports clubs, we have activated the operation of school sports clubs, expanded the operation of face-to-face and virtual school sports clubs, and linked schools with public and designated sports clubs. In addition, we supported teachers' professional competence in physical education to strengthen the professional competence of teachers and physical education leaders.

In response to the need to build a comprehensive platform to support future online and offline physical education classes and develop content to support future classes, we supported online and offline blended physical education classes. To this end, we developed and distributed remote content for 30 sports classified in five levels of achievement standards to help improve the quality of online and offline classes. In addition, we developed and distributed a 'movement analysis app' that analyses student performance and provides feedback on movement to support effective online classes (Kim, 2021).

Dimension 4: Plans for Feasibility and Accessibility of Physical Education (PFAPE)

The goal of physical education in Korea is to develop physical activity competence to lead an active and creative life, a healthy and proactive life, enjoy a culture of physical activity, and lead a desirable and shared life in society. The Sports Instructor Placement Project for Elementary and Special Schools, which has been in place since 2009, selects professional sports instructors with a certain level of qualification to teach regular classes and after-school sports clubs alongside physical education teachers.

Primary school sports instructors must be qualified as sports instructors (sports instructors, health and exercise managers, sports instructors for the disabled, youth sports instructors, and sports instructors for the elderly) according to Article 2 (6) of the National Sports Promotion Act. In addition, as survival swimming education has been implemented for all grades of elementary schools, there has been a growing demand for improving the quality of survival swimming education, and theoretical and practical education centered on survival functions, which is the core function of survival swimming, has helped students strengthen their self-rescue and self-protection capabilities.

The basic directions for promoting girls' physical activity are to create a gender-equitable environment for physical activity, select sports that consider girls' physical abilities and preferences, and run girls-specific programs to promote girls' participation in sports. To this end, at the elementary school level, girls' preferred sports and sports that stimulate girls' emotions and are easy for them to participate in are used in classes, and in mixed classes in middle and high schools, girls and boys are taught separately or sports that can be run as mixed classes are used.

Meanwhile, the Korea Sports Federation has been running sports classes for girls in elementary, middle, and high schools across the country to expand opportunities for girls to participate in sports. The government is also supporting the expansion of indoor gymnasiums and the installation of changing rooms so that girls' preferred sports and those that are easier for them to participate in can be played indoors by reconfiguring the space to encourage girls' active participation in physical education activities (Ministry of Education, 2023).

Dimension 5: Social Norms and Cultural Practice (SNCP)

The core values of future education of the Seoul Metropolitan Office of Education are: education to learn that all people are human beings with dignity through participation and practice in solving everyday problems; education to foster diversity so that our beliefs and values do not lead to discrimination against minorities; and education to develop the ability to coexist as connected beings in the global ecological system beyond humans.

Therefore, we need citizenship that extends the values of coexistence and common good from the national level to the global level, so we conduct global citizenship education for global coexistence to overcome the limitations of national-based citizenship. Global citizenship education is an extension of the content and methods of international understanding education and sustainable development education, and it goes beyond understanding and respecting differences and places greater emphasis on action and responsibility in the sense that it cultivates the knowledge, skills, values, and attitudes necessary for learners to contribute to creating a more inclusive, just, and peaceful world (UNESCO Korean Commission, 2024).

Dimension 6: Governmental Input for Physical Education (GIPE)

To activate the operation of the school sports governance and support system, a council between relevant ministries, local governments, and related organizations is operated on a permanent basis to strengthen responsiveness to cooperation issues. The council is composed of the Ministry of Education, the Ministry of Culture, Sports and Tourism, city and provincial education offices, the Korean

Sports Federation (sports organizations, city athletic associations), and related institutions (School Sports Promotion Association, Sports Ethics Centre).

The city-provincial council is a systematic consultative body between the Ministry of Education and provincial education departments to improve and promote inclusive school physical education policies. In addition, the scale of human and material resources to support school physical education has been expanded and subdivided into consulting groups for each school level and province. The Ministry of Education has established a comprehensive portal for school physical education to upgrade the comprehensive platform for school physical education information, and is also supporting school physical education activities through the aggregation of school physical education and student-athlete data, a congratulatory website, and a unified statistical survey system, as well as providing training materials and contents for teachers and physical education leaders, and linking with the National Institute of Education and Training and K-SpoEdu, the national sports promotion agency, to improve access to training and expand participation.

The Korea Sports Federation supports the operation of the I-League, a regular league for youth clubs to promote youth health, lays the foundation for sports participation, and expands the popularity of daily sports. Until 2021, the I-League was run as a youth football league combining football and various cultural and educational contents, and in 2022, it was expanded to seven sports, including baseball, tennis, badminton, table tennis, basketball, and billiards. In collaboration with relevant organizations, we aimed to lay the foundation for the operation of school-local sports clubs by providing sports facilities and professional sports resources through a regional network to support the operation of various school sports clubs. To support the development of this school and local sports club activities, use of scientific data will be very important. One of the examples is the use of Youth Martial Arts activities data for sport development (Cho, 2023). The scientific use of data will be the future foreseeable strategy for sport development.

Dimension 7: Cognitive Skill Development (CSD)

To eradicate school violence and deviant behavior caused by academic stress, games, etc., as well as the increase of 'corona blues' due to the prolonged COVID-19 outbreak, and the reduction of physical activity opportunities for students, it is necessary to create a lively school atmosphere by fostering good character through school sports. In addition, it is necessary to improve the operation of the PAPS to establish a self-directed health practice system that enables students to diagnose, check, and manage their own physical fitness level regardless of their athletic ability. For this reason, the MOE provides a student physical fitness promotion program to improve students' individual health management capabilities (Incheon Metropolitan Office of Education, 2022). In addition, the government is promoting the 'Fit for Life' project to overcome the intersection of physical inactivity and mental health inequalities and is encouraging support to increase participation in various physical activities and create a better life through 'Fit for Life'. The lack of physical activity among young people has been linked to a reported 200% increase in mental stress, including a spike in anxiety and depression, and there is a need to restore their health.

The PAPS is conducted once a year at the beginning of the school year for students in grades 5–6, middle school, and high school, and at least once a year for students in grades 4–5 after the health and physical fitness class is held, to minimize the proportion of students with low physical fitness. The measurement area measures five physical fitness factors (cardiopulmonary endurance, flexibility, strength and muscular endurance, quickness, and obesity) and can be distributed in consideration of school conditions (Incheon Metropolitan Office of Education, 2024). Measurement equipment and personnel are provided free of charge through the 'Visiting PAPS Classroom' of the Physical Fitness Certification Centre of the Korea Sports Authority, an agency of the Ministry of Culture, Sports and Tourism.

Dimension 8: Habituated Behavior in Physical Activities (HBPA)

The school sports promotion now turns to be mandatory and operates as school sports clubs to provide students with a variety of physical activity opportunities (Jeong & Jin, 2023). As a result, 'one student, one sport' is highly encouraged, and class-based school sports club leagues are actively organized during after-school hours and lunch breaks. To promote school sports clubs, all students are encouraged to participate in at least one sport, and class-based school sports clubs centered on 'team sports' are encouraged so that a large number of students can participate. In recent years, there has been a trend to encourage 'one-teacher-one-sport matching' so that general education teachers, in addition to physical education teachers, can also coach one or more school sports clubs, and promote class-based school sports club leagues where a dedicated teacher oversees the overall management of the league and student-led competitions.

Since 2020, the National School Sports Club Festival has been a sports festival that promotes friendship and unity among students. This Festival has abolished ranking awards in favor of fair play awards, abolished tournaments, and introduced various league systems. The tournaments are held in the following order: intramural tournaments, education support agency tournaments, provincial tournaments, and national tournaments.

Based on the experience of separating in-person celebrations before COVID-19 and non-personal celebrations during COVID-19, we aimed to revitalize the operation of school sports clubs by linking in-person and non-personal school sports clubs with leagues and celebrations. To achieve this objective, we first operated in-person school sports clubs and linked them with leagues and celebrations. In addition, an 'in-school and out-of-school' physical education program was implemented to support students' ongoing sports activities. The program consists of an 'in-school programme' that focuses on sports for which facilities are available in schools, as well as an 'out-of-school programme' that focuses on sports such as swimming, bowling, golf, and horse riding that are difficult to experience in schools (Ministry of Education, 2023).

Conclusion

Physical education in South Korea has been established as part of the existing school curriculum and has developed into an institutionalized system and structure. In that sense, it has been continuously supported by the state and society as a 'quality guarantee'. However, in the wake of COVID-19, there is still a lack of discourse on how to reset the practical value of physical education. Beyond the various competencies and skills to be taught to students, the question is whether an environment is created in which they can enjoy the things they deserve as healthy students. In recent years, there has been an ongoing debate in Korea about 'student-athletes' and 'athlete-students'. The task of defending the role and value of school physical education in the midst of this debate is not simple, and it is therefore important to make a cross-national comparison of the above eight perspectives of QPE. The eight dimensions of QPE which developed from the scholars' cooperation work, are not only suitable barometers for comparison of the global circumstances of PE, but also a country can investigate their own PE environment with the 'common' and 'legitimated' reviews of academia. Based on this evidence, I believe that in this time of the population cliff, humanity will eventually make wise decisions for its survival. It is believed that Korea will be able to go beyond the many existing trials and errors and conflicts among stakeholders and eventually accept a forward-looking paradigm shift in terms of 'individual development' for quality school physical education in terms of fostering healthy future generations.

References

Cho, Hyunjoo. (2023). *Study on How to Use Youth Martial Arts Activity Data. UNESCO International Martial Arts Center.* www.sports.re.kr/front/research/project/orginView.do?menu_seq=594&pageno=1&artctrlno=CR_615440&bibctrlno=CR_615440&lib_seq=.

Ho, W., Ahmed, Md. D., & Kukurova, K. (2021). Development and validation of an instrument to assess Quality Physical Education. *Cogent Education*, 25 pages. Article ID: 8:1864082. https://doi.org/10.1080/2331186X.2020.1864082

Ho, W., Ahmed, D., Rafeal, K., de D'Amico, R. L., Antala, B., Liu, M., Dong, X. X., & Xie, Y. Y. (2023). Quality Physical Education (QPE) measuring tool development. *International Sports Studies*, *45*(2), 6–27. https://doi.org/10.30819/iss.45-2.02

Incheon Metropolitan Office of Education. (2024). *Basic Plan for the 2024 Student Health and Physical Assessment System (PAPS)*. www.ice.go.kr/ice/na/ntt/selectNttInfo.do?mi=11790&nttSn=3284066.

Jeong, H. W., & Jin, Y. K. (2023). Exploring the direction of improvement through historical considerations of school sports clubs. *Journal of the Korean Society of Sports Education*, *30* (2), 67–89. doi: 10.21812/kjsp.2023.4. 30.2.67

Kim, Cheol-hoe. (2021). *Lesson Improvement Measures to Improve Students' Physical Strength.* https://nas.na.go.kr/nas/info/study_report.do.

Ministry of Culture, Sports and Tourism. (2022). *2022 Sports White Paper (11-371000-000015-10)*. www.mcst.go.kr/kor/s_policy/dept/deptView.jsp?pDataCD=0417000000&pSeq=1827.

Ministry of Culture, Sports and Tourism. (2024). 2024 Policy Implementation Plan of the Ministry of Culture, Sports and Tourism. MoCST. www.mcst.go.kr/english/policy/businessPlan.jsp

Ministry of Education. (2023). Plans to Promote School Sports in 2023. www.moe.go.kr/boardCnts/viewRenew.do?boardID=316&lev=0&statusYN=W&s=moe&m=0302&opType=N&boardSeq=95698.

Ministry of Education (2024). *Korean Education System*. MoE. https://english.moe.go.kr/sub/infoRenewal.do?m=0301&page=0301&s=english#:~:text=Korean%20Education%20System,their%20social%20status%20or%20position

Office for National Statistics. (2024). *Statistics Korea*. KOSTAT. https://kostat.go.kr/anse/

UNESCO Korea Committee. (2024). *UNESCO-Listed Heritage Online Teacher Training Content Provided by Elementary and Secondary Teachers Nationwide*. https://unesco.or.kr/240613_03/.

Chapter 23

Quality Physical Education in Spain

Antonio Campos-Izquierdo, María-Dolores González-Rivera, and María Gutiérrez-Conejo

Introduction

General Background in Spain

Spain is a country with an area of 504,782 km² and is the second largest country in the European Union. It is made up of 17 autonomous communities and the autonomous cities of Ceuta and Melilla and is located on the Iberian Peninsula in the southeast of Europe. Two of its autonomous communities are archipelagos: the Balearic Islands in the Mediterranean Sea and the Canary Islands in the Atlantic Ocean (Spanish Presidency, Council of the European Union, n.d.).

According to the National Statistics Institute (INE, 2024), the population of Spain on 1 April 2024 was 48,692,804, of whom 23,858,956 were men and 24,833,848 women, making it the fourth most populous country in the European Union (Spanish Presidency of the Council of the European Union, n.d.).

Spain's political system is a parliamentary democracy and a constitutional monarchy. Spain is a full member of the United Nations and the European Union. In July 2023, Spain will assume the Presidency of the Council of the European Union for the fifth time since it joined the EU in 1986.

The official language of Spain is Spanish (the second most widely spoken native language in the world), and it has four co-official languages (Spanish Presidency, Council of the European Union, n.d.).

Regarding the Spanish education system, there has been a succession of different education laws in line with the changes, mainly political, that have taken place. Since 1970, there has been a succession of eight education laws. Currently, the Spanish education system is governed by Organic Law 3/2020, of 29 December, which modifies Organic Law 2/2006, of 3 May, on education. This law establishes the starting point for the curricula of the different subjects set out in the royal decrees for the Organisation of Minimum Education, according to the stages of education, and it is the responsibility of the autonomous communities to specify the curriculum corresponding to their territorial scope, with the aim of adapting it to the characteristics of each community. Based on this curriculum specification, schools

DOI: 10.4324/9781003513582-25

adapt the curriculum to the characteristics of the center, and, finally, teachers adapt it to the reality of the classroom (González-Rivera and Campos-Izquierdo, 2014).

Quality Physical Education (QPE) Development in Spain

The Spanish constitution is the fundamental pillar of the legal and social structure of Spain, and article 43.3 states that "the public authorities shall promote health education, physical education (PE), and sport" (p. 10), which shows the importance given to PE in Spain (Spanish Constitution, 1978).

The QPE has been and continues to be a central element in the various publications that deal with the subject of PE, both in terms of its organization and in terms of its development and professional intervention. In this sense, from the 1960s, with the texts of José María Cagigal, to the present day, a large number of studies have been published on the subject of PE, which, directly or indirectly, develop and reflect on its quality, aiming to improve some of its elements.

Similarly, the quality of PE in Spain has been linked to the demands of the profession to improve various aspects, such as the compulsory nature of this subject, the work schedule, the objectives, content, competences and working, and professional conditions of teachers, as well as the facilities, material and economic resources for PE, and the practice of physical and sports activities in the schools.

The teacher is the key to the quality of PE and has an influence on other important elements for the quality of this subject, and it depends on him/her for the comprehensive development of students in this subject through knowledge, procedures, skills, and attitudes, as well as multiple and diverse educational, social, and health benefits. Likewise, the PE teacher contributes to and encourages students to acquire active, daily, healthy, and autonomous life habits through the practice of regular and appropriate physical and sports activities. Consequently, this chapter deals with these elements that influence quality, emphasizing the intervention (performance) of the PE teacher.

Currently, all levels of primary education, compulsory secondary education, and the first year of the baccalaureate have 2 hours of PE per week. However, in some autonomous communities, it has 3 hours per week. In addition, in some autonomous communities and in some schools, these hours are complemented, up to 4 or 5 hours per week, with an optional subject related to PE, physical activity, and sports at different educational levels. This variation in the number of hours is because Spain is a decentralized state, and each autonomous community, through its decrees, establishes the schedule to be fulfilled in each subject, and each school, in the exercise of its school autonomy, can increase the number of hours of PE.

In the case of the baccalaureate, PE is compulsory in the first year, and in the second year, it can be an optional subject in some schools. This is due to the fact that in the Royal Decree 243/2022 of April 5, which establishes the organization and the minimum curriculum of the baccalaureate, article 14 states that "the educational administrations are responsible for regulating the offer of optional subjects" and that "schools may propose other optional subjects within the framework of the provisions of the corresponding educational administration" (p. 46054).

To improve the quality of PE and its benefits for students, the number of hours should be increased. In addition, the benefits of this subject will be achieved if the practice of physical activity and sport is promoted through the development of a coherent and educational physical activity in extracurricular activities in such a way that there is an adequate connection and extension with PE classes. To this end, schools and PE teachers should be adequately involved in the promotion, organization, and development of school sports, and these activities should be included in school plans. However, studies carried out in Spain show that, in some cases, schools do not favor this connection (González-Rivera and Campos-Izquierdo, 2014). However, studies conducted in Spain show that, in some cases, schools do not promote this connection (González-Rivera and Campos-Izquierdo, 2014). This is despite the fact that the Spanish Education Law (Organic Law 3/2020), in its 46th additional provision, states that

> in order to promote and consolidate healthy lifestyles, the said administrations [the education administrations] will encourage the daily practice of sport and physical activity by students during the school day [...] to encourage a healthy and autonomous life, promoting healthy eating habits and active mobility, reducing sedentary lifestyles [...]. The design, coordination, and supervision of the measures adopted for these purposes shall be carried out by teachers with appropriate qualifications or specialization in these areas.
>
> (pp. 100–101)

Regarding the initial training of PE teachers, the qualifications are a degree in elementary education at the elementary level and a degree in physical activity and sports sciences at the compulsory secondary and baccalaureate levels, as well as the university master's degree in teacher training for compulsory secondary, baccalaureate, vocational and language education. However, the initial training required for the teaching of PE in compulsory secondary education and the baccalaureate is not specific, as the Education Law (Organic Law 3/2020), in its ninth additional provision on the requirements for entry into the civil service of teaching, states that "in addition to pedagogical and didactic training, it will be necessary to hold a university degree or an equivalent qualification for teaching purposes [...] and to pass the corresponding selection procedure" (p. 63). Therefore, to guarantee all the benefits of physical activity and sport, it should be specified that PE teachers at secondary school and baccalaureate level must have a degree in physical activity and sports sciences, together with the required official master's degree. It should be noted, however, that in practice, the vast majority of PE teachers have this qualification.

For the professional performance of PE teachers, especially in secondary education, to have a direct impact on the quality of this subject, it would be necessary for them to acquire and master, in their initial and continuing training, the following areas of specific competencies identified by Campos-Izquierdo and Martín-Acero (2016). These competencies were subsequently established in the Resolution of the General Secretariat of Universities of September 18, 2018 (pp. 91211–91214):

- Educational intervention.
- Intervention for prevention, adaptation, and improvement of physical sports performance and health through physical fitness and physical exercise.
- Promotion of healthy and autonomous habits through physical activity and sport.
- Intervention through the manifestations of human movement.
- Planning, evaluation, and management-organization of resources and physical activity and sport.
- Methods and scientific evidence in professional practice.
- Performance, deontology, and professional practice in the context of interventions.

In addition, it should be noted that these areas of specific competencies are the backbone that guides the permanent achievement of an appropriate, efficient and quality professional intervention of the PE teacher and, therefore, directly affect and contribute to a QPE (Campos-Izquierdo and Martín-Acero, 2016).

Regarding the development of students' skills and physical awareness through PE, the Education Law (Organic Law 3/2020) includes the development of sports and healthy habits among the objectives of education (Article 2, h). Specifically, in primary education, this law states that one of the objectives is: "To value hygiene and health, to accept one's own body and that of others, to respect differences and to use PE, sports and nutrition as a means of promoting personal and social development" (Article 17, k, p.14), and in compulsory secondary education, one of the objectives of this stage of education is:

> To know and accept the functioning of one's own body and that of others, to respect differences, to strengthen body care and health habits and to use physical education and the practice of sports to promote personal and social development. To know and appreciate the human dimension of sexuality in all its diversity. Critically evaluate social habits related to health, consumption, care, empathy and respect for living beings, especially animals, and the environment, and contribute to their preservation and improvement.
>
> (Article 23, k, p. 28)

Therefore, based on these objectives, PE is of great importance in the Spanish educational system, as it contributes to the integral development of students through the knowledge, procedures, skills and attitudes acquired in this subject, through the enrichment of motor situations and the acquisition of an active, healthy and autonomous lifestyle (Campos-Izquierdo, 2016). However, these educational objectives need to be put into practice through the development of factors and resources for quality teaching in PE.

To this end, in the Spanish education system, an essential element of the curriculum is the key competencies, as defined in the Council Recommendation of 22 May 2018 on key competencies for lifelong learning (2028). In this way, all subjects must address, in a balanced way, the achievement of the eight key competencies at the different stages of education. These key competencies are:

1 Linguistic communication competence.
2 Multilingual competence.
3 Mathematical competence and competence in science, technology, and engineering.
4 Digital competence.
5 Personal, social, and learning competencies; and civic competence.
6 Entrepreneurial competence.
7 Cultural awareness and expression.

Likewise, the royal decrees that establish the curriculum for each subject at the different levels of education establish specific competencies. In PE, these specific competencies at the level of compulsory secondary education are (Royal Decree 217/2022, of March 29, which establishes the organization and the minimum curriculum of compulsory secondary education, pp. 41630–41633):

1 To adopt an active and healthy lifestyle by consciously choosing and incorporating physical and sports activities into the daily routine, based on a critical analysis of the body's patterns [...].
2 To adapt their physical, perceptual-motor, and coordinative abilities, as well as their motor skills and abilities, with progressive autonomy in their performance [...].
3 Sharing spaces for physical and sports practice, regardless of cultural, social, gender and ability differences, prioritizing respect among participants and respect for rules over results, adopting a critical attitude [...].
4 Practicing, analyzing, and valuing the different manifestations of motor culture, using the expressive possibilities and resources of the body and movement, and studying the consequences of sport as a social phenomenon [...].
5 To adopt a sustainable and eco-socially responsible lifestyle, applying individual and collective safety measures in physical and sporting practice in accordance with the environment, and developing collaborative and cooperative community service actions related to physical activity and sport [...].

Therefore, these skills are intended to promote habits of physical behavior, social norms, and cultural practices, and PE teachers plan and design their lessons accordingly so that students can acquire them.

In the same way, the corresponding curriculum developments for each educational level (royal decrees) define the basic knowledge (content) that will help teachers design the activities in their classes and acquire specific competencies. In

PE, they are divided into six blocks of content that should be developed in different contexts to create varied learning situations so that, together with the acquisition of specific competencies, QPE can be achieved. These blocks of content are as follows:

A Active and healthy lifestyles.
B Organization and management of physical activity.
C Problem-solving in motor situations.
D Emotional self-regulation and social interaction in motor situations.
E Manifestations of motor culture.
F Efficient and sustainable interaction with the environment.

To this end, and in accordance with the current Education Law, teachers are guided by pedagogical principles that consider the different learning rhythms of students, promote their ability to learn independently, encourage teamwork and collaborative problem-solving, and strengthen self-esteem, autonomy, reflection, and responsibility. This will help students develop their cognitive skills, improve their critical thinking, problem-solving, and independent thinking skills, and develop their moral values and behaviors.

Similarly, with regard to social norms and cultural practices, the Education Law integrates a transversal approach to the teaching of values that should contribute to the development of all subjects. This transversal approach includes sustainable development, gender equality, equal treatment, and non-discrimination, as well as the prevention of violence against girls and women, bullying and cyberbullying, and the culture of peace and human rights. In this way, the PE teacher must ensure that this cross-curricular approach is adequately addressed through the content of the subject itself and in coordination with teachers of other subjects.

All these elements of the curriculum are planned and designed by PE teachers so that students acquire the necessary knowledge and skills. This planning is mandatory according to the current Education Law, which expresses that the functions of the educational inspection are the supervision and control of the programs from a pedagogical and organizational point of view, as well as the monitoring of the teaching process (González-Rivera et al., 2023). In this sense, the study by González-Rivera et al. (2023) shows that a high percentage of Spanish PE teachers carry out a detailed written plan (90.6%).

With regard to facilities and standards in PE, the regulation of facilities for sports use is found in Law 39/2022 on Sports (Article 14, e), which states that the government, through the National Sports Council, establishes the technical standards for sports facilities and their equipment, paying particular attention to compliance with the requirements established for safety and universal accessibility, free of architectural barriers (p. 193328). These technical standards are also a reference for quality compliance in school sports areas, where there is a strong tendency to comply with these technical standards. The safety of these areas is mandatory according to the different technical regulations, both general and specific. Regarding accessibility, the Spanish Federation of Municipalities and Provinces (2009) states that the physical sports areas of the educational center must be accessible so that everyone can approach, access, practice, and manage physical activity and sports without difficulty.

Similarly, the fifth article of Law 39/2022 on Sports establishes that the public authorities will contribute to the following measure, among others: "The planning and dimensioning of school spaces available for physical activity, adapted to the needs of the child and adolescent population, and ensuring that these spaces are safe and accessible to girls and adolescents" (p. 193323).

As far as school sports facilities are concerned, they must comply with the minimum requirements for adequate space for PE, as set forth in Royal Decree 132/2010 of February 12, which establishes the minimum requirements for centers that teach the second cycle of infant, primary and secondary education and establishes that all schools that teach these subjects must have

> a playground, partially covered, suitable for use as a multisport field, with a surface area commensurate with the number of school places. In no case may it be less than 900 square meters. In addition, there must be a gymnasium with a surface area appropriate to the number of school places.
> (Article 3.3, p. 24833)

In terms of continuous training, it is very important to train PE teachers to adapt to new methodologies to implement quality, student-centered PE programs, adapting to the characteristics and needs of students and promoting their inclusion, and it is essential to promote constant reflection, scientific rigor, and orientation towards excellence and innovation in professional practice. In this way, it will be possible to achieve quality in PE (González-Rivera and Campos-Izquierdo, 2023). To this end, PE teachers must be enthusiastic, creative, and adaptable to the new educational needs of society throughout their professional careers (González-Rivera and Campos-Izquierdo, 2014). Therefore, it is of great interest to analyze the continuing education of PE teachers (González-Rivera and Campos-Izquierdo, 2023).

The study by Campos-Izquierdo (2014) (the results of which are part of the Fundamental Research Project DEP2009-12828 funded by the Ministry of Science and Innovation (Spain) and coordinated by Campos-Izquierdo) found that most of the PE teachers participated in continuous training activities, among which: most of them (72%) attended courses and conferences (48%), and the less common training activity was participation in working groups within schools (30%).

Therefore, most of them participated in training programs outside of school. Compared to other studies (Bernabé et al., 2018; Gutiérrez-Conejo et al., 2024) that have analyzed the continuous training of other physical activity and sports professionals (i.e., sports instructors, professionals working with people with disabilities), PE teachers are the ones with the highest percentage of continuous training. This may be because educational legislation in Spain establishes that continuous training is a right and an obligation, with the aim of improving the quality of teaching and the functioning of schools through research, experimentation, and continuous improvement of teaching processes (González-Rivera and Campos-Izquierdo, 2014).

In any case, studies show that training outside schools sometimes does not meet their expectations or needs because it does not provide knowledge for practical teaching (González-Rivera and Campos-Izquierdo, 2023). Therefore, schools should promote more working group activities and educational research, and PE teachers should be more involved in these activities, focusing on the topics in which teachers have been trained through courses and conferences to transfer knowledge from courses and conferences to working groups, under the principle of collaboration and teamwork, and to participate in educational research processes. In this sense, educational administrations are increasingly promoting this type of in-service training in schools.

Conclusion: Strategies and Challenges for Improving the Quality of Physical Education

Based on the previous sections of this chapter, different strategies and challenges can be addressed to improve the quality of PE in Spain:

- Continue to increase the number of compulsory hours of PE to 5 hours a week. It is also necessary to establish an effective link with out-of-school physical and sports activities.
- Strengthen incentives for PE teachers to participate in the organization, design, and development of out-of-school and in-school physical and sports activities.
- Promote the school (during school and non-school hours) as an essential component of the "Comprehensive system of promotion and intervention of physical and sporting" activity for health, quality of life, well-being, and individual and social development, also commonly referred to as "physical exercise and sports prescription". This strategy is already being developed, but it is essential that it is increased and expanded because of its great benefits for students and citizens.
- Promote the joint and comprehensive development of PE with other subjects to contribute, through physical activity and sport, to the acquisition of knowledge and skills in mathematics, social sciences, languages, etc.
- Integrate a "motor and quality of life competence" as a key competence across the curriculum in all subjects, together with the eight key competencies in the current education system.
- Promote, as a complement to the compulsory minimum of 3 hours of PE per week, a varied offer of optional subjects in each educational stage related to PE, physical activity, and sport, with a view to the acquisition by pupils of autonomous and healthy habits.

- Ensure that the subject of PE is taught by graduates in physical activity and sports sciences in secondary education and in the baccalaureate, although this is already the case in the vast majority of cases.
- Continue to encourage further in-service training for PE teachers with a stronger connection to real classroom practice through educational innovation and research projects, and encourage frequent national collaboration schemes and learning opportunities for teachers.
- Encourage comprehensive, inclusive, and diverse school physical activity and sports projects to promote active and healthy lifestyles for students, involving PE teachers. Together with this action, it is important to promote the school as a promoter of physical activity and sport in all its forms and for all its purposes, for students and the whole population (outside school hours), in connection with the social and community environment.

References

Bernabé, B., González-Rivera, M.D., & Campos-Izquierdo, A. (2018). Formal Continuing Education of Spanish Physical Activity and Sport Instructors. *Apunts. Educació Física i Esports*, *134*, 134–145.

Campos-Izquierdo, A. (2014) (director). *Memoria del Proyecto de Investigación Fundamental de I+D+i* "Estructura ocupacional y organizativa de los recursos humanos de actividad física y deporte en España" *(DEP2009-12828)*. Ministerio de Ciencia e Innovación.

Campos-Izquierdo, A. (2016). La formación de los profesionales de actividad física y deporte en España. *Movimento*, *22*(4), 1351–1364.

Campos-Izquierdo, A., & Martín-Acero, R. (2016). Percepción de las competencias profesionales de los graduados en Ciencias de la Actividad Física y del Deporte. *Revista de psicología del deporte*, *25*(2), 339–346.

Council Recommendation of 22 May 2018 on key competences for lifelong learning (Text with EEA relevance.). (2018, May). *Official Journal*, C 189, 1–13. CELEX. https://eur-lex.europa.eu/legal-content/EN/TXT/?uri=CELEX:32018H0604(01)

González-Rivera, M. D., & Campos-Izquierdo, A. (2014). *La intervención docente en educación física en secundaria y en el deporte escolar*. Editorial Síntesis.

González-Rivera, M.D., & Campos-Izquierdo, A. (2023). Training Physical Education Teachers. In H. Walter, U. Nair, G. Kishore, S. Prajapati, P. Dutta, & R. López de D'Amico (eds.). *State of the Art in Physical Education, Sport and Physical Activity in the International Context. Book of abstracts from the 22nd Biennial Conference of International Society for Comparative Physical Education and Sport* (p. 64). EDUFISADRED Civil Foundation "Physical Education, Recreation and Sport" – ISCPES – Lakshmibai National College of Physical Education.

González-Rivera, M.D., Campos-Izquierdo, A., Hall, N.D., & Villalba-Pérez, A.I. (2023). Planning and assessment practices among Spanish physical education teachers according to experience and teaching level. *European Physical Education Review*, *29*(3), 438–454. https://doi.org/10.1177/1356336X231158916

Gutiérrez-Conejo, M., González-Rivera, M.D., & Campos-Izquierdo, A. (2024). Planning and evaluation of sport programmes for people with disabilities. *Retos*, 53, 472–480.

INE. (2024, April). Estadística Continua de Población (ECP). 1 de abril de 2024. Datos provisionales. https://ine.es/dyngs/INEbase/es/operacion.htm?c=Estadistica_C&cid=1254736177095&menu=ultiDatos&idp=1254735572981

Law 39/2022, of December 30, 2002, on Sport. (BOE. no. 314, December 31, 2022). www.boe.es/boe/dias/2022/12/31/pdfs/BOE-A-2022-24430.pdf

Organic Law 3/2020, of 29 December, which modifies Organic Law 2/2006, of 3 May, on Education. (BOE. no. 340, December 30, 2020.). www.boe.es/buscar/pdf/2020/BOE-A-2020-17264-consolidado.pdf

Resolution of the General Secretariat of Universities of September 18, 2018, publishing the Agreement of the Council of Universities of September 17, 2018, establishing recommendations for the proposal by the universities of verification reports of the official degree in Physical Activity and Sport Sciences. (BOE No. 228, September 20, 2018). www.boe.es/boe/dias/2018/09/20/pdfs/BOE-A-2018-12774.pdf

Royal Decree 132/2010 of February 12, which establishes the minimum requirements for centers that teach the second cycle of infant, primary and secondary education. (BOE. No. 12 of March 2010). www.boe.es/boe/dias/2010/03/12/pdfs/BOE-A-2010-4132.pdf

Royal Decree 217/2022, of March 29, which establishes the organization and the minimum curriculum of compulsory secondary education. (BOE No. 76, of March 30, 2022). www.boe.es/buscar/pdf/2022/BOE-A-2022-4975-consolidado.pdf

Royal Decree 243/2022 of April 5, which establishes the organization and the minimum curriculum of the Baccalaureate. (BOE No. 82, of April 6, 2022). www.boe.es/boe/dias/2022/04/06/pdfs/BOE-A-2022-5521.pdf

Spanish Constitution (1978). (BOE. no.311, December 29, 1978). www.boe.es/buscar/pdf/1978/BOE-A-1978-31229-consolidado.pdf

Spanish Federation of Municipalities and Provinces (2009). *Buenas Prácticas en Instalaciones Deportivas*. Consejo Superior de Deportes. https://cid.csd.gob.es/es/documentacion/instalaciones/83-manual-de-buenas-practicas-de-las-instalaciones-deportivas/file

Spanish Presidency, Council of the European Union. (n.d.). Presidencia. Descubre España. Retrieved July 14, 2024, from https://wayback.archive-it.org/12090/20240620135147/https://spanish-presidency.consilium.europa.eu/es/presidencia/descubre-espana/

Chapter 24

A Glance at Quality Physical Education in Venezuela

Rosa López de D'Amico, Argenira Ramos, and Alixon Reyes Rodríguez

Introduction

The Bolivarian Republic of Venezuela is located in the north of South America, in the Caribbean region. It borders Colombia, Guyana, and Brazil and in the north with the Caribbean Sea. Venezuela has a privileged geographical location with nearly a million kilometers square, an important geographical and biological diversity that places it among the top mega-diverse countries in the world (Sistema Venezolano de Información sobre la Diversidad Biológica, 2021). It is a state democratic country with five public powers: Executive, Legislative, Judicial, Electoral, and Citizens Power (Constitución de la República Bolivariana de Venezuela [CRBV], 2009). It is divided into 23 states and one capital District; it has 335 municipalities.

The economy of the country is mostly based on petroleum extraction, its derivatives, and its commercialization in the international market, not to mention that it has the largest reserves of oil in the world. Besides, it also exports gas and other minerals such as bauxite, gold, diamond, iron, aluminum, coal, and coltan, among others. In recent years, since 2013, the economy has been deeply affected by the imposed blockade on the country, and therefore, the unemployment rate and the inflation have been in deficit. However, the United Nations Economic Commission for Latin America and the Caribbean (CEPAL, 2022) estimates that there will be a 10% increase in the economy in the coming years, and it will provoke an expansion of the national economy.

Demographically speaking, in the latest national census in 2011, Venezuela had a population of 28,946,101 people (Instituto Nacional de Estadística, 2014). But according to the System on Educational Trends in Latin America (SITEAL, acronym in Spanish), the projection by 2018 was 31.6 million people (Sistema de Información de Tendencias Educativas en América Latina, 2019). However, since 2017, there has been a big migratory tendency.

Education is a social right and, according to the law, is a priority for the state (CRBV, 2009). The education system is structured in subsystems. The basic education subsystem is formed by initial education (maternal 0–3 years old and preschool 4–6 years old), primary (grades 1 to 6 – 7 to 12 years old), and secondary school (years 1 to 5 or 6). The university subsystem has undergraduate (bachelor) and graduate programs (specialization, master doctorate). It also has several modalities, such as special education, education for adults, education in the borders areas, rural education, education for the arts, military education, and intercultural bilingual education (Ley Orgánica de Educación [LOE], 2009).

Brief Review of the Historical Development of Physical Education in Venezuela

The subject in the education system is known as physical education (PE). This semantic nomenclature responds to the national norms and curricular and administrative policies; it also follows a marked disciplinary tradition in the West (Ley Orgánica de Deporte, Actividad Física y Educación Física [LODAFEF], 2011). The relevance of the physical culture comes directly from one of the fundamental references in the ideology of Venezuelan education, Simón Bolivar, as it was he who, on the occasion of the Angostura Constitution (Second Venezuela constitution), declared the well-known Moral Power in 1819, an adjunct document of that Constitution. It indicated that the education chamber was in charge of the children's physical and moral education from birth until the age of 12 (Carrero, 2020). The compulsory character of the curricular subject was present in the Code of Popular Instruction and the Decrees of Public Instruction since the late nineteenth and early twentieth century. In the 1920s, the National Regulation for Physical Education was approved, making it compulsory for students between the ages 7 and 21. It went through some changes, but it has always been present as a subject in the education system (Ramírez, 2014). Since the early twentieth century, the training of PE instructors was coordinated by the Ministry of Education in charge until the 1940s when the first teachers training higher education institute was created 'Instituto Pedagógico Nacional', and since then, many other universities have been created which there are undergraduate and graduate programs in the discipline (Scharagrodsky & López de D'Amico, 2023). The pioneer in training PE teachers is the Universidad Pedagógica Experimental Libertador.

The PE syllabus has gone through different approaches; it started with general gymnastics, hygienic tendency, sports skills, and psychomotor education (Reyes-Rodríguez, 2021). The discipline is nurtured by the humanistic approach that is the base of the national education system. PE is understood as a holistic quality education that embraces equity inclusion and looks at the consolidation of human values that are linked to the disciplinary dynamics of the field, such as the notions of well-being, health, hygiene, the adoption of healthy lifestyles, and the achievement of physical exercise habits (LOE, 2009).

Many activities have been developed in the last 20 years (2004–2024) to fulfill the law, such as the National Survey for Quality Education in 2014, the National Training and Research System for Teachers, the Bicentennial Text Books for Basic Education, the Canaima project, PE Class Festival, Pedagogical Congresses, National School Food Service, new training teachers program, e.g., Micomisión Simón Rodríguez, new universities, e.g., Universidad Nacional Experimental del Magisterio 'Samuel Robinson', Observatory for Quality Education (OCEV), to mention but a few. The curriculum transformation in secondary school (Ministerio del Poder Popular para la Educación, 2016) provided a new glance at the PE subject and other spaces in the curriculum (López de D'Amico & Guerrero, 2018; Reyes-Rodríguez, 2021; Reyes-Rodríguez & Reyes, 2020). Therefore, the PE sessions were three times per week with a total of 6 hours weekly, and the other 2 hours for areas of interest in which physical activity, sport, and recreation were created so students could develop their potential.

After the COVID-19 pandemic, some changes occurred. The latest guidelines indicate the following class time distribution (Ministerio del Poder Popular para la Educación, 2024):

Initial level: 3 sessions per week, 30 minutes each.
Primary level: From grade 1 to 3, twice per week, each of 45 minutes
   From grade 4 to 6, twice per week, each of 90 minutes
Secondary level: 3 sessions per week, 80 minutes each.
Technical level has some more guidelines related to the specialization area.

Dimension Analysis and Discussion

To look at the situation of PE in relation to the concept of quality physical education (QPE), it was decided to follow Ho et al. (2023) study as it provides clear indications related to QPE based on teacher's perception. The latest is of relevance as teachers could inform supported by their own experience and knowledge. However, it was also triangulated with literary review, so it follows a mixed methodology (Haag, 2004). The questionnaire (Ho et al., 2021) was applied to 345 teachers – 184 men and 152 women – with experiences working in different levels of the education system: 110 primary, 149 secondary, and 77 from university level or administrative positions. The informants were from five different cities and states: Maracay (Aragua), Valencia (Carabobo), San Fernando de Apure (Apure), Calabozo (Guárico), Margarita Island (Nueva Esparta) (López de D'Amico et al., 2024). The results were supported by literature and research from the country that supported the dimensions under study. The dimensions are: Skill Development and Bodily Awareness (SDBA), Facilities and Norms in PE (FNPE), Quality Teaching of PE (QTPE), Plans for Feasibility and Accessibility of Physical Education (PFAPE), Social Norms and Cultural Practice (SNCP), Governmental Input for PE (GIPE), Cognitive Skill Development (CSD), and Habituated Behaviour in Physical Activities (HBPA). The media and standard deviation of all the data were calculated.

Dimension 1: Skill Development and Bodily Awareness (SDBA)

The results indicate a mean of 5.3 and a standard deviation of 2.9 (Table 24.1); the majority of the respondents promote physical activity, motor abilities, and sports in their pedagogical praxis for the benefit and health care of the students to

Table 24.1 Average mean and standard deviation of the dimensions

Dimensions	Mean	Standard Deviation
SDBA	5.3	2.9
FNPE	5.8	2.8
QTPE	6.1	3.4
PFAPE	7.8	2.7
SNCP	6.8	2.6
GIPE	5.6	2.7
CSD	5.3	2.7
HBPA	5.7	3

SDBA = Skill Development and Bodily Awareness; FNPE = Facilities and Norms in PE; QTPE = Quality Teaching of PE; PFAPE = Plans for Feasibility and Accessibility of Physical Education; SNCP = Social Norms and Cultural Practice; GIPE = Governmental Input for PE; CSD = Cognitive Skill Development; HBPA = Habituated Behaviour in Physical Activities.

improve their quality of life. According to Ramos (2010), teachers have a central role in transferring the written policy into practice such as understanding students' needs and interests, multidisciplinary planning with teachers from other subjects, school-community integration, and pedagogical supervision, among others, and it was observed that they did have the knowledge to plan actions and activities. The curriculum incorporates the basic elements to develop motor abilities. Ramos et al. (2014) indicated that in the practical classes in PE, there are innovative programs implemented in schools and communities to develop habits and behaviors of a healthy lifestyle so they can use or practice them every day (e.g., Gil-Lugo, 2024).

Dimension 2: Facilities and Norms in Physical Education (FNPE)

The media is 5.8, and the standard deviation is 2.8, this means that teachers acknowledge the existence of norms and legal policies to guarantee that PE is quality, inclusive, and accessible to all. In addition to that, educational institutions should have appropriate spaces, facilities, and resources, among others, to develop the teaching-learning process. PE is compulsory at all levels of the education system, and there is no discrimination based on ability/disability, gender, sexual orientation, age, culture, race/ethnicity, religion, or social or economic condition. The State has several legal documents, such as the Law of Sport, Physical Activity and Physical Education (2011), National Sport, Physical Activity and Physical Education Plan 2013–2025 (PND by its acronym in Spanish), General Guidelines for the Economic and Social Development Plan, among others. The purpose is to enforce a legal framework to support the development of Venezuela as a potential educational and sportive nation. However, Romero (2014) indicated that the PND had to be reviewed to organize its content and indicate concrete objectives to be fulfilled. López de D'Amico et al. (2013) reinforce this aspect by suggesting that municipal and state teams need to work together to have only one organized structure working to apply and achieve the official guidelines.

The universities promote the training of PE teachers, and in the last 20 years, there has been an awareness of the differences between sports science and physical education professionals, which is evident in the syllabus of the universities; there are more places to train professionals in the field (López de D'Amico & Mizrahi, 2015). However, it is still not enough; more PE teachers are needed to answer the demands of the education system. New initiatives have been promoted by the Ministry of Education to train teachers in service and to create opportunities to train new PE teachers all over the states in the country, an example of this is the Micromision Simon Rodríguez, nowadays Universidad Nacional Experimental del Magisterio Samuel Robinson (UNEM) which is a teachers' training university (Guerrero et al., 2018).

Morillo (2019) indicated that educational institutions should look for self-management and become sustainable, so all the members of the community become co-responsible and look for solutions to solve problems such as poor resources or adequate space to develop the PE class.

Dimension 3: Quality Teaching of Physical Education (QTPE)

The results indicate a median of 6.1 and a standard deviation of 3.4 (Table 24.1); the tendency is that teachers acknowledge that in PE, students must acquire healthy living habits that could help them understand and value the conscious care of their body in their different life periods. Ramos (2010) found that Venezuelan teachers value the knowledge and the interaction with the physical world. PE provides notions and skills about healthy habits that will benefit the student's daily life, particularly those physical qualities associated with the improvement of physical condition and health, such as cardiovascular endurance, strength endurance, and flexibility, among others. On the other hand, responsible use and basic understanding of the natural environment should be encouraged through physical activities carried out in nature. Physical activities are an effective means to facilitate integration and promote respect, and at the same time, they contribute to the development of cooperation, equality, communication, and teamwork.

Portela et al. (2013) indicate that the practice and organization of collective sports activities require integration into a common project and acceptance of the differences and limitations of the participants, following democratic norms in the organization of the group, and each member assuming their own responsibilities. Compliance with the rules and regulations that govern sporting activities contributes to the acceptance of the codes of conduct of a society. PE helps significantly to achieve autonomy and personal initiative.

According to the curriculum (Ministerio del Poder Popular para la Educación [MPPE], 2016), PE activities are considered a fundamental element in health promotion programs as they allow understanding of the different physiological, cognitive, and biological functions, among others, in human beings. At the same time, it contributes to the acquisition of cultural and artistic competence. The appreciation and understanding of cultural facts are done through the recognition and valuation of the cultural manifestations, such as sports, traditional games, expressive activities, or dance, and their consideration as part of the country's cultural heritage or region. It allows the expression of ideas or feelings creatively through the exploration and use of body movement, as well as to the acquisition of perceptual skills, especially from the sensory and emotional experiences inherent to the activities of bodily expression. On the other hand, the knowledge of recreational, sports, and body expression manifestations typical of other cultures allows the acquisition of an open attitude toward cultural diversity.

Dimension 4: Plans for Feasibility and Accessibility of Physical Education (PFAPE)

The results indicate a median of 7.8 and a standard deviation of 2.7 (Table 24.1). This is meaningful as PE demands all, particularly governments, intergovernmental organizations, and sports organizations, among other entities, to adhere to international policies and national ones to make it a reality for all citizens. According to Andueza (2013), UNESCO and its collaborators play an important role in the transformation of educational policies towards equity, social mobility, and productive development. Examples of these are the diverse initiatives mentioned before to train more PE teachers and the latest creation of the OCEV.

Ramos (2010) highlighted that PE as a subject in the education system has a crucial role in promoting the well-being of all students; PE provides opportunities for physical activity, social interaction, practical learning, and, in short, meaningful chances for personal development. The celebration of national sports school games provides access to all students. However, some considerations have to be given as not all the attention should turn to the Games, this is one of the constant reminders that researchers indicate.

Ramírez (2009) indicated that there should be more support for PE teachers, particularly in acknowledging their responsibility for public health and adopting a holistic physical activity school program supported by the authorities. Besides, the author also highlights that it is needed a closer follow-up to what is planned for the corporal-physical activity development of society.

The State has had important inputs to the training of more teachers, graduate programs for teachers in service, international agreements, and support for research. However, it is also necessary to indicate that in the last six years, the support has been reduced as a consequence of the economic crisis the country has been facing in the last 8 years.

Dimension 5: Social Norms and Cultural Practice (SNCP)

The replies indicate a median of 6.8 and a standard deviation of 2.6; this is considered positive because teachers acknowledge the existence of norms for PE and sports that fulfill a fundamental role in the holistic training of the citizens without discrimination.

Reyes-Rodríguez (2021) points out that the teacher must provide spaces for criticism dialogic that surpasses the curriculum, a student conscious and capable of causing sociocultural changes and political-economic transformation in the region, in schools, and in communities. Facilitating in students their awareness of identity to move towards integrity, understanding the bodily entity, and realizing these aspirations in the curricular, legislative, and political contexts, but even more so, at the level of social consciousness, social representations, values, practices, speeches, beliefs, among other aspects. Women have joined sports activities and have demolished the myths and sociocultural barriers of inequality in relation to the male sex, as well as highlighting the morphophysiological benefits that such practices provide to increase the level of their quality of life (García et al., 2008). However, Hernández (2013) observed that at the high school level PE class, many girls try to avoid class and be more aware of beauty and cosmetics than physical exercise. Culturally speaking, the subject suffers, as it happens in many places of the world, from the stereotype that it is not as important as other subjects, however, in the norms and policies in place, it is clearly stated that it is as important as any other subject.

Dimension 6: Governmental Input for Physical Education (GIPE)

Media 5.6 and standard deviation 2.7 represent that the respondents pointed out the relevance of PE in the education system. This is based on the recognition by the State with policies and actions to guarantee the progressive incorporation of all citizens into the practice of PE, physical activities, and sports, as well as the creation of public training of human resources necessary to work in this educational area.

In Venezuela, PE is a compulsory subject of the school curriculum, and it is considered an important component of comprehensive education that forms the construction of knowledge through movement. The learning context is characterized by defined didactics, which also involve scientific foundations with interdisciplinary links in relation to the approach to the bio-psychosocial dimensions of the student (Navarro et al., 2019). The government, in the first decade of 2000, supported a significant number of young students to be trained as PE teachers abroad, besides master and doctoral fellowships to study with the Cuba–Venezuela partnership, not to mention the creation of universities to train sports science and physical activity professionals (López de D'Amico & Mizrahi, 2015). Since 2015 the government has created training programs to train more new PE teachers and provide continuous professional development to teachers in service with the possibility to do graduate studies (specialization, master and doctoral level) with no or minimum cost (Guerrero et al., 2018; Reyes-Rodríguez & Reyes, 2020).

Dimension 7: Cognitive Skill Development (CSD)

With the median being 5.3 and the standard deviation 2.7, the teachers understand that from a pedagogical point of view, there are multiple ways to achieve the development of cognitive skills through PE classes.

Reyes-Rodríguez (2021) commented that PE, from a critical perspective, implies a pedagogy based on the needs and interests of the students when carrying out planning, evaluation, and selection of resources, among other aspects. Therefore, planning from this context must aim at the transformation of the conditions in which knowledge is generated, its socialization, and the consolidation of a communication system in learners. Garbán (2008) stated that the teacher is a mediator of learning and pays attention to the individual differences of his students, that is, he or she projects his praxis, taking into account the diversity of sociocultural concepts of these students. According to Ramos (2010), physical activities are a means of expression used by students to communicate something about themselves that characterizes them; it is an expression of a way of life, thoughts, and emotions. They also allow actions to be established to stimulate imagination, spontaneity, and creativity in students. Their implementation fosters a critical personality, in addition to the implementation of deep and complete communications.

Dimension 8: Habituated Behaviour in Physical Activities (HBPA)

The replies indicate a median of 5.7 and a standard deviation of 3; the respondents expressed that in the pedagogical praxis, the teacher must promote varied physical and sports activities so that students are able to select those they like and do them inside or outside of school. In this sense, Dun (2019) pointed out that to promote healthy living habits, the use of sports, physical, and healthy strategies is essential, which will produce changes in attitude in students, as well as contribute to the improvement of their life relationships at the school, family and social level. Ramos et al. (2014) declared that educational action focused on interdisciplinary and transdisciplinary approaches has as its purpose to make the student responsible, able to decide about the physical activities of their preference, aware of the prevention of diseases, and enjoy health. Romero (2015) pointed out that the sports practice carried out in the university space has great potential for the training of the student because these provide ethical growth, encourage the development of identity, and promote the ability to make decisions; it enhances plurality in students and encourages participation and commitment in social projects.

Figueira (2020) proposes to develop actions involving members of the university community to discuss alternatives and address the needs of students fundamentally with regard to their quality of life. In this sense, it points out that the systematic practice of physical activity helps to improve the individual and social life of students, as well as improves health and interpersonal relationships, both physical and psychological. That is why the author suggests the formation of work teams for the development of physical activity programs with the integration of public and private organizations.

Final Comments

At the policy level, there are important documents that support the presence of PE in the education system, and this is evident from the results, and its presence in the syllabus is of relevance. There have been significant initiatives that have been developed for the development of PE, and perhaps it is important to assess them; there is a good chance with the Observatory for Quality Education. There are programs in place to train PE teachers; however, more teachers are needed to attend to the demand for basic education. PE is an inclusive subject, but there are aspects that need to be improved, such as access to facilities. More strategic alliances, particularly in the region, can be generated, e.g., ALBA, MERCOSUR, CELAC, UNASUR, and CLACSO, to push for more quality PE not just in the country but also in the region. There are important initiatives for education in general, and if the economic situation improves, it will definitely have a positive impact on the education sector and, as a consequence, on PE.

Acknowledgment

We appreciate the support of the following colleagues who were instrumental in the data collection: Grisell Bolívar, Mary Camacho, Mónica Pino, Delfín Vasquez y Roraima Solórzano.

References

Andueza, Y. (2013). Construcción del episteme de educación inclusiva para la formación del docente en educación inicial. [Doctoral Thesis, Universidad Pedagógica Experimental Libertador Rafael Alberto Escobar Lara, The Bolivarian Republic of Venezuela].

Carrero, M. (2020). *Bolívar y el Poder Moral. Proyecto para una República Popular.* Venezuela: Centro de Estudios Simón Bolívar.

Constitución de la República Bolivariana de Venezuela (CRBV) (2009). *Gaceta Oficial N° 5908 Extraordinario.* February 19, 2009.

Dun, R. (2019). Hábitos y prácticas físico-deportivas en la promoción del estilo de vida saludable en los estudiantes de la UNELLEZ Municipalizada Elorza. [Master's Thesis, UNELLEZ, The Bolivarian Republic of Venezuela]. https://cuts.top/Dhyi

Figueira, F. (2020). Actividades físicas, deportivas y recreativas para el fortalecimiento de las relaciones inter-personales entre los estudiantes de primer año de derecho sección B de la Universidad Nacional Experimental de los Llanos Occidentales Ezequiel Zamora del Municipio San Fernando, Estado Apure. [Master's Thesis, UNELLEZ Apure, The Bolivarian Republic of Venezuela]. http://opac.unellez.edu.ve/doc_num.php?explnum_id=1471

Garbán, Y. (2008). Los nuevos enfoques que fortalecen la Educación Física en Venezuela. *Lecturas en Educación Física y Deportes*, *13*(121). www.efdeportes.com/efd121/la-educacion-fisica-en-venezuela.htm

Gil-Lugo, J. (2024). Los deportes urbanos: una visión de integración y socialización de los jóvenes en el territorio. [Unpublished Doctoral Thesis, Universidad Pedagógica Experimental Libertador, The Bolivarian Republic of Venezuela].

Guerrero, G., López de D'Amico, R., Hojas, J., & Pateti, J. (2018). La Micromisión Simón Rodríguez en el área de Educación Física. In: R. López de D'Amico (Ed.). *Aproximación a la historia de la Micromisión Simón Rodríguez y los programas iniciales* (pp. 128–149). CENAMEC

Haag, H. (2004). *Research Methodology for sport and exercise science*. Germany: Die Deutsche Bibliothek.

Hernández, G. (2013). Factores que inciden en la participación activa de las estudiantes en la clase de educación física. [Unpublished Master's Thesis, Universidad Pedagógica Experimental Libertador, The Bolivarian Republic of Venezuela].

Ho, W., Ahmed, D., Kukurová, K., López de D'Amico, R., Antala, B., Liu, M., Dong, X.X., & Xie, Y. (2023). Quality Physical Education (QPE) Measurement tool development. *International Sport Studies*, *45*(2), 6–27. https://doi.org/10.30819/iss.45-2.02

Ho, W.; Dilsad, A., & Kukurova, K. (2021) Development and validation of an instrument to assess quality physical education. *Cogent Education*, *8*(1), 1–25. https://doi.org/10.1080/2331186X.2020.1864082

Instituto Nacional de Estadística (2014). *XIV Censo Nacional de Población y Vivienda*. Ministerio del Poder Popular del Despacho de la Presidencia. https://cuts.top/Dhy4

Ley Orgánica de Deporte, Actividad Física y Educación Física (2011). *Gaceta Oficial N° 39741*, August 23rd, 2011.

Ley Orgánica de Educación (LOE) (2009). *Gaceta Oficial N° 5929 Extraordinario*. August 15th, 2009.

López de D'Amico, R., & Guerrero, G. (2018). Transformación curricular y pedagógica en educación media en Venezuela: Caso Educación Física. *Revista Alesde*, *9*(2), 119–133. https://cuts.top/D6TA

López de D'Amico, R., Guerrero, G., Hojas, J., & Murillo, J. (2013). El desarrollo del deporte municipal en la República Bolivariana de Venezuela. In: D. Martínez. (Coord.). *La gestión deportiva municipal en Iberoamérica: historia, teoría y práctica* (pp. 489–512). ESM.

López de D'Amico, R., Ho, W., Rafael, K., Ceballos, O., Bolivar, G., D'Amico, A., Camacho, M., Vasquez, L. D., Pino, M., & Solorzano, R. (2024). Percepciones de docentes acerca de la Educación Física de Calidad: Caso Venezuela. *ACCION*, 20 (Especial XXV). https://accion.uccfd.cu/index.php/accion/article/view/317/862

López de D'Amico, R., & Mizrahi, E. (2015). Estado, Deporte y Educación en Venezuela. In: Hernández, C. M. C., Enríquez Caro, C. L. C., Nogales, H. E. G., Perez, I. S., Díaz, I. F., & López de D'Amico, R. (Eds.). *Psicología, Deporte y Actividad Física. Investigaciones Aplicadas* (pp. 326–346). EDUFISADRED.

Ministerio del Poder Popular para la Educación (MPPE) (2016). *Proceso de transformación curricular en educación media*. Author.

Ministerio del Poder Popular para la Educación (MPPE) (2024). *Cuadernillo Pedagógico. Área de Formación Educación Física*. Author.

Morillo, S. (2019). Estrategias gerenciales de autogestión en la adquisición de insumos deportivos para el voleibol master del municipio Guacara-Carabobo. [Master's Thesis, Universidad de Carabobo, The Bolivarian Republic of Venezuela]. http://mriuc.bc.uc.edu.ve/bitstream/handle/123456789/8367/laular.pdf?sequence=1

Navarro, J., Ramos, C., & Varguillas, C. (2019). Educación Física en Venezuela: Pertinencia teórica y viabilidad de la reforma del currículo 2016–2018. *Educación Física y Ciencia, 21*(4), 107. https://dx.doi.org/https://doi.org/10.24215/23142561e107

Portela, Y, Rodríguez, E., & Lemos, C. (2013). La comunicación y la Educación Física en la Universidad de las Ciencias Informáticas. *Lecturas en Educación Física y Deportes. 18*(182). www.efdeportes.com/efd182/la-comunicacion-y-la-educacion-fisica.htm

Ramírez, E. (2014). *Aventura del movimiento. Los senderos de la Educación Física.* Fundación BetCRIS.

Ramírez, J. (2009). Bases legales y de organización estructural de la educación Física, el deporte y la recreación en Venezuela. *Lecturas en Educación Física y Deportes, 14*(133). https://cuts.top/BrQw

Ramos, A. (2010). Educación física, curriculum y práctica escolar. [Doctoral Thesis, Universidad de León, Spain]. https://dialnet.unirioja.es/servlet/tesis?codigo=25848

Ramos, A., López de D'Amico, R., & Guerrero, G. (2014). Educación física y su relación con la salud en la formación integral. Experiencia desde el contexto educativo en Venezuela. *Revista Iberoamericana de Psicología del Ejercicio y el Deporte, 9*(2), 303–322. www.redalyc.org/pdf/3111/311131093003.pdf.

Reyes-Rodríguez, A. D. (2021). Educación Física crítica: experiencias, aplicaciones y posibilidades. El caso venezolano. *Ágora para la Educación Física y el Deporte,* 23, 29–51. https://doi.org/10.24197/aefd.0.2021.29-51

Reyes-Rodríguez, A. D., & Reyes, C. (2020). Formación de profesores en educación física en la Micromisión Simón Rodríguez. Caso: Monagas-Anzoátegui. *Trenzar. Revista de Educación Popular, Pedagogía Crítica e Investigación Militante, 4*(2), 105–126. https://revista.trenzar.cl/index.php/trenzar/article/view/63

Romero, I. (2014). Aportes al plan nacional del deporte en Venezuela. *Lecturas en Educación Física y Deportes 18*(188). www.efdeportes.com/efd188/plan-nacional-del-deporte-en-venezuela.htm.

Romero, J. (2015). Las actividades deportivas en la universidad como espacio de formación ciudadana: caso UCV. [Bachelor thesis, Universidad Central de Venezuela, The Bolivarian Republic of Venezuela] http://saber.ucv.ve/bitstream/10872/18817/1/COMPLETA.pdf

Scharagrodsky, P., & López de D'Amico, R. (2023). Debatiendo la educación física a partir del congreso panamericano, Venezuela, 1987. *Motricidades*, 7(1), 29–43. http://dx.doi.org/10.29181/2594-6463-2023-v7-n1-p29-43

Sistema de Información de Tendencias Educativas en América Latina (2019). *Venezuela.* IIPE-UNESCO. https://cuts.top/BhBf

Sistema Venezolano de Información sobre la Diversidad Biológica (2021). *Megabiodiversa Venezuela.* Author. https://cuts.top/D6XL

United Nations Economic Commission for Latin America and the Caribbean (CEPAL) (2022). *Estudio Económico de América Latina y el Caribe.* Del autor. https://cuts.top/BhB2

Chapter 25

Quality Physical Education in Zambia

Katongo Bwalya and Mwangala Kebby Liseka

Introduction

Geographical Information

Zambia is a landlocked country located in Southern Africa that is bordered by eight countries: Tanzania to the northeast, Malawi to the east, Mozambique to the southeast, Zimbabwe and Botswana to the south, Namibia to the southwest, Angola to the west, and the Democratic Republic of the Congo to the north. The country covers an area of approximately 752,612 square kilometres, characterized by diverse landscapes including high plateaus, mountains, and river valleys. Zambia gained independence from British colonial rule on October 24, 1964. It has a democratic form of government with a multiparty political system. The capital city is Lusaka, which is also the largest city.

The current political climate is relatively stable, with regular elections and peaceful transitions of power. Zambia's economy is heavily reliant on mining, particularly copper mining, which constitutes a significant portion of its gross domestic product (GDP) and export earnings. Agriculture, tourism, and manufacturing are also important sectors. Despite its rich natural resources, Zambia faces economic challenges, including high poverty rates, unemployment, and a need for economic diversification. Zambia has a population of approximately 19 million people, with a youthful demographic profile; nearly half of the population is under the age of 15 years. The official language is English, but there are numerous local languages spoken across the country. The population is diverse, with over 70 ethnic groups (Mudenda, 2006).

Physical Education in Zambia

The journey of physical education and sport (PES), as it is recognized in Zambia, is a blend of influences and developments. Mwanakatwe (2013) confirms that physical education was one of the subjects enlisted on the first national curriculum after independence in 1964, although much uncertainty exists on the content and context of the subject in the period immediately after independence (Alexander, 1997;

Bwalya, 2022). Amusa and Triola (2010) however, note that, following independence, the PE syllabi for most African countries remained significantly unchanged from the one before independence because the 1933 European syllabus still formed the bedrock of physical education.

Over the years, various factors have shaped or contribute to shaping PES in Zambia, either through assimilation or adaptation. Although PES appears on the national curriculum, it largely remains unimplemented. Despite the recognized importance of PES, there are significant disparities in its implementation and quality across the educational landscape. For instance, PES has been on the national school curriculum from independence, but, like elsewhere in much of sub-Saharan Africa, it was regarded with varying degrees of importance (Mwanakatwe, 1968). One of most significant turning points or watershed moments emerged in 2005 during the second Next Step conference in Livingstone, where then-President Levy Mwanawasa declared as mandatory the teaching of PES in all of Zambia's schools (Mubita, 2017). After the presidential decree, the Ministry of Education set in motion a series of policy measures aimed at implementing the directive. Opportunely so, in 2006, at the University of Zambia (UNZA), the Department of In-Service Education and Advisory Services (ISEAS) was split into the Advisory Unit for Colleges of Education (AUCE) and Department of Primary Education (DPE). DPE continued to offer in-service teacher's degree programmes as had previously been the case, but with a renewed focus on practical subjects with the PES programme being one of the popular choices.

Over the course of the next few years, PES generally witnessed a surge in status and appeal, and the future of the subject appeared bright. Both the government and Zambia's development partners' offered financial support to the subject, with remarkable progress. In line with the aforementioned, Zambia, in 2007, along with India, Brazil, Azerbaijan, and Palau benefited from a programme called International Inspiration Programme which was a legacy programme developed out of a commitment by UK Sport, United Nations Children's Emergency Fund (UNICEF), British Council, and partners to help transform the lives of children in schools and communities through physical education and sport (ECORYS, 2014). It was envisioned that, through the programme, children and young people would benefit from the improved delivery of PES lessons in school as a consequence of the capacity building of teachers, school principals, and youth leaders. The programme was designed to ensure not only that PES was embedded within the school curriculum and practised more regularly in schools, but also that it proved more attractive and suitable for different groups of young people.

In 2011, Mwanawasa's Movement for Multiparty Democracy (MMD) government which was in power since 1991 was defeated in a general election by the opposition Patriotic Front (PF) led by Michael Sata. The new government moved to introduce a series of educational reforms that resulted in the enactment and implementation of a revised education curriculum in 2012. One of the major outcomes of the reforms was the Zambia Education Curriculum Framework of 2013 (ZECF) which reversed Mwanawasa's 2005 decree and effectively restored PES to its pre-2005 position. This essentially ended the 'compulsory' status PES had enjoyed the preceding few years (Curriculum Development Centre, 2013a).

Currently, at the lower primary level (grades 1–4), physical education is part of Creative and Technology Studies which is a collective of Technology Studies, Home Economics, and Expressive Arts. At upper primary (grades 5–7), it is part of Expressive Arts consisting of music, art and design. This combination denotes a complex overlap of practical subjects which might be appropriated by the strength of a teacher and time allocation.

The secondary school level (grades 8–12) has two career pathways: academic and vocational. The academic pathway is meant for learners with passion for academic subjects and desire for careers in that direction. The vocational career pathway is for learners with ambitions and interests in technical and practical jobs. Vocational subject options include Agriculture, Technology, Performing and Creative Arts (PCA), PES, and Home Economics and Hospitality (HEH). This policy direction essentially permits school managers of secondary schools to either offer or not offer PES against other vocational career pathway subjects. In the absence of adequate infrastructure, lack of qualified human resources, and administration preference, PES as a career pathway in secondary schools is less likely to be offered. Therefore, even with policy and curriculum frameworks, the implementation of PES still remains the preserve of local school authorities.

Dimensions of Quality Physical Education (QPE)

Skill Development and Bodily Awareness (SDBA)

From early childhood education (pre-grade) through to secondary levels, the Zambian PES curriculum is designed to contribute towards the holistic development of the learner. PES at early childhood level focuses on physical development with particular attention to fine and gross motor skills development. According to the curriculum framework, the emphasis of Expressive Arts syllabus in early childhood education is to promote creativity, critical thinking, problem solving, positive interpersonal relationships, health and well-being, self-expression, self-confidence, awareness of space, and assertiveness. The syllabus encourages learning through the exploration of different media and the response to a variety of sensory experiences.

At lower primary, PES places emphasis on the development of practical skills and enhancement of talents, creativity, self-expression, life skills, and sense of aesthetic. On the other hand, at upper primary, the syllabus provides opportunities for the individual and the group to learn activities that cultivate healthy habits, team work, determination, and resolve. Here learners are encouraged to participate in sport such as netball, volleyball, basketball, football, and traditional games both for leisure and competition.

The approach taken at secondary school level is to use PES for the acquisition of the analytical knowledge, physical skills, life skills, right attitudes, and values toward the pursuit of a lifelong physically active and healthy lifestyle. The PES programme secondary schools is additionally designed to be a major stepping stone to providing opportunities for learners to participate in a variety of physical activities such as sports and games and to acquire the concepts and the skills that will enable them to participate in these sports and games both for leisure and competition and as a means of livelihood. In addition, PE provides a natural platform and valuable opportunities to develop self-management skills, social and cooperative skills, and build character. It serves to complement other educational areas in promoting the desired outcomes of education.

As noted earlier, the role of PES after independence was multifaceted. One of the sectors in which PES was utilized in terms of awareness interventions is health. At the height of the HIV pandemic, physical education and sport were used not only as tools of information communication but also as approaches for knowledge acquisition and health development (Abell et al, 2005). In Zambia, PES lessons have quite often provided a platform to address current or trending societal issues commonly referred to as crosscutting issues in the curriculum framework. PES within the national curriculum has been used in leveraging the appeal of sport and play as means to address social development challenges such as HIV/AIDS, COVID-19, cholera outbreaks, etc.

Facilities and Norms in Physical Education (FNPE)

Overall, there is irrefutable evidence to indicate that Zambian public schools have limited sports facilities, equipment, and appropriately qualified human resources to offer quality PES. PES as an academic subject is funded by the MoGE through annual budgetary allocations. Once the funding has been disbursed to the 10 provinces of the country, at provincial level, planners are summoned from all districts to allocate resources to schools and training colleges according to the stipulated standard criteria for each area. Although the government determines the generic focus areas such water and sanitation, desks, text books, etc., schools have the liberty to make the final decision on what to spend the money on within the identified most needy areas. With the continually growing population and the recent introduction of free education, PES is hardly prioritized and often is the one of the least funded subject areas (MoGE, 2019a; UNESCO, 2017).

Quality Teaching of Physical Education (QTPE)

Currently, all teacher training institutions in Zambia, both public and private, that offer PES teacher qualifications at Early Childhood Education Teachers' Diploma level, Primary Teachers' Diploma, and the Junior Secondary Teachers' Diploma and Bachelor's Degree levels have been mandated to use curricula that was recently reviewed and coordinated by the MoGE in 2021. Teachers are expected to get familiar with the curriculum framework in their teaching. Such expectation was already well written in the document on Standards of Practice for Teaching Practice for the Teaching Profession (MoGE, 2019b). This was done to harmonize the content that all teachers across the country were exposed to and to link the teacher–education curriculum to the revised school curriculum. The goal was to ensure that graduate teachers are familiar with the revised school curriculum and have the knowledge and skills required for delivery at school level. Some teacher training colleges have additionally begun to train teachers that specifically focus on pupils with visual impairments, hearing impairments, and other physical disabilities.

Despite the many positive strides that have been taken by the government to improve teacher training, there are still a number of challenges in PES teacher training that require redress if quality PES delivery is to be achieved. There is, for instance, need to raise the quality of students that are enrolled as PE student teachers. Many students have enrolled into PES teacher training under the assumption that it is a less academic subject and therefore lack the intellectual proficiency to grasp some complex content in PES courses such as Biomechanics and Kinesiology found in the PES teacher training syllabus. Other student teachers lack physical preparedness and hence their inability to demonstrate the accurate execution of sport skills to the learners.

An additional challenge in relation to the teachers training is that quite often, private universities and colleges are more interested in the number of paying students enrolled rather than the calibre of students. This tends to compromise the quality of PES student teacher enrolled because they focus on the quantity rather than the quality.

Plans for Feasibility and Accessibility of Physical Education (PFAPE)

According to the MoGE, the physical education syllabus is designed to promote physical activity, self-discipline, and teamwork among students (Curriculum Development Center, 2013b). However, challenges such as insufficient infrastructure, limited funding, and inadequate teacher training affect the implementation of effective PES programmes. A survey conducted by the Zambia National Education Coalition (ZANEC, 2021) found that only 20% of students engage in regular physical activities within the school environment, a statistic that raises concerns over the effectiveness of PES programmes and student health outcomes. School going children have cited inadequate facilities as a reason for their disengagement in PES (Mundia & Nkhata, 2018).

The feasibility and accessibility of PES in Zambia remains fraught with challenges that must be addressed to optimize health outcomes for children. By focusing on infrastructure development, teacher capacity, community engagement, and policy reform, Zambia can create a more equitable and effective physical education landscape for its youth.

Social Norms and Cultural Practice (SNCP)

Zambia is a country characterized by rich cultural diversity and significant socioeconomic challenges, and the dynamics of physical education are deeply influenced by cultural practices, gender norms, and economic disparities.

Zambia is home to over 70 ethnic groups, each with distinct cultural practices and beliefs. Traditional attitudes towards sports and physical activity can either encourage or inhibit participation in physical education. For instance, communities that value collective participation in traditional games might foster a positive attitude towards physical activity. However, the prevalence of certain cultural beliefs may discourage girls from engaging in sports, viewing such activities as inappropriate or contrary to gender roles (Musonda & Muma, 2020). Research indicates that in some Zambian cultures, physical activity is often seen as a male domain, whereas females are expected to focus on domestic roles (Chanda & Chanda, 2019). This cultural bias can directly impact school attendance and participation in PE, where gender segregation may lead to lower enrolment rates among girls. Gender inequality is a pervasive issue in Zambia, affecting educational opportunities, health outcomes, and economic participation. According to the Zambia Demographic and Health Survey (ZDHS) 2018, only 54% of females aged 15–24 years are literate compared to 74% of males (Central Statistical Office, 2019). This educational gap extends to physical education, where girls are often marginalized in both school settings and community sports. This corresponds with a study by Njovu (2021) which highlighted that female students were less likely to participate in school sports, with only 30% of girls regularly engaging in physical activities compared to 70% of boys. Factors contributing to this disparity include societal norms that prioritize academic success over physical activity for girls and safety concerns regarding harassment during travel to school and sports facilities.

Upon reading through key texts on PES in Zambia, it became evident that indigenous elements of knowledge and their impact on learners' cognitive abilities and physical fitness have received considerable attention. One of the earliest authors to discuss traditional games in the school education system in Zambia is Inyambo Mufalali. Mufalali (1974) pointed to some of the ways in which Zambian traditional games are similar to the western sport though he authoritatively advanced his preference of the local games over the western sports and games citing the impractical application of western sport. According to him, western sport comes with highly complex rules, regulations, and expensive equipment, and in many instances takes away the African sense of belonging. This is also exemplified in the work undertaken by Kakuwa (2005) who focused on the Zambian traditional games and their social benefits. In his work, Kakuwa particularly gives an account of common traditional games accompanied with songs from various parts of the country highlighting the value of the games in the social development of those that take part in these games both in and out of school.

The incorporation of life skills and traditional games into the PES curriculum has endeavoured to localize the subject. It has been observed that the linkages of indigenous and foreign practices have increased the appreciation of PES.

Cultural, gender, and economic factors significantly influence physical education in Zambia, creating a complex landscape that shapes the experiences of young people in this domain. To enhance the effectiveness and inclusivity of PES programmes, stakeholders must address these multifaceted challenges. Strategies could include community engagement to challenge cultural attitudes towards gender roles in sports, increased investment in infrastructure and resources for school sports, and targeted programs aimed at fostering female participation in physical activities. As Zambia continues to develop, a holistic approach to physical education that considers these factors will be essential for nurturing healthy, active, and well-rounded citizens.

Governmental Input for Physical Education (GIPE)

Economic challenges significantly hinder the implementation of quality physical education programmes in Zambia. The country's per capita income was about $1,442 in 2021, with a significant portion of the population living below the national poverty line (World Bank, 2021). Many schools lack adequate funding, which leads to insufficient sports facilities, equipment, and trained personnel necessary for effective PES programmes.

Additionally, families facing economic hardship may prioritize academic subjects over physical education, perceiving sports as a luxury rather than a necessity. Previous discussion revealed that children from lower socioeconomic backgrounds were less likely to participate in organized sports, which could adversely affect their health and social development (Nielesani et al., 2015). A profound moment in the development of PES was the recommendation to make it an examinable subject. Local literature and stakeholders interviewed suggest that making PES an examinable subject increased its prominence while reviewing the need for more investments and involvement, both as a field of study and an area of practice.

Collaborative partnerships between sport non-governmental organizations (NGOs) and the government through the Ministry of Education have similarly played a crucial role in transforming and making PES a priority area within and out of school settings. These concerted efforts seem not to have been limited to local stakeholders but extended to international bodies such as the Norwegian Olympic and Paralympic Committee. The significant and positive correlation between sport NGOs and the scaling up of PES in the Education section has supported school sport infrastructure development, information sharing, and the provision of continuing professional development opportunities, especially for teachers.

Conclusion

The key findings of this review indicate that PES in Zambia has been influenced by a number of factors such as presidential directive, curriculum reforms, as well as collaborative efforts amongst stakeholders. It was noted that the curriculum changes have created a level of prominence for PES through it being an examinable and timetabled subject. The study also revealed the need for social cultural alignment in PES curriculum. For instance, continuous training and revision of content materials. The findings underscored several systemic issues affecting PES in Zambia. Despite the comprehensive national strategy outlined in the Zambia Education Curriculum Framework of 2013, the integration of PES with economic, cultural, health, and social strategies remains insufficient. The quality of PES teacher education is compromised by a lack of practical training, inadequate infrastructure, and insufficiently qualified lecturers. Furthermore, the curricula in some local universities have not been updated in line with revised school curricula, resulting in a mismatch between teacher training and classroom needs.

Funding emerged as a major challenge, impacting the availability of resources, facilities, and equipment necessary for effective PES delivery. The study highlighted the need for policy frameworks to prioritize PES infrastructure and resource sharing with local communities, ensuring accessibility for all pupils, including those with disabilities. Research on PES in Zambia is limited, pointing to a need for stronger research networks and collaborations among educational institutions, government ministries, and local universities. Such networks would support evidence-based policy development and program implementation, fostering continuous improvement in PES.

References

Abell, J. E., Hootman, J. M., Zack, M. M., Moriarty, D., & Helmick, C. G. (2005). Physical activity and health related quality of life among people with arthritis. *Journal of Epidemiology & Community Health, 59*(5), 380–385.

Alexander, D. (1997). Problems of educational reform in Zambia. In *1982 Conference Proceedings*, unknown date (pp. 77–103). Edinburgh: Scutrea.

Amusa, L. O., & Toriola, A. L. (2010). The changing phases of physical education in Africa: Can a uniquely African model emerge?. *African Journal for Physical Activity and Health Sciences, 16*(4), 666–680. www.ajol.info/index.php/ajpherd/article/view/64095

Bwalya, K. (2022). A historical analysis of physical education development in Zambia: 1991–2021. Phd thesis, University of Zambia.

Central Statistical Office. (2019). *Zambia demographic and health survey 2018*. Lusaka: Government of Zambia.

Chanda, M., & Chanda, T. (2019). Gender and participation in physical education in Zambian schools: A cultural analysis. *Journal of African Education, 5*(2), 34–45.

Curriculum Development Centre (2013a). *Zambia Education Curriculum Framework 2013*. Ministry of Education, Science, Vocational Training and Early Education. www.giakonda.org.uk/wp-content/uploads/2018/05/ZECF-FINAL-COPY.pdf

Curriculum Development Center (CDC). (2013b). *Physical Education Syllabus grade 8-9*. Ministry of Education, Science, Vocational Training and Early Education. www.giakonda.org.uk/wp-content/uploads/2018/05/Physical-Education-Syllabus-8-9.pdf

ECORYS. (2014). *Final evaluation of the International Inspiration Programme.* ECORYS. file:///G:/Research%20and%20presentation/Resources/PEin%20Zambia/ecorys_international_inspiration_final_review_2014_1.pdf

Kakuwa, M. (2005). *Zambian traditional games and activities.* Oslo: Kicking AIDS Out

Ministry of General Education (MoGE). (2019a). *Physical education curriculum framework.* Lusaka: Government of Zambia.

Ministry of General Education (MoGE) (2019b). *Standards of practice for teaching practice for the teaching profession.* MoGE. file:///G:/Research%20and%20presentation/Resources/PEin%20Zambia/Standards-of-Practice-for-the-Teaching-Profession-in-Zambia-2019-r1705418802.pdf

Mubita, A. (2017). A history of physical education in Zambia. *Physical Culture and Sport. Studies and Research, 76*(1), 47–54. https://sciendo.com/article/10.1515/pcssr-2017-0029

Mudenda, M. M. (2006). *The challenges of Customary Land Tenure in Zambia.* Munich, Germany: Shaping the Change XXIII FIG Congress.

Mufalali, I. (1974). *Physical Education in Primary Schools.* Lusaka: NECZAM.

Mundia, L., & Nkhata, M. (2018). Physical education and health outcomes in Zambian schools. *Zambia Medical Journal, 1*(2), 50–58.

Musonda, C., & Muma, M. (2020). Cultural influences on sports participation among Zambian youth. *Zambia Journal of Sport and Education, 12*(1), 76–90.

Mwanakatwe, J. M. (1968). *The growth of education in Zambia since independence.* London: Oxford University Press.

Mwanakatwe, J. M. (2013). *The growth of education in Zambia since independence* (Revised ed.). Lusaka: University of Zambia Press.

Njelesani, J., Gibson, B. E., Cameron, D., Nixon, S., & Polatajko, H. (2015). Sport-for-development: A level playing field? *Forum Qualitative Sozialforschung/Forum: Qualitative Social Research, 16*(2), Art. 12, http://nbn-resolving.de/urn:nbn:de:0114-fqs1502120

Njovu, H. (2021). The impact of gender on participation in physical education in Zambia: A case study of secondary schools in Lusaka. *International Journal of Educational Research, 92,* 102–112.

UNESCO (2017). *Situation analysis of physical education and sport in Zambia - Towards Quality Physical Education (QPE) policy framework.* UNESCO. https://en.unesco.org/inclusivepolicylab/system/files/teams/document/2017/8/SITAN_0_0_0_0_0.pdf

World Bank. (2021). *Zambia economic update: COVID-19 and the future of work.* Washington, DC: World Bank Publications.

Zambia National Education Coalition (ZANEC) (2021). *Continuity of Learning Survey Final Report 2021.* Ministry of General Education. https://zanec.org.zm/wp-content/uploads/2022/03/FINAL-CONTINUITY-OF-LEARNING-SURVEY-REPORT-2021-2.pdf

Part III
Conclusion and Forward

Chapter 26

Quality Physical Education and the Global Perspectives
Conclusion and Future Outlook

Walter Ho, Klaudia Rafael, Selina Khoo, Usha Sujit Nair, Rosa Lopez de D'Amico, and Ling Qin

The chapter on Quality Physical Education Global Perspectives takes us on a journey traveling different corners of the world exploring physical education and its intervening nature to the healthy living of our next generations. Physical education is a classroom activity with sports and exercises as the main teaching activities to achieve healthy growth of students. Some of the authors in their chapters mentioned its origin of development with links to war preparation. The development of physical education in Colombia was officially established in 1928 under the decree 710 of 1928, the country inherited the Spanish tradition in physical and sports practices with purpose for development of healthy lifestyle habits and preparation of war. In Japan, physical education (*taiiku*) was initiated during the early Meiji period under the appellation of "*taijutsu* (i.e., physical technique)", and subsequently transformed into "*taiso* (i.e., gymnastics)". It served with the functions to prepare for war and taught with contents on physical and military training. For many European countries, the main goal of physical education was to prepare their youth for the army. For example, Law 4371 in Greece recognized the significance of physical education and made it compulsory for this reason.

As time passed, there was the gradual change of focus from military purpose to other concerns. The author from the Dominican Republic had this comment to their country's development in physical education. The way of conceiving and teaching physical education has changed, reflecting advances in the knowledge of human development and social needs with focus on the holistic approach that promotes the physical, emotional, and social development of students. While the authors from Mexico mentioned the developmental progress of physical education, there was the focus of physical education program in basic education with the military approach in 1940, then sports in 1960, psychomotor in 1974, organofunctional in 1988, motor of dynamic integration in 1993, global motor skills in 2011, and building motor competence in 2018. Similar evolution description could be found in the India chapter that the National Education Policies of 1968, 1986, and 2020 had significantly changed to reflect India's educational landscape by emphasizing holistic development, inclusivity, and the integration of sports and physical education into the curriculum, reflecting the government's commitment to comprehensive

DOI: 10.4324/9781003513582-29

education in the current reform. The development process of physical education in Zambia will be another example to see the change of concern to match the latest focus of students' needs.

The modern development of physical education usually has the focuses on learners' needs. For example, in China, under the "Health First" philosophy, there was the establishment of standards for compulsory physical education and health curricula in schools and the standards were divided into four levels of sports participation, namely sports skills, physical and mental health, and social adaptability. In Australia, students were expected to develop their skills, knowledge, and understanding to strengthen their sense of self, build on personal and community strengths to assist their well-being through the curriculum of Health Physical Education. In Nigeria, the learning of physical education is based on scientific aspects of sports performance, physical fitness, and healthy living and at the same time to equip students with the knowledge, skills, and confidence to engage in lifelong physical activity. When in Madagascar the country hosted the First Regional Meeting of African Ministers on the Implementation of the Kazan Action Plan in Africa in 2019, the Antananarivo Recommendations were announced, outlining the necessary actions to advance work on QPE. In response to this initiative, the Ministre De L'Education Nationale in Madagascar started to introduce the national curriculum in physical education to include various topics in health maintenance, talent identification, extracurricular activities, and literacy development in values, competition, and group responsibility.

To support the development of physical education, countries usually establish the subject with compulsory status or implemented with mandatory standard time and duration to protect the right for physical education. In Malaysia, Physical and Health Education is a compulsory subject in primary and secondary schools. The time allocated for physical education is more than for health education. There are 42 weeks in the school year and the minimum allocation for physical education is 32 hours a year for primary school and 48 hours a year for secondary school. In Spain, all levels of primary education, compulsory secondary education, and the first year of the Baccalaureate have 2 hours of physical education per week. In some autonomous communities in Spain, the allocation for physical education can be up to 3 hours per week. In Chile, there is the allocation of 4 hours per week for physical education courses from the first to fourth year of basic education. Between fifth and eighth year, it is reduced to 2 hours per week. In the Philippines, time allotted for physical education consists of 40 minutes per week for grades 1–6, 60 minutes per week for grades 7–10, and 120 minutes per week for grades 11–12. In Slovakia, physical education is taught at all levels of primary and secondary education as a compulsory subject with 2 hours per week to all grades. This is divided between two separate lessons of 45 minutes each, and additional courses (swimming, skiing, and a course on human and health protection) can be organized in additionally teaching time out of the compulsory two lessons. In Venezuela, according to the law, there are three physical education sessions per week totaling 6 hours weekly, and additional 2 hours for topics in which physical activity, sport, and recreation are introduced for students to develop their potential. In Puerto Rico, physical education became a compulsory subject within the public education curriculum in 1990 and with all students required to participate in three sessions, totaling 3 hours per week. Puerto Rico's system provides a model worth considering for implementation elsewhere. Under this mandatory program, physical education teachers are assigned to schools with permanent classrooms and appropriate facilities for physical education. Every school in Puerto Rico must have at least one specialized physical education teacher. If a school's enrolment exceeds 250 students, an additional physical education teacher is assigned for every additional 250 students. This approach helps reduce the workload on teachers and allows them more time to focus on students in need. This method supports physical education in school as it reduces the heavy workload in teaching this subject and teachers can have more time to students. Such examples are worthy of further discourse as the question of staffing issue is always the concerns in relation to the quality teaching in class. There is no doubt that when staffing issue is managed properly, it can be the catalytic agent for successful implementation of QPE.

The provision of compulsory structure for physical education seems to be the right step toward the establishment of the subject as a human right issue. Nevertheless, there is the need of caution to allow the opportunities of learning with equal access to all students. The case from South Korea seems to protect equality rights by means of rules and regulation. Their Minister of Education established basic guidelines necessary for the activation of girls' physical education activities and informed the superintendent of education and school principals to formulate and implement planning of girls' physical education activities every year in accordance with the basic guidelines. In places with religious concern, there is the need of other arrangement to make physical education possible for both genders. In Jordan, there is the awareness of this issue and understands the Islam culture to support sports participation for both genders and that the policy is to have segregated class for each gender to study. Similar action is also recognized in Saudi Arabia and in 2017, the Ministry of Education made a historic decision to allow girls to participate in physical education. Primary school students are allocated 112 minutes per week of physical education for girls, whereas secondary school students are having 45 minutes per week.

While taking note of all these developments, it offers an optimistic picture for the work of QPE development. Nevertheless, the establishment is confronted by different challenges with relationship to our perception, social condition, geographical location, political stability, and economic development. It happens, for example, in Australia, the hours allocated lesson of Health and Physical Education vary according to the state and year level. In Madagascar, the country is immersed with the crisis on child labor and gender inequality issues. Urgent action seems to be needed in assisting students to go back to school. Yet, this problem cannot be solved by political decision but needs to review the social and economic condition. In Malaysia, there was the challenge on the perception that some school administrators and parents regarded physical education was not an important subject when compared to other examination subjects such as Mathematics and Science. There were other challenges that include limited budget for physical education, qualified physical education teachers not teaching physical education, and non-physical education specialists teaching physical education. The authors from Philippines voiced the common scenarios with wider perspectives of poverty, armed conflicts, lack of resources and infrastructure to support the development, overwork in teachers, and job burnout and low salaries as the barriers to slow down our success.

Hardman (2008) commented on the mixed message that nation had the desire to commit the development through legislation but slow in translating the expected goal into action through actual implementation and assurance of quality of delivery. There are many issues that impede the progress of success in QPE. This is also the reason for the ISCPES research team to conduct the study in QPE with the core focus to answer "How far has QPE been achieved?". The 10 years of work from 2010 to 2019 identified 48 items in 8 dimensions as the basic factors for us to understanding the concerns in QPE development. It was a huge undertaking to identify the dimensions, and two papers (Ho et al, 2021, 2023) were published to summarize its development. After the successful identification of the items and dimensions, the research team launched a pilot study 2020 and invited researchers from around the world to complete a questionnaire in QPE. The 48 items in 8 dimensions were used as the basic materials in this survey. Readers who are interested in these dimensions can read the related materials from the two papers to check the scientific work behind the development of the 48 items and 8 dimensions.

This book comprises cases from 24 countries to provide a snapshot of the current situation of the 8 dimensions. When discussing these dimensions, the authors from these countries praise the success but also indicate the shortfalls. Most of the countries have made effort in the curriculum development of sport and physical education and recognize the difficulties mostly from the dimensions in relation to teachers' training, facilities and venue building, government input, cognitive development, inclusion, and habitual behavior in exercises. The authors from Mexico mentioned that most public elementary schools in Mexico had sports facilities for physical education classes. However, they were not sufficient, and the budget for their acquisition was limited. For this reason, teachers from Mexico had to buy materials with their own money or used recycled materials. While the Indian team mentioned the number of teachers enrolled in each year, it had the figures of (as of March 31, 2022) intake as follows: D.P.Ed = 9495; B.P.Ed = 47860; M.P.Ed = 7415 in teachers' training. Although there was the large number of teachers receiving training, it is still "falls significantly short of the annual demand". In Zambia, there was the cultural bias and had direct impact to school attendance and hence, participation in physical education, where gender segregation may lead to lower enrolment rates among girls. Gender inequality is a pervasive issue in Zambia, affecting educational opportunities, health outcomes, and economic participation. In Greece, the authors discussed the development of habitual behavior of students in exercises and sport but went with the comments of the development of habituated behavior until now, the goals have been partially achieved. In the Philippines, the implementation of QPE posed a big challenge while considering the many issues of limited government support, inadequate facilities and equipment, lack of qualified physical education teachers in many schools, time allotment, resource materials, and the long-standing problem of undervaluing physical education among others.

The case studies of the different countries seem to indicate that strong legislative efforts are important in improving the quality of physical education; however, it should not be focused only on the compulsory provision of physical education to students but there is a need to adopt strategies to ensure professional development of physical education teachers and specialists, infrastructure building, and practical practice for inclusion and equality in education. Providing high-quality physical education programs involves developmental dimensions which are different from legislative efforts. QPE is of great relevance to contribute to a healthy society. It is not just physical but also mental well-being. Worldwide the relevance of physical education is still diminished, and other subjects are more valued in societies. Physical education in an interdisciplinary subject that allows the holistic comprehension of theory and practice of the social and biological phenomena. Governments should look closely at the international agreements in which they have ratified in and the fulfilment of them. For this, we would like to highlight some suggestions from the various chapters to conclude the outlook of QPE development in future.

The Japan chapter highlighted the essential elements for building high-quality physical education programs, including teacher training, curriculum design, the introduction of advanced technology, support for lifelong learning, enrichment of extracurricular activities, and research in physical education. Managing and developing of these elements in a comprehensive way seems to be the key to the success of high-quality physical education. Yet, we need to think of the balanced concept in applying the comprehensive strategy. The Malaysia chapter alerts us to the importance of balanced development in a country. Funding should be available and provided to schools in rural areas which do not have enough fundamental equipment to conduct physical education classes. In fact, similar call was written in the China chapter. China's eastern region, which is home to the country's most economically developed provinces, had demonstrated a higher level of development in the eight key dimensions of QPE compared to the national average. This imbalance may have the link with the differences in economic development, prevailing concepts of education, and investment in sports venues and facilities. The need of strategies to transfer the knowledge and resources from the region with successful implementation experiences to the needed area seems to be the agenda as QPE is supposed to be a global development, not a regional success.

In conclusion, we invite readers, school administrators, policy makers, and frontline teachers to consider the information of QPE development in this book. This book contains relevant information and records of what we are working in developing physical education as the best desirable means for education. We want to see the change and to quote the comments from the partners in South Africa; QPE plays a pivotal role in advancing the transformative agenda of the education system. To make it a serious agenda that would be essential especially when UNESCO has the call for "Fit for Life" as action for the future world of healthy living. There is no doubt that proper QPE provides the basic and fundamental support for this initiative to be successful in future development of active living of our next generation. The Australia chapter gives us the way of how to treat the materials in this book. Her writing tries to link QPE in Australia with the Australian Curriculum: Heath Physical Education content, showing the context-specific of what QPE should looks like. While she makes the debates of what QPE means, it is indeed to call the action and attempts to unpack what QPE implies in different countries. This is what we wish for you, while you are reading the book, unpack the knowledge and think what it means to you, to your class, to your school, to your city, and to your country. For that, we believe there is the way for us to improve the works of physical education as the best educational activities for the health growth of our next generation.

References

Hardman, K. (2008). Physical education in schools: A global perspective. *Kinesiology, 40*(1), 5–28. www.academia.edu/19622196/Physical_education_in_schools_A_global_perspective

Ho, W., Ahmed, Md. D., & Kukurova, K. (2021). Development and validation of an instrument to assess Quality Physical Education. *Cogent Education, 8*(1), 1864082. https://doi.org/10.1080/2331186X.2020.1864082

Ho, W., Ahmed, D., Rafael, K., de D'Amico, R.L., Antala, B., Liu, M., Dong, X.X., & Xie, Y.Y. (2023). Quality Physical Education (QPE) measuring tool development. *International Sports Studies, 45*(2), 6–27. https://doi.org/10.30819/iss.45-2.02

Index

Association for Physical Education 4
Australia: Active and Healthy Schools Committee 20; Australian Council for Health, Physical Education and Recreation 20; Australian National Health and Physical Education Curriculum (AC: HPE) 15, 16–17, 18, 19, 20–21, 22–23, 278; Australian Professional Standards for Teachers 21; Australian Sports Commission 20; cognitive skill development in PE 22; colonial legacy in education 16; disabled students 20; ethical behaviour education 18–19; emotional education 19; facilities and norms in PE 18–19; fitness tests 17; geography of 15; goals of HPE 16–17; governmental input for PE 21; habituated behaviour in physical activities 22–23; healthism discourse, HPE criticised as 17; Health-Related Quality of Life programme 23; history of 15–16; inadequate allocated curriculum time and resources 18; Indigenous knowledge 21; intercultural understanding education 20–21; lack of coherent pedagogical approach 7; Lunchtime Enjoyment Activity and Play intervention 23; origins of PE 16; personalised student plans 17; plans for feasibility and accesibility of PE 20; quality teaching of PE 19; refining movement skills 19; safety education 18, 22–23; skill development and bodily awareness 17–18; social diversity of Australians 16, 20; social interaction skills 22; social norms and cultural practice 20–21; Sporting Schools 20; Victorian HPE curriculum 4, 20; Western Australia HPE curriculum 16
Austrian National Method 28

Bolivar, Simón 251
Bolivarian Alliance for the Peoples of the Americas (ALBA) 74, 258
Brazil: Agita Sao Paulo Program 35; biological-functional conception of physical fitness 30; cognitive skill development in PE 34; Coordination for the Improvement of Higher Education 34; dance 29; developmental and holistic PE perspectives, emergence of 30; European gymnastics methods, pre-1940s dominance of 28; facilities and norms in PE 32; gender division of PE classes 29; geography of 27; governmental input for PE 34; habituated behaviour in physical activities 34–35; history of 27–28, 30; inclusive and responsive principles, PE anchored in 28, 33–34, 35; International Inspiration Programme 262; Law of Guidelines and Bases of National Education (1996) 29, 30; National Common Curricular Base (BNCC) 31, 32, 34; National Physical Education Council 33; National Research and Technology Council 34; National School of Physical Education and Sports 28; origins of PE 28; plans for feasibility and accesibility of PE 33; *Programa Segundo Tempo* 32; public–private school resource gap 32, 33; quality teaching of PE 32–33; School of Physical Education (State University of Sao Paulo) 28; skill development and bodily awareness 31; social diversity of Brazilians 27–28, 33; social norms and cultural practice 33–34; teacher qualifications for PE 32; technical sports concept, dominance of 29, 30; women, restrictions on sports

participation 30; women in Brazilian society 28
British Council 169

Cajigal, José María 61
Canada 4
Chile: Centro de Perfeccionamiento, Experimentación e Investigaciones Pedagógicas (CPEIP) 38, 39; Choose to Live Healthy program 41; cognitive skill development in PE 43; current curriculum reform proposal 38, 42, 43, 44; Curricula for Basic Education and Secondary Education (MINEDUC) 38; evaluation of the eight dimensions of QPE in Diguillín province 39–44; evaluation of PE, not coherent with paradigms of PE 39, 44; facilities and norms in PE 42; geography of 37; governmental input for PE 44; habituated behaviour in physical activities 43; history of 37; human motor sciences as current paradigm for PE 38, 39; National System of Professional Teacher Development 42; optionality of PE in upper secondary schools 37, 41, 43; Pedagogical and Disciplinary Standards for Physical Education and Health Pedagogy Careers 38; plans for feasibility and accesibility of PE 44; Programa de Evaluación de Desempeño 39; Promotion of Active and Healthy Lifestyles 41; Prueba Nacional de Desempeño Escolar 38; quality teaching of PE 41–42, 44; sedentary lifestyles and obesity 37, 42; Sistema de Evaluación de la Calidad de la Educación 39; Sistema de Medición de la Calidad de la Educación 39; Sistema Nacional de Evaluación de Resultados de Aprendizaje 38; skill development and bodily awareness 42–43; social norms and cultural practice 43–44; time allowance for PE in curriculum 38, 274
China: cognitive skill development in PE 53, 54, 56; development of QPE 50; facilities and norms in PE 51; geography of 49; governmental input for PE 52; *Guiding Opinions on Promoting the Reform of the Educational Methods of Ordinary Senior High Schools in the New Era* 53; habituated behaviour in physical activities 53–54; 'Health First' philosophy 49, 274; information technology resources for PE 52, 54; 'Learning to Learn' reforms in Hong Kong 5; low physical activity among youth 4–5; *Medium- and Long-Term Youth Development Plan* 49; myopia rates 51; national survey 4–5; *Opinions on Comprehensively Strengthening and Improving School Physical Education in the New Era* 49; *Outline of Healthy China 2030 Plan* 53; *Physical Education and Health Curriculum Standards for Compulsory Education* 54; plans for feasibility and accesibility of PE 54; project-based learning 52; 'quality education' reforms 5; quality teaching of PE 52–53; regional variations in economic resources and QPE development 54–56, 277; sedentary lifestyles and obesity 53; skill development and bodily awareness 51; sports venue infrastructure 52; State General Administration of Sports 52; structured and situational curriculum ideas 52–53; textbooks for PE 52; university students 5
Colombia: curricular diversity in PE 67; Curricular Guidelines 65; disability rights 64; European gymnastics movements 60–61, 67; facilities and norms in PE 62; geography of 59–60; governmental input for PE 66–67; hermeneutic exaltation of subjectivities and new bodily practices 65, 66; human motor sciences as current paradigm for PE 61; individual and collective class participation 65, 66; lack of PE professionals at some schools 61–62; military training, PE as 60, 273; literacy rate 60; Ministry of National Education (MEN) 60, 66, 67; origins of PE 60; Paralympic sports 65; Physical Education Development Centers 62; plans for feasibility and accesibility of PE 63–65; postgraduate PE training 67; public–private school differences 61–62; quality teaching of PE 62–63; Secretaries of Education 66; sedentary lifestyles of schoolchildren, trend toward 67; skill development and bodily awareness 61; social diversity of Colombians 60; social

norms and cultural practice 65–66;
Sports and Recreation Institutes 66–67;
time allowance for PE in curriculum 63, 67
Common Market of the South
 (MERCOSUR) 74, 258
Community of Latin American and
 Caribbean States (CELAC) 74, 258
Convention on the Rights of Persons with
 Disabilities 106
COVID-19 pandemic 147, 155, 180, 209,
 233, 234, 236, 237, 252, 264

Declaration of Berlin 175
Dominican Republic: Catholicism 74;
 cognitive skill development 43, 75;
 constitutional right to sport 72, 73;
 economic constraints on education
 74; facilities and norms in PE 42, 72;
 General Law of Sport 72, 73; geography
 of 70; governmental input for PE 44,
 74–75; habituated behaviour in physical
 activities 43, 75; history of 70; holistic
 approach to PE, emergence of 70, 76,
 273; inclusion and equality challenges,
 persistence of 76; Instituto Nacional de
 Educación Física (INEFI) 72; Instituto
 Superior de Formación Docente Salomé
 Ureña 75; Ministry of Sports and
 Recreation 72, 75; National Action
 Plan for Physical Activity 73; National
 Intersectoral Physical Activity Plan 71;
 National Report on the Evolution of
 Education Expenditure 74; plans for
 feasibility and accessibility of PE 44, 73;
 quality teaching of PE 41, 73; regional
 education networks and initiatives 74;
 skill development and bodily awareness
 43, 71; social diversity of Dominicans
 70; social norms and cultural practice
 43, 73–74; time allowance for PE in
 curriculum 73; Universidad Autónoma
 de Santo Domingo 75

Ecuador 41, 42, 43, 44
European gymnastics movements 28,
 60–61, 67

Federation Internationale d'Education
 Physique 7

gender issues in physical education 29,
 94–95, 97, 105, 107, 112, 114, 116, 118,
 127, 137, 138, 146, 147, 160, 170, 181,
 194, 198, 199–200, 203, 204, 205, 212,
 218, 219, 256, 266, 267, 275
Generalized Sports Method 28
Global Index of Quality Physical Education
 39, 124
Global Voices in QPE 7–8
Greece: Adapted PE 84; Aesop Platform
 for Digital Teaching Scenarios 87–88;
 Analytical Program (Ministry of
 Education) 82, 88; cognitive skill
 development 87–88; compulsory PE
 at all school levels 83; constitutional
 commitment to PE 80; dance, traditional
 85; 'Detailed Program of PE in primary
 schools 82; elementary curriculum
 82, 83; EU guidelines for PE 80–81,
 82; EVZIN program 83; facilities and
 norms in PE 83–84 former military
 orientation of PE 81, 273; geography
 of 80; governmental input for PE
 86–87; habituated behaviour in physical
 activities 88–89, 276–277; Hellenic
 Institute of Educational Policy 82,
 84, 86; high school curriculum 83;
 history of 80; inclusivity 84, 86, 89;
 interdisciplinary initiatives 88; Law 1566
 (1985) 81; Law 4371 (1929) 81; National
 Academy of PE 81; Olympic Education
 85, 86, 87; physical literacy 82; plans
 for feasibility and accessibility of PE
 86; public–private school resource gap
 83–84; quality teaching of PE 84–85;
 school autonomy 82; skill development
 and bodily awareness 82–83; skills
 workshops 88; social norms and
 cultural practice 86; Special Education
 schools 84; swimming 82, 83; teacher
 training and assessment 83, 86; working
 group for upgrade of PE (Ministry of
 Education) 86–87

human right, QPE as 32, 212, 230, 275

India: Annual Status of Education Report
 93; caste system 91; Central Board of
 Secondary Education (CBSE) 92–93;
 cognitive skill development 96; complex
 structure of education system, as barrier
 to effective PE programs 97; Department
 of Education 91; facilities and norms
 in PE 92–93; Fit India Movement 94;

gender disparity in physical exercise 94–95, 97; gender inequality 91; Global School-Based Student Health Survey 96–97; governmental input for PE 95–96; habituated behaviour in physical activities 96–97; inclusivity 96, 273; *Khelen Bhi Aur Khilen Bhi* 95–96; Khelo India movement 95, 96; National Education Policy (NEP) 92, 95, 98; plans for feasibility and accessibility of PE 94; quality teaching of PE 93–94; regional diversity 91; research gap on PE 98; sedentary behaviour 96–97; shortage of qualified PE teachers 97, 276; skill development and bodily awareness 92; social norms and cultural practice 94–95; time allowance for PE in curriculum 92–93; universal primary education, progress toward 91–92; urban–rural disparity in physical exercise 95, 97; yoga 92, 93, 96

Inter-American Planning Center of the Organization of American States 74

International Association of Physical Education and Sport for Girls and Women 7

International Baccalaureate Diploma Programme 213

International Charter of Physical Education and Sport (UNESCO) 3, 6, 97

International Committee of Sport Pedagogy 7

International Council for Health, Physical Education, Recreation – Sports and Dance 134

International Federation of Adapted Physical Activity 7

International Inspiration Programme 262

International Monetary Fund 75, 80

International Physical Education Conference 180

International Society for Comparative Physical Education and Sport (ISCPES) 7, 124, 276

Japan: cognitive skill development 107–108; combination of physical and health education 104–105; disabled and special needs students 106–107; discussion scenes 107; evolution of PE concept 102, 108; facilities and norms in PE 104–105; former military focus of PE 102, 273; gender disparity in PE 105, 107; geography of 101; governmental input for PE 106–107; habituated behaviour in physical activities 108; history of 101; ICT in classrooms 107; integration of teaching and assessment 102–103, 109; Japan Society of Physical Education 105–106; Japan Society of Sports Education 106; martial arts 104; National Institute for Educational Policy Research 107; National School Physical Education Research Federation 106; physical fitness tests 104; plans for feasibility and accessibility of PE 105–106; prefectural variation in curricula 103; quality teaching of PE 105; religion 106; skill development and bodily awareness 104; social cohesion of Japanese society 106; social norms and cultural practice 106; Standards for the Establishment of Schools 104; time allowance for PE in curriculum 103, 105; universal primary education, early achievement of 101

Jordan: after-school sports activities 113, 115; British colonial legacy 112; cognitive skill development 117–118; curriculum framework for PE 116–117; emergence of PE 112; facilities and norms in PE 113–114; First National Conference for Education Reform 112; GCSE, PE excluded from 112, 114, 116, 119; gender disparity in PE 112, 114, 116, 118, 275; governmental input for PE 116–117; habituated behaviour in physical activities 118–119; Health Competent Project 113; health-promoting schools initiative 116, 117, 118; Islam 111, 112, 118, 275; King Abdullah II Award for Physical Fitness 117, 118–119; Madrasati initiative 115, 117; Ministry of Education PE guidelines 114; Nashatati Program 115, 117; National Center for Curriculum Development 116; National Strategy for Human Resource Development 111; obesity, rise of 111, 115, 116, 117–118; plans for feasibility and accessibility of PE 115; quality teaching of PE 113, 114–115; Royal Health Awareness Society 117, 118; Right to Play initiative 116, 117; sedentary lifestyles 115–116,

118; skill development and bodily awareness 113; social norms and cultural practice 115–116; theoretical part of PE neglected 114–115, 119; time allowance for PE in curriculum 112, 114, 119

Keleher, Julia 194

Latin American Social Sciences Council (CLACSO) 74, 258

Madagascar: Antananarivo Recommendations 124, 274; child labor problem 124, 275; cognitive skill development 128; facilities and norms in PE 127–128; French colonial legacy in education system 123, 124; gender inequality 127, 275; GIQPE survey 124–126; governmental input for PE 127–128; habituated behaviour in physical activities 128; health education through PE 126; Human Development Index ranking 128; national PE curriculum, introduction of 124, 274; plans for feasibility and accessibility of PE 127; poverty, violence and natural disasters 123, 128; religion 127; quality teaching of PE 128; research gap on PE 124, 126, 129; sedentary lifestyles 128; shortage of qualified teachers 129; skill development and bodily awareness 128; social norms and cultural practice 127; team sports, potential benefits of 127; underinvestment in secondary education 124

Malaysia: after-school sports activities 135; cognitive skill development 138–139; Curriculum and Assessment Standard Document 134; disabled students 135–136, 137; facilities and norms in PE 135–136; gender disparity in PE 137, 138; geography of 133; Global School-Based Student Health Survey 137; governmental input for PE 138; habituated behaviour in physical activities 139; holistic development as goal 136–137, 138; National Education Philosophy 134, 138, 139; National Physical Fitness Standard Test 136; National Strategic Plan for Active Living 139; 'One Student, One Sport' policy 138; plans for feasibility and accessibility of PE 137; psychomotor domain, PE emphasis on 134; quality teaching of PE 136–137; safety guidelines for PE 136; sedentary lifestyles 139; skill development and bodily awareness 134–135; social norms and cultural practice 137–138; standard-based curriculum, adoption of 134; Standard School Curriculum for Physical and Health Education 133–134, 135; Sultan Idris Education University 136; Teaching Games for Understanding 136; time allowance for PE in curriculum 133, 274

Mexico: cognitive skill development 147–148; COVID-19 pandemic 147; development of education system 143; disabled students 146; evolution of PE 143, 273; facilities and norms in PE 145, 276; gender disparity in PE 146, 147; geography of 142; governmental input for PE 147; habituated behaviour in physical activities 148; New Mexican School 142–143, 144; obesity, prevalence of 148; obsolete pedagogy 146; plans for feasibility and accessibility of PE 146; quality teaching of PE 145–146; QPE survey 144; shortage of trained PE teachers 143; skill development and bodily awareness 144–145; social norms and cultural practice 147; socioeconomic inequalities 142, 145; sports accidents 145; time allowance for PE in curriculum 143; 'Towards a National Strategy for the Provision of Physical Education in the Mexican Educational System' 145
Michigan Department of Education 4
military motivations for PE 60, 81, 102, 273
motor praxeology 61
Muñoz Marin, Luis 188
Mwanawasa, Levy 262, 263

New Zealand: Balance Is Better 155, 156, 157, 163; bodily awareness 158; cognitive skill development 162; community partnerships 156, 157, 158, 159, 163, 164; COVID-19 pandemic 155, 156; digital tools for health and fitness 155, 164; disabled students 159; environmental awareness through PE 154, 156; facilities and norms in

PE 157–158; Football New Zealand 157; gender stereotypes as ongoing challenge 160; geography of 153, 157; governmental input for PE 161–162; habituated behaviour in physical activities 163; Hauora 153, 154, 158, 160; Health and Physical Education Curriculum 153, 154–155, 156, 157, 160; holistic approach to health and well-being 154; inclusive PE practices 156, 157, 158, 161, 164; interdisciplinary approach to teaching health and PE 159, 162, 164; Māori values 160; mental health through physical activity 155; movement skills 158; national sporting culture 153; Netball New Zealand 156; New Zealand Cricket 157; New Zealand Physical Activity Guidelines 154; outdoor education 156, 157; out-of-school promotion of physical activity 159, 163; Pacific Island cultures 160; plans for feasibility and accessibility of PE 159; quality teaching of PE 158–159; Rugby New Zealand 156; safety measures 158; skill development and bodily awareness 156–157; social norms and cultural practice 160; Sport New Zealand 155, 156, 157, 158, 159, 161, 163–164; time allowance for PE in curriculum 154; Tū Manawa 155, 156, 158, 159

Nigeria: cognitive skill development 171; colonial education legacy 167; economic constraints on PE 170, 171; facilities and norms in PE 168–169; geography of 166; governmental input for PE 170, 172; habituated behaviour in physical activities 171; Islamic gender disparities in PE 170; National Education and Research Development Council 169; National Policy on Education 167; Nigeria Association for Physical, Health Education, Recreation, Sports and Dance 170; optionality of PE in secondary school 169; origins of PE 167; out-of-school children 166; plans for feasibility and accessibility of PE 169–170; quality teaching of PE 169; Safe School Initiative 168; Science Teachers Association of Nigeria 170; scientific PE approach, recent shift toward 167–168, 274; shortage of teachers 166, 169, 171; skill development and bodily awareness 168; social norms and cultural practice 170; special schools 169; training of PE teachers 167; Universal Basic Education Commission (UBEC) 166, 170; time allowance for PE in curriculum 168
Norwegian Olympic and Paralympic Committee 267

obesity 37, 42, 53, 111, 115, 116, 117–118, 148, 176, 193, 195
Organization for Economic Cooperation and Development (OECD) 74, 102, 208, 229, 230

Pakistan 7
Parlebas, Pierre 61
Philippines: cognitive skill development 182; Commission on Higher Education 182; constitutional commitment to PE 176; Department of Interior and Local Government 182; disabled students 179; facilities and norms in PE 178–179; Galaw Pilipinas 183; gender-sensitive teaching 181; governmental input for PE 182; habituated behaviour in physical activities 182–183; health and movement-related approach to PE 177, 182; learner-centered education 178; low status of PE 177, 183, 277; MATATAG Curriculum 178, 179, 181, 182, 183; Mother Tongue-Based Multilingual Education program 181; multi-ethnicity 181; National Calisthenics Exercise Program 183; National Coaching Certification Program 182; National Educator Academy of the Philippines 180; National Physical Education Teachers' Convention 180; National Sports Associations 181; Palarong Pambansa 179; Philippine Olympic Committee 181; Philippine Sports Commission (PSC) 181, 182; Philippine Sports Institute 182; plans for feasibility and accessibility of PE 180–181; poverty and lack of resources 177, 183, 276; quality teaching of PE 179–180; religion 181; School-Based Training of Teachers in Physical Education 180; Schools Physical Education and Sports Development Act 176; shortage of PE teachers 179–180, 277; skill

development and bodily awareness 177–178; social norms and cultural practice 181; Sports Club Program 179, 183; time allowance for PE in curriculum 177, 183, 274, 277; traditional and indigenous sports and games 181
Physical and Health Education Canada 4
Professional Perceptions Toward Quality Physical Education 8
Puerto Rico: academic training for PE teachers 190–191; Adapted Physical Education (APA) 189, 195: Americanization of education system 188; Association for Physical Activity, Physical Education, and Dance of Puerto Rico (AEFR PUR) 193, 194; cognitive skill development 194; College of Pedagogy 188; Council of Higher Education 188; Department of Education 189, 192, 194; disabled students 193; emergence of PE as discipline 189; facilities and norms in PE 193–194; gender disparity in PE, overcoming of 194; geography of 187; governmental input for PE 194; habituated behaviour in physical activities 194–195; history of 187; Hurricane Maria schools damaged and closed by 193–194, 195; Industrial Normal School 188; mandatory PE, adoption and abandonment of 190, 194, 195; Longitudinal Strategic Plan 192 for PE program 192; obesity 193, 195; Personal Meaning curricular model for PE 191–192; plans for feasibility and accessibility of PE 194; political fluctuations in education policy 188–189, 190, 193, 194, 195; quality teaching of PE 194; shortage of teachers 189, 195; skill development and bodily awareness 193; social norms and cultural practice 194; Spanish educational legacy 187–188; standards of PE program 192; University of Puerto Rico 188, 195; time allowance for PE in curriculum 190, 275

quality evaluation in education, complexity of 38
Quality Physical Education (QPE): compulsory and comprehensive QPE in schools, importance of 4, 6, 224, 274–275; definition of 7, 15; eight-dimensions model of 8, 221, 222, 225; as foundational to lifelong engagement in active living 3, 4, 175; growing consensus on importance of 6; health and well-being, contribution to 277; holistic development 4, 19, 219, 221, 223, 277; inadequate allocated curriculum time and resources 6, 18, 175–176, 218; international agreements by governments 277; legislative support, importance of 277; origins of 3, 39; professional development of PE teachers 277; six-factor model of 221–225; teacher shortage as ubiquitous issue 275; transcendence of mere physical activity 223; transferring successes to underresourced regions 277
Quality Physical Education: Guidelines for Policy Makers (UNESCO) 4, 39, 134, 146, 210, 221, 224

Saudi Arabia: cognitive skill development 203; compulsory PE at schools and universities 198, 205; disabled students 203; emergence of PE 197–198; facilities and norms in PE 199–200, 201; First Development Plan 197; gender in PE and sports 198, 199–200, 203, 204, 205, 275; General Presidency of Youth Welfare 198; geography of 197; governmental input for PE 204; habituated behaviour in physical activities 201–203; Islam 197, 198, 275; non-communicable diseases, rise of 204; plans for feasibility and accessibility of PE 203; quality teaching of PE 200, 202; research gap in PE 199; Saudi Vision 2030 198, 203, 204–205; sedentary lifestyles 203, 204; skill development and bodily awareness 199, 200; social norms and cultural practice 204; time allowance for PE in curriculum 198, 205; traditional Saudi games 204; training of PE teachers 198, 205
sedentary lifestyles 37, 42, 53, 67, 96–97, 115–116, 118, 128, 139, 203, 204
Sergio, Manuel 61
Singapore 5–6
Slovakia: Association of Physical and Sports Education Teachers 208–209; Central Committee for the Educational Area Health and Movement 209, 214; Coaches at School project 210; cognitive skill development 212;

Committee of Physical and Sports Education Subject 209; COVID-19 pandemic 209; Curriculum Council 209; disabled students 212; facilities and norms in PE 210–211; gender disparity in PE 212; governmental input for PE 212; habituated behaviour in physical activities 212; Health and Movement curriculum proposal 214–216; Ministry of Education, Science, Research, and Sport of the Slovak Republic (MSVVS SR) 209, 211; plans for feasibility and accessibility of PE 213; quality teaching of PE 211; QPE survey 210; recent curricular reform 213–214; skill development and bodily awareness 211; Slovak Football Association 209; Slovak Olympic and Sports Committee 209; Slovak Tennis Association 209; social norms and cultural practice 212; Sports Support Fund 209; testing physical abilities of elementary school children 209; time allowance for PE in curriculum 208, 211, 216, 274

South Africa: compulsory PE, failure to ensure 7, 218, 224; Curriculum and Assessment Policy Statement 218; diverse school approaches to PE 220; educational value of PE, perceptions of 223; gender disparity in physical activities 218; gender-segregated PE in Apartheid era 219; holistic development through PE, hindered by resource challenges 223–224; knowledge and skill development through PE, perceptions of 223; Life Orientation (LO) paradigm for PE 219, 220; non-communicable diseases 218; outcomes-based education, shift to 219; policy and collaboration, failure of for QPE 224; Raymond Mhlaba Local Municipality QPE study 220–221; safe and conducive PE environments, lack of 224–225; sedentary lifestyles 218–219; shortage of qualified PE teachers 219, 220, 223; time allowance for PE in curriculum 219

South Korea: cognitive skill development 236–237; competency-based PE curriculum 232; COVID-19 pandemic 233, 234, 236, 237; demographics, economy and politics of 229; educational rankings of 229–230; evolution of PE 230–231; facilities and norms in PE 233; female PE initiatives 231, 234, 235, 275; Fit for Life project 236; fostering global citizenship through PE 232, 235; governmental input for PE 235–236; government construction projects 231, 233; habituated behaviour in physical activities 237–238; 'human-centeredness and harmony of values' as educational philosophy 230; I-League 236; information technology for PE 234; Korea Sports Federation 235, 236; National Sports Promotion Act 234; Physical Activity Promotion System (PAPS) 232, 236–237; plans for feasibility and accessibility of PE 234–235; quality teaching of PE 233–234; Revised Curriculum for Physical Education and Sports 231, 232; school sports, governance of 230, 232, 235–236, 236–238; School Sports Promotion Act 231, 232; skill development and bodily awareness 232–233; social norms and cultura practice 235; Sports Instructor Placement Project for Elementary and Special Schools 234; student health and fitness assessments 233; survival swimming 234–235; Tailored Programme for Low-Fitness Students 233; training of PE teachers 230, 231, 234; value-based PE curriculum, retiring of 231, 232; virtual PE classes 234

Spain: basic knowledge in PE curriculum 244–245; constitutional basis for PE 241; continuous training of PE teachers 246–247, 248; evolution of PE 241; facilities, technical standards for 245–246; geography of 240; integrating PE with other subjects 247; key competencies for lifelong learning 244, 247; lesson planning for PE 245; national curriculum 240–241; objectives of PE 243; 'physical exercise and sports prescription' strategy 247; qualifications of PE teachers 242, 248; school sports, linking PE to 242, 247; specific competencies for PE students 244; specific competencies for PE teachers 242–243; time allowance for PE in curriculum 241–242, 247, 274; transversal approach to teaching of

values 245; working group activities and educational research projects for PE teachers 247, 248
Sport Education Model 19, 223

Taiwan 6–7
Teaching for Personal and Social Responsibility 19
Teaching Games for Understanding 19
Trigo, Eugenia 61

UNESCO: cognitive skills of students, emphasis on 75; Declaration of Berlin 175; 'Fit for Life' project 236, 278; International Charter 3, 6, 39, 97; King Sejong Literacy Prize 229; Madagascar, assessment of 129; pivotal role in transformative education systems 278; *Quality Physical Education: Guidelines for Policy Makers* 4, 134, 146, 210, 221, 224; Regional Bureau of Education for Latin America and the Caribbean 74; Saudi Arabia, report on 205; training, provision of 170; in Venezuela 255; Worldwide Survey 6; youth policy advocacy 56
UNICEF 115, 117, 124, 169, 262
Union of South American Nations (UNASUR) 74, 258
UNRWA 116, 117

Venezuela: cognitive skill development 257; COVID-19 pandemic 252; cultural competence through PE 255; economy of 250; education system, structure of 250–251; environmental awareness through PE 254; evolution of PE 251; facilities and norms in PE 253–254; gender disparity in PE 256; geography of 250; governmental input for PE 256; habituated behaviour in physical activities 257–258; health promotion through PE 254–255, 257; holistic and humanistic approach to PE 251, 255; interdisciplinary teaching of PE 256, 257; Observatory for Quality Education (OCEV) 251, 255, 258; personal development through PE 255; plans for feasibility and accessibility of PE 255; policy framework for PE 253–254; quality teaching of PE 254–255; regional initiatives, need for 258; shortage of PE teachers 254; skill development and bodily awareness 252–253; social development through PE 254, 257; social norms and cultural practice 255–256; time allowance for PE in curriculum 252, 274; training of PE teachers 254, 255, 256; UNESCO, policy influence of 255

World Bank 75, 92, 166, 169–170
World Health Organization (WHO) 4–5, 72, 81, 108, 116, 118, 134, 139
Worldwide Survey of School Physical Education (UNESCO-NWCPEA) 6

Zambia: colonial legacy in PE 262; COVID-19 264; Creative and Technology Studies umbrella for PES 263; cultural diversity 266; disabled students 265; disparities in implementation of PES 262, 263; economy of 261, 267; evolution of PES 262; 'examinable subject' status for PES 267, 268; facilities and norms in PE 264; gender disparity in PES 266, 267, 276; geography of 261; governmental input for PE 267; health awareness through PES 264; HIV pandemic 264; holistic approach to PES 263, 267; international collaborations 267; International Inspiration Programme 262; mandatory PES, abolishment of 262–263; mandatory PES, establishment of 262; plans for feasibility and accessibility of PE 265; quality teaching of PE 264–265; research gap on PES 268; skill development and bodily awareness 263–264; social norms and cultural practice 266–267; sport NGOs, government collaboration with 267; traditional games 266–267; training of PES teachers 264–265, 267, 268; underfunding of PES 264, 267, 268; Zambia Education Curriculum Framework 262–263, 268

For Product Safety Concerns and Information please contact our EU representative GPSR@taylorandfrancis.com Taylor & Francis Verlag GmbH, Kaufingerstraße 24, 80331 München, Germany

Printed and bound by CPI Group (UK) Ltd, Croydon, CR0 4YY
09/06/2025
01897932-0002